WordPress for Web Developers

An Introduction for Web Professionals

Stephanie Leary

ISBN-13 (pbk): 978-1-4302-5866-7

ISBN-13 (electronic): 978-1-4302-5867-4

Trademarked names, logos, and images may appear in this book. Rather than use a trademark symbol with every occurrence of a trademarked name, logo, or image we use the names, logos, and images only in an editorial fashion and to the benefit of the trademark owner, with no intention of infringement of the trademark.

The use in this publication of trade names, trademarks, service marks, and similar terms, even if they are not identified as such, is not to be taken as an expression of opinion as to whether or not they are subject to proprietary rights.

While the advice and information in this book are believed to be true and accurate at the date of publication, neither the authors nor the editors nor the publisher can accept any legal responsibility for any errors or omissions that may be made. The publisher makes no warranty, express or implied, with respect to the material contained herein.

President and Publisher: Paul Manning
Lead Editor: Michelle Lowman
Production Editor: Douglas Pundick
Technical Reviewer: Chris Wiegman
Editorial Board: Steve Anglin, Ewan Buckingham, Gary Cornell, Louise Corrigan, Morgan Ertel,
    Jonathan Gennick, Jonathan Hassell, Robert Hutchinson, Michelle Lowman, James Markham,
    Matthew Moodie, Jeff Olson, Jeffrey Pepper, Douglas Pundick, Ben Renow-Clarke, Dominic Shakeshaft,
    Gwenan Spearing, Matt Wade, Tom Welsh
Coordinating Editor: Kevin Shea
Copy Editor: James Fraleigh
Compositor: SPi Global
Indexer: SPi Global
Artist: SPi Global
Cover Designer: Anna Ishchenko

Distributed to the book trade worldwide by Springer Science+Business Media New York, 233 Spring Street, 6th Floor, New York, NY 10013. Phone 1-800-SPRINGER, fax (201) 348-4505, e-mail orders-ny@springer-sbm.com, or visit www.springeronline.com.

For information on translations, please e-mail rights@apress.com, or visit www.apress.com.

Apress and friends of ED books may be purchased in bulk for academic, corporate, or promotional use. eBook versions and licenses are also available for most titles. For more information, reference our Special Bulk Sales–eBook Licensing web page at www.apress.com/bulk-sales.

Any source code or other supplementary materials referenced by the author in this text is available to readers at www.apress.com. For detailed information about how to locate your book's source code, go to www.apress.com/source-code/.

Contents at a Glance

Contents

About the Author

Stephanie Leary has been building sites with WordPress since 2004, and has always used WordPress for more than just blogs. She worked at Texas A&M University for over 10 years, where she established accessibility and web standards and pioneered the use of blogging software (first Movable Type, then WordPress) as full content management systems for departments' websites.

Stephanie is now a full-time freelance WordPress developer. She is a frequent speaker at higher education conferences, WordPress Meetups, and WordCamps. In between conferences, she can be found giving concise WordPress tips on Twitter.

About the Technical Reviewer

 **Chris Wiegman** is a Senior Developer for Springbox in Austin, TX where he works on WordPress sites both big and small. In addition, he is the developer of the Better WP Security plugin and an adjunct faculty member at St. Edward's University, where he teaches courses such as information security in the Computer Science department.

Acknowledgments

I owe a huge debt of thanks to Jared Atchison, Andrea Rennick, Mika Epstein, Shelley Keith, Helen Hou-Sandí, Andrew Nacin, and Bill Erickson and for hanging out in IRC and on Twitter, providing suggestions and encouragement.

Thanks also to everyone who wrote to me about the first edition or stopped to chat with me at a WordCamp. Your enthusiasm prompted me to write this edition, and your comments and suggestions have made this a better book.

I had a wonderful technical reviewer, Chris Weigman, and a great team at Apress, Michelle Lowman, Douglas Pundick, Kevin Shea, and James Fraleigh.

Thanks also go to my son (although he won't understand why for a few years yet) for giving up some Mommy time in the evenings while I wrote. And thank you to my husband, Michael, for everything.

—Stephanie Leary

Introduction

WordPress became my CMS of choice because it's so easy for end users to learn how to manage their own sites. In this book, you'll learn how to install, configure, and customize WordPress to make it the perfect CMS for your next project. I'll walk you through the complete development of a WordPress site, whether you're importing content from another CMS or writing your own. You'll learn how to create custom themes that give you complete control over your site's appearance. You'll see how to extend WordPress with custom post types when you find that posts and pages aren't enough, and you'll learn to write your own plugins when your needs outstrip the built-in features.

Who This Book Is For

This book is for the professional web developer who already understands HTML, CSS, and maybe a little PHP, but has never used WordPress before. If you're comfortable building sites without a content management system, or with a CMS other than WordPress, this book will teach you how to begin building comparable sites using WordPress.

How This Book Is Structured

I've arranged this book into three parts.

Chapters 1 through 7 provide an introduction to WordPress and a detailed tour of its administration screens. Along the way, you'll also learn about various plugins that might be helpful in specific situations. No particular expertise is needed in these chapters; they are intended to be useful to all site owners and administrators.

Chapters 8 through 10 cover more advanced administration functions involving server configurations and database operations.

Chapters 11 through 14 provide an introduction to WordPress theme and plugin development. Here, some knowledge of HTML, CSS, and PHP is required. You'll also see a few MySQL queries, but you won't need to write any of your own to follow the examples. Each chapter's introduction includes a list of the specific technical topics that will be relevant, along with a list of books and online resources you can use to brush up on the subjects, if needed. Chapters 11 through 14 end with a list of articles for further reading on each subject.

Conventions

Throughout the book, I've kept a consistent style for presenting HTML markup and PHP code. Where a piece of markup, a function, or a WordPress hook is presented in the text, it is presented in fixed-width Courier font, such as this:

```
<?php get_sidebar(); ?>
```

Downloading the Code

The code for the examples shown in this book is available on the Apress web site, `www.apress.com`. A link can be found on the book's information page under the Source Code/Downloads tab. This tab is located underneath the Related Titles section of the page.

Contacting the Author

Should you have any questions or comments—or even spot a mistake you think I should know about—you can contact me at `stephanieleary.com`.

CHAPTER 1

Getting Started

WordPress has grown enormously in the last few years, going from the most popular blogging software to the most popular web-based software, period. At 2012's Signal Conference, it was estimated that WordPress powered 16% of the entire web (http://sleary.me/wp1).[1] A study by the Royal Pingdom blog showed that of the top 100 sites on the web, nearly half of them ran on WordPress (http://sleary.me/wp2).[2]

What is this thing, and how did it get so popular?

Why WordPress?

WordPress is one of many content management systems that allow you to update your site through a simple Web interface instead of editing and uploading HTML files to a server. Most other systems emphasize either blog posts or web pages. WordPress is best known as a blogging system, but in fact it treats posts and pages equally. It is therefore ideal for dense reference sites that also have a news section, or news-oriented sites that have a few informational pages. It is a flexible system that can be used to create sites for businesses, project collaborations, university departments, artist portfolios, and (of course!) personal or group blogs.

A developer familiar with WordPress's application programming interfaces (APIs)—which you will be, too, once you've finished this book!—can even use WordPress as an application development platform. Yuri Victor, describing how the *Washington Post* uses WordPress (http://sleary.me/wp3),[3] writes:

> *The Washington Post uses WordPress for blogging and to quickly build products and prototypes because while being a lightweight system, WordPress is a good foundation for what we need . . . The crazy thing [is] we've only been using WordPress for about six months. I don't think The Post has ever launched so many products, so quickly with such success.*

wordpress.com vs. wordpress.org

WordPress comes in two distinct flavors, usually referred to as .com and .org.

On wordpress.com, anyone can sign up for a free, hosted site running on WordPress. The service comes with a few limitations, however: you'll have to choose from one of the approved themes (although there are a lot of them), and you can't install any plugins. On the other hand, you never have to worry about backing up your data or upgrading the software; all of that is handled for you.

---

[1]http://socialmediatoday.com/socialmktgfella/475399/102-people-power-16-web
[2]http://royal.pingdom.com/2012/04/11/wordpress-completely-dominates-top-100-blogs/
[3]http://yurivictor.com/2013/01/09/why-the-washington-post-uses-wordpress/

If you need more flexibility than wordpress.com offers, you can go to wordpress.org, download the software for free, and install it on your own server, along with any themes and plugins you desire. You will be responsible for backing up your data, installing upgrades when they become available, and making sure your site is secure (all of which you will learn how to do in later chapters).

Most commercial Web hosts support WordPress, although only three are recommended on wordpress.org. There are a handful of managed WordPress hosting services that try to combine the benefits of wordpress.com (handling backups, upgrades, and security for you) while giving you the flexibility of wordpress.org (custom themes and plugins). If the prospect of backing up and restoring a MySQL database makes you tremble, these hosts might be the answer for you. The Vandelay Design blog has a good comparison of the managed WordPress hosting services (http://sleary.me/wp4).[4]

This book covers only the self-hosted version of WordPress available from wordpress.org.

Everything You Need

WordPress is famous for its five-minute installation. In fact, if you have your database connection details in hand before you begin, it might not even take you that long! WordPress's system requirements (discussed in more detail in Chapter 2) are modest, allowing it to run on most commercial shared hosting plans that include PHP and MySQL.

WordPress comes with everything you need to set up a basic web site, including:

- *Posts and pages.* In the most traditional use of WordPress, a blog (composed of posts) will feature a few "static" (but still database-driven) pages, such as "About." However, as you'll see throughout this book, you can use these two primary content types in a number of other ways.

- *Media library.* The post and page editing screens allow you to upload files and insert them into your content: images, audio, video, Office documents, PDFs, and more.

- *Categories and tags.* WordPress includes both hierarchical and free-form taxonomies for posts.

- *User roles and profiles.* WordPress users have five possible roles (Subscriber, Contributor, Author, Editor, and Administrator), with escalating capabilities and a basic workflow for editorial approval. User profiles include a biography, e-mail address, URL, and a Gravatar (a user image stored in a central service).

- *RSS and Atom feeds.* There are RSS and Atom feeds available for just about everything in WordPress. The main feeds include recent posts and comments, but there are also feeds for individual categories, tags, authors, and comment threads.

- *Clean URLs.* WordPress supports search engine-friendly URLs (or permalinks) on both Apache and IIS servers, with a system of tags that allow you to customize the link structure.

- *Spam protection.* The WordPress download package includes the Akismet plugin, which provides free industrial-strength filtering of spam comments for personal sites. (Nonpersonal sites can use it for a small monthly fee.) Because it uses a central web service, it constantly learns and improves.

- *Automatic upgrades.* WordPress displays an alert when a new version is available for the core system or for any themes or plugins you have installed. You can update any of these with the click of a button (although it's always a good idea to back up your database and files first).

- *Multiple sites from one installation.* You can expand your WordPress installation into a network of connected sites. The setup process is just a little more involved than the basic installation, and your host has to meet a few additional requirements, which I'll go over in Chapter 2.

---

[4]http://vandelaydesign.com/blog/wordpress/hosting

Easy to Use

WordPress has an amazingly user-friendly administration interface. Even Web novices can begin updating content with very little training.

- *Rich text editing*: WordPress includes the popular TinyMCE editor, which provides you with an interface similar to Microsoft Office products. For those who prefer to work with markup directly, WordPress has a basic HTML view as an alternative. The editor includes tools to import content and remove embedded styles from Office documents.

- *Media uploads and embeds*: The content editing screens include a media uploader. You'll be prompted to provide titles, captions, or other metadata based on the file type, and you can easily link to the media files or insert them directly into the document. WordPress includes a basic image editor that allows you to rotate or resize the image. It also generates thumbnails automatically that can be used in place of the full-size image. Images can be aligned left, right, or center, and can include captions as well as alternative (alt) text. It's easy to embed audio and video files from other sites into your content—just paste the URL as you edit, and when your post or page is published, the address will be replaced with the appropriate media player.

- *Menu management*: You can let WordPress build navigation menus automatically based on your pages' hierarchy, or you can define custom menus that link to the content you specify, including posts, pages, categories, tags, and links to external URLs.

Easy to Extend

WordPress offers a robust template system as well as an extensive API. Anyone with experience in PHP can change a site's appearance or even modify WordPress's behavior. At `www.wordpress.org`, you can download thousands of themes and plugins to do just this.

- *Themes* determine your site's appearance and how content is displayed. WordPress is designed to let you switch themes without changing the underlying content. Theme files are simply HTML documents containing some WordPress-specific PHP functions that display information from the WordPress database. A theme can be as simple as a single `index.php` file with a stylesheet, or it might contain separate, specific templates for posts, pages, archives, search results, and so on. It might also include images, JavaScript files, and Web fonts.

- *Plugins* can add functions, template tags, or widgets; modify existing functions; and filter content. A plugin could add administration screens that give you access to new settings, or it might change WordPress's usual behavior—alphabetizing your posts instead of sorting them by date, for example.

- *Widgets* are drag-and-drop components that can be added to your site's sidebars. For example, there are widgets to display polls, Flickr photos, and Twitter streams. You can use widgets to list pages, posts, and links; provide a search box; add arbitrary HTML; or display an RSS feed. Some themes come with their own widgets; other widgets can be installed as separate plugins.

Advanced users can extend the basic types of content in WordPress by adding custom fields to the standard title, content, and excerpt fields. You can even define your own content types in addition to posts and pages. And if the built-in category and tag system isn't enough for your site, you can create custom taxonomies for posts, pages, or media files. I'll go over custom fields, taxonomies, and content types in Chapter 14.

To see just how far you can go using themes and plugins, visit `buddypress.org`. BuddyPress is a set of themes and plugins for WordPress that turns a basic site into a complete social network with member profiles, friends, private messages, forums, and activity streams. The transformation is amazing!

The Business Benefits of WordPress

Because WordPress has built-in support for clean and canonical URLs, microformats and rich snippets, categories and tags, and standards-based themes, it does a stellar job of optimizing sites for search engines. At the 2009 WordCamp in San Francisco, Google's Matt Cutts explained to the audience that WordPress is the best blogging platform for search engine optimization purposes, and that choosing WordPress would be a good first step for any small business seeking to build an online presence.

It's easy to integrate moneymaking features into WordPress sites. Thanks to the vibrant plugin developer community, there's probably a plugin to help you integrate any third-party marketing services, ad servers, or affiliate codes you would want to use. There are even a number of e-commerce plugins that will let you turn your WordPress site into a storefront.

Sites Built with WordPress

These are just a few examples of WordPress sites. As you'll see, there are virtually no limits to the designs you can create with WordPress. For more examples, visit the Showcase at `wordpress.org/showcase`.

Web Experts and Open Source Projects

Many of the Web's most famous designers have adopted WordPress: Jeffrey Zeldman, Eric Meyer, Jason Santa Maria, Douglas Bowman, Dan Cederholm, and Aarron Walter are a few. Famous geeks Robert Scoble, Chris Pirillo, and Leo Laporte use WordPress, too.

WordPress powers the web sites of other open source projects, too. For example, it's the basis for the jQuery site (Figure 1-1), including the documentation.

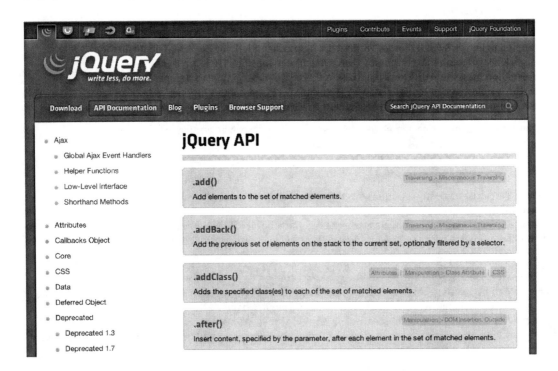

Figure 1-1. *The jQuery project uses WordPress categories to organize its documentation*

Government Web Sites

Budget-crunched government offices are turning to open source content management systems—and the results are not as dull as you might expect. The Milwaukee Police News site (Figure 1-2) is one of the most stylish WordPress sites on the Web today. Scroll down the entire home page to see their fantastic use of photos.

Figure 1-2. *The Milwaukee Police News blog uses an innovative parallax scrolling design to mix news, statistics, and photos into a compelling presentation*

Personal Sites

Tons of public figures use WordPress for their sites. Some of their sites look more or less like blogs (Figure 1-3); others are video libraries or design showcases.

Figure 1-3. *Author Jennifer Crusie's site is a standard blog with a quirky navigation menu*

Blog Networks

The *New York Times,* Edublogs, and `wordpress.com` are large sites with anywhere from a few dozen to hundreds of thousands of individual blogs. These sites use the WordPress Multisite feature, hosting all their blogs from a single WordPress installation.

Some of these blogs include the most viewed sites on the Web. FiveThirtyEight, part of the *New York Times* network (Figure 1-4), was the star of the 2012 election.

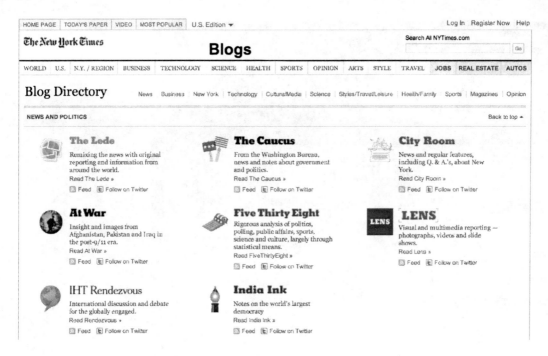

Figure 1-4. *The New York Times blog network includes some of the busiest blogs on the Web*

Social Networks

Using the BuddyPress suite of plugins, a WordPress site can be turned into a complete social network in just a few minutes. Niche networks built on BuddyPress include FilmmakerIQ (Figure 1-5), Vivanista, Nourish Network, and Hello Eco Living.

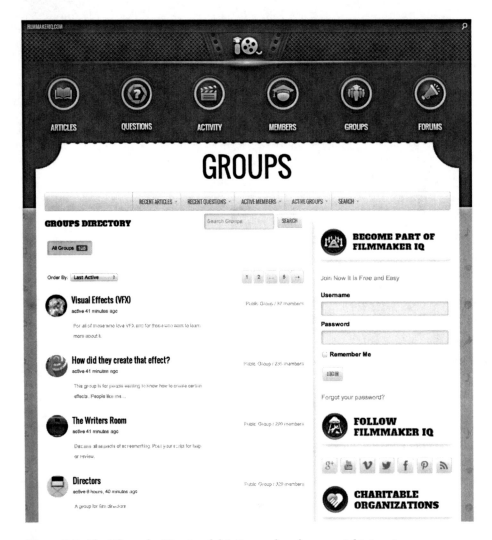

Figure 1-5. The FilmmakerIQ network lets its members form special-interest groups

Colleges and Universities

Bates College (Figure 1-6), the University of Arkansas at Little Rock, Texas Tech University, and Queens College at the University of Melbourne all use WordPress to maintain their schools' web sites. A number of schools use WordPress for individual departments, such as the Yale School of Drama, Vanderbilt University Alumni Relations, the University of Virginia Department of Environmental Sciences, Cornell Department of Music, Duke University, and Texas A&M University—just to name a few.

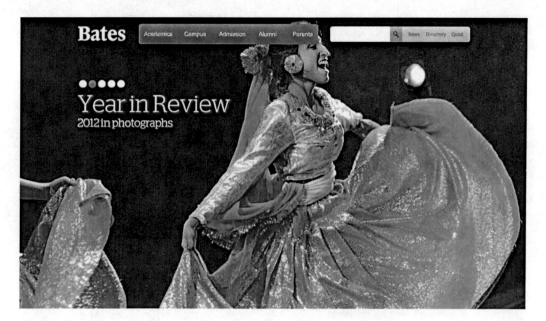

Figure 1-6. *The Bates College home page uses a stunning full-screen photo slideshow—and little else*

Universities using WordPress Multisite to create a unified presence for their main sites and departments include the University of Maine, Southern Arkansas University, Wesleyan University, Wheaton College, and Missouri State University. Many universities also use Multisite to provide blog networks for students and/or faculty.

WordPress is also a popular choice among secondary and higher-education teachers for providing students with blogs for their classroom writing projects.

Small Businesses

Wandering Goat Coffee and IconDock (Figure 1-7) are among the many small businesses using WordPress to run their main business sites.

Figure 1-7. *The IconDock site is a store featuring a clever drag-and-drop shopping cart*

WordPress Tour

When you install WordPress for the first time (see Chapter 2), you'll have a simple site dressed in the lovely new Twenty Twelve theme (Figure 1-8). (If this theme is not your cup of tea, don't worry. In Chapter 2, I'll show you how to install other themes, and in Chapter 12, I'll show you how to create your own.)

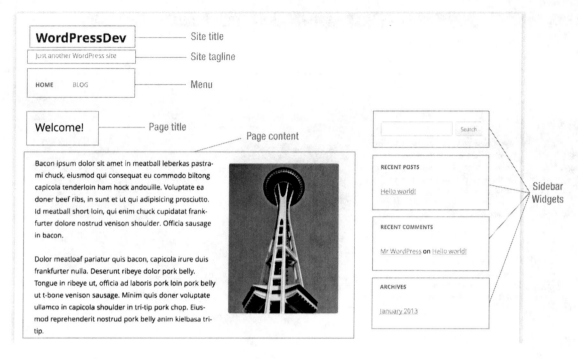

Figure 1-8. *A simple WordPress home page using the Twenty Twelve default theme*

Let's break down this page and see how WordPress put it together.

At the top of the page, you'll see the site title you chose when you installed WordPress (see Chapter 2). Off to the right is the tagline ("Just another WordPress site"), which you can specify in the theme customizer or on the General Settings page (see Chapter 3).

The row of links just under the site tagline is a navigation menu. You can specify which links appear in your menu, and you can create additional menus to use elsewhere on your site. This example uses the default menu: a list of all the pages in the site.

Below the header and the menu, you have two columns: the content area and the sidebar. This content area shows a page. In later chapters, I'll discuss a number of ways you can change what appears here.

This site's sidebar contains four widgets: Search, Recent Posts, Recent Comments, and a list of archives. You can add and remove widgets by dragging them into the sidebars on the Widgets administration screen in the Appearance section. These four widgets are part of WordPress's built-in set. Some of the themes and plugins you install will provide you with additional widgets, and in Chapter 13, I'll show you how to create your own.

Anatomy of a Page

Take another look at the content area, and compare it to the page editing screen (Figure 1-9).

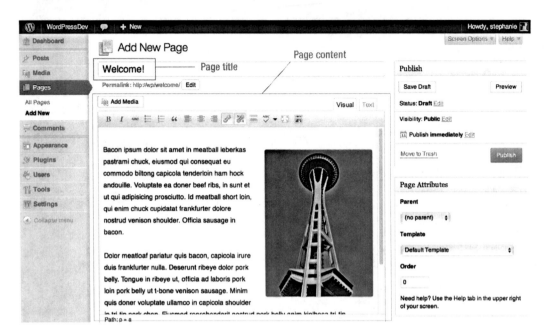

Figure 1-9. *The page editing screen*

Here you can see how each page is built behind the scenes. You enter your page's title and content, and the theme determines how that information is displayed. You can change the display by switching themes, or by modifying the theme you have.

Template tags are PHP functions, so if you're familiar with PHP syntax, you'll have no trouble learning to modify WordPress themes. Even if you've never used PHP before, you can begin modifying your site by copying template tags from the WordPress Codex (codex.wordpress.org) or a tutorial. As you grow more comfortable with the language, you'll find yourself making bigger changes with confidence.

Summary

In this chapter, I've introduced you to WordPress. I've shown you how WordPress is easy to install, easy for you and your content authors to use, and easy to customize. I've discussed the accolades WordPress has won, and I've shown you just a few examples of the wide variety of sites that can be built with WordPress. I've gone over the components of a basic WordPress site and explained some of the terminology (like themes, sidebars, and widgets) you'll see often throughout this book.

In Chapter 2, I'll show you the famous five-minute installation process. You'll learn the extra configuration steps needed to expand your WordPress installation into a network of sites. I'll show you how to upgrade your site when new versions of WordPress are released, and how to install and upgrade themes and plugins. I'll also go over some common installation problems and troubleshooting tips.

■ ■ ■

Installing and Upgrading WordPress

WordPress is famous for its five-minute installation. Many commercial web hosts offer one-click installation from their account control panels. If your host does not, you can upload the WordPress files to your web directory and complete the installation using the web interface.

System Requirements

WordPress's requirements are modest. At minimum, your server should support:

- PHP version 5.2.4 or greater

- MySQL version 5.0 or greater

- For clean URLs, a URL rewriting module that understands .htaccess directives, such as mod_rewrite on Apache or URL Rewrite on IIS 7

Your host should list these features and version numbers in the description of hosting plans or the support area (or both).

Your host might also offer one-click installers for many web software packages, including WordPress. If you are taking advantage of this option, skip to the Initial Settings section.

Otherwise, it's time to create a database and upload some files.

Installation Using the Web Interface

To install WordPress, you'll need to create a database, upload the files, and run the installer. I'll walk you through the most common ways to accomplish these tasks.

First, you'll need to set up a database for WordPress to use. If your host has already created one for you, simply locate the database name, username, password, and host you were provided (usually in the welcome e-mail you received when you signed up).

Otherwise, create a new database according to your host's instructions. Figure 2-1 shows how to do this in phpMyAdmin (the MySQL web interface most commonly used by commercial hosting companies). If you are asked to specify a character set, choose UTF-8, which will support any language. If you are asked to specify a collation, choose utf8-general-ci. These are the language and character settings WordPress expects, but some old MySQL installations use more restrictive character sets as their default.

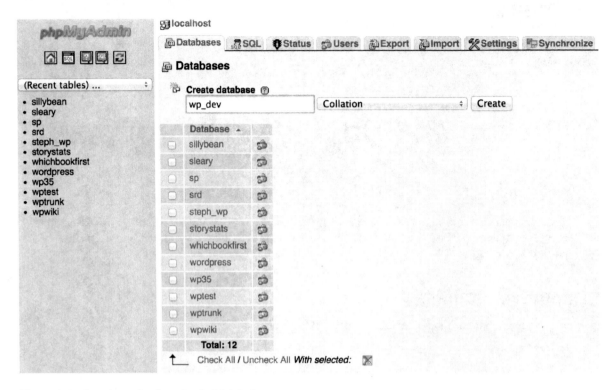

Figure 2-1. *Creating a database in phpMyAdmin*

If you have the option to create a new database user, you should do so. Be sure to grant the new user all permissions on your database, as shown in Figure 2-2. In phpMyAdmin, you'll go to the Users tab and edit the appropriate user, or create a new one. Users are associated with particular hosts; here, my username is appended with @localhost. If you are creating a new user, and your database is hosted on the same server as your web files, localhost is usually the hostname you should use. Otherwise, the IP address of your WordPress installation is a safe choice.

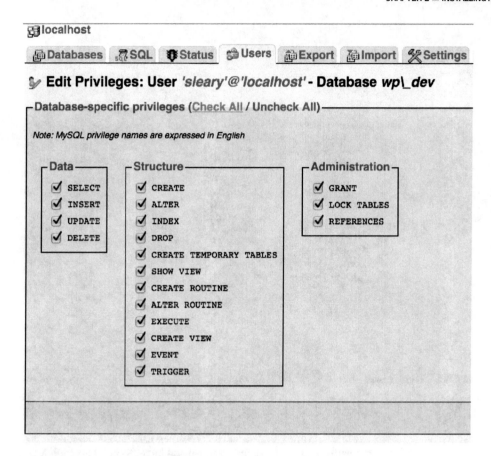

Figure 2-2. *Granting user privileges on the new database in phpMyAdmin*

■ **Note** Throughout this book, you'll see that my example site's address is http://wp. This is because I'm hosting WordPress locally on my laptop using MAMP, a Mac application that sets up PHP, Apache, MySQL, and phpMyAdmin in an easy-to-install package. Windows users can do the same using XAMPP. With your desktop server in place, you can create simple hostnames like localhost or, in this case, wp, rather than using fully qualified domains. See http://sleary.me/wp5[1] for details on installing WordPress with MAMP.

Once you have your database credentials in hand, you're ready to install WordPress.

Download the installation package from wordpress.org, unzip the files, and upload the files to your web host using your favorite FTP client software (I like Transmit for the Mac, as shown in Figure 2-3, but Filezilla, WinSCP, or another program would be fine). Simply place the files where you want your WordPress site to be located; that is, if you want the site to be located at mysite.com, upload the files to your web root folder. If you want the site to be located at mysite.com/blog, create a folder called blog and upload the WordPress files to that folder instead.

---

[1]http://codex.wordpress.org/Installing_WordPress_Locally_on_Your_Mac_With_MAMP

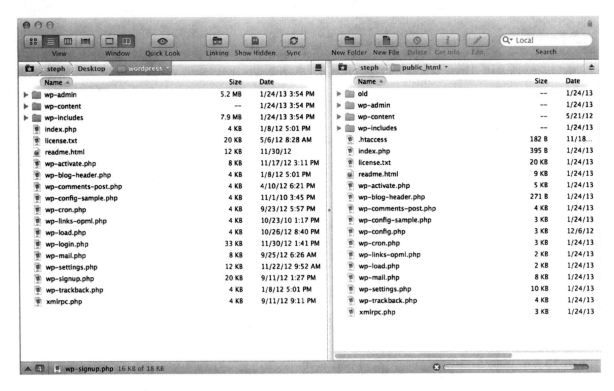

Figure 2-3. *Uploading files via FTP in Transmit*

Once you have uploaded the files, visit the site in a web browser. You will be prompted to create a configuration file (Figure 2-4). Fill in the requested information (Figure 2-5) as shown in Figure 2-6 and press Submit to complete the installation.

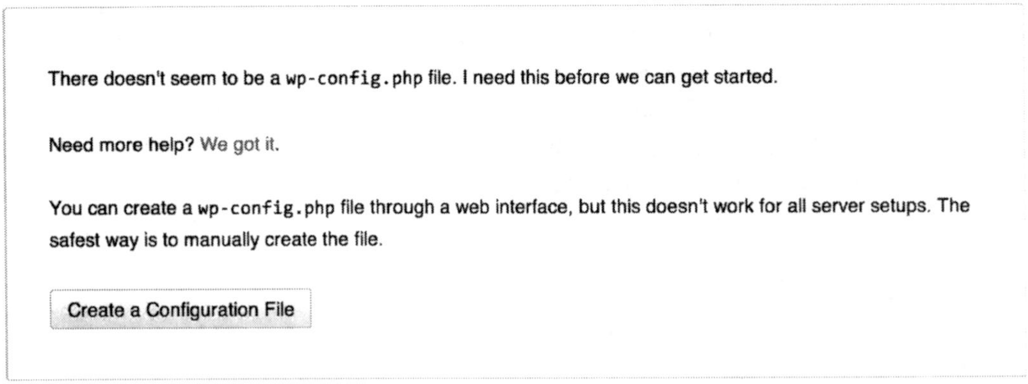

There doesn't seem to be a `wp-config.php` file. I need this before we can get started.

Need more help? We got it.

You can create a `wp-config.php` file through a web interface, but this doesn't work for all server setups. The safest way is to manually create the file.

Create a Configuration File

Figure 2-4. *Configuration file prompt*

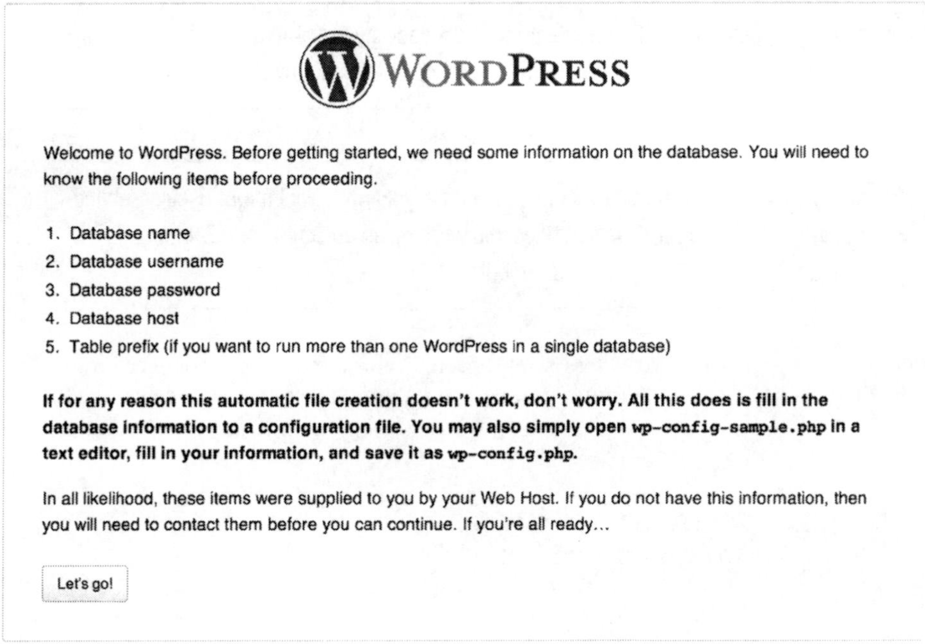

Welcome to WordPress. Before getting started, we need some information on the database. You will need to know the following items before proceeding.

1. Database name
2. Database username
3. Database password
4. Database host
5. Table prefix (if you want to run more than one WordPress in a single database)

If for any reason this automatic file creation doesn't work, don't worry. All this does is fill in the database information to a configuration file. You may also simply open `wp-config-sample.php` in a text editor, fill in your information, and save it as `wp-config.php`.

In all likelihood, these items were supplied to you by your Web Host. If you do not have this information, then you will need to contact them before you can continue. If you're all ready…

Let's go!

Figure 2-5. *Information you need before installing*

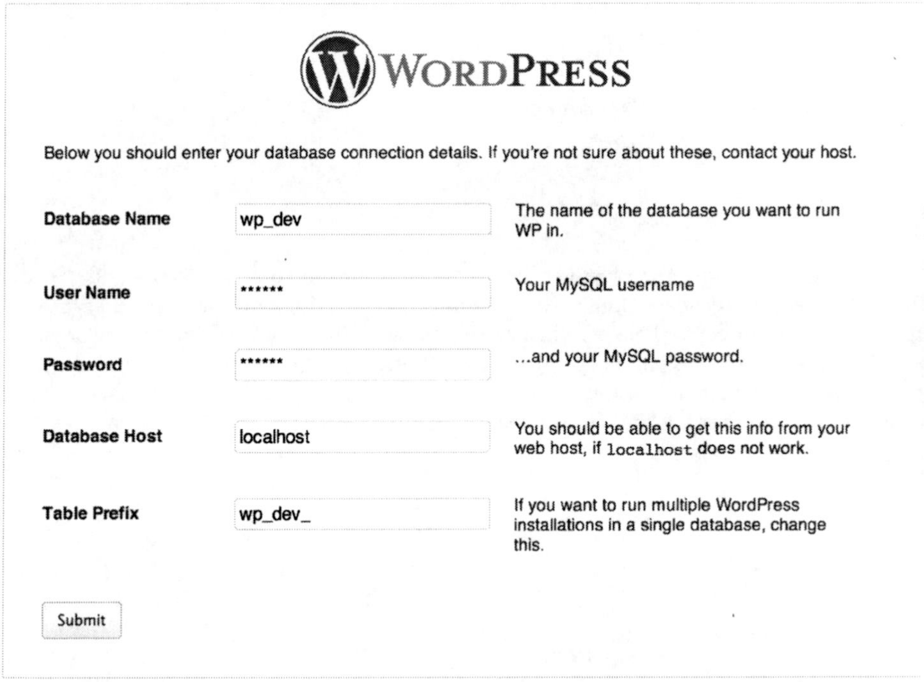

WORDPRESS

Below you should enter your database connection details. If you're not sure about these, contact your host.

Database Name	wp_dev	The name of the database you want to run WP in.
User Name	******	Your MySQL username
Password	******	…and your MySQL password.
Database Host	localhost	You should be able to get this info from your web host, if `localhost` does not work.
Table Prefix	wp_dev_	If you want to run multiple WordPress installations in a single database, change this.

Submit

Figure 2-6. *Filling in the database connection information*

■ **Caution**　The configuration screen suggests wp_ for the table prefix. As a security precaution, you should always change this prefix to something else. See Chapter 9 for more information on database security.

■ **Note**　While localhost is the most common setting for the database host, your web host might use something different—even if the host was not included in the database settings you were given. GoDaddy and Dreamhost, for example, do not use localhost. Check your web host's documentation.

If you entered all the correct information and WordPress is able to connect to your database, you'll be prompted to complete the installation (Figure 2-7). If not, you'll need to double-check the database connection details with your host.

All right sparky! You've made it through this part of the installation. WordPress can now communicate with your database. If you are ready, time now to...

    Run the install

Figure 2-7.　*Successful database connection and installation prompt*

Initial Settings

Once the installation is complete, you'll have the opportunity to create your account, as shown in Figure 2-8. In previous versions, the first user was always called admin, but you should choose a different username. Because that username is so common, it's an easy target for hackers who use automated tools to guess account passwords. In April 2013, an enormous distributed attack was launched against WordPress (and other MySQL-based content management systems), in which repeated login attempts were made with the username admin and a thousand or so common passwords. Choose a username other than admin, and see Chapter 9 for more information on securing your WordPress installation.

Welcome

Welcome to the famous five minute WordPress installation process! You may want to browse the ReadMe documentation at your leisure. Otherwise, just fill in the information below and you'll be on your way to using the most extendable and powerful personal publishing platform in the world.

Information needed

Please provide the following information. Don't worry, you can always change these settings later.

Site Title   WordPressDev

Username   stephanie

Usernames can have only alphanumeric characters, spaces, underscores, hyphens, periods and the @ symbol.

Password, twice

A password will be automatically generated for you if you leave this blank.

●●●●●●●●●●

●●●●●●●●●●

Strong

Hint: The password should be at least seven characters long. To make it stronger, use upper and lower case letters, numbers and symbols like ! " ? $ % ^ &).

Figure 2-8. *Creating the admin account*

Now, visit your site's Dashboard. Its URL is the URL of the directory in which you installed WordPress, plus /wp-admin. That is, if you installed WordPress in the root directory of example.com, you would go to example.com/wp-admin/ to log in.

Log in using the password you just created (Figure 2-9). You should see the Welcome screen shown in Figure 2-10. We'll go over the Dashboard and the rest of the WordPress settings in the next chapter.

Username

stephanie

Password

●●●●●●●●●●

☐ Remember Me   Log In

Lost your password?

← Back to WordPressDev

Figure 2-9. *The WordPress login screen*

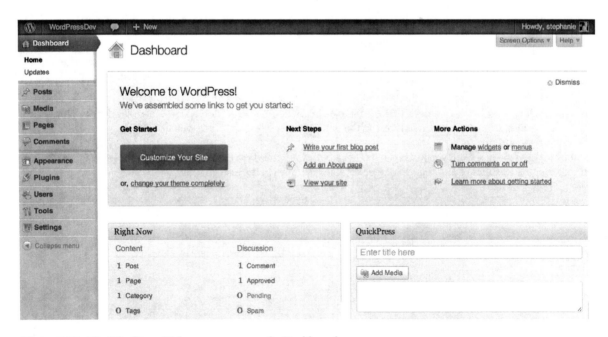

Figure 2-10. *The WordPress Welcome message on the Dashboard*

Troubleshooting the Blank White Page

On most web hosts, PHP errors are logged rather than printed to the screen. This is good security; it prevents you from accidentally exposing your database password or other sensitive information if you mess up your code. However, this feature also prevents you from seeing what's gone wrong if there was a problem during your installation. Instead of a login screen, you'll just see a blank white page.

If you know where your PHP error log is, you can check its last line to see what the problem was. If you don't know where the log is, you can check your web host's documentation to find out, or you can simply turn on the error display until you resolve the problem. WordPress will not display your database connection information even if there is an error.

To display errors, find the `wp-config.php` file in your WordPress directory. Look for the WP_DEBUG constant, below your database settings. Change it from `false` to `true` (Listing 2-1).

Listing 2-1. Debugging with `wp-config.php` (Partial)

```
// ** MySQL settings - You can get this info from your web host ** //
/** The name of the database for WordPress */
define('DB_NAME', 'my_wp_db');

/** MySQL database username */
define('DB_USER', 'my_wp_db_user');

define('WP_DEBUG', true);
```

Visit your site again, and you should see the problem. Ignore any warnings and notices, and look for fatal errors. Is there an unknown function? Look for a missing file, or simply re-upload the entire WordPress package.

Listing 2-2 shows the kind of error message you would see if one of the files from wp-includes were missing–in this case, `capabilities.php`. The first message, a warning, could be safely ignored, but in this case it provides us with a clue as to why the second error occurred. The fatal error is the showstopper. Resolve that problem, and WordPress should work correctly.

When you've solved the problem, switch the value of WP_DEBUG back to `false`.

Listing 2-2. Fatal Error Due to a Missing File

Warning: require(/Users/steph/Sites/wp/wp-includes/capabilities.php): failed to open stream: No such file or directory in **/Users/steph/Sites/wp/wp-settings.php** on line **108**

Fatal error: require(): Failed opening required '/Users/steph/Sites/wp/wp-includes/capabilities.php' in **/Users/steph/Sites/wp/wp-settings.php** on line **108**

You can also log errors instead of displaying them on the screen. This is especially useful when you begin developing your own themes and plugins. To log errors, add the WP_DEBUG_DISPLAY and WP_DEBUG_LOG constants to your configuration file as shown in Listing 2-3.

Listing 2-3. Turning on Error Logging in `wp-config.php` (Partial)

```
// ** MySQL settings - You can get this info from your web host ** //
/** The name of the database for WordPress */
define('DB_NAME', 'my_wp_db');

/** MySQL database username */
define('DB_USER', 'my_wp_db_user');
```

```
define('WP_DEBUG', true);
define('WP_DEBUG_LOG', true);
define('WP_DEBUG_DISPLAY', false);
```

See the Codex (the WordPress documentation wiki) page on wp-config.php, http://sleary.me/wp6,[2] for more debug log options and PHP configuration settings that might help with debugging.

Installing Themes

Once you have WordPress installed, you'll want to make it look good! You can change themes at any time.

You can download theme files from www.wordpress.org/themes and upload them to your wp-content/themes folder if you wish, or you can use the automatic theme installer.

From your Dashboard, visit Appearance ➤ Themes. On this screen, you'll see two tabs, Manage Themes and Install Themes. Under Manage Themes, you'll see all the currently installed themes. Click Install Themes, and you'll see a search screen. Here, you can search for themes by name, or you can check off a list of the features you want (color, number of columns, etc.) as shown in Figure 2-11. You'll get a list of results with links allowing you to preview and install the themes (Figure 2-12).

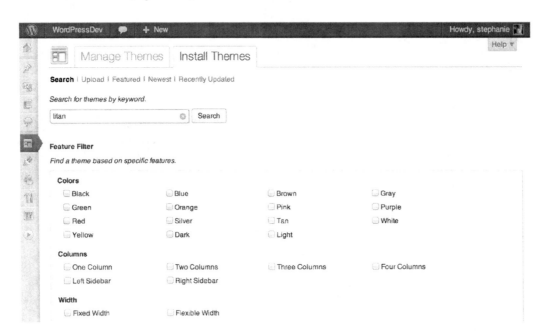

Figure 2-11. *Choosing themes*

---

[2]http://codex.wordpress.org/Editing_wp-config.php#Debug

Figure 2-12. *Installing and previewing themes*

Once the themes have been installed, they'll appear in your list of themes under Appearance. Click the theme's thumbnail image to see a preview of the theme on your site. Here, the Theme Customizer (Figure 2-13) appears. You can see how the theme will look on your site, and you can adjust your title, tagline, and the settings that relate to your site's appearance. You'll see more settings in Chapter 3.

Figure 2-13. *The Theme Customizer*

If you're happy with the theme, click the blue Save & Activate button at the top of the screen. Otherwise, you can cancel and try another theme.

■ **Caution**   If you decide not to use a theme you have installed, you should delete it. Even themes that are not active can allow hackers to gain access to your site if the theme contains a vulnerability.

Installing Plugins

While WordPress includes most of the features you would want in a basic site, sooner or later you'll probably find that you want something more. Visit `www.wordpress.org/plugins` to see all the things you can add to your site. You'll see more about working with plugins in Chapter 6.

You can download the plugin files and upload them to your `wp-content/plugins` folder, just as you did with themes. However, there is also an automatic plugin installer. From your Dashboard, visit Plugins ➤ Add New. On this screen (Figure 2-14), you can search for plugins by keyword or author name.

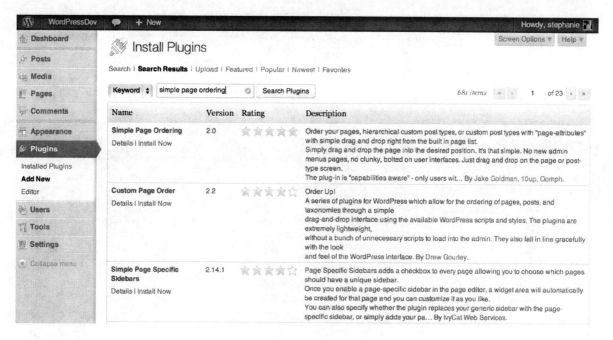

Figure 2-14. *Searching for the Simple Page Ordering plugin*

Once a plugin has been installed, it will appear in your plugin list. You'll see a brief description of what the plugin does, a link to its home page, and a link to activate it.

■ **Caution** Every plugin you add to your WordPress site represents a potential security problem. See Chapter 6 to learn how to use the ratings and other plugin details to evaluate plugins before you install them.

Try activating Hello Dolly, the sample plugin that comes with WordPress, using the Activate link under the plugin's name. When the plugin list reloads, you'll get a message confirming the activation. You should also see a lyric from "Hello, Dolly" in the upper right corner of your screen, as shown in Figure 2-15.

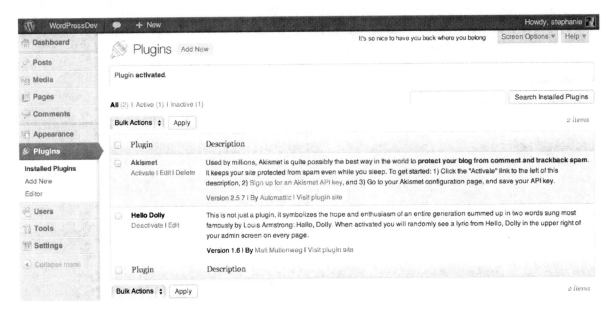

Figure 2-15. *Plugin list after activating Hello Dolly*

Some plugins will not activate. They might contain coding errors, or they might conflict with something else you've installed, or they might not run properly with your version of PHP. When a plugin will not activate, you'll see a message containing the PHP error that caused the problem, as shown in Figure 2-16.

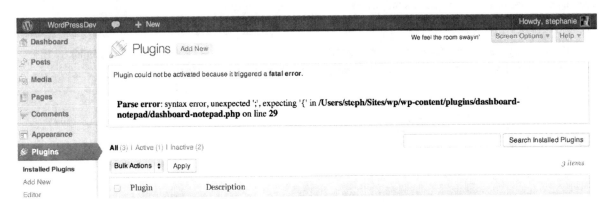

Figure 2-16. *Fatal error during plugin activation*

Even the problem is simple (in this case, a typo) and you can fix it yourself based on the information shown in the error message, you should still visit the plugin's support forum on wordpress.org and let the author know what happened.

■ **Note**　All the plugins mentioned in this book are listed in Appendix A. Plugins hosted in the official plugin repository at wordpress.org/plugins are referenced by name only, and you can find them by searching the repository for the plugin name. URLs are provided for any plugins that are not part of the repository.

Upgrading WordPress, Themes, and Plugins

New versions of WordPress are released often. In addition to providing you with new features, the updated version often includes corrections for newly discovered security problems. Keeping your installation up to date is the most important thing you can do to prevent your site from being hacked.

When a new version of WordPress is available, you'll see a message on every administration screen. You'll also see a number next to your site's name in the admin bar. Newer versions of your themes and plugins are also included in this number, as shown in Figure 2-17.

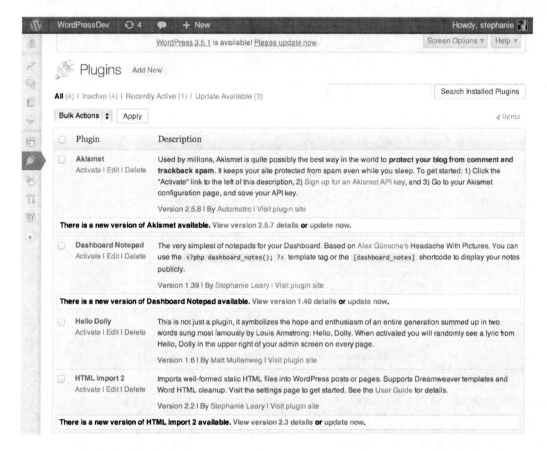

Figure 2-17. *WordPress and plugin updates available*

Bulk Upgrades

If you have several plugins that need to be upgraded, you can process them all at once. Put a checkmark next to the plugins' names, then choose Upgrade from the Bulk Actions dropdown at the top of the plugin list (Figure 2-17). Or, on the Updates screen (Figure 2-18), check off the plugins you want to update and press the Update Plugins button at the top of the list.

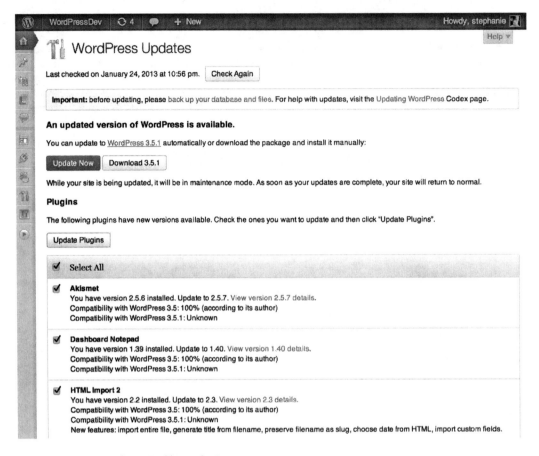

Figure 2-18. *Upgrading WordPress plugins*

WordPress will place your site into maintenance mode automatically, then upgrade each plugin in turn. You'll see a running status report as each plugin is upgraded, and when they're all finished, WordPress will take your site out of maintenance mode.

If you don't plan to log in to your WordPress site very often, you might want to subscribe to the RSS feed or the e-mail announcement list for new releases. You can find both at wordpress.org/development/. The WordPress blog includes general news as well as release announcements. If you want alerts about new versions only, subscribe to the Releases category instead, at http://sleary.me/wp7.[3]

WordPress can upgrade itself automatically, or you can download the files and upload them to your web server. See the Manual Upgrades section later in this chapter.

Troubleshooting Automatic Upgrades: FTP Credentials

In order for the automatic upgrades to work, all the files in your WordPress installation must be owned by the same user the web server runs under. If you're prompted to enter connection information when you try to upgrade, WordPress doesn't have permission to write the new files to the server. There are two ways to fix it: you can enter the information and let WordPress upgrade through an FTP or SSH connection, or you can change the file owner.

---

[3]http://wordpress.org/development/category/releases/feed/

Changing the owner is the fastest way to solve the immediate problem. However, it might not be the best choice if you're on a shared server. It might be a hassle: you'll have to create a group that includes you and the system user so you can still write to the directory, and you'll have to make sure to change the owner again on any new files you upload.

However, if you simply fill in the requested information on the upgrade screen, it won't be saved, and you'll have to enter it again every time you upgrade the WordPress core, a theme, or a plugin.

A far better option is to save your connection information in your `wp-config.php` file, as shown in Listing 2-4. With your connection settings saved, WordPress won't have to prompt you every time you upgrade. You'll need to fill in the full path to your WordPress installation as well as your `wp-content` and `plugins` directories.

Listing 2-4. FTP Connection Settings in `wp-config.php`

```
define('FTP_BASE', '/home/user/wordpress/');
define('FTP_CONTENT_DIR', '/home/username/wordpress/wp-content/');
define('FTP_PLUGIN_DIR', '/home/username/wordpress/wp-content/plugins/');
define('FTP_USER', 'username');
define('FTP_PASS', 'password');
define('FTP_HOST', 'ftp.example.com:21');
define('FTP_SSL', false);
```

If your files are no longer visible to the public after you upgrade using FTP, ask your host if default permissions are set on newly uploaded files when using FTP. On many servers, a `umask` setting is in place. This is a way of adjusting permissions on newly uploaded files. If this is the case on your server, you'll need to ask the host to change this setting for you, or you'll need to upgrade WordPress through some other method.

If the SSH library for PHP is available on your server, the upgrade screen will give you an option to use SSH instead of FTP. To use SSH, leave the password field blank. Instead, generate a pair of keys: one public, one private. Place both files on your server, and fill in their locations to your configuration file, as shown in Listing 2-5. See `http://sleary.me/wp8`[4] for more details on generating SSH keys for use in WordPress.

Listing 2-5. SSH Connection Settings

```
define('FTP_BASE', '/home/user/wordpress/');
define('FTP_CONTENT_DIR', '/home/username/wordpress/wp-content/');
define('FTP_PLUGIN_DIR', '/home/username/wordpress/wp-content/plugins/');
define('FTP_USER', 'username');
define('FTP_PUBKEY', '/home/username/.ssh/id_rsa.pub');
define('FTP_PRIKEY', '/home/username/.ssh/id_rsa');
define('FTP_HOST', 'ftp.example.com:21');
define('FTP_SSL', false);
```

■ **Tip** Pass phrase protected keys do not work properly in WordPress. You should generate your SSH keys without a pass phrase.

---

[4]`http://wpforce.com/wordpress-tutorial-ssh-install-upgrade/`

Troubleshooting Automatic Upgrades on IIS

On some IIS servers, automatic upgrades will fail with this error message: "Destination directory for file streaming does not exist or is not writable." This sounds like a permissions problem, but it's not; WordPress is trying to use the wrong directory to store the downloaded upgrade files. Add the line in Listing 2-6 to your `wp-config.php` file to solve the problem.

Listing 2-6. Defining `wp-content` as the Temporary Directory

```
define( 'WP_TEMP_DIR', ABSPATH . 'wp-content/' );
```

Manual Upgrades

If you can't get automatic upgrades to work, or if you're uncomfortable letting WordPress doctor its own innards, you can always upgrade your files manually. Simply download the new version, unzip it, and transfer the files to your host, just as you did when you first installed WordPress.

To make sure I don't accidentally overwrite my themes, plugins, and uploaded media files, I always delete the `wp-content` directory from the downloaded package before I upload the files to my web server.

Even though it's faster to use my FTP client's synchronize feature to upload only the files that have changed, I usually delete all the standard WordPress files from the server–everything except `wp-config.php` and the `wp-content` directory–before uploading the new copies. Otherwise, strange errors can occur due to duplicated functions, as files are sometimes eliminated and functions deprecated between versions. If a function has been deprecated (and therefore moved to `wp-includes/deprecated.php`) but you still have the original function in an old copy of its original file, you'll get fatal errors when you visit the site because the function has been declared twice within WordPress.

■ **Tip** Make sure the /wp-includes and /wp-admin/includes directories are completely uploaded. When things don't work correctly in the administration screens (menus don't appear, widgets can't be moved, Quick Edit doesn't work) after an upgrade, the problems are almost always caused by missing or corrupted files in these two directories.

If you decide to upload the new files yourself, you'll need to deactivate your plugins first, remove the `.maintenance` file if it exists, and reactivate your plugins when you're done. See the Codex page on upgrading (`http://sleary.me/wp9`[5]) for step-by-step instructions.

Summary

In this chapter, you've learned how to install and upgrade WordPress. I've talked about things that can go wrong and how you can correct the problems. You've also learned how to install themes and plugins, and how to keep your WordPress installation up to date.

You're ready to begin building your site! In the next chapter, I'll go over the options that will determine how your site will work.

---

[5]`http://codex.wordpress.org/Upgrading_WordPress`

CHAPTER 3

Dashboard and Settings

Once you've logged in and changed your password, it's time to go exploring. In this chapter, I'll take you on a tour of the WordPress administration screens (often collectively referred to as the Dashboard, although only the introductory screen actually goes by that name). You'll learn about all the administrative settings and how they affect the display of your site.

The Dashboard

Most of the time, the Dashboard is the first thing you see when you log in. It shows you a welcome screen (until you dismiss it), a snapshot of statistical information about your site, and some updates about WordPress development and plugins (see Figure 3-1).

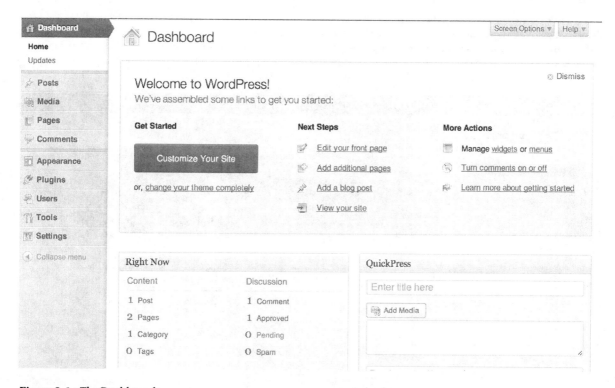

Figure 3-1. The Dashboard

Each box on the Dashboard (Right Now, QuickPress, Recent Comments, etc.) is a widget. If you've just installed WordPress, you'll see the widgets displayed in two columns. Click the Screen Options tab (to the top right of your Dashboard) as shown in Figure 3-2, and you'll see that you can specify the number of columns. You can also turn off widgets altogether by unchecking them here.

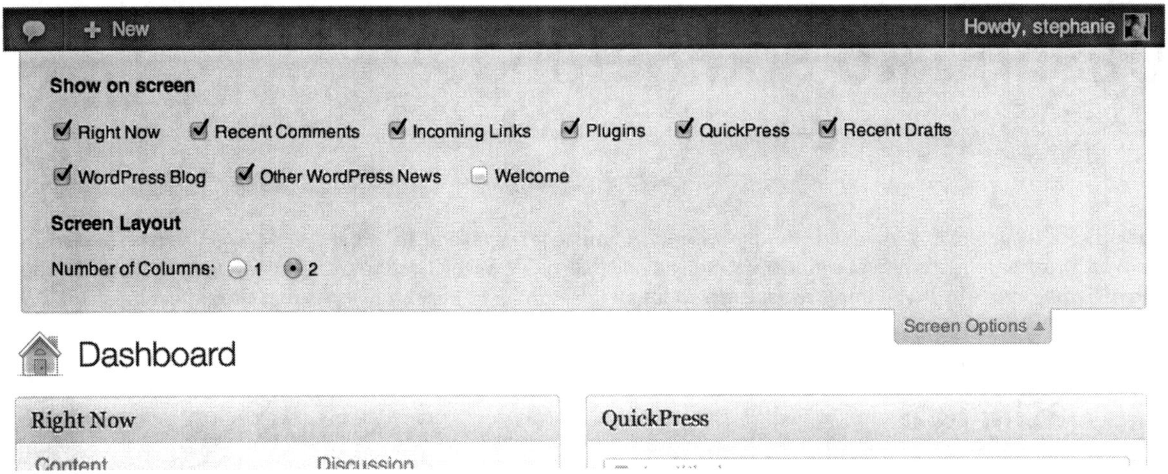

Figure 3-2. *Dashboard screen options*

You can drag widgets around to rearrange them (Figure 3-3). You can also collapse them so only the titles are displayed using the down arrow that appears to the right of the title when you hover your mouse over the title area. Some of the widgets, like Incoming Links and Development News, have configurable options. You'll see a Configure link next to the arrow if you hover over these widgets' titles. Let's take a look at what some of these widgets do.

Figure 3-3. *Moving Dashboard widgets*

QuickPress

The QuickPress widget lets you write a blog post right from the Dashboard. It's handy but limited; you can use tags but not categories, media uploads but not the rich text editor, and you can't change the post's publication date or status. Still, if you need to dash off a quick missive to your readers, QuickPress can save you a step. You'll see the full post editing screen in Chapter 4.

Incoming Links

The Incoming Links widget is set up to show you Google Blog Search results for your site's URL. The widget is configurable (Figure 3-4), so if you'd rather see results from some other service, or if you want to change the number of search results displayed, click Configure in the widget's title bar and edit the settings.

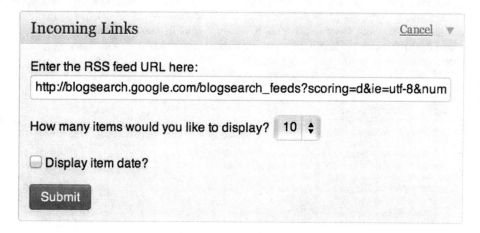

Figure 3-4. Configuring the Incoming Links Dashboard widget

■ **Tip** The Incoming Links, WordPress Development Blog, and Other WordPress News widgets are all just RSS readers with some preconfigured options. If you want to show other RSS feeds instead of these three, click Configure and replace each widget's URL with the feed URL you want to use.

WordPress News Blog

This widget displays headlines from the blog at `http://sleary.me/wp10`.[1] New releases, including security updates, will be announced here. If you decide to configure this widget to use another feed, you should subscribe to the WordPress News blog feed (`http://sleary.me/wp11`)[2] in your RSS reader or sign up for e-mail notifications at `http://sleary.me/wp12`.[3]

---

[1]`http://wordpress.org/news`
[2]`http://wordpress.org/news/feed`
[3]`http://wordpress.org/download`

Dashboard Widget Plugins

Some of the plugins you will install (see Chapter 2) might add more widgets to your Dashboard. These widgets behave exactly like the built-in Dashboard widgets; you can drag them around, configure them, or turn them off altogether using the Screen Options.

Screen Options are personal settings; that is, while you might turn off some Dashboard widgets, they'll still be visible to all other users. There are several plugins you can use to turn off widgets for all users who might be confused by the developer-specific information, particularly the News Blog, the Plugins, and the Other WordPress News. See Appendix A for a list of Dashboard-related plugins.

The Administration Menu and the Admin Bar

You've probably noticed the navigation menu along the left side of your screen. Did you notice that it has two formats? By default, each menu option displays an icon and text (as shown in Figure 3-5), and you can click each option to expand the submenu below. Once you learn your way around, though, you might find that you recognize the icons alone and it's faster to hover over the main menu options to reach the submenus. You can switch to the icons-only, hover-style menu using the small arrow below the menu.

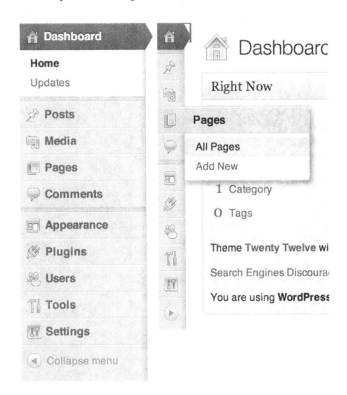

***Figure 3-5.** The two menu styles, wide (left) and collapsed (right)*

The admin bar (Figure 3-6) is the dark gray bar that appears at the top of every page, both in the administration screens and on your site's pages, as long as you're logged in. If you would prefer not to see the admin bar when viewing your site, you can turn it off under Users ➤ Your Profile. The admin bar includes quick links to the most common administration screens: creating new content, managing comments, and updating WordPress core files, plugins, and themes.

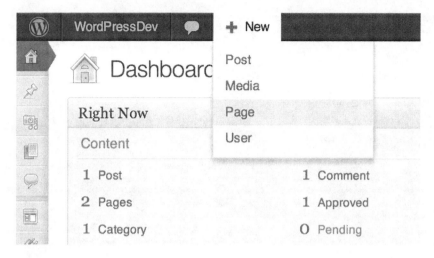

Figure 3-6. *The admin bar*

I'll go over all the sections in the administration menu by the end of this book, but for now let's skip to the last section, Settings.

Settings

The Settings panels give you control over almost every aspect of your site. In addition to the options below, many plugins will add settings panels with even more options. There's a lot to cover in the Settings panels, so let's dig in.

General Settings

The General Settings are shown in Figure 3-7. You've already seen the first few options: the blog title and URLs shown here are the ones you chose during the installation process. The tagline is a brief description of your site that might be displayed near your blog title, depending on the theme you choose.

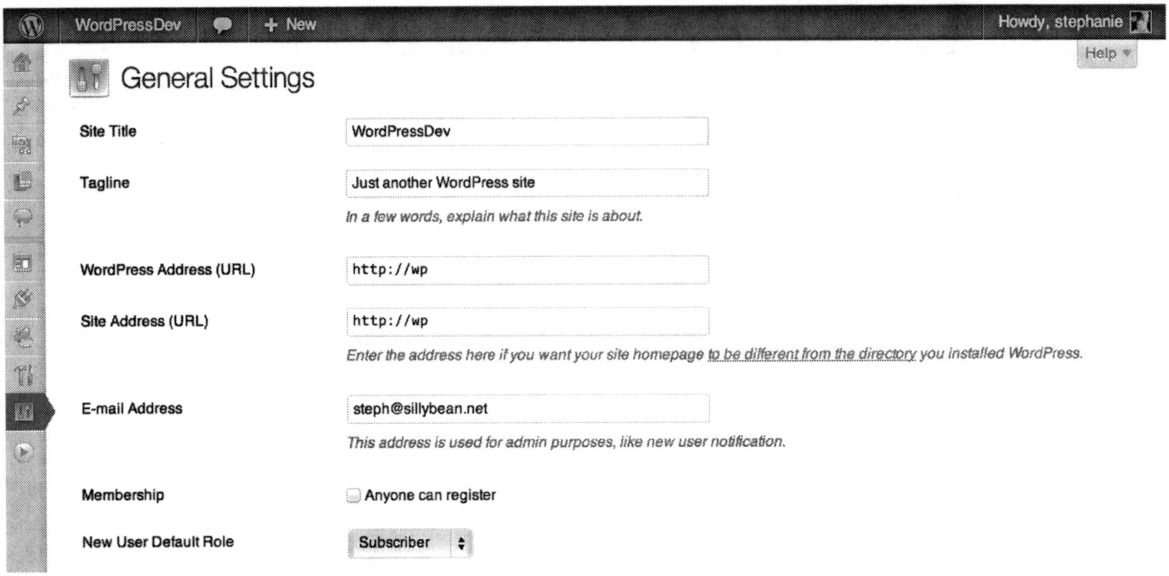

Figure 3-7. *The General Settings screen (top half)*

The Membership and Default Role options are useful if you want to start a group blog. If you allow visitors to sign up as users, you can allow them to contribute posts to your blog. I'll discuss WordPress user roles in depth in Chapter 7, but for now, here's a quick overview:

Subscribers can edit their own profiles and not much else.

Contributors can submit posts for editors' approval, but can't publish anything.

Authors can write and publish posts.

Editors can write and publish posts and pages. They can also publish posts and pages submitted by other users.

Administrators can do everything.

These five roles apply only to registered users. General visitors to your blog have no role at all. No matter what you choose as the default new user role, you can promote users later in the Users panel.

The rest of the settings on the General Settings page deal with date and time formats (Figure 3-8). You can set your local time zone and choose the date format you prefer. WordPress dates are formatted with the same strings that PHP's date() function uses; see http://php.net/date for all your options. The Week Starts On setting changes the way calendar grids are displayed. If you use a calendar archive widget in your sidebar (which you will see in Chapter 5), this setting determines which day begins the week.

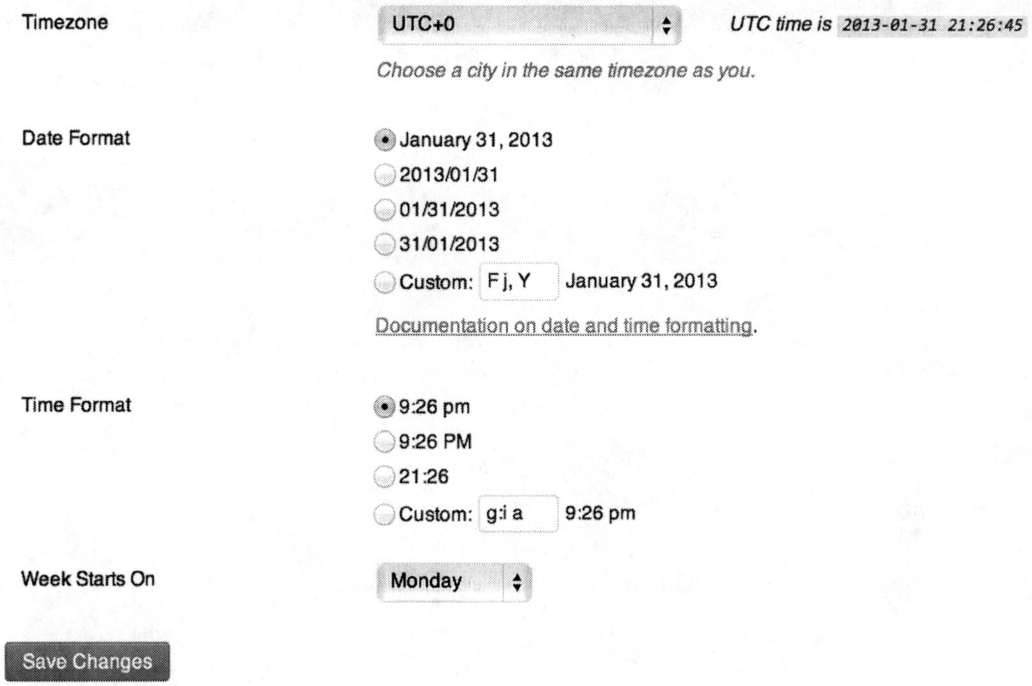

Timezone	UTC+0 ⬍	*UTC time is* `2013-01-31 21:26:45`
	Choose a city in the same timezone as you.	

Date Format

- ◉ January 31, 2013
- ◯ 2013/01/31
- ◯ 01/31/2013
- ◯ 31/01/2013
- ◯ Custom: `F j, Y` January 31, 2013

Documentation on date and time formatting.

Time Format

- ◉ 9:26 pm
- ◯ 9:26 PM
- ◯ 21:26
- ◯ Custom: `g:i a` 9:26 pm

Week Starts On   Monday ⬍

Save Changes

Figure 3-8. *The time and date section of the General Settings page*

Writing Settings

The first three options you'll see on the Writing Settings screen (Figure 3-9) have to do with the editor you'll see on the Post and Page Edit screens. WordPress uses the popular TinyMCE editor (`http://www.tinymce.com`) for its rich text option. The HTML view uses normal markup, but line breaks are converted automatically: one becomes a `<br />` tag; two denotes a break between paragraphs.

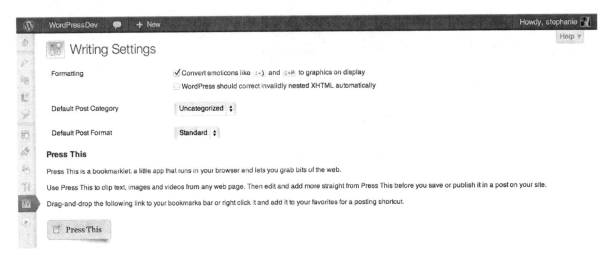

Figure 3-9. Writing Settings (top half)

The next two options determine how the editor will handle emoticons (a complete set of smilies is included in WordPress) and any XHTML you enter.

■ **Tip** TinyMCE doesn't always handle advanced markup well. If the Visual editor drives you crazy, look on your user profile page (Users ➤ Your Profile) for a check box that allows you to turn it off altogether.

WordPress requires posts to be assigned to at least one category. Here, you can specify which categories should be checked by default when you create new posts. You probably haven't set up any categories yet, but you can always return to this page after you've read the next chapter.

Press This is a bookmarklet for faster blogging. Try it out! It selects content from the web page you're viewing and pastes it into the post editor. This makes it easy to quote someone or repost an image.

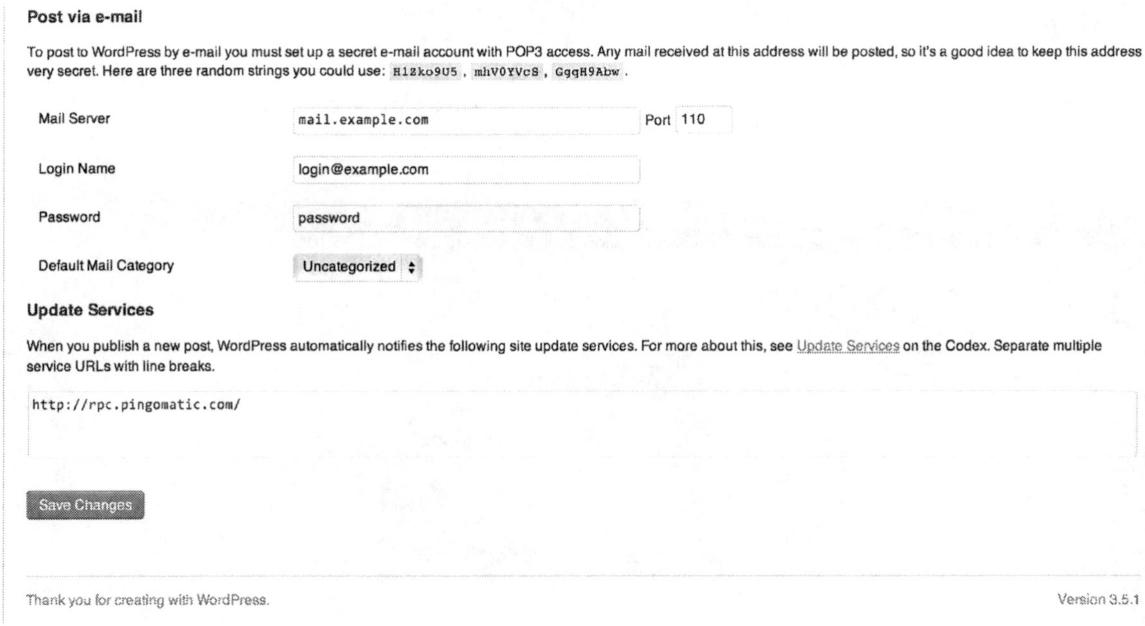

Post via e-mail

To post to WordPress by e-mail you must set up a secret e-mail account with POP3 access. Any mail received at this address will be posted, so it's a good idea to keep this address very secret. Here are three random strings you could use: `H12ko9U5` , `mhV0YVc8` , `GgqH9Abw` .

Mail Server	`mail.example.com`	Port `110`
Login Name	`login@example.com`	
Password	`password`	
Default Mail Category	Uncategorized ⬍	

Update Services

When you publish a new post, WordPress automatically notifies the following site update services. For more about this, see Update Services on the Codex. Separate multiple service URLs with line breaks.

```
http://rpc.pingomatic.com/
```

[Save Changes]

Thank you for creating with WordPress.   Version 3.5.1

Figure 3-10. *Writing Settings (lower half)*

Posting by E-mail

Posting by e-mail is possible, but somewhat limited. HTML tags will be stripped from e-mail messages. Attachments are not converted to media uploads, but are instead included as raw data. The post will be assigned to the default category specified in this section, if different from the usual default category, unless your e-mail subject begins with [n], where *n* is the ID of another category.

In addition to filling in the e-mail account details listed on this screen, you'll also need to set up a way for WordPress to check that mailbox periodically: cron, the WP-Cron plugin, Procmail, or .qmail. Check `http://sleary.me/wp13`[4] for detailed instructions.

Update Services

There are a number of ping services that aggregate information about recently updated blogs. In other words, they let people know that you've posted something new. If you've just installed WordPress, you'll see one service listed here, Ping-O-Matic. It's a central site that feeds into lots of other services.

If you want to go beyond Ping-O-Matic, take a look at the list of ping services maintained by Vladimir Prelovac at `http://sleary.me/wp14`.[5] If you use Feedburner, Google's service for publicizing and tracking RSS feeds, you should also add their PingShot service to your list.

---

[4]`http://codex.wordpress.org/Post_to_your_blog_using_email`
[5]`http://www.prelovac.com/vladimir/wordpress-ping-list`

Reading

The Reading settings (Figure 3-11) determine how your posts appear to your visitors. This is where you can determine whether your site works like a blog, with the most recent posts on the home page, or displays something else. (There are more advanced ways of doing this, which I'll cover in Chapter 12.)

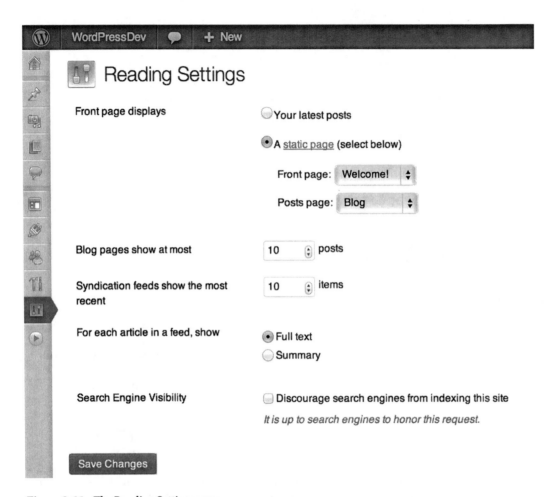

Figure 3-11. *The Reading Settings screen*

Under *Front page displays,* if you select a page as your home page, you'll have the option to display your blog posts on another page. Anything you've entered into the body of that page will not be shown; instead, it will be replaced with your most recent posts.

The next setting, *Blog pages show at most,* determines how many posts per page appear on the blog home page, archive pages, and search results. You can choose a different number of posts to appear in your Atom and RSS feeds, if you wish.

If you want to make your feed subscribers click through to your site to read your complete posts, you may choose to show them only a summary of each post. Keep in mind, however, that the feed summaries strip the HTML formatting from your posts, including things like lists and images. If your unformatted excerpts wouldn't make sense, consider leaving this setting on "Full text."

If you choose *Discourage search engines from indexing this site,* WordPress does the following:

- Adds `<meta name='robots' content='noindex,nofollow' />` to your `<head>` content

- Responds to requests for a `robots.txt` file with one that disallows all user agents—but only if a `robots.txt` file doesn't already exist *and* WordPress is installed in your site root directory.

- Prevents you from pinging linked blogs or blog update services when writing a post.

- Hides the Update Services section on the Writing settings panel.

These privacy options apply only to search engine crawlers and other machines. They do not prevent human visitors from seeing your site. When you write posts and pages, you'll have the option to make them private or password-protected on an individual basis. If you want to make your whole WordPress site private, you'll need to install a plugin such as Registered Users Only (see Appendix A).

■ **Note** The `robots.txt` file (`http://sleary.me/wp15`)[6] is a standard convention web site owners can use to ask search engines not to index parts of a site. Search engines' compliance with the standard is entirely voluntary. That is, you can ask search engines to ignore parts of your site, but unless you password-protect those pages, the search engines could index them anyway.

Discussion

The Discussion settings (Figure 3-12) allow you to control how your site handles comments and trackbacks: whether comments and/or trackbacks are allowed, how they're moderated, who's allowed to comment, how you get notified of new comments, and whether commenters' avatars are displayed. This is a dense screen with a lot of settings. I'll go through each section in detail.

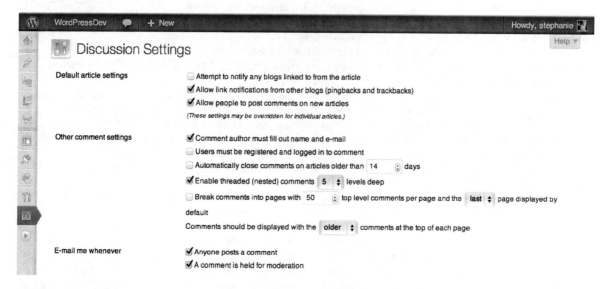

Figure 3-12. *The Discussion Settings screen (top third)*

---

[6]`http://www.robotstxt.org/robotstxt.html`

Comments vs. Trackbacks

Comments are readers' responses to your posts. They are written in a small form on your post or page (usually at the bottom of the screen) and, once approved, are displayed in a list below your post.

Trackbacks are automated alerts that someone has referenced your post or page on their own site. When another blogger includes a link to your post, their site will send a notice to WordPress, including a link to their article and a very brief excerpt. In most WordPress themes, these notices are displayed in your list of comments.

When you write an article, you have the option of sending these automated notices to the sites you've mentioned.

Default Article Settings

You've probably noticed by now that posts and pages in WordPress are usually labeled as such, so the word *article* here is a tip that these settings apply to both posts *and* pages. These three options will be the default settings for any new posts or pages you write, but all of them can be changed on individual posts or pages if you need to deviate from the norm.

If *Attempt to notify any blogs linked to from the article* is checked, WordPress will scan your post or page for links to other blogs. If it finds any, it will ping them—that is, it will send trackbacks to the linked sites—in addition to the Update Services options you selected in the Writing settings. The next option is the inverse: It allows you to decide whether to allow other bloggers to ping your articles when they link to them.

The third option determines whether comments are open by default on new posts and pages. Changing this option will not affect the comment status of any posts and pages you've already published; you'll have to change those from the Post or Page Edit screens using the Bulk Edit feature (see Chapter 4).

Other Comment Settings

The first three settings in this section are designed to help you eliminate unwanted comments. First, you'll have to decide how much information a commenter must provide. By default, they have to leave a name and an e-mail address. If you uncheck this option, only the commenter's IP address will be recorded.

If you are planning a community site, you might choose to allow comments only from registered users. This option is not on by default, and it overrides the previous one.

You can have WordPress automatically close the comment threads on older posts. This is a useful anti-spam feature, since spambots are indiscriminate about which posts they target, but most of the real discussion on a blog post generally takes place in the first few days after it's published. You can adjust the number of days to suit your readership; if you notice that comments are lively for two months before dropping off, turn this setting on and change the number of days to 60. Note, however, that the word *article* appears again here: this setting applies to pages as well as posts. If you want to allow comments on your pages indefinitely, you'll want to leave this setting off.

The next three settings determine how comments are displayed on your site: threaded or linear, nested or flat, and chronological or reversed. Not all themes take advantage of these features.

If comments are threaded, your visitors have the option of responding to individual comments as well as your post. Each comment will have its own Reply link.

In a nested comment list, replies to individual comments are shown indented underneath. In a flat list (and in all versions of WordPress prior to 2.7), comments are simply listed chronologically, no matter whether they are responding to the post or another comment.

WordPress also supports paging for very long lists of comments. If your post or page contains many comments, you can choose how many you'd like to display at one time. Once the number of comments exceeds your per-page setting, visitors will see navigation links allowing them to browse through the additional pages of comments.

Most sites show comments in their original chronological order. However, if you have a post or page with many comments, you might want the newest comments to appear first. Choose Older or Newer from the drop-down box in this last setting as needed, and if you have chosen to split your long comment lists into pages, decide whether the first page will show the newest or oldest comments.

Comment E-mail Notifications

The two settings in this section are checked by default. Unless you turn them off, the author of a post or page will receive an e-mail for every comment posted. Every comment that's held for moderation will generate a notification to the e-mail address you specified in the General Settings panel (Figure 3-6).

Comment Moderation

The next three sections (Figure 3-13) determine which comments are held for moderation. This means that they will not appear on your site as soon as the comment author submits them; instead, they'll go into a queue in the administration area, and you'll have to approve them before they're published.

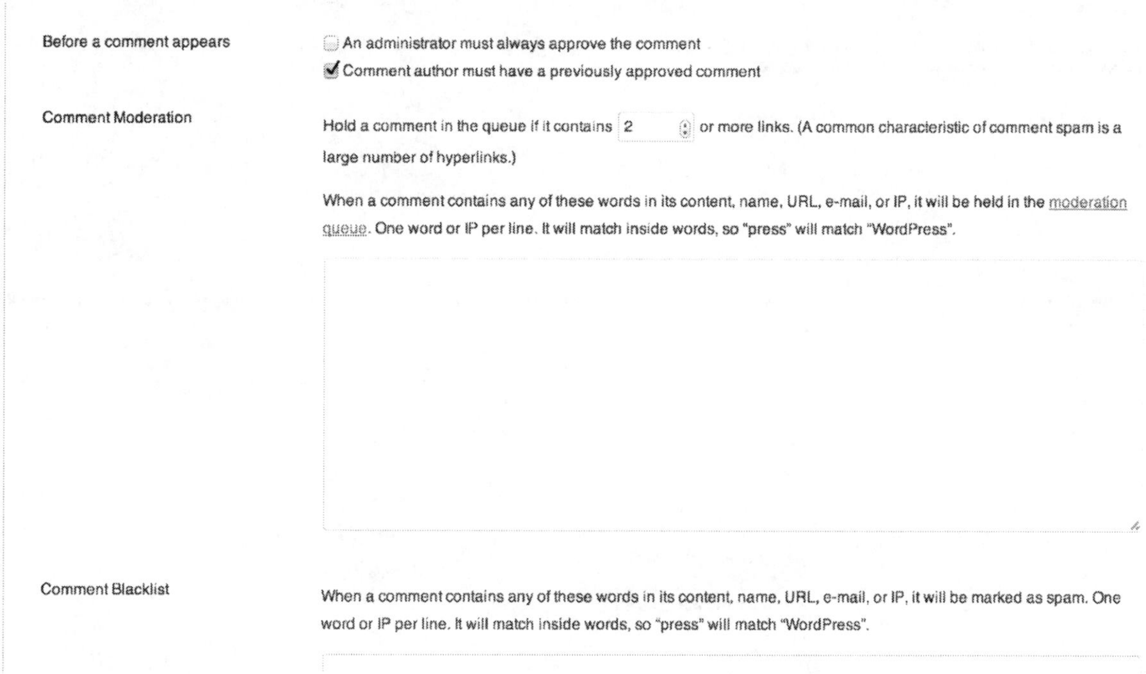

Before a comment appears

☐ An administrator must always approve the comment
☑ Comment author must have a previously approved comment

Comment Moderation

Hold a comment in the queue if it contains 2 ⬍ or more links. (A common characteristic of comment spam is a large number of hyperlinks.)

When a comment contains any of these words in its content, name, URL, e-mail, or IP, it will be held in the moderation queue. One word or IP per line. It will match inside words, so "press" will match "WordPress".

Comment Blacklist

When a comment contains any of these words in its content, name, URL, e-mail, or IP, it will be marked as spam. One word or IP per line. It will match inside words, so "press" will match "WordPress".

Figure 3-13. *Discussion settings (middle third)*

You can require that all comments be held for moderation. This is not the default behavior, and for a typical blog, it would slow the pace of the discussion while inundating you with notification e-mails. A less restrictive choice would be to require that comment authors have at least one previously approved comment. This setting lets your trusted repeat readers comment without your intervention, so you need only worry about the first-time commenters.

You can moderate comments based on their content as well as their author. Since spam comments typically contain long lists of links, by default WordPress will hold a comment for moderation if it contains more than two links. You can adjust the number here if you find that your legitimate comments often contain more links than you have allowed.

In addition to the number of links, you can specify a list of words, names, e-mails, and IP addresses that will be held for moderation. This lets you throttle known spammers, but it's also useful for keeping your discussions on track. If you know that certain topics tend to spark flame wars, list the relevant keywords here, and comment authors will quickly find that they can't discuss those subjects without your explicit approval. Note that these settings apply only to the WordPress comment system. If you are using a plugin to allow comments from other sites, like Facebook, or to replace the built-in comment system with a commenting service like Disqus or IntenseDebate, those systems' settings will override the WordPress moderation settings.

Avatars

Avatars—those little user images on Twitter, Facebook, instant messenger clients, and so on—are all over the internet. They're on your blog, too, unless you turn them off in this section (Figure 3-14). Keep in mind that your choice of theme also has a lot to do with avatar display; some themes don't support them at all, regardless of the setting here. Most themes that do support avatars display them only in comments, not for post or page authors.

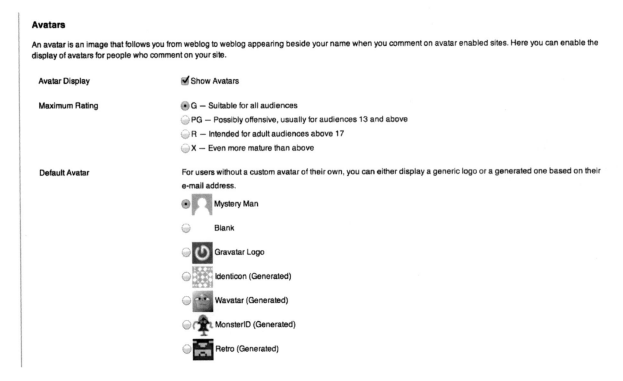

Figure 3-14. Discussion settings (bottom third)

If you allow avatars, you have some control over the kinds of avatars that appear on your site. WordPress uses Gravatars (http://sleary.me/wp16)[7], a central service where people can choose avatars to be associated with their e-mail addresses. Gravatars include content ratings loosely based on the MPAA system for movie ratings: G for child-friendly images, PG for audiences over 13, R for audiences over 17, and X for explicit images. By default, only G-rated Gravatars are allowed on your site.

---

[7]https://en.gravatar.com/

You can also choose the image that's used for comment authors who don't have a Gravatar. The options include several generic settings (e.g., blank, Mystery Man) and three randomized selections: Identicon, Wavatar, and MonsterID.

Identicons are computer-generated geometric patterns. A unique pattern will be assigned to each commenter's e-mail address, so the same pattern will be used every time they comment. MonsterID uses the same concept, but draws images of monsters instead of geometric designs. Wavatar assembles avatar images from a pool of pieces (faces, eyes, noses, hair), rather like assembling a Mr. Potato Head toy.

Media

The Media Settings screen (Figure 3-15) allows you to determine the maximum dimensions of your uploaded images and videos. When you upload images to be embedded in your posts and pages, WordPress generates several copies of the image at different sizes: thumbnail, medium, and large, in addition to the original size. You'll be able to include the smaller sizes in your post and link to the original if your image would otherwise be too large to fit in your layout, or if you don't want to make your visitors download the full size until they've seen a preview. Set your default image dimensions based on your site's layout: if you're using a fixed-width layout, and your post area will be 600 pixels wide, use 600 as the max width for your large size. If your image is small to begin with, only those sizes smaller than the original will be generated.

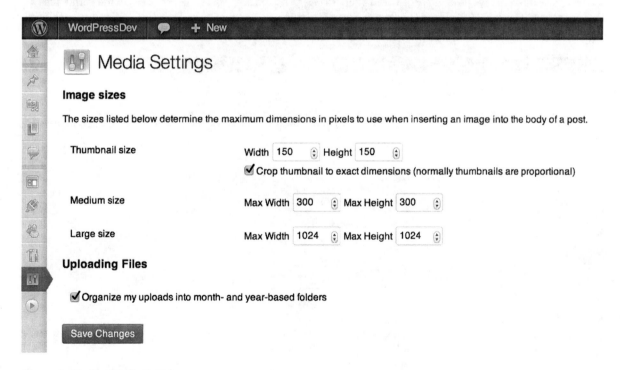

Figure 3-15. *The Media Settings screen*

Note that the default settings for thumbnails result in a 150-pixel square, even though (as the screen says) "normally thumbnails are proportional." Square thumbnails are ideal for magazine-style themes, but you might find that your photos are badly cropped using these settings. If you decide later that square thumbnails are not ideal, you can change this setting.

If you change the image dimensions later, there are several plugins you can use to correct the thumbnails for images you've already uploaded. See Appendix A for a list of media-related plugins.

45

Uploading Files

At the bottom of the Media Settings screen, you can choose whether WordPress creates date-based subdirectories for your upload files. By default, WordPress will create subdirectories for each year, and within those for each month. Your files will be stored according to the dates they were uploaded. For example, if you upload a file called `image.gif` in December 2010, it would be stored as `wp-content/uploads/2010/12/image.gif`. If you uncheck this option, all of your uploaded files will be stored in your specified upload directory. Our example file would be stored as `wp-content/uploads/image.gif` whether you uploaded it in December or June.

When you upload a file with the same name as one that's already in the media library, WordPress will automatically append numbers to the new file's name (e.g., `image1.gif`). If you search the media library for the original name, you won't find it because WordPress has renamed it for you.

Various operating systems have different limits on the number of files and subdirectories a directory can contain. Over time, your media library could grow to the point where your server has trouble showing you a list of all your uploaded files. Using the date-based subdirectories helps you avoid this issue.

I *highly* recommend letting WordPress sort your uploads into date-based subdirectories.

Permalinks

By default, WordPress uses post and page IDs in query strings in its URLs: `example.com/?p=123`. On the Permalinks Settings screen (Figure 3-16), you can choose a custom URL structure (also known as *clean URLs* or *pretty permalinks*) if you have installed WordPress on one of the following servers:

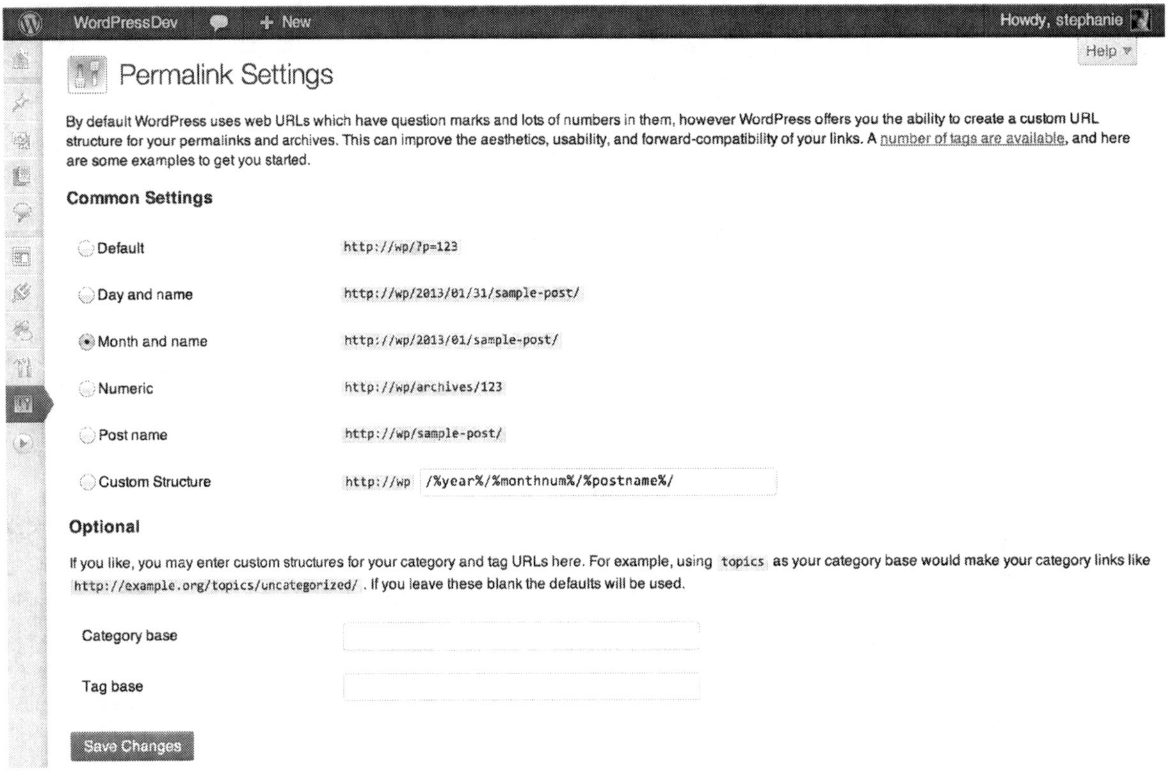

Figure 3-16. *The Permalinks Settings screen*

- Apache or LiteSpeed with the `mod_rewrite` module installed

- Microsoft IIS 7, with the URL Rewrite module 1.1 or higher and PHP 5 running as FastCGI

- Microsoft IIS 6, using a 404 handler or a third-party rewrite module

- Lighttpd, using a 404 handler, `mod_rewrite`, or `mod_magnet`

- Nginx, with the Nginx Helper plugin for full permalink support

If your server meets these conditions, you can switch to one of the other URL structures shown in Figure 3-16, or create your own using the available tags.

If your server uses `.htaccess` files to manage URL rewrites, WordPress will attempt to create or modify your `.htaccess` file when you save your Permalink options. If WordPress can't write to the file, you'll see the necessary rewrite rules displayed, and you'll be asked to edit the file yourself.

If you're using IIS 7, you'll need to add a rule to your `web.config` file after saving your Permalink structure. See `http://sleary.me/wp17`[8] for detailed information.

■ **Tip** Once you've chosen your permalink structure, you should adjust your file permissions so that WordPress can no longer write to `.htaccess`. A number of common exploits involve altering your `.htaccess` file to redirect your visitors to other sites or append unwanted links to your WordPress pages. If changes to `.htaccess` are needed, they'll be displayed and you'll be asked to edit the file yourself.

If you are using any permalink structure other than the default for your posts, your pages will use pretty permalinks as well. The permalink structures use the page name (no matter what structure you've chosen for posts), and they form a directory-like chain based on the page hierarchy. Parent pages appear in the URL as if they were parent directories of static files. In Chapter 4, you'll see how to set up parent pages to create a hierarchy for your site content.

Table 3-1 shows a sample page structure and the resulting page archive URLs.

Table 3-1. *Parent and Child Permalinks for Pages and Categories*

Page/Category	Permalink
WordPress *(page)*	`http://example.com/wordpress/`
Plugins	`http://example.com/wordpress/plugins/`
Themes	`http://example.com/wordpress/themes/`
Books *(category)*	`http://example.com/category/books/`
Fiction	`http://example.com/category/books/fiction/`
Mystery	`http://example.com/category/books/fiction/mystery/`

---

[8]`http://codex.wordpress.org/Using_Permalinks`

You can change your permalink structure at any time. WordPress will store your previous permalink structure and will automatically redirect visitors from the old location to the new one using HTTP's 301 redirect protocol. However, it stores only one previous structure, so if you've changed it a few times, your visitors (and any search engines that indexed your site) might get lost. Since WordPress uses full URLs in linking to its own posts and files, any internal links in your old posts could stop working if you change your permalink structure more than once.

Pick a permalink structure that will work for your site over the long term, and avoid changing it unless absolutely necessary.

■ **Tip**   URLs that contain a page's keywords tend to rank higher on most search engines. If you are interested in optimizing your site for search engine results, choose a permalink structure that includes the post name: Day and Name, Month and Name, or Post Name.

Short Links

If you have included your post name in your permalink structure, or if you have deeply nested pages with long titles, your permalinks can get very long. Sometimes you'll want shorter URLs to paste into an email or Twitter message. A number of URL-shortening plugins are available; Short URL is one of the most popular.

However, you don't need a plugin to get a shorter URL. No matter what permalink structure you have chosen, the default ("ugly") structure will always work. To use it, just find the ID of your post or page—it's in the URL in the Edit Post/Page screen, among other places. There's also a "Get Shortlink" button on the individual post editing screen, as you'll see in Chapter 4.

Category Base

Category and tag archive pages contain a permalink "base," which by default will be "category" for categories and "tag" for tags (e.g., http://example.com/tag/humor/). It's possible to remove the category base—for search engine optimization purposes, to keep your URLs short, or just because you don't like the way it looks—using a plugin such as No Category Base. However, you'll have to be careful to avoid using identical names for categories and pages. Without a category base, categories and pages with the same titles will have identical URLs. Visitors trying to reach your category archive will end up on the page instead.

Summary

Once you've combed through all these settings, you should have a pretty good idea of how your blog is going to work. You've decided how you want the editor to behave when you write new posts and pages, and you've determined how visitors will see your posts displayed. You've set up your comments, decided how they will be moderated, and chosen a set of avatars for your commenters. You're all set to begin adding content to your site!

■ ■ ■

CHAPTER 4

Working with Content

WordPress comes with several basic content types: posts, pages, and media files. In addition, you can create your own content types, which I'll talk more about in Chapter 14.

Posts and pages make up the heart of your site. You'll probably add images, audio, video, or other documents like Office files to augment your posts and pages, and WordPress makes it easy to upload and link to these files.

WordPress also automatically generates a number of different feeds to syndicate your content. I'll talk about the four feed formats, the common feeds, and the hidden ones that even experienced WordPress users might not know about.

Since WordPress is known for its exceptional blogging capabilities, I'll talk about posts first, and then discuss how pages differ from posts.

Posts

Collectively, posts make up the blog (or news) section of your site. Posts are generally listed according to date, but can also be tagged or filed into categories.

At its most basic, a post consists of a title and some content. In addition, WordPress will add some required metadata to every post: an ID number, an author, a publication date, a category, the publication status, and a visibility setting. There are a number of other things that may be added to posts, but the aforementioned are the essentials. Figure 4-1 shows the basic post editing screen.

Figure 4-1. *The post editing screen, using the Visual editor*

Occasionally, a plugin or widget will ask you to enter the ID of a post or page, but it won't be visible on any of the Edit screens. To find the ID, take a look at your URL while you're editing a post or page or while you hover over a post on the Edit screen. The ID is the number at the end of the URL. In this case, the URL is `example.com/wp-admin/post.php?action=edit&post=12`, which means the ID is 12. If you prefer, you can install a plugin like Simply Show IDs, which will display the IDs next to the post titles on the Edit Posts screen.

Post Formats

If your theme supports post formats—all the default themes do—you'll see a meta box below the Publish box that lists the available formats. You can ignore them and continue adding your title and content if you want to write a standard blog post; that's the default format. However, if you want to make something else the focus of your post—an audio or video file, a link, a quote—you can choose the corresponding format.

Figure 4-2 shows a post using the audio format. You can choose an audio file from the media library or enter a URL into the post content. When you publish the post, an audio player will replace the file's URL in the post content.

Figure 4-2. *The audio post format*

Theme support for post formats varies. Some treat all formats the same way; others, like the new Twenty Thirteen default theme, display specialized designs for each format. Figure 4-3 shows an audio post format in the Twenty Thirteen theme.

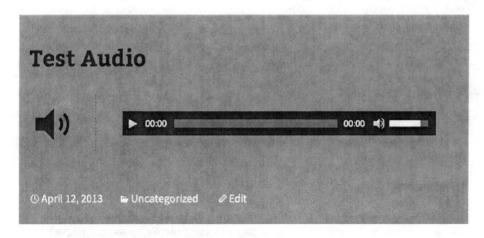

Figure 4-3. *Twenty Thirteen's audio post format*

The post formats available are:

- Standard (text)
- Image
- Image gallery
- Link
- Video
- Audio
- Chat transcript
- Status (a brief update)
- Quote (a quote, its source, and a link URL)
- Aside

The Visual Editor

The content box lets you edit your content in a rich text editor (the Visual tab, which is on by default) or work with the underlying source code (the Text tab). Most people are comfortable writing in the Visual editor. It behaves more or less like familiar desktop word processors, allowing you to add formatting (bold, italic, lists, links) without having to write HTML. Of course, if you know HTML, you can check the Visual editor's work by switching to the Text view. In either view, the editor automatically converts single line breaks to <br/> tags and double line breaks to properly nested paragraphs. If you include <p> and <br/> tags in the Text view, they'll be removed unless they include attributes. For example, <p> would be removed, but <p class="caption"> would not.

The last button in the Visual editor's toolbar is labeled Show/Hide the Kitchen Sink (Figure 4-4). Press this button and a second row of tools will be revealed, including a dropdown that lets you create headings, addresses, and preformatted text using the appropriate HTML tags.

Figure 4-4. Expanding the Visual toolbar

The Visual editor does not include tools for working with tables, subscripts, superscripts, or other relatively unusual formats. If you need these tools, use the TinyMCE Advanced plugin to add them to your toolbar. Install the plugin as described in Chapter 2, then go to Settings ➤ TinyMCE Advanced to configure your toolbars. You'll be able to create up to four rows of buttons. Simply drag the buttons you don't want to use out of the toolbar areas and drop in the ones you do.

Dealing with Content from Microsoft Office

Even those who have been using WordPress for a while might have overlooked the handy Paste from Word button (Figure 4-5) on the second row of the Visual editor's toolbar. If your Visual editor's toolbar has just one row of buttons, press the one labeled Show/Hide Kitchen Sink. In the second row, you'll see a clipboard with the Word logo on it. Press this button, and you'll get a pop-up screen where you can paste the contents of your Word file (see Figure 4-6). It works well with Excel tables, too, and even does a decent job with text copied from Adobe PDF documents.

Figure 4-5. *The Paste from Word button*

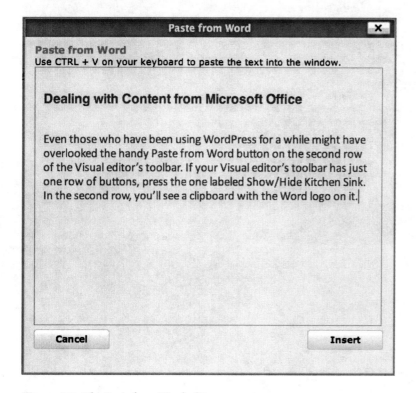

Figure 4-6. *The Paste from Word editor*

Press Insert, and your post will now contain the cleaned-up contents of your Word file. The editor will attempt to retain the structure of your document. It will translate headings from Word's style menu into proper HTML headings, and it will preserve lists and tables. It will remove the Word-specific markup that would clutter your document if you pasted it into the editor without using this tool, such as extraneous `<div>` tags, `MsoNormal` classes, inline styles, and smart tags.

■ **Tip** If Paste from Word is not as thorough as you'd like, save your Word document as HTML, then run the resulting source code through the cleanup tool at `wordoff.org` before pasting it into your post's HTML view.

Shortcodes

WordPress allows developers to define shortcodes—bracketed words that are replaced with content when the post is displayed to visitors. Shortcodes work like text macros in Microsoft Word. WordPress itself uses shortcodes to insert some forms of media (photos with captions, image galleries). A typical image caption shortcode is shown in Figure 4-7, and the resulting image display is shown in Figure 4-8.

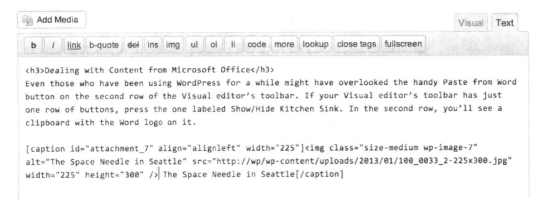

Figure 4-7. *An image caption shortcode*

The Space Needle in Seattle

Figure 4-8. *The image display resulting from the caption shortcode*

Permalinks

Assuming you have enabled permalinks in your Settings, you'll see a Permalink field on each post and page. The portion highlighted in yellow is derived from the title, with spaces replaced by hyphens and other punctuation removed. This is called the slug. Posts, pages, categories, and tags all have slugs. If you don't like the generated slug or if it's too long, you can edit it using the Edit button to the right. This turns the slug into an editable field as shown in Figure 4-9. Note that you can't edit the rest of the URL; it's constructed based on the pattern you chose on the Permalink Settings panel.

Figure 4-9. *Editing the post slug*

If you edited your permalink and later decide you'd like to get the generated slug back, you can just delete everything in the slug field and press the Save button. WordPress will fill in the blank.

Publish Settings

In the Visibility section, you can choose who's allowed to see your post. The default setting is public, which means that anyone can read it. Just below this option, you'll see a checkbox labeled *Stick this post to the front page*. Making a post "sticky" means that it always appears at the top of lists, including archives, as well as your home page.

The other two Visibility settings are not as intuitive as they appear to be. A private post is one that only registered users of your site can read, if they have permission (or in WordPress parlance, the *capability*) to read private posts. By default, only editors and administrators have this capability. You'll learn more about roles, and how to change them, in Chapter 7.

A password-protected post is not public, but visitors don't have to be registered users in order to read it. When you choose the *Password protected* option in the Visibility box, you'll be asked to provide a password for the post. This is unique to the post, and has no relationship to any users' passwords. You can then give that password to anyone you like (in an e-mail, let's say). When they visit your site, they'll see the title of the post but not the content. In place of the content, there will be a password field. When your visitors enter the correct password, they'll see the post content.

The Status setting provides a rudimentary workflow for your posts. When you begin a new post, it remains in Draft status until you press the blue Publish button. At that point, the status changes to Published and the post becomes visible to your visitors. A contributor, who doesn't have the ability to publish posts, would see a Submit for Review button instead of Publish. The contributor's post status would then change to Pending Review, and an Editor would have to approve and publish the post.

You can leave posts in Draft mode indefinitely. If you need to close the editing screen before you've finished writing, press the Save Draft button rather than Publish.

■ **Note** While the Permalink, Visibility, Status, and Publication Date fields have their own OK buttons, none of your changes to these settings will take effect until you press the blue Publish (or Update) Post button.

Publication Date and Scheduling Posts

When you press Publish, the post becomes visible to the public and its publication date is set to the current date and time. However, you can easily change the date if you need to backdate a post or schedule it to appear in the future.

To change the date, immediately press Edit next to Publish in the Publish Settings box. An extra set of form fields will appear, as shown in Figure 4-10. Enter your desired publication date—note the 24-hour time format!—and press OK. If the date is in the past, the post's publication date will be adjusted, and it will appear in the archives according to the new date. If you chose a date in the future, the post will be scheduled to publish at that time. The Publish button will change to Schedule, and the post will not be visible on your site (or in your feeds) until the time you specified.

Figure 4-10. *Scheduling a future post*

■ **Note** WordPress's cron system is actually a pseudo-cron system. That is, it runs only when someone visits the site (either the public pages or the administration screens). Scheduled tasks therefore run as soon as someone visits the site after the scheduled time. On a busy site, the difference might be negligible. On a site with only a handful of visitors per day, tasks might run several hours after their scheduled time.

Categories

Categories can be a powerful tool for organizing your posts. Many magazine-style themes for WordPress rely on categories to break articles into divisions, much like a magazine's departments or a newspaper's sections. You can also get a feed for each of your categories (see the "Feeds" section of this chapter). By styling your categories differently and publicizing the otherwise hidden feeds for individual categories, you can create the illusion of multiple blogs for your visitors, even though behind the scenes you're maintaining just one. You'll learn how to do this in Chapter 12.

To manage categories, go to Categories under Posts in the main menu. You'll be able to add, edit, or delete categories. You'll also be able to add descriptions, change slugs, or even convert categories to free-form tags (Figure 4-11).

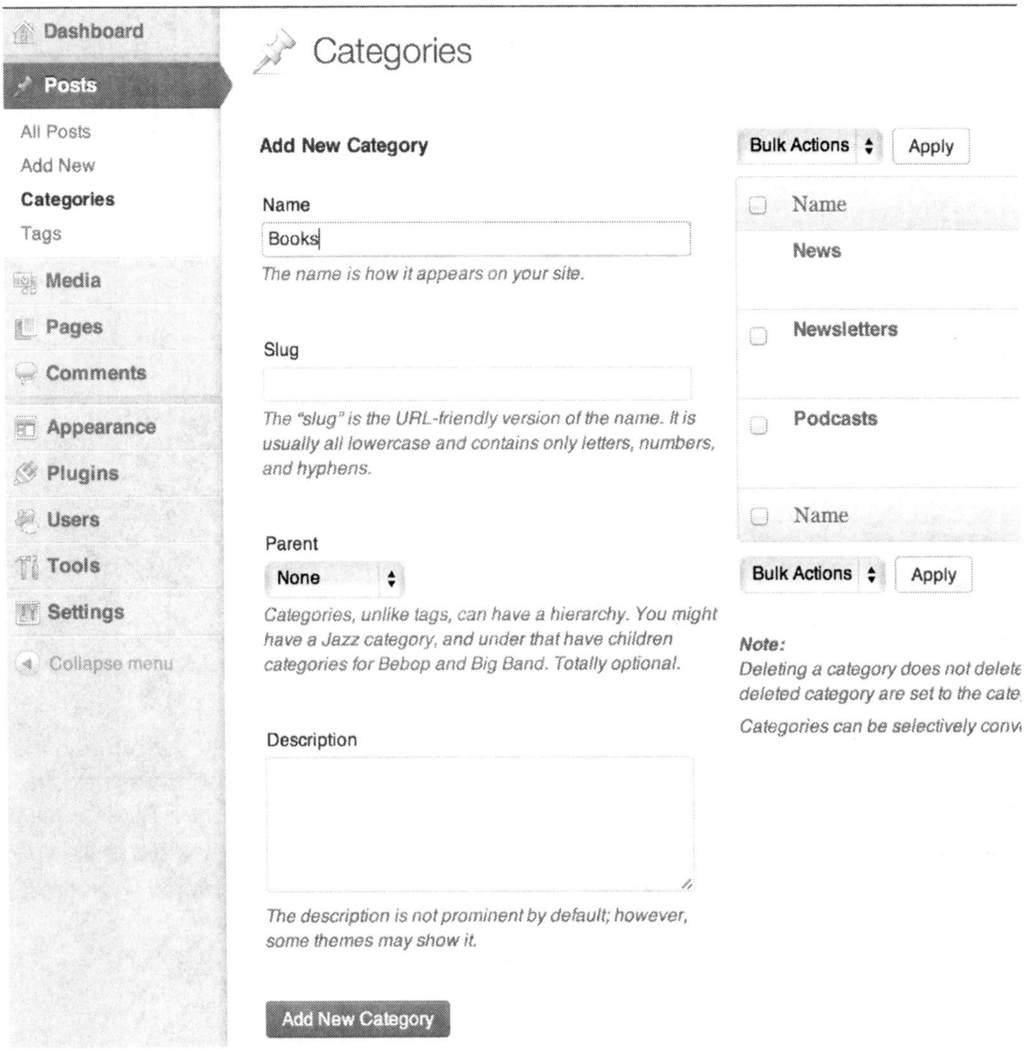

Figure 4-11. *Managing categories*

Categories can be arranged into hierarchies. When you create a new category, you'll have the option to make it a child of an existing one. There is no limit to the depth of your categories.

Categories must have distinct slugs. Even if two categories have different parents and would therefore have different permalinks, you can't assign them the same slug. If you choose a slug that's already in use, WordPress will discard your new category and highlight the existing one that uses that slug.

When you're editing an individual post, the Categories box shows a hierarchical list of all your categories. If you don't check one, the default category you chose in your Writing Settings will be checked for you when you save the post. All posts in WordPress must have at least one category selected. However, you can select as many as you like.

Tags

If you're familiar with good old meta keyword tags (the kind that used to drive search engine optimization) or the concept of tagging from social media sites like Flickr, YouTube, or Delicious, the tag entry box holds no surprises for you. Tags are subject keywords, just like categories, but where categories must be set up ahead of time by an editor or administrator, authors are free to create new tags simply by typing them into the Tag box while writing a post (Figure 4-12). If a tag already exists on another post, WordPress will suggest it once you've typed a few characters.

Figure 4-12. *Editing tags on a post*

Note that after you've added new tags, you must press Add in order to apply them. Then, you still have to press the blue Publish/Update button before your changes take effect.

To manage your tags, go to Post ➤ Tags in the main menu. Here, you can add or delete tags, edit slugs, add descriptions, or convert tags to categories. Like categories, tag slugs must be unique—and since categories and tags share the same pool of slugs (they're both considered taxonomies), a category and a tag can't share a slug, even if they have the same name.

You can get feeds for each of your tags, as you'll see in the "Feeds" section of this chapter.

Featured Images

The featured image (formerly known as the post thumbnail) is an image that represents your post. It might be shown by itself, or alongside the post content or excerpt, depending on how your theme displays posts.

I'll cover uploading images in the "Media Files" section of this chapter.

If you don't see a Featured Image box on your Edit Posts screen (Figure 4-13), your theme probably doesn't support them. You can enable them by adding a line to your theme's functions.php file. See Chapter 12 for details.

Figure 4-13. Setting a featured image

Excerpts

An excerpt is, as the box says in WordPress, a summary of your post. Some themes show excerpts rather than the full content when posts are listed, either on the home page or in archives. If a theme calls for an excerpt and none is specified, it will be generated automatically from the post content. However, any HTML formatting will be removed. If your content contains lists or tables, the results might be very odd. You can preserve HTML formatting in excerpts using the Advanced Excerpt or the_excerpt Reloaded plugins.

Excerpts are shown with a continuation string. By default, '[. . .]' is appended to your excerpt text, which is 55 words long. Both the string and the excerpt length can be modified with a few lines of code in your theme or plugin; see Chapter 12.

Comments and Trackbacks

In Chapter 3, you set your preferences regarding comments and trackbacks. Here, you can override those settings for the current post. If you're editing an existing post that has comments, you'll see the comments listed, and you can edit them right from this screen.

Trackbacks are automated notifications (pings) from other sites that have mentioned your post. They let you (and your readers) know that conversations are taking place elsewhere about something you wrote. Trackbacks are usually displayed alongside comments on a post (see Figure 4-14). Here on the Edit screen, you'll see a list of any trackbacks your post has received.

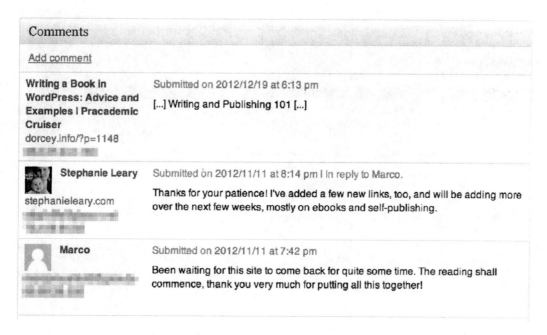

Figure 4-14. A trackback and a comment on a post

In the Trackbacks box, you'll be able to ping sites about your post. Keep in mind the list of sites you chose to ping for all your posts in the Update Services section of your Writing settings. Also, if you chose on that screen to ping linked sites, any links included in your post will be pinged automatically. If you want to ping any sites in addition to your Update Services list and the sites linked in your post, you can add the URL in the Trackback section, as shown in Figure 4-15. If your post has already been published, this box will display a list of the sites that have already been pinged.

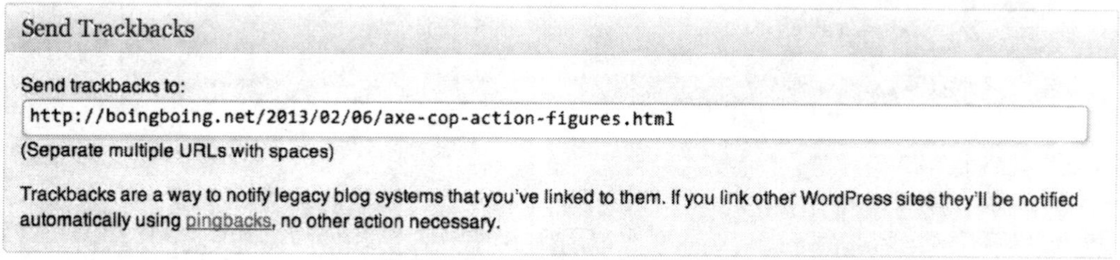

Figure 4-15. Sending additional trackbacks from the Edit Post screen

Revisions

WordPress saves every revision of your posts and pages, including the most recent autosave, if there is one. If you messed something up and need to revert to a previous version, use the Screen Options to turn on the Revisions box (Figure 4-16). Then, scroll down the editing screen to the Revisions box near the bottom. There you'll see a list of all the revisions. Click one to view it. The title, content, and excerpt (for posts) will be shown (Figure 4-17). These fields, along with the author, are the only ones stored for each revision. At the bottom of this screen, there's another list of all the revisions, but this time you'll see radio buttons allowing you to select two revisions for comparison. Each revision also has a restore link on this page.

Figure 4-16. *Turning on Revisions in the Screen Options*

Figure 4-17. *Comparing revisions*

Restoring a post or page actually creates *another* revision. WordPress copies the revision you chose, saves it as a new version, and marks it as the current revision. In other words, if you revert a post and later realize that you really do need the newer copy, it's still there. Just look in the revision list for the corresponding date.

As you might imagine, storing all these revisions can inflate the size of your WordPress database. If you're concerned about storage space, you can limit the number of revisions WordPress stores by adding the following line to your wp-config.php file:

```
define('WP_POST_REVISIONS', 3);
```

To turn off revisions altogether, set the number to zero:

```
define('WP_POST_REVISIONS', 0);
```

There are also several plugins that will handle this setting for you. They provide a Settings screen where you can make changes without having to edit your config file. Revision Control is a good one.

Custom Fields

Custom fields allow you to create new attributes for your posts and pages. Some common uses for custom fields include adding a mood to each blog post, providing custom CSS for posts or pages, listing what music you're currently listening to or the books you're reading, or setting an expiration date for posts.

The custom fields box is not visible by default. If you need it, you can turn it on using the Screen Options. The field values are stored in the database but are not shown in most themes. You'll have to add a template tag to your theme file or use a plugin to display your custom field data.

The built-in custom field interface (Figure 4-18) is not very user-friendly. Often, developers create custom meta boxes with a more intuitive interface for entering custom field data. You'll learn how to do this for your own themes and plugins in Chapter 14.

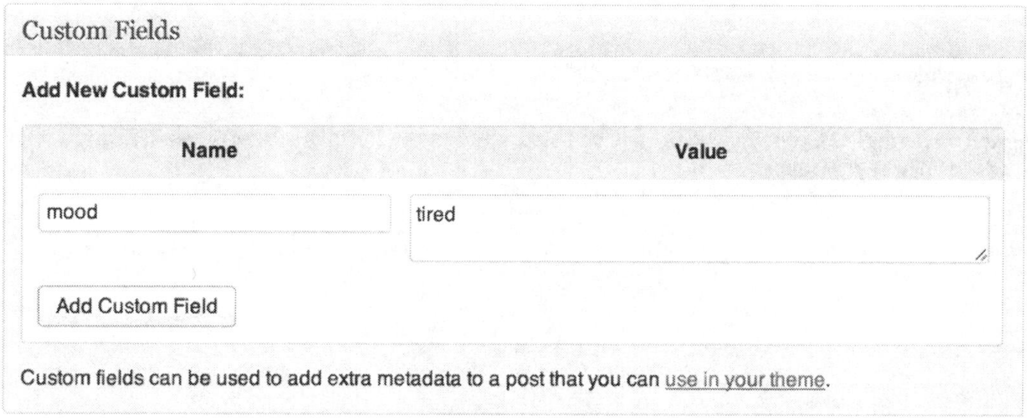

Figure 4-18. *Custom fields*

Pages

Pages in WordPress are for information that is not part of a blog—that is, content where the publication date is (mostly) irrelevant. You'll notice that your first page, Sample Page, was created for you during installation.

Pages are much like posts: you need a title and some content, and that's about all. The ID, author, date, publication status, and visibility will be set for you when you publish the page. However, there are some important differences. The publication date is not displayed for pages in most themes, and pages are not organized by date. Also, you probably noticed that categories and tags are not available for pages. Pages can be organized into a hierarchy, but since they exist outside the collection of posts, they don't share the same metadata.

Page Attributes: Parents, Templates, and Order

You can arrange your pages into filesystem-like hierarchies by making them children of parent pages (Figure 4-19). In the Attributes box on any single page's Edit screen, you'll be able to select another existing page as the parent. That page could, in turn, have another parent, and so on.

Figure 4-19. *Pages arranged in a parent/child hierarchy*

If you've turned on permalinks, your page's URL will be built by adding its slug to that of its parent and any other page ancestors, as shown in Figure 4-20.

Figure 4-20. *The slug of a page with a parent*

As you'll see in Chapter 5, WordPress themes can have multiple templates for pages. When you create a new page template, it becomes available as an option in the parent drop-down portion of the Page Attributes box (Figure 4-21). To use your new template instead of the default page template, select it here and update the page.

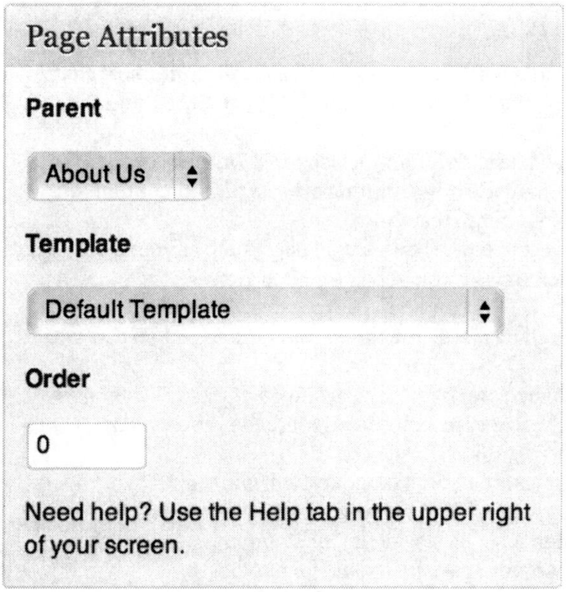

Page Attributes

Parent

About Us ⬍

Template

Default Template ⬍

Order

0

Need help? Use the Help tab in the upper right of your screen.

Figure 4-21. *Page Attributes*

When custom menus have not been specified, WordPress builds menus by listing pages, and it uses the order field to sort them. Numbering them using this field is a bit like programming in BASIC; inevitably, you'll find that you need to insert a new page between two existing ones, and then you'll have to redo the numbering for all the pages. To avoid the problem, you can use a numbering scheme that leaves you plenty of room between pages (111, 222, 333, etc.). If you prefer, there are plugins that provide a drag-and-drop screen where you can rearrange your pages without having to count. Simple Page Ordering (Figure 4-22) is one of the best. If you plan to use the custom menu feature, the order of your pages probably doesn't matter much, and you can simply leave the order field blank.

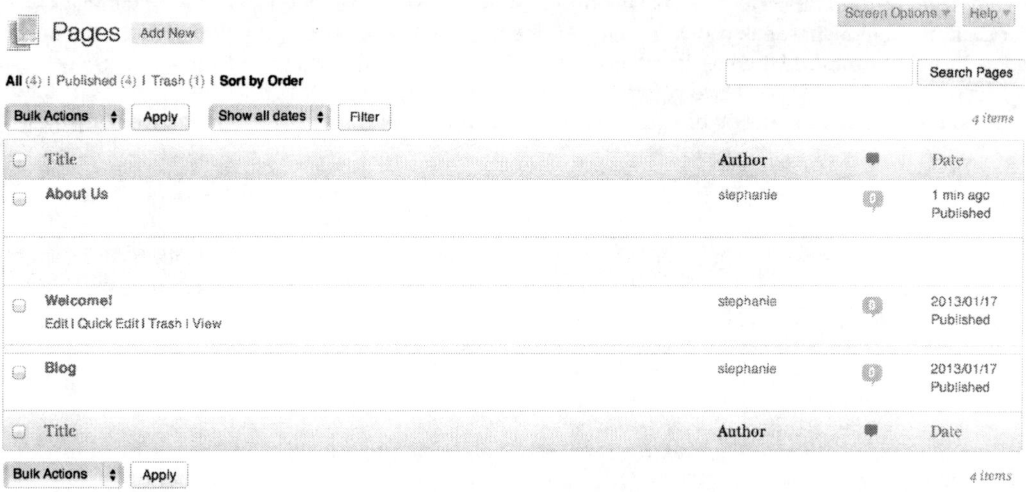

Pages Add New

Screen Options ▾ Help ▾

All (4) | Published (4) | Trash (1) | **Sort by Order**

Search Pages

Bulk Actions ⬍ Apply   Show all dates ⬍ Filter

4 items

☐ Title	Author	💬	Date
☐ About Us	stephanie	0	1 min ago Published
☐ Welcome! Edit I Quick Edit I Trash I View	stephanie	0	2013/01/17 Published
☐ Blog	stephanie	0	2013/01/17 Published
☐ Title	Author	💬	Date

Bulk Actions ⬍ Apply

4 items

Figure 4-22. *Simple Page Ordering lets you drag and drop pages to rearrage their order*

Posts vs. Pages: Same, but Different

Sometimes it's not immediately clear whether your content would work best as a post or a page. On the surface, they are much the same in WordPress: they share a similar editing screen and both can accept comments and trackbacks. How do you decide which to use?

In general, posts are ideal for date-based content: blogs, podcasts, columns, newsletters, journals, or a press release archive. In short, for news of any kind, you should definitely use posts. Putting the rest of your content into pages will provide a logical division for both your visitors and your content authors.

Posts are shown in a chronological sequence (usually newest to oldest) on a single page, such as your home page or an archive of posts from a particular month or category. Once your visitors select a post to view by itself, they'll be able to read the comments as well as your content.

Pages are generally not grouped in chronological order. Each page will appear on its own screen. You can create a list of pages using a widget or a menu (see Chapter 5).

If your site consists mainly of articles that will not often change and need to be arranged in a simple hierarchy, like files in folders, then pages will probably work well for you. In this case, you could ignore the post screens altogether or create a basic "What's New?" blog as an adjunct to the main site.

If no such clear division exists in your content, think about your content taxonomy and your subscribers' needs. Pages do not have tags or categories. They can be arranged in a parent/child hierarchy, but if you need a more complex or flexible taxonomy, posts would probably work better. Also, pages are not included in feeds. Will your readers want to be notified every time you add a document? If so, your content should go into posts.

Posts Are Pages; Pages Are Posts

Posts and pages in WordPress are essentially the same thing. They share the same table in the WordPress database (wp_posts), with one field to distinguish them: type, which could be "post" or "page." (In fact, media files also share this table, as you'll see later.) Posts and pages use most of the same fields in that table. The big difference is in the way they're presented to you. Even though all the database fields are available to each type of content, only some of those fields appear in the Edit panels.

As with nearly everything in WordPress, this default behavior can be changed using plugins. For example, you can add excerpts, categories, and tags to pages.

Pages do not have excerpts, even though they have a database field for them. Since pages never appear in archive lists, excerpts would never be used for pages in a typical WordPress site. However, excerpts can be useful for pages as well as posts. For example, you might tweak your search results theme file to display excerpts rather than the full post content. Also, some heavily customized themes do list pages in archive-like lists. You can use a plugin such as PJW Page Excerpt or Excerpt Editor to add excerpts to your pages.

In Chapter 14, you'll see how you can add categories and tags, as well as new custom taxonomies, to your pages.

Editing Posts and Pages

You can filter the list of posts by category or date using the drop-down menus at the top of the list. You can also search your posts and pages using the box at the top right side of the Edit screens, but beware: it searches not only the titles but also the complete content of posts and pages.

Autosave

WordPress does save your posts automatically, once per minute, as you write. You can adjust this timing by adding this line to your wp-config.php file:

```
define('AUTOSAVE_INTERVAL', 120 );  // autosave every two minutes
```

■ **Note** The autosave function will not continue to work if you close your browser window or go offline.

If you leave a post open in your browser after you've published it, WordPress might autosave a revision. The next time you edit this post, you'll see a warning that a newer revision exists. Use the comparison tool to check the revision. If it's no different from the published version, you can dismiss the warning by deleting the revision or updating the post.

Screen Options

Like the Dashboard, the Edit Posts and Pages panels have Screen Options available. You can choose which columns you want to see; the post/page title will always display, but the author, categories, tags, comments, and date columns are optional. You can also choose how many posts or pages you'd like to see per page (Figure 4-23). Twenty is the default, but you can increase it if you have lots of content and you'd like to scroll through it faster. Keep in mind that the more posts or pages you put on each screen, the longer it will take WordPress to generate the screens.

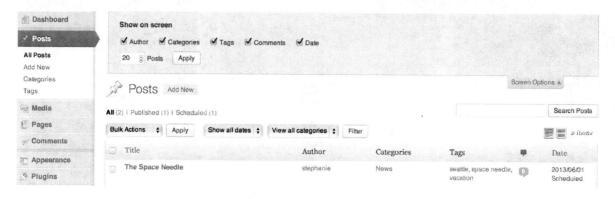

Figure 4-23. *Screen options for the Edit Posts screen*

Screen options are also available when editing individual posts and pages (Figure 4-24). If you're working on a small screen or a monitor with a low resolution, you might want to switch your editing layout to a single column. You can also choose to enable boxes that are turned off by default, like Revisions and Custom Fields.

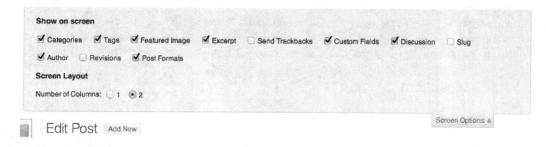

Figure 4-24. *Screen options for an individual post*

Quick Edit

If you need to change the attributes of a post or page without editing the content, you can do so quickly using the Quick Edit feature. Go to Edit Posts (or Pages) and hover your mouse over the post you want to modify. A row of links will appear below the title: Edit, Quick Edit, Delete, and View. Choose Quick Edit, and the table row will transform into a miniature editing form (Figure 4-25) that lets you change nearly everything about the page except the content, excerpt, and custom fields.

Figure 4-25. *The Quick Edit feature*

Bulk Edit

What do you do when you need to change the attributes of many posts or pages at once? Again, go to your list of Posts (or Pages). Select the checkboxes next to the posts you want to edit, then choose Edit from the Bulk Actions drop-down above the list of posts and press Apply. (If you want to select all the posts on the page, just use the checkbox in the gray table header.)

The Bulk Edit form (Figure 4-26) offers fewer options than Quick Edit. Things that would be illogical to change for multiple posts, like titles and publication dates, are not available. You can edit the categories and tags (for posts), parent and template (for pages), and the comment, trackback, visibility, and publication status settings.

Figure 4-26. *Bulk editing posts*

Media Files

WordPress allows you to upload virtually any kind of file and attach it to your post or page (as long as your host allows file uploads). You can add files using the uploader found on the individual post/page editing screens and in the Media Library section. You can insert links directly to the media files into your posts, or you can link to an attachment page, a dedicated view showing details about the file and a link to the source.

Edit any individual post or page, and you'll see that there's an icon labeled Add Media above the content box. Click it and a pop-up box should appear with two tabs across the top: Upload Files and Media Library. On the right side of this window you'll have options to create a gallery, set the featured image, or insert a file from a URL.

Uploading a File from Your Computer

The media uploader lets you choose multiple files from your computer, or just drag them from your desktop into the empty area in the middle of the uploader window. Once WordPress has processed the file, you'll see a dialog (Figure 4-27) where you can fill in details: a title, a caption, a description, a link URL, and some alignment and size options.

Figure 4-27. *Uploading an image from your computer*

Title: This is for internal use only. When you're browsing your media library, you'll see this title next to a tiny thumbnail of the image. If you don't fill in a title, the file name will be used.

Caption: This will be shown beneath the image, audio file, or video in your post. The exact formatting will depend on your theme's stylesheet.

Alternate Text: For images, this is the text that will be displayed if the image is missing. It will be read aloud to visually impaired users browsing your site with a screen reader.

Description: This will be displayed in your media library. It will also be displayed on the file's attachment page.

Link URL: This lets you specify whether your file is linked, and if so, where it leads. Linking to the file URL is a great way to let your visitors see the full-size image if you're inserting a smaller version. If your post discusses another site, you might choose to paste that URL here instead.

Alignment: Choose whether an image should be aligned to the left, the right, in the center, or not at all. If you choose left or right alignment, your post text will wrap around the image. If you choose center, your image will appear on its own line.

Size: You can insert the full-size image into your post. WordPress will generate up to three smaller sizes (based on the dimensions you choose in your Media Settings), and you can choose any of these if one will fit better in your post content.

Below these fields, you'll see a blue button that lets you insert the image into your post.

Some themes do not support image alignment. If your images are not aligned correctly, add the lines in Listing 4-1 to your theme's `styles.css` file. These CSS rules correspond to the classes WordPress inserts into image tags; with these styles in place, your images will be aligned according to the settings you choose in the upload screen.

Listing 4-1. Image Alignment Styles

```
img.alignright, a img.alignright { float:right; margin: 0 0 1em 1em}
img.alignleft, a img.alignleft { float:left; margin:0 1em 1em 0}
img.aligncenter, a img.aligncenter { display: block; margin: 1em auto; }
```

If you chose multiple files, you'll see all these options for only the first file. Simply click another file to edit its details. The file you are currently editing will be highlighted in blue (Figure 4-28).

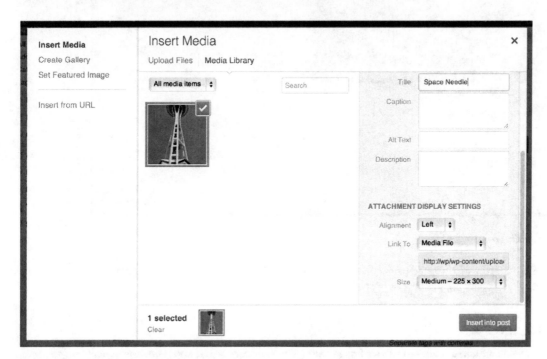

Figure 4-28. *Adding an image from the Gallery*

Inserting an Image from a URL

You can use images hosted on another site without downloading them to your computer and uploading them into WordPress. Instead of selecting files to upload, click the Insert from URL tab. You'll be asked for the source URL in addition to the caption, alt text, alignment, and link fields (Figure 4-29). However, WordPress won't generate other sizes; you have to use the image as-is.

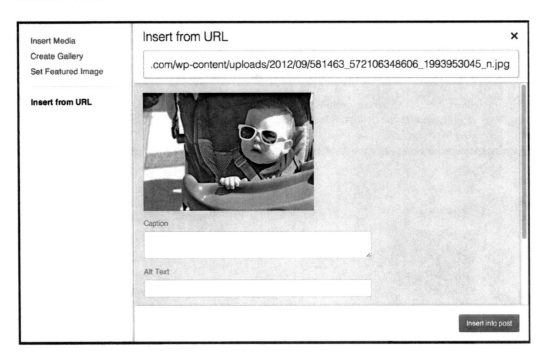

Figure 4-29. *Adding an image from a URL*

Keep in mind that images inserted from URLs are not copied to your server. If the owner of the original file moves or deletes it, it will no longer appear in your post.

Editing Images

The WordPress media uploader includes a basic image editor. You can crop, resize, and rotate the images you've uploaded. To begin, click the Edit Image button next to the thumbnail shown in the image details. A simple editing interface will appear (Figure 4-30). Click the image once, then drag your cursor to choose an area to crop. If you want to scale or crop the image to a precise number of pixels, use the numeric scaling and cropping forms to the right of the image.

Figure 4-30. *Cropping an uploaded image*

Galleries

If you have several images to add, you can do them all at once and create a gallery rather than inserting them one at a time. Galleries are automatically formatted into neat grids of thumbnails that link to the larger versions of the images.

When you're finished uploading files, choose the Create Gallery tab (Figure 4-31). You'll see all the images in your media library; if you prefer, you can use the dropdown just above the images to limit your selections to the images that have been uploaded for this post. Clicking an image will add it to your selections, shown at the bottom of the window. When you're done, click the "Create a new gallery" button.

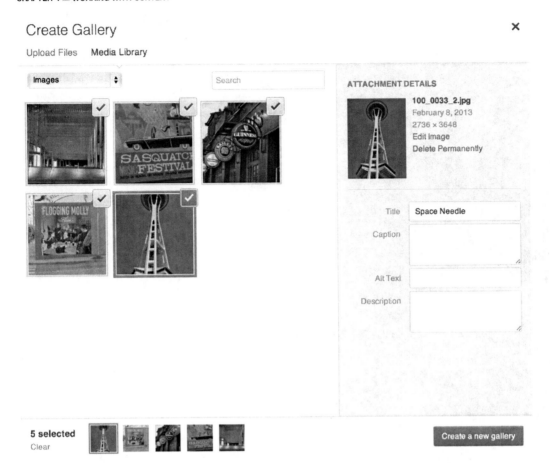

Figure 4-31. *Selecting images to create a gallery*

On the subsequent Edit Gallery screen, you'll be able to add captions, rearrange the images, and choose some display options for your gallery, like the number of columns and whether the thumbnails link to the full-size images or attachment pages. When you press "Insert gallery," you'll see that "[gallery]" has been added to the post's text (possibly with some attributes like a list of IDs, depending on the options you chose). Just leave that shortcode on its own line and type whatever else you'd like to say. When you publish the post, a thumbnail-sized copy of each photo appears in the post, as shown in Figure 4-32.

This entry was posted in News and tagged seattle, space needle, vacation on June 1, 2013. Edit

Figure 4-32. *An image gallery as shown in the default theme*

Audio

Uploading audio is fairly straightforward, too: choose the file, and you'll be asked to fill in the title, description, caption, and link URL. When you press Insert into post, an [audio] shortcode will be inserted into your post. When you view the post, you'll see that the shortcode has been replaced with a player (Figure 4-33). This is an HTML5 interface created using MediaElement.js (`http://sleary.me/wp18`[1]), and its appearance can be customized using CSS in your theme. In older browsers, it will fall back to a Flash or Silverlight interface.

An Audio File

Leave a reply

Play the audio file:

This entry was posted in Uncategorized on April 12, 2013. Edit

Figure 4-33. *The [audio] shortcode turns into an HTML5 player*

---

[1]`http://mediaelementjs.com`

Podcasting

Podcasting with WordPress is relatively easy. If you've inserted your audio file into your post (even as a simple link), WordPress will automatically add the proper enclosures to your feeds. However, if you want to include your podcast in the iTunes podcast directory, you'll need a plugin to configure some additional fields for your feed. Blubrry PowerPress Podcasting is the most popular, but there are several podcasting plugins available; see Appendix A.

■ **Tip**   The various podcasting plugins work for both audio and video podcasts.

Video

When you upload a video, you'll be asked to fill in the four basic attributes: title, description, caption, and link URL. Inserting the file into the post results in a [video] shortcode. When the post is viewed, this turns into a HTML5 player similar to the audio player.

oEmbed

Embedding video from other sites is quite easy. WordPress supports the oEmbed standard. What this means is that you don't have to paste the complicated HTML provided by sites such as YouTube. Instead, you can simply paste the URL of the video page into your post on its own line. Try it out now! Grab a URL from YouTube, save your post (Figure 4-34), and view it. If everything is working as expected, your plain text URL should have been replaced with a video player, as shown in Figure 4-35.

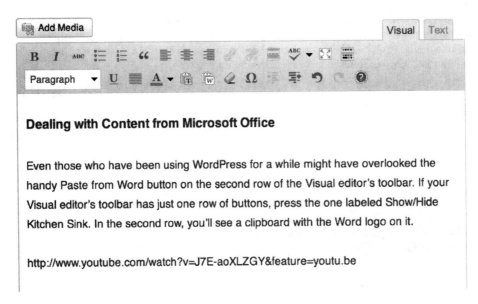

Figure 4-34. Embedding a YouTube video is as easy as pasting the URL into your post

Dealing with Content from Microsoft Office

Even those who have been using WordPress for a while might have overlooked the handy Paste from Word button on the second row of the Visual editor's toolbar. If your Visual editor's toolbar has just one row of buttons, press the one labeled Show/Hide Kitchen Sink. In the second row, you'll see a clipboard with the Word logo on it.

This entry was posted in News and tagged seattle, space needle, vacation on June 1, 2013. Edit

Figure 4-35. *The YouTube video embedded from the URL*

oEmbed works with a number of video providers. See http://sleary.me/wp19[2] for a complete list. This page also contains instructions on adding other video providers, if your favorite is not already included.

Other File Types

For all other kinds of files, you'll have just a few attributes: title, caption, description, and link URL. As with audio and video files, inserting another file type will result in a simple link to the original file.

Unfortunately, there is no easy way to list all the files attached to a post, unless they're images. The [gallery] shortcode doesn't work with documents like Word or PDF files. You can use the List Child Attachments plugin, which provides both a template tag and a shortcode to list all attached files. See Appendix A for more plugins that help out with attachments.

---

[2]codex.wordpress.org/Embeds#oEmbed

File Sizes and Upload Permissions

If you are working with other users, occasionally your content authors might get an error message when uploading unusual file types. While the error might mention the file size as a potential problem, more likely the real issue is the unfiltered upload capability in WordPress user roles. You'll quickly find, for example, that only administrators can upload Flash videos (.flv). To get around the problem, you can use a role-editing plugin like Members to allow unfiltered uploads for other user roles, or you can use a plugin like PJW Mime Config that allows you to specify individual MIME types that will be allowed.

Of course, it's possible that the file size really is the problem. If you have access to your server's php.ini file, increase the file_uploads, upload_max_filesize, and post_max_size values. If you can't modify php.ini, you can try adding the value to wp-config.php using PHP's ini_set() function. If that still doesn't work, check with your server administrator.

Sometimes, file uploads fail not because they're too large, but because the permissions are not set correctly on your uploads directory or one of the month-based subdirectories. See Chapter 9 for the correct permissions settings.

The Media Library

You can see and edit the details for all the media files currently on the site (Figure 4-36) by choosing the Media Library option in the main navigation menu. You can add files to the library directly. They won't be associated with any posts or pages, but individually they can be inserted into posts and pages from the Media Library tab in the upload dialog box.

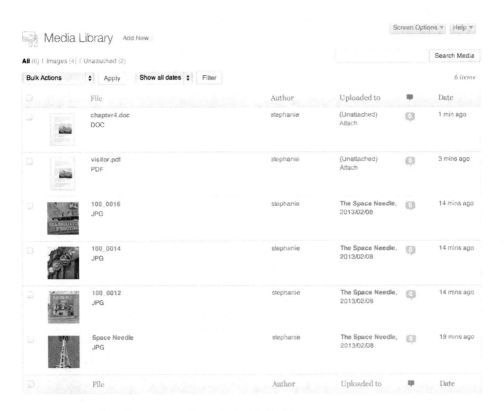

Figure 4-36. *All media types are shown in the Media Library*

Feeds

WordPress generates RSS and Atom feeds automatically for your posts and comments. Links to these feeds are available in the Meta widget, which you'll see in Chapter 5. If you're using a browser that discovers feeds automatically, you'll see that your post and comment feeds are available on every page of your site. Post feeds display your most recent posts, as determined by the number you chose on the Reading Settings panel. If you've set up permalinks, you can find your feeds by adding /feed (for RSS) or /feed/atom to your site's URL. If you haven't set up permalinks, you can use the query string URL format instead: /?feed=rss2 or /?feed=atom.

The comment feeds are located at /comments/feed/ or /?feed=comments-rss2 for RSS and /comments/feed/atom or /?feed=comments-atom for Atom. The number of comments displayed, like the number of posts, is based on the number you chose in the Readings Settings panel.

WordPress generates a number of other feeds in addition to those for posts and comments (see Table 4-1). There's a feed for each of your categories and tags. You can get feeds of the posts written by an individual author. You can even get feeds for search results! Since WordPress doesn't advertise these hidden feeds, you'll have to do a little URL manipulation to find them. In general, you can go to any archive page and add /feed (or /feed/atom) to its URL, and you'll get the corresponding feed. For example, if you have a Recipes category and its URL is http://example.com/category/recipes, its RSS feed will be http://example.com/category/recipes/feed.

Table 4-1. *Hidden Feeds in WordPress*

Feed Type	Default URL	Clean URL
Posts RSS 2.0 (default)	/?feed=rss2	/feed or /feed/rss2
Posts Atom 1.0	/?feed=atom	/feed/atom
Posts RSS 0.92	/?feed=rss	/feed/rss
Posts RDF	/?feed=rdf	/feed/rdf
Comments	/?feed=comments-rss2 /?feed=comments-atom	/comments/feed /comments/feed/atom
Category ID: 1 slug: news	/?feed=rss2&cat=1 /?feed=atom&cat=1	/category/news/feed /category/news/feed/atom
Tag slug: book	/?feed=rss2&tag=book /?feed=atom&tag=book	/tag/book/feed /tag/book/feed/atom
Multiple Tags slugs: book, apress	/?feed=rss2&tag=book+apress /?feed=atom&tag=book+apress	/tag/book+apress/feed /tag/book+apress/feed/atom
Custom Taxonomy Term taxonomy: genre term: mystery	/?feed=rss2&genre=mystery /?feed=atom&genre=mystery	/genre/mystery/feed /genre/mystery/feed/atom
Author ID: 2 username: joe	/?feed=rss2&author=2 /?feed=atom&author=2	/author/joe/feed /author/joe/feed/atom
Search Results term: apress	/?feed=rss2&s=apress /?feed=atom&s=apress	/search/apress/feed /search/apress/feed/atom
Custom Post Type slug: course	/?feed=rss2&post_type=course /?feed=atom&post_type=course	/course/feed /course/feed/atom

Of course, once you've located your feeds, you can place the links somewhere in your theme so your visitors can find them too. In Chapter 12, you'll see how to add a `<link>` tag to a new feed in your theme, which allows browsers and RSS readers to discover the feed automatically.

Summary

If you've been playing along at home, your new WordPress site is now chock-full of delicious content. In Chapter 5, I'll talk about how to make that content look good by customizing your theme—and in Chapter 12, you'll learn how to build your own.

Things to keep in mind:

- When choosing between posts vs. pages, any content that's organized by date or anything that belongs in a feed should be stored as a post.

- Stored revisions can drastically increase the size of your database. Limit the number of revisions WordPress keeps if you're concerned about storage space.

- Use your screen options, bulk edit, and quick edit features when you need to make fast changes to groups of posts or pages.

- New in 3.6: audio and video uploads are no longer treated as links, but are displayed with a complete player interface.

While WordPress generates lots of feeds for you, most of them aren't visible to your users. Create links in your theme files or a text widget if you want to make them available.

CHAPTER 5

Working with Themes

Now that you've configured your site and created some content, it's time to make it look good! First, you'll learn a few ways to change your site's appearance: using the theme customizer, widgets, the menu manager, and uploading custom header and background images.

In Chapter 12, you'll learn how to build your own theme.

Using the Customizer

The theme customizer is a relatively new feature in WordPress (see Figure 5-1). It lets you not only preview a theme, but also make changes to your settings and see the effects in real time. To try it out, go to Appearance ➤ Themes. Click the Customize link under your active theme or the Live Preview link under any other theme.

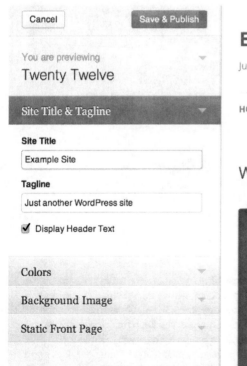

Figure 5-1. *The theme customizer*

Several of the settings you chose when you set up your site are presented here again: your site's title, tagline, and front page settings. If your theme supports custom backgrounds and/or headers, you'll see sections for those here as well. If your theme includes menu locations, you can set a menu here. Backgrounds, headers, and menu locations all exist in other parts of the Appearance section, as you'll see later in this chapter. The customizer merely gathers all the appearance-related settings into one place. Any changes you make in the customizer will update those settings throughout the site.

Once you've made your changes, click the blue Save & Publish button at the top of the customizer pane to save your settings.

Using Widgets

Widgets offer a powerful way to change up your site without touching a line of code. WordPress comes with a dozen built-in widgets. You can download many more from the plugin repository, and some themes come with their own widgets. Figure 5-2 shows the basic widgets you'll find under Appearance ➤ Widgets.

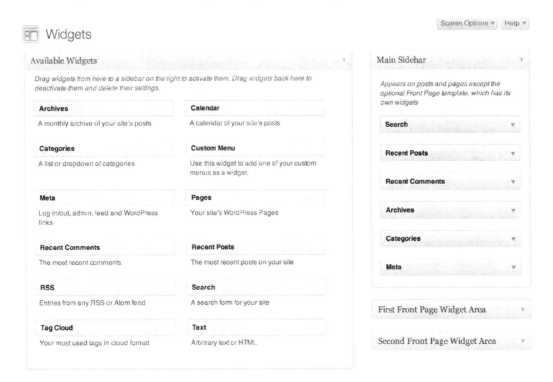

Figure 5-2. *The widget management screen*

On the main page, you'll see a bank of available widgets. Below the available widgets, there's another bank of inactive widgets. On the right, you'll see a drop zone for each sidebar—that is, each widget area defined in your theme, regardless of whether they actually appear on the sides. The number of sidebars varies; some themes have just one, while others (like Twenty Twelve) have five or six. Sidebars can include descriptions to help you keep track of which is which, but the description is optional, as you'll see in Chapter 13, and not all theme or plugin authors will include them.

To get started, drag a widget from the available bank into one of the sidebars, as shown in Figure 5-3. Once you've placed the widget in the sidebar, the widget options screen will open. Most widgets have some options that let you customize their display. For example, the category widget lets you turn the plain linked list into a drop-down, or show the categories in nested lists reflecting the parent/child hierarchy, or include the number of posts assigned to each category. Once you've changed the options, be sure to press the Save button. Otherwise, your changes will be lost when you leave the widget manager screen.

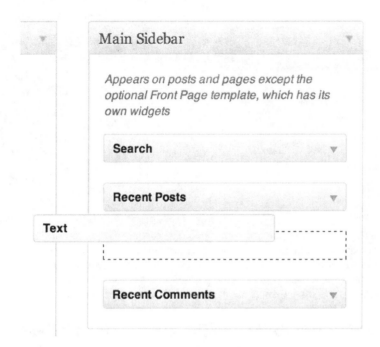

Figure 5-3. *Dragging widgets into place*

When you drag a widget to the inactive area, it will no longer be displayed in your theme, but all its settings will be preserved. This is useful when you want to temporarily disable a widget or try out an alternative without losing your previous work. If you remove a widget from a sidebar by dragging it somewhere other than the inactive area, its settings will be lost.

When you change your theme, all the active widgets you were using will be preserved if your new theme's sidebars have the same names as your old theme's. Otherwise, your widgets will be moved to the inactive area. All their settings will be saved, so all you have to do is drag them back into the appropriate sidebars in your new theme.

You'll learn how to create your own widgets in Chapter 13.

Using Menus

To get started with your custom menu, go to Appearance ➤ Menus. To create your first menu, enter a name in the Menu Name area (Figure 5-4) and press the Create Menu button.

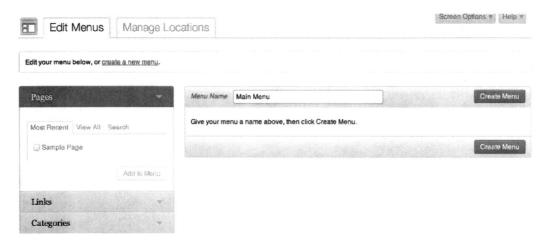

Figure 5-4. *Creating a new menu*

Use the checkboxes on the right side of the page to add new items to your menu. You can add almost any kind of content as a menu item. By default, the menu management page shows pages, categories, and custom links to URLs you specify. However, in this page's screen options (Figure 5-5), you can turn on the boxes that will let you add posts, tags, custom content types, and custom taxonomies. (You'll learn how to create custom post types and taxonomies in Chapter 14.) You can add multiple items quickly by checking them all at once and pressing the Add to Menu button.

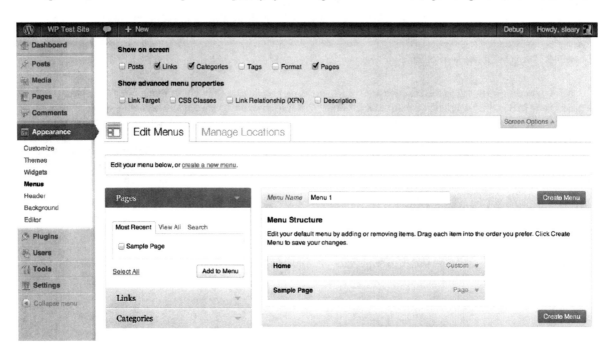

Figure 5-5. *Menu screen options*

Once you have a few menu items in place, you can create a hierarchy by dragging items to the right. In most themes, the subsections of the menu will be displayed as drop-downs.

Now that you've created a menu, there are two ways you can display it on your site. Some themes include theme locations for menus. If your theme does, you'll see a Theme Location box at the top of the left column on the menu page (Figure 5-6). Select your menu, save the location, and preview your site to see how it looks.

Figure 5-6. Theme locations for menus

■ **Caution**   Be sure to press the blue Save Changes button before leaving this screen! Otherwise your menu changes will be lost.

If your theme doesn't have preset locations, or if you don't want to use them, you can add a menu to any sidebar using the menu widget.

Editing Menu Items

To edit an item's details or delete it from the menu, use the arrow on the far right side of the item to show the detail editing box (Figure 5-7). By default, the menu item will display the title of the page or the name of the category. However, you can change both the label (the linked text) and the title attribute (the tooltip shown on hover). The original title will always be shown at the bottom of the menu item detail box, so you won't lose track of the item's source.

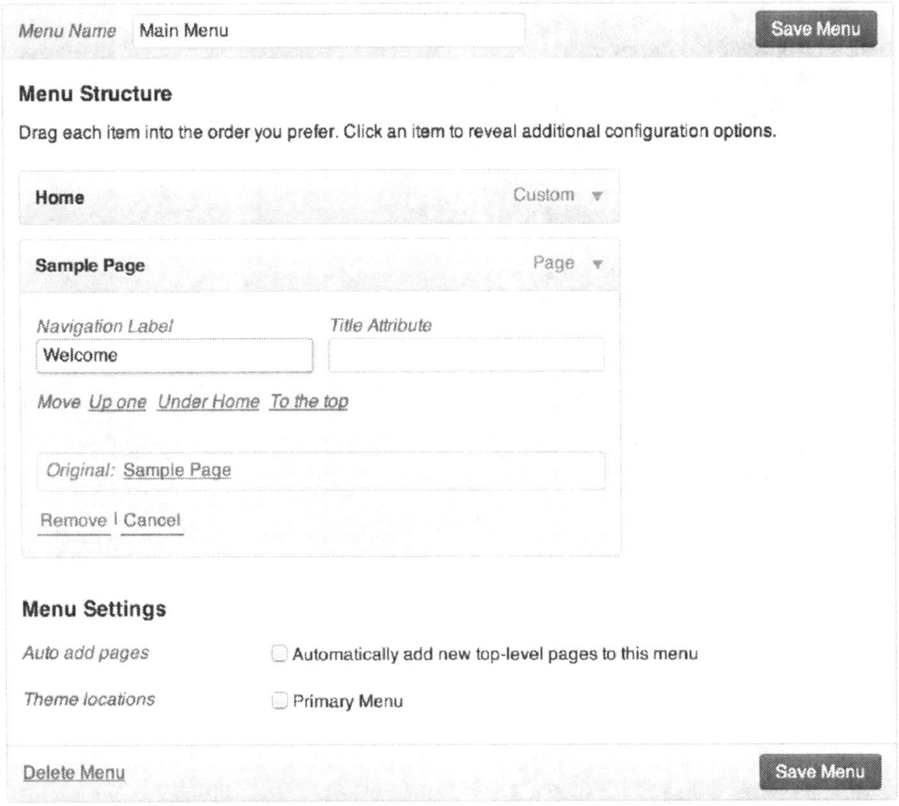

Figure 5-7. *Editing menu item details*

In the screen options, you can turn on some additional attributes for each menu item: the link target (whether the link opens a new browser window), CSS classes, link relationships (using the XFN microformat), and a description (which could be displayed below the link if your theme supports it).

You can create more than one menu using the link at the top of the page. The second menu will become active, and you can begin adding items to it. You can switch back to the first menu using the drop-down at the top of the screen (Figure 5-8).

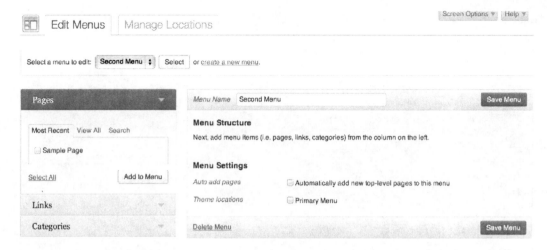

Figure 5-8. *Editing a second menu*

Using Header and Background Images

If your theme supports custom header and background images, you'll see two additional menu items under Appearance. Let's start with backgrounds. Go to Appearance ➤ Background to get started. Figures 5-9 and 5-10 show the process of uploading a background image and setting the display options.

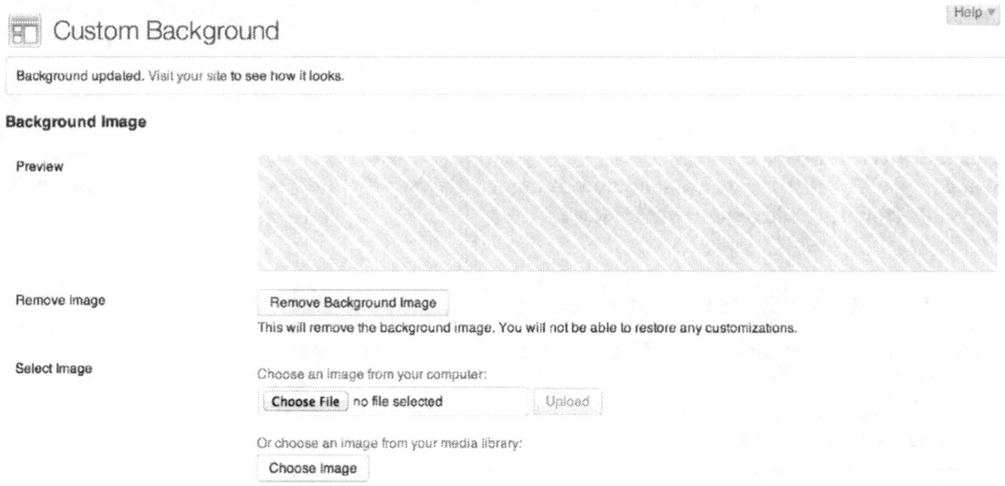

Custom Background   Help ▼

Background updated. Visit your site to see how it looks.

Background Image

Preview

Remove Image

Remove Background Image

This will remove the background image. You will not be able to restore any customizations.

Select Image

Choose an image from your computer:

Choose File   no file selected   Upload

Or choose an image from your media library:

Choose Image

Figure 5-9. *Uploading a background image*

Display Options

Position	⦿ Left ◯ Center ◯ Right
Repeat	◯ No Repeat ⦿ Tile ◯ Tile Horizontally ◯ Tile Vertically
Attachment	⦿ Scroll ◯ Fixed
Background Color	Select Color

Save Changes

Figure 5-10. *Setting the background image display options*

Setting a header works much the same way. Once you've chosen your image, you'll have the option to crop it to fit your theme's header area, if necessary.

You can choose whether or not to display your site's title and tagline as well as the image you've uploaded. If so, the text will be superimposed on the image.

Making Other Changes to Themes

If you're an experienced web developer, you're probably itching to change other things at this point—and you might have noticed the Editor section under the Appearance menu, which leads to a very basic editor for all your theme files. But beware: while you can edit a theme's files to make the changes you want, you probably shouldn't. When WordPress upgrades a theme, it overwrites the entire theme subdirectory, replacing it with the new files. That means your changes will be lost.

There are two ways to handle the problem. If you just need to make some small CSS changes, you can do so using a plugin. Jetpack includes a custom CSS module.

For larger changes, you'll need to create a child theme. I'll show you a simple one later in this chapter, and you'll learn how to create more complex child themes in Chapter 12.

Adding CSS Without Editing the Stylesheet Using Jetpack

Jetpack is a huge plugin that offers self-hosted WordPress sites (that's us!) some of the same features as sites on wordpress.com. It comes with a ton of modules, but for now, all we're interested in is the custom CSS section. Once you have installed Jetpack, you'll see an Edit CSS option under the Appearance menu.

On this page (Figure 5-11), you'll find a much more advanced CSS editor than the one that's built in to WordPress. It will check your styles as you write them and alert you to any errors.

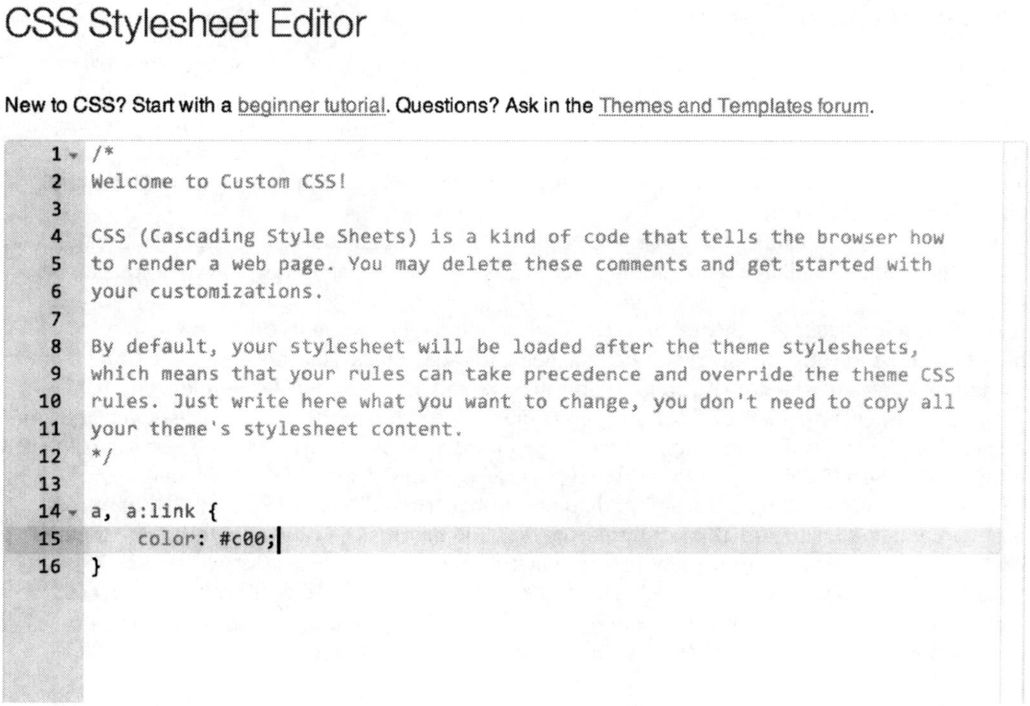

CSS Stylesheet Editor

New to CSS? Start with a beginner tutorial. Questions? Ask in the Themes and Templates forum.

```
 1  /*
 2  Welcome to Custom CSS!
 3
 4  CSS (Cascading Style Sheets) is a kind of code that tells the browser how
 5  to render a web page. You may delete these comments and get started with
 6  your customizations.
 7
 8  By default, your stylesheet will be loaded after the theme stylesheets,
 9  which means that your rules can take precedence and override the theme CSS
10  rules. Just write here what you want to change, you don't need to copy all
11  your theme's stylesheet content.
12  */
13
14  a, a:link {
15      color: #c00;
16  }
```

Figure 5-11. *The Jetpack CSS editor*

Normally, you'd use the editor to make minor changes, leaving the plugin in its default Add-on mode. If for some reason you need to replace the entire theme stylesheet with your own CSS, you can do so by changing the plugin's mode (Figure 5-12). However, creating a child theme is probably a better option.

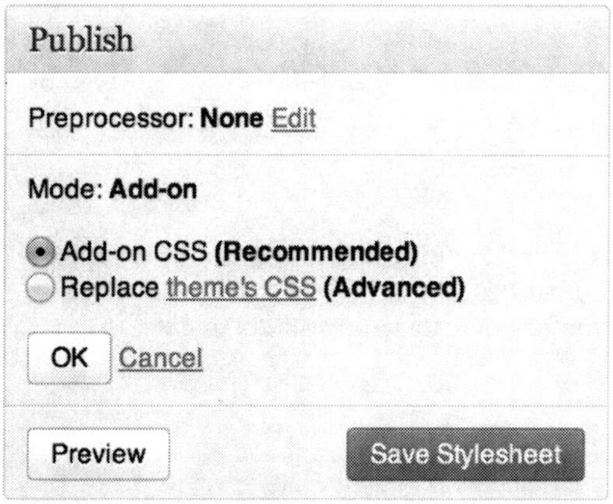

Publish

Preprocessor: **None** Edit

Mode: **Add-on**

● Add-on CSS **(Recommended)**
○ Replace theme's CSS **(Advanced)**

OK   Cancel

Preview   Save Stylesheet

Figure 5-12. *Overriding the theme stylesheet with your Jetpack CSS edits*

Adding CSS with a Child Theme

To illustrate what child themes are and why they're needed, consider the following scenario. You know that it's essential to keep your themes and plugins up to date. However, you just needed to make a few tiny modifications to your theme. You've edited the files to make these changes. Now an update is available from the original theme author, and it includes security improvements. But, if you upgrade the theme, you'll lose the changes you've made. You're faced with two unpalatable options: redo your changes every time there's an update to the original theme, or simply put off upgrading and risk being hacked.

You can solve the problem by making changes to your original theme without editing its files. How? Create a child theme! A child theme inherits all the files of its parent theme, but has its own stylesheet in which you can add your own rules.

Themes are stored in the `wp-content/themes` directory. Each subdirectory represents a different theme. Most contain many files, although only two are required for a theme to work: `index.php` and `style.css`. Child themes can have just one, the stylesheet. In Chapter 12, you'll see how to make complex child themes by adding more files.

The child theme's stylesheet imports the rules of the parent theme's. To understand how this works, you need to understand CSS specificity. If you need to brush up, the HTML Dog tutorial on Specificity (`http://sleary.me/20`)[1] is excellent, and Andy Clarke's Specificity Wars (`http://sleary.me/21`)[2] is a fun way to remember the rules.

For our purposes, the important thing to remember right now is that, if two CSS rules exist, the later one takes precedence. Child themes take advantage of this fact by placing the child theme's CSS rules after the parent theme's. This allows child theme authors to override any rules that exist in the parent theme's stylesheet.

To create a child theme, simply create a new subdirectory in `wp-content/themes`. Add a file called `style.css`. This file must contain two things: a comment block defining the theme, and an import of the parent theme's stylesheet. In the comment block, you need a Template line, giving the name of the parent theme's directory. Listing 5-1 shows the style.css file of a child theme of Twenty Thirteen.

Listing 5-1. A Twenty Thirteen Child Theme `style.css` File

```
/*
Theme Name: Party Like It's Twenty Thirteen
Description: Child Theme of Twenty Thirteen
Author: Stephanie Leary
Author URI: http://stephanieleary.com
Template: twentythirteen
Version: 1.0
*/


/* Import Parent Theme */
@import url('../twentythirteen/style.css');
```

To override Twenty Thirteen styles, or simply add new rules, you can begin writing your CSS after the @import line. Switch to this new theme, and you should see Twenty Thirteen plus your additions.

With all your changes confined to your child theme stylesheet, you're free to install any future updates to Twenty Thirteen as soon as they're released.

---

[1]`http://www.htmldog.com/guides/css/intermediate/specificity`
[2]`http://www.stuffandnonsense.co.uk/archives/css_specificity_wars.html`

Starter Themes and Theme Frameworks

As you browse the long list of themes available for WordPress, you'll see two more special kinds of themes in addition to child themes. Starter themes and theme frameworks are very similar.

Starter Themes

Most starter themes are intended to be modified directly, not used as parent themes, although of course you could do so. You can edit them to your heart's content in order to create a custom theme.

Great starter themes include:

- Underscores (http://underscores.me)

- Bones (http://themble.com/bones)

- Starkers (http://viewportindustries.com/products/starkers)

- Toolbox (http://wordpress.org/extend/themes/toolbox)

- Thematic (http://wordpress.org/extend/themes/thematic)

- Sandbox (http://wordpress.org/extend/themes/sandbox)

- Skeleton (http://demos.simplethemes.com/skeleton)

- Foundation (https://github.com/drewsymo/Foundation)

Reading through the code of any one of these themes would be an excellent introduction to WordPress theme development.

Theme Frameworks

Frameworks are robust themes that offer the user lots of options. A framework is not just a simple theme that supports blogging, but also one that can be used on many kinds of sites. Frameworks generally offer extra page templates, different layouts, color scheme choices, and perhaps new custom widgets.

One of my favorite examples of a theme framework comes from Boston University (Figure 5-13). Their design catalog (http://sleary.me/wp22)[3] beautifully illustrates how child themes can modify a parent theme, keeping a consistent style while allowing for variations.

---

[3]http://www.bu.edu/tech/comm/websites/www/wordpress/design-options

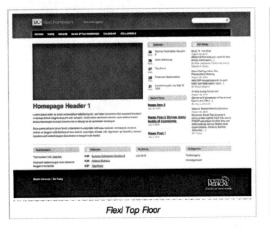

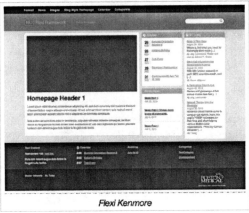

Flexi Top Floor   Flexi Kenmore

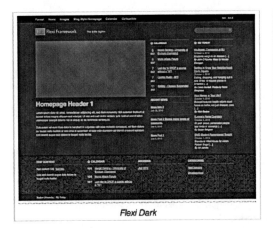

Flexi Dark   Flexi Comm Ave

Figure 5-13. *Child themes of Boston University's Flexi framework*

There are many theme frameworks available, including:

- Hybrid (http://themehybrid.com)
- Genesis (http://www.studiopress.com/themes/genesis)
- Headway (http://headwaythemes.com)
- Gantry (http://www.gantry-framework.org)
- Carrington (http://carringtontheme.com)
- Whiteboard (http://whiteboardframework.com)
- UpThemes (http://upthemes.com/upthemes-framework)

■ **Note**   Several of these theme frameworks are commercial endeavors. While they are open source, you do have to purchase them.

Summary

In this chapter, you've seen how to make some changes to your site's appearance without editing your theme files. In the next chapter, you'll learn more about making changes to your site using plugins, and in Chapter 13, you'll learn how to create your own custom themes.

■ ■ ■

CHAPTER 6

Working with Plugins

Most of the time, working with plugins is straightforward. The plugin developer has written a readme file with comprehensive description of the plugin's features, good installation instructions, and a FAQ. The installation goes smoothly and what you see matches the plugin's screenshots.

Sometimes it's not that easy.

In this chapter, you'll learn where to look for plugins' settings and data, how to evaluate plugins, how to test their performance, and what to do when a plugin breaks your site.

There are many places to find WordPress plugins, but beware: because WordPress offers a lot of flexibility to plugin developers, it's easy for unscrupulous developers to take advantage of the system to insert spam or malware into your site. You'll learn more about security in Chapter 9. In the meantime, I don't recommend getting plugins anywhere but the official repository at wordpress.org, where plugins are reviewed and vetted before being listed.

First, let's look at all the things plugins can do.

How Plugins Work

WordPress plugins use hooks—places in the core code where WordPress allows extra functions to operate. Hooks are placed throughout the WordPress code. They allow plugins to do the following:

- Insert things (text, images, social media links, etc.) above or below a post's content
- Change RSS feed content
- Add things like new <meta> tags to a page's <head> area
- Display information from other sites or services
- Add widgets
- Add options to existing Settings screens, or create whole new Settings screens
- Add extra fields to posts and pages
- Create new post types and taxonomies
- Send extra email notifications
- Change user roles
- Change administration menus
- Add Dashboard widgets
- Add importers for other blogging formats or services

- Expose hidden features

- Monitor visitors, WordPress users, and other plugins

- . . . and many other things.

In Chapter 11, you'll learn how to use hooks to write your own themes and plugins.

Where Plugins Store Their Data

If a plugin has settings, it probably stores them in your database's options table (`wp_options`, unless you chose another prefix during the installation). Most plugins, when activated, add a row to this table containing their default settings. Some plugins will write a separate row for each of their settings; others will compress their settings into an array and store it in a single row. Some plugins that need to store a lot of data—audit logs, for example—create whole new tables in your WordPress database.

If the plugin was properly written, deleting it from the Plugins screen will remove its data as well as its files. For this reason, it's a good idea to use the Delete link (or the Delete option in the Bulk Actions menu, if you're removing more than one) to get rid of unused plugins, rather than just removing their files from your server.

Where to Find Plugin Settings

Well-behaved plugins put their settings screens in the Settings section of the admin menu. A few, especially those aimed at developers, add their screens to the Tools section (Figure 6-1). A plugin should add screens to other parts of the menu only in limited situations. A plugin that lets you edit user roles, like Members, might reasonably add its screen to the Users section of the menu.

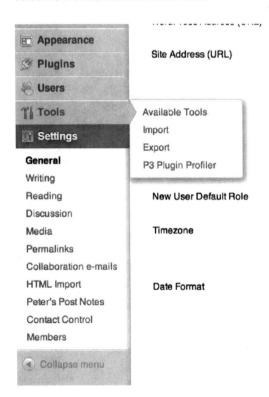

Figure 6-1. *Most of this site's plugin settings are in Settings, but P3 Plugin Profiler is under Tools*

Some plugins have no settings. Clean Notifications, for example, simply changes your email notifications to a friendly HTML format as soon as it's activated.

Evaluating Plugins

A handful of very old plugins still work beautifully with current versions of WordPress. However, those plugins are rare. Most of the time, very old plugins won't work: they won't activate at all, or they'll display errors, or the thing they're trying to modify doesn't exist anymore and they simply don't do anything. Plugins that haven't been updated in over two years will show up with a warning on wordpress.org, and they won't show up at all when you search for plugins in your site's Plugins ➤ Add New screen.

Take a look at the plugin's ratings and the number of downloads (Figure 6-2), but be aware that both can be misleading. A very good plugin might have few ratings simply because it fills a small niche; a plugin with thousands of downloads might be churning out minor updates every few weeks. In a recent change, the ratings system now requires the user to leave a review. As a result, ratings have been somewhat unreliable in the past, but should be much better from now on.

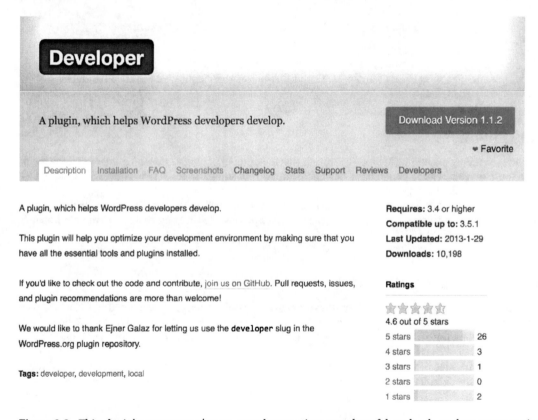

Figure 6-2. *This plugin's page on* wordpress.org *shows ratings, number of downloads, and support questions*

The Support tab on the plugin's wordpress.org page is a much better indicator of quality. Are there a lot of reports that the plugin doesn't work? Are questions to the plugin developer going unanswered? If so, you might want to find another plugin that serves your needs.

Once you have downloaded and activated the plugin, there are a number of other things to look for:

- Do JavaScript-based administrative functions (like Bulk Edit, Quick Edit, and the admin menu flyouts) still work?

- Does your site slow down?

- Does the plugin add warnings to the top of every administration screen? If so, are they sensible warnings ("This plugin needs to be configured"), or just invitations to buy things and/or promote the company on your social media networks?

- Does it add spam links to your source code? Check the site in another browser, one where you are not logged in to WordPress. Visit the home page and view source. Look through the HTML, especially near the bottom of the page.

- Does it put ads on your admin screens—even those for other plugins' settings? Does it add a Dashboard widget full of links to the developer's other products?

- Does it add text to your site's footer ("Powered by My Awesome Plugin!") without your permission?

- Does its settings screen blend in with the WordPress Dashboard, or does it look completely different?

Of course, the best way to evaluate a plugin is to simply open up its files and read the code. That might seem intimidating now, but once you've finished Chapters 11, 12 and 13, you'll be sufficiently well-versed in WordPress functions to spot obvious problems.

How Many Plugins?

People worry about installing too many plugins. The truth is that the number of plugins doesn't matter nearly as much as the quality of those plugins. A good plugin has a negligible impact (but still *some* impact) on your site's load time. A bad one can bring the whole site crashing down.

You can run twenty, thirty, forty, or more well-coded plugins and your site will be just fine. Of course, not all plugins are written well. If you've noticed that your site is slower with lots of plugins installed, it's time to do some troubleshooting to locate the problem.

Troubleshooting Plugins

Plugins can introduce a world of trouble to your WordPress site. Not only can they cause problems with core WordPress functions, but they can trip over each other, causing conflicts with CSS and JavaScript files or conflicting functions.

If you notice a problem immediately after you install a new plugin, simply deactivate it and see if the problem goes away.

If the problem appears later, or you can't remember which plugin you installed most recently, deactivate all your plugins, switch to one of the default themes—themes can conflict with plugins, too!—then turn the plugins back on one by one.

If your site is simply too slow, try installing the Plugin Performance Profiler (P3). (Yes, it's somewhat ironic to use a plugin to diagnose a problem with plugins.) This plugin will scan your site (automatically visiting its pages, or allowing you to visit specific pages in a separate window) and report how your plugins affected the site's load time.

Once it's installed, you'll find its scanner under Tools ➤ P3 Plugin Profiler. Press Start Scan to begin. When the scan is complete, you'll see a report like the one in Figure 6-3. There's more detailed information behind each of the report's tabs, but the most important information is in the pie chart: which plugins took the longest to load?

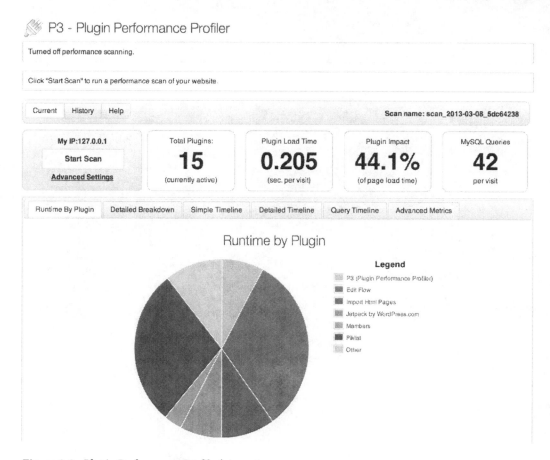

Figure 6-3. *Plugin Performance Profiler's report*

Once you've found the culprit, you have a few options. You can keep the plugin and live with its problems. You can contact the plugin's developers, tell them about the problem you had, and wait to see if they fix it. Or you can find another plugin that does something similar. There are well over 10,000 plugins in the official repository alone; chances are good that there's more than one that will serve your needs.

Summary

You've learned a little bit about the way WordPress plugins interact with the core system. You've learned where to find plugins and how to evaluate them. You've learned where to look for plugins' settings and how to troubleshoot misbehaving plugins.

In the next chapter, you'll learn how to work with users, roles, and workflow in WordPress.

CHAPTER 7

■ ■ ■

Working with Users

WordPress has five built-in user roles with escalating permissions. The basic role and notification systems work well for many blogs. For more complex content management, you can change the fields in the basic user profile, modify roles, create whole new roles, and add notifications using a couple of plugins. I'll look at the built-in features first, and then show you the plugins required to extend them.

Users

If you changed your password just after you installed WordPress, you've already seen the user profile page (Figure 7-1). You can reach it by going to Users ➤ Your Profile in the navigation menu. You might not have noticed, but you were assigned the administrator role.

Figure 7-1. *A user profile (part 1 of 2)*

In the Personal Options section, you can determine how the WordPress administration screens will work for you. You can disable the visual (rich text) editor on the content editing screens and you can switch the color scheme to blue. See http://sleary.me/wp23[1] for the full list of comment moderation shortcuts you'll have if you enable keyboard shortcuts for comment moderation.

Note that the username you chose when you installed WordPress cannot be changed unless you edit the database field directly (with PHPMyAdmin, for example). You could also create another user, give it the administrator role, and log in with that account instead. You could then delete the original account, which might offer your site a little added security. The user ID 1 is often the target of hacker attacks, since almost all sites have one.

The first and last name fields should be self-explanatory. The nickname field works much like a post's slug. It's used in the URL to your author archive page. The display name setting determines how your name will appear on your site: in your post/page bylines, on your author archive pages, and in your comments (if you're logged in when you leave a comment).

Your e-mail address (Figure 7-2) will be used for all the notifications you, personally, will receive from WordPress. While the e-mail you specified in Settings ➤ General will be used for system notifications, you'll be notified at the address you provide here about every comment on posts you've written, if you've checked the appropriate setting in Settings ➤ Discussion. If you forget your password, you'll be able to reset it by having a new one sent to this address. Note that users can't have duplicate e-mail addresses; if you need to create additional accounts for yourself as you test various features, you'll have to use a different address for each one.

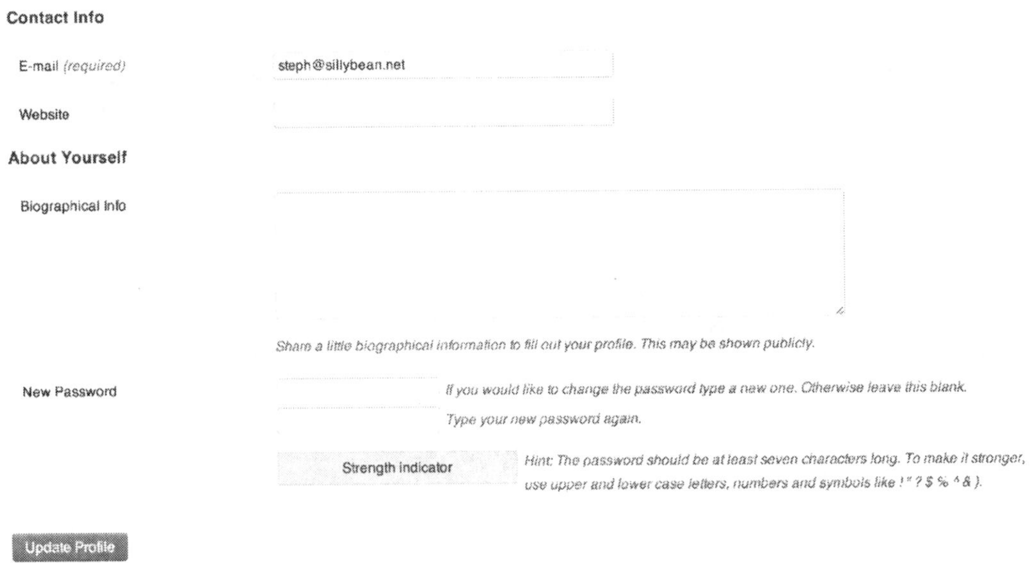

Contact Info

E-mail *(required)*   steph@sillybean.net

Website

About Yourself

Biographical Info

Share a little biographical information to fill out your profile. This may be shown publicly.

New Password   *If you would like to change the password type a new one. Otherwise leave this blank.*

Type your new password again.

Strength indicator   *Hint: The password should be at least seven characters long. To make it stronger, use upper and lower case letters, numbers and symbols like ! " ? $ % ^ &).*

Update Profile

Figure 7-2. *A user profile (part 2 of 2)*

The URL you enter here will be used if your theme supports author links in bylines. Your name will also be linked to this URL if you are logged in when commenting.

The biography field is not often used in themes, but some display it as a post footer in a multi-author blog or in the sidebar of the author archive template. This field accepts a limited set of HTML tags—the same ones allowed in comments, in fact. All other tags will be removed. The allowed tags (and attributes) in all filtered HTML fields are shown in Listing 7-1.

---

[1]http://codex.wordpress.org/Keyboard_Shortcuts

Listing 7-1. HTML tags and Attributes Allowed in Filtered HTML Fields, Including the User Biography

```
<a href="" title="">
<abbr title="">
<acronym title="">
<b>
<blockquote cite="">
<cite>
<code>
<del datetime="">
<em>
<i>
<q cite="">
<strike>
<strong>
```

WordPress uses Gravatars (`gravatar.com`) for its user avatars. If a user has a Gravatar associated with his or her e-mail address, it will be shown in the administration screens and in any theme that supports avatars.

Changing Profile Fields with a Plugin

There are a number of plugins you can use to add fields to user profiles. I like Advanced Custom Fields. It has a number of other uses, as you'll see in Chapter 14. In Figure 7-3, I've created a new group called Address and added three fields to it. Figure 7-4 shows how the user profile looks after I've saved my new field group. Any groups you add to the user profile will appear at the bottom of the screen, below the password fields.

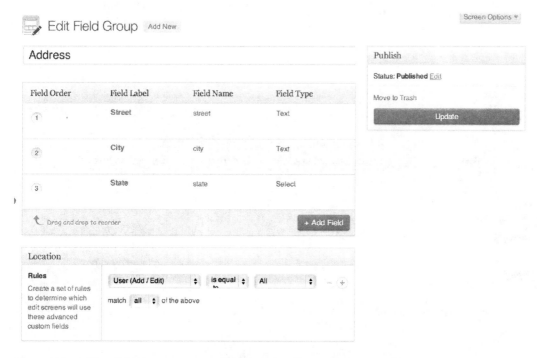

Figure 7-3. *Adding fields to a new user profile group in Advanced Custom Fields*

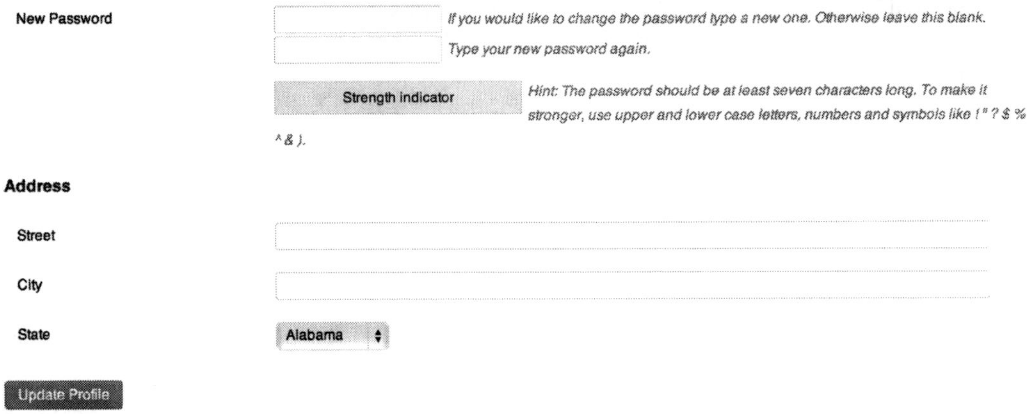

New Password		*If you would like to change the password type a new one. Otherwise leave this blank.*
		Type your new password again.
	Strength indicator	*Hint: The password should be at least seven characters long. To make it stronger, use upper and lower case letters, numbers and symbols like ! " ? $ % ^ &).*

Address

Street	
City	
State	Alabama ⬍

Update Profile

Figure 7-4. A user profile with the new fields

The fields in the Contact Info section are special. E-mail and Website can't be changed, but the rest can. To add or remove them, you can use my User Contact Control plugin (Figure 7-5). In Chapter 13, you'll learn how to do this with just a few lines of code in your own plugin.

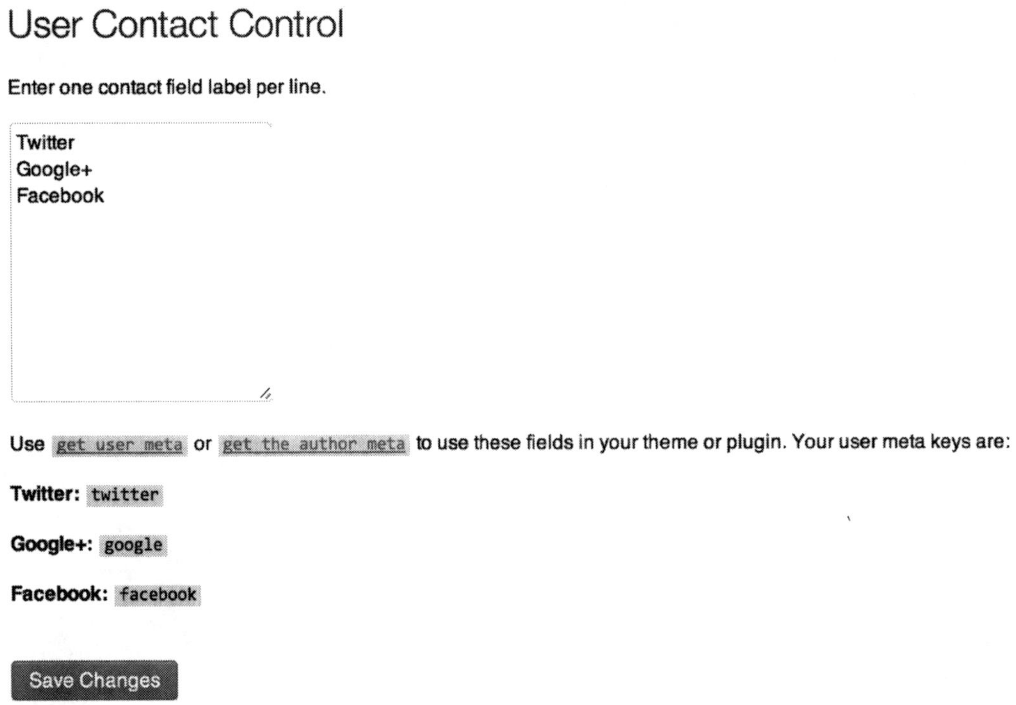

User Contact Control

Enter one contact field label per line.

```
Twitter
Google+
Facebook
```

Use `get_user_meta` or `get_the_author_meta` to use these fields in your theme or plugin. Your user meta keys are:

Twitter: `twitter`

Google+: `google`

Facebook: `facebook`

Save Changes

Figure 7-5. Editing the Contact Info fields with User Contact Control

104

Roles

WordPress has five built-in user roles. Each has a set of capabilities (or permissions):

1. *Administrators* can do anything in the WordPress administration area: write, edit, and delete posts, pages, links, and comments; upload media files of any type; import content; manage the Dashboard; create, edit, and delete other users; enable and configure plugins and themes; change the site's theme; and manage all the available options. If you installed WordPress, you are an administrator.

2. *Editors* can publish, edit, and delete posts and pages written by any user. They can upload some kinds of files, and they can write HTML without restrictions. They can manage links and categories, and they can moderate comments. Editors and administrators are also the only users allowed to read private posts and pages.

3. *Authors* can publish, edit, and delete their own posts. They cannot write pages. They can upload some kinds of media files, and they are allowed to use only the limited set of HTML tags shown in Listing 7-1.

4. *Contributors* can write their own posts but may not publish or delete them. Their HTML is limited to the set of allowed tags and they cannot upload media files. Contributors' finished posts are saved as Pending Review until an editor or administrator approves and publishes them.

5. *Subscribers* can manage their own profiles, but can do virtually nothing else in the administration area.

Visit http://sleary.me/wp24[2] for a detailed list of all the capabilities assigned to each role. There are a few additional roles in multisite WordPress installations, which you'll see in Chapter 8.

Features that are not available to users will not appear in their administration screens. For example, see Figure 7-6, where the navigation menu is fully expanded to show the options available to authors. While the author can see all the existing posts, he can't edit those written by other users.

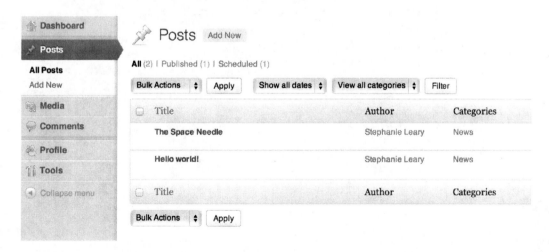

Figure 7-6. *The Edit Posts screen as it appears to an author*

---

[2]http://codex.wordpress.org/Roles_and_Capabilities

Roles in Action: Notifications, Moderation, and Workflow

For administrators and editors, publishing posts and pages is simple: write the content, press Publish. For contributors, it's a little more complicated. Since they are not allowed to publish their own posts, they must submit them for review, as shown in Figure 7-7. Editors and administrators will then see the pending posts on the Posts ➤ Edit screen, as shown in Figure 7-8. They will not get an e-mail notification (unless you add a plugin, as you'll see in the next section).

Publish
Save Draft   Preview
Status: **Draft**
Visibility: **Public**
Move to Trash   Submit for Review

Figure 7-7. Contributors don't have a Publish button; instead, they submit posts for review

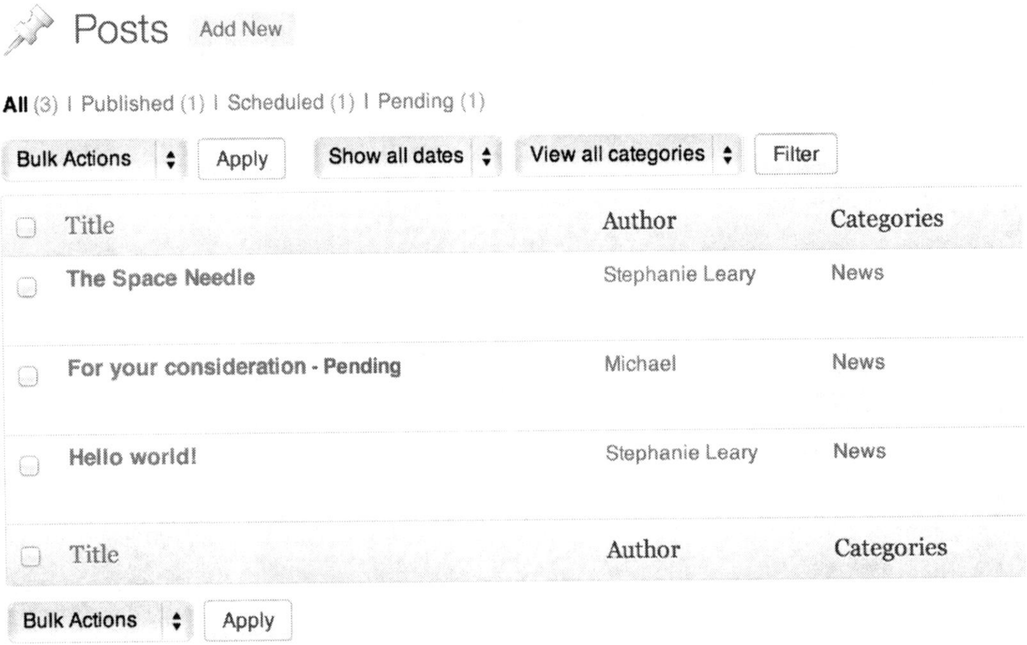

Posts   Add New

All (3) | Published (1) | Scheduled (1) | Pending (1)

Bulk Actions ⬍   Apply   Show all dates ⬍   View all categories ⬍   Filter

	Title	Author	Categories
☐	**The Space Needle**	Stephanie Leary	News
☐	**For your consideration - Pending**	Michael	News
☐	**Hello world!**	Stephanie Leary	News
☐	Title	Author	Categories

Bulk Actions ⬍   Apply

Figure 7-8. Pending posts from the administrator's view

Improving Workflow with Plugins

For very busy sites with many authors and editors, the built-in notifications and post scheduling features often prove inadequate. There are several plugins you can install to provide your users with a more robust workflow.

■ **Note** E-mail notifications rely on the server's mail settings. PHP uses sendmail on most UNIX-based operating systems. If you're on Windows, or sendmail doesn't work, install a plugin to send mail via SMTP instead. See Appendix A for a list of possible plugins. If your host does not allow sending e-mail at all, you'll need a third-party service such as AuthSMTP or Sendgrid.

Notification of Posts Pending Review

WordPress does not send e-mail notifications to editors and administrators when a post is pending review; the pending posts simply wait under Posts ➤ Edit until a reviewer logs in. If you do want e-mails of pending posts, install the Peter's Collaboration E-mails plugin. It allows you to add administrators and editors to the general notification list, as shown in Figure 7-9, and it provides options to set up notifications for categories or groups of users.

Manage collaboration e-mails

Set the moderators who should be e-mailed whenever Contributor users submit pending posts.

Default moderators

These users will be e-mailed if none of the rules below match. Note that they must be either editors or administrators.

☑ General admin (steph@sillybean.net)

☐ Add: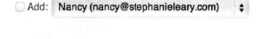

[Update]

Figure 7-9. *Peter's Collaboration E-mails options*

Notifying All Administrators

If you are sharing administration duties with a partner, you might become frustrated with the fact that comment notifications are sent only to the address saved in Settings ➤ General. If you want all administrators to get an e-mail, add the Notifications to All Administrators plugin. It has no options; just install it and wait for the notification e-mails to arrive.

Viewing Scheduled Posts

Normally, posts scheduled for future publication are displayed in the same list as your other posts, under Posts ➤ Edit. When you have many future posts, this list becomes unwieldy. The Editorial Calendar plugin allows you to visualize your scheduled posts. It places a new screen under the Posts menu (Figure 7-10) where you'll see a few weeks' worth of posts at a time. (You can configure the number in the Screen Options tab.) Move your cursor near the top or bottom of the calendar to scroll through additional dates.

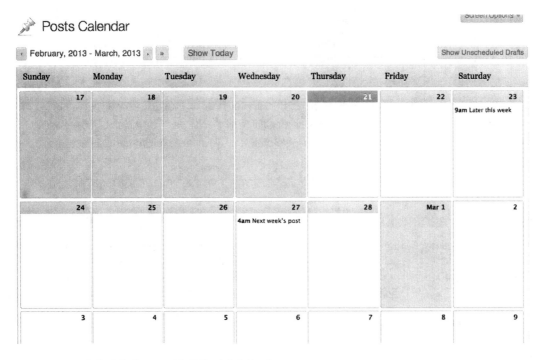

Figure 7-10. *Scheduled posts with Editorial Calendar*

■ **Note** Like many other CMSs, WordPress's `cron` tasks run only when someone visits the site (either the public pages or the administration screens). The schedule is therefore inexact. A task might not run at precisely its scheduled time, but it will run as soon as someone visits the site after the scheduled time.

You can add a post by clicking a day's header, and if you hover over the posts on the calendar, you'll see a row of links allowing you to edit, delete, or view the post. To reschedule a post, click and drag its title to another day.

Complete Workflow

Even with Peter's Collaboration E-mails, WordPress's notification features are just not what they should be. For example, when an editor approves a post for publication, the author isn't notified! The creators of the Edit Flow plugin aim to collect all of the missing role and notification features into a single plugin. Designed for newsrooms, Edit Flow includes custom post statuses (Figure 7-11), including Assigned, Pitch, and Waiting for Feedback; editorial comments on the post editing screen; and e-mail notification any time a post's status changes. The plugin allows you to create groups of users who can subscribe to updates on a post and to configure recipients for all the notifications.

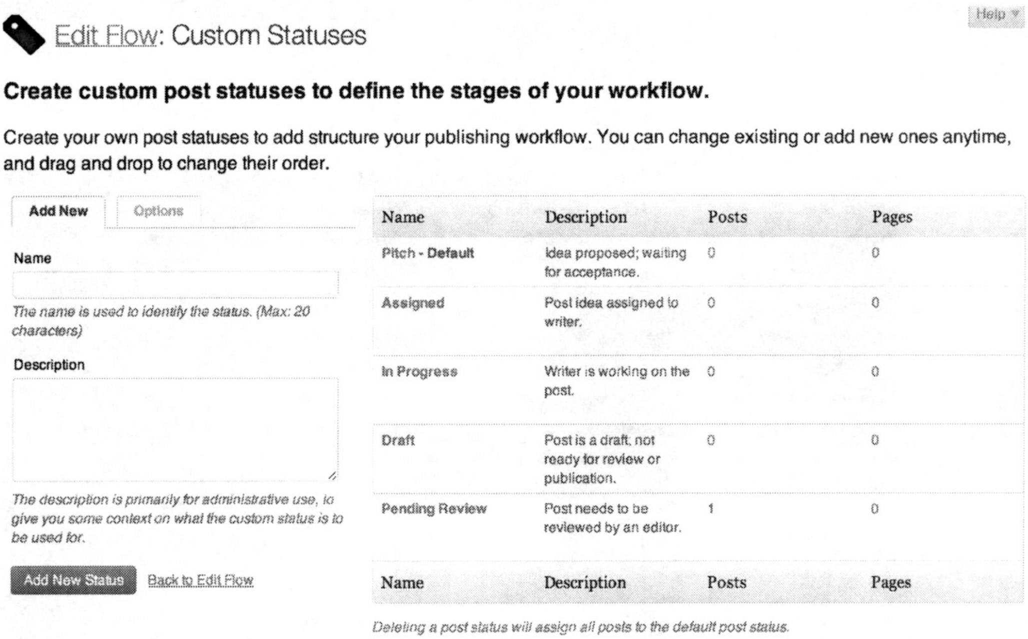

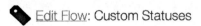 **Edit Flow**: Custom Statuses

Create custom post statuses to define the stages of your workflow.

Create your own post statuses to add structure your publishing workflow. You can change existing or add new ones anytime, and drag and drop to change their order.

Add New Options

Name

The name is used to identify the status. (Max: 20 characters)

Description

The description is primarily for administrative use, to give you some context on what the custom status is to be used for.

[Add New Status] Back to Edit Flow

Name	Description	Posts	Pages
Pitch - Default	Idea proposed; waiting for acceptance.	0	0
Assigned	Post idea assigned to writer.	0	0
In Progress	Writer is working on the post.	0	0
Draft	Post is a draft, not ready for review or publication.	0	0
Pending Review	Post needs to be reviewed by an editor.	1	0
Name	Description	Posts	Pages

Deleting a post status will assign all posts to the default post status.

Figure 7-11. *Custom post statuses in Edit Flow*

Edit Flow also contains a calendar feature, although it's not quite as polished as Editorial Calendar's.

Managing Roles with Plugins

The WordPress role system is very granular; individual capabilities can be added and removed, and whole new roles created—but none of this can be done through the administration screens; it's all hidden away, intended for developers' use only. Fortunately, there are several plugins that make role management a much easier task by providing a complete user interface.

■ **Caution**   Always give users the fewest capabilities they need to accomplish their work on your site. Be very careful with the delete_*, edit_*, install_*, manage_*, publish_*, and remove_users capabilities in particular. Refer to the Codex if you can't remember what a capability means, and don't grant anyone a capability you don't recognize and understand.

The Members plugin is the most complete and up to date plugin for managing roles and capabilities. In addition to managing roles, it adds other features, such as privacy controls for individual posts and an option to make the entire site private. Figure 7-12 shows the Members screen allowing you to edit the administrator role.

Figure 7-12. *Editing the administrator role with the Members plugin*

Creating Roles

Sometimes, rather than adding capabilities to an existing role, you need to create a whole new role. Let's imagine a new scenario. You're building a large site, and you, the programmer, are sharing responsibilities with a graphic designer. You want to give your designer complete control over the content and theme design, but you don't want him editing other users, adding plugins, or importing content from other sites. You might create a Designer role, as shown in Figure 7-13.

Add New Role

Role Name	designer
	Required: The role name should be unique and contain only alphanumeric characters and underscores.
Role Label	Designer
	Required: The role label is used to represent your role in the WordPress admin.
Role Capabilities	**Optional:** Select the capabilities this role should have. These may be updated later.

☐ activate_plugins   ☐ add_users   ☐ create_roles

☐ create_users   ☐ delete_others_pages   ☐ delete_others_posts

☐ delete_pages   ☐ delete_plugins   ☐ delete_posts

☐ delete_private_pages   ☐ delete_private_posts   ☐ delete_published_pages

☐ delete_published_posts   ☐ delete_roles   ☐ delete_themes

☐ delete_users   ☐ edit_dashboard   ☐ edit_files

☐ edit_others_pages   ☐ edit_others_posts   ☐ edit_pages

☐ edit_plugins   ☐ edit_post_subscriptions   ☐ edit_posts

☐ edit_private_pages   ☐ edit_private_posts   ☐ edit_published_pages

☐ edit_published_posts   ☐ edit_roles   ☑ **edit_theme_options**

☑ **edit_themes**   ☐ edit_usergroups   ☐ edit_users

☐ ef_view_calendar   ☐ ef_view_story_budget   ☐ export

☐ import   ☐ install_plugins   ☑ **install_themes**

☐ list_roles   ☐ list_users   ☐ manage_categories

☐ manage_links   ☑ **manage_options**   ☐ moderate_comments

Figure 7-13. *Creating a new role and assigning its capabilities*

Summary

In this chapter, I've looked at the built-in user profiles. I've shown you a few ways to change and extend the profiles, and how to display user information in themes. I've also covered the built-in roles, how roles define the editorial workflow, and how to change that workflow with plugins. Last, you learned how to modify and create roles with the Members plugin.

At this point, you know how to set up and manage a single WordPress site. In the next chapter, you'll learn how to create a whole network of WordPress sites from one installation.

CHAPTER 8

■ ■ ■

Setting Up Multisite Networks

Up to this point, you've looked at using WordPress to manage a single website. However, WordPress can be used to create a network of related sites similar to wordpress.com or edublogs.com. Even if you don't need to create a whole network of user sites, you could use the network features to manage multiple sites rather than installing WordPress separately for each one. This would be especially useful if your group of sites shares the same pool of users, since they would each have one account instead of several.

While the network-enabled WordPress (known as multisite mode) looks mostly the same, there are some differences in the requirements, the user management, and plugin and theme activation. There are also a few consequences for your original site. You'll no longer be able to install themes and plugins from the Appearance and Plugins section of the admin menu; you'll have to go to the new Network Dashboard instead. You'll also be subject to any limits you set on uploads (in addition to the server's limits) in the network settings: the maximum size of each file, the maximum total space used for each site's uploads, and the types of files allowed.

Multisite Requirements

In general, WordPress's multisite mode has the same requirements as WordPress itself. However, you'll need to decide how you want your network site's addresses to work. You can choose subdomains (http://subsite.example.com) or subfolders (http://example.com/subsite/), and each requires something a little different.

Subdomains

If you are planning to allow users to sign up for their own sites on your network, you need to set up wildcard DNS, and you must be able to create wildcard aliases.

In most cases, setting up wildcard DNS is something your hosting provider must handle for you. The general idea is that, in addition to accepting requests for example.com and www.example.com, your domain must be able to accept requests for all other subdomains—*.example.com—without your having to add each one individually to the DNS record.

Similarly, your server must be set up to direct traffic for all unspecified virtual hosts to your WordPress site. In Apache's configuration, you would add ServerAlias *.example.com to your WordPress site's virtual host definition. Again, this is generally something your hosting provider can help you with.

If you are not planning to allow users to create new sites on their own, you do not need to set up wildcard DNS or aliases. For example, if you are managing a network of university departments, you would not necessarily want any authorized users to be able to create new sites without your approval. In that case, you would want to create the new subdomains one at a time.

Subfolders

We've talked about .htaccess files quite a bit throughout this book, so you probably have one set up. However, if you've gotten away without one until now, you'll need it in order to use the subfolder option on your network. WordPress won't create any new physical subfolders for your new sites; they'll all be virtual folders created using rewrite rules, with all incoming requests routed through WordPress.

Activating the Network

You don't have to download anything extra to gain access to the network features; they're just hidden until you turn them on. You need to add a constant to the wp-config.php file, WP_ALLOW_MULTISITE, as shown in Listing 8-1.

Listing 8-1. Turning On Multisite

```
define( 'WP_ALLOW_MULTISITE', true );
```

Save the file, and when you log back in to the Dashboard, you'll see that there is now a Network menu under Tools. Go to it, and you'll see the initial page of the network setup process, as shown in Figure 8-1.

Figure 8-1. *The network setup screen*

First, choose subdomains or subdirectories for your setup, keeping in mind the requirements I've discussed. Then, enter a title for your network. You'll be asked to enter an administrator e-mail address again; this one will be used for notifications related to new sites, and it does not have to be the same as the address you chose for your initial WordPress installation (which will be used for comment notifications and so on related to that site only).

Click Install!

On this second screen (Figure 8-2), you'll be given a set of constants to copy into your wp-config.php file. This is not the entire file, so don't overwrite the whole thing! Just add these few constants. I recommend creating a network section.

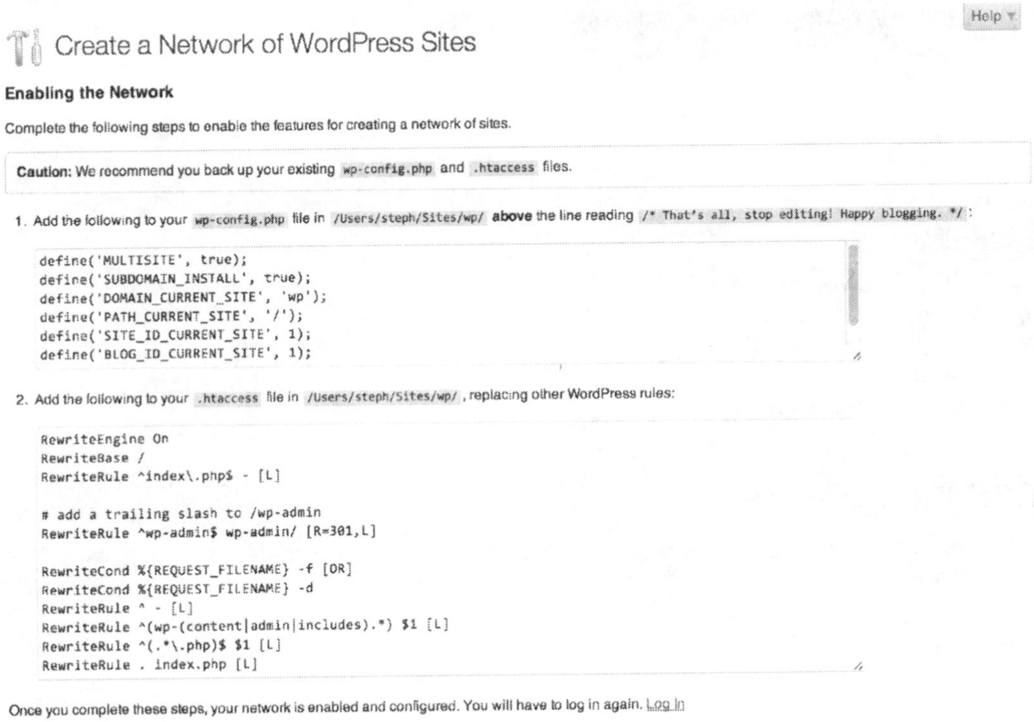

Help ▼

Ti Create a Network of WordPress Sites

Enabling the Network

Complete the following steps to enable the features for creating a network of sites.

Caution: We recommend you back up your existing `wp-config.php` and `.htaccess` files.

1. Add the following to your `wp-config.php` file in `/Users/steph/Sites/wp/` **above** the line reading `/* That's all, stop editing! Happy blogging. */` :

```
define('MULTISITE', true);
define('SUBDOMAIN_INSTALL', true);
define('DOMAIN_CURRENT_SITE', 'wp');
define('PATH_CURRENT_SITE', '/');
define('SITE_ID_CURRENT_SITE', 1);
define('BLOG_ID_CURRENT_SITE', 1);
```

2. Add the following to your `.htaccess` file in `/Users/steph/Sites/wp/` , replacing other WordPress rules:

```
RewriteEngine On
RewriteBase /
RewriteRule ^index\.php$ - [L]

# add a trailing slash to /wp-admin
RewriteRule ^wp-admin$ wp-admin/ [R=301,L]

RewriteCond %{REQUEST_FILENAME} -f [OR]
RewriteCond %{REQUEST_FILENAME} -d
RewriteRule ^ - [L]
RewriteRule ^(wp-(content|admin|includes).*) $1 [L]
RewriteRule ^(.*\.php)$ $1 [L]
RewriteRule . index.php [L]
```

Once you complete these steps, your network is enabled and configured. You will have to log in again. Log In

Figure 8-2. *The second step of the network setup*

You'll also be given a new set of rewrite rules for your `.htaccess` or `web.config` file. Paste these in; they can replace the WordPress section that's already there. A typical set of `.htaccess` rewrite rules is shown in Listing 8-2.

Listing 8-2. `.htaccess` Rewrite Rules for Multisite

```
# BEGIN WordPress
<IfModule mod_rewrite.c>
RewriteEngine On

RewriteBase /
RewriteRule ^index\.php$ - [L]

# uploaded files
RewriteRule ^files/(.+) wp-includes/ms-files.php?file=$1 [L]

RewriteCond %{REQUEST_FILENAME} -f [OR]
RewriteCond %{REQUEST_FILENAME} -d
RewriteRule ^ - [L]
RewriteRule . index.php [L]
</IfModule>
# END WordPress
```

Once you've saved both files, return to the Dashboard. You'll have to log in again.

On the left, you'll see that there's a whole new section of the admin bar, My Sites (Figure 8-3). The settings pages under this section of the menu will allow you to configure your network, and I'll walk you through each of them.

Figure 8-3. *The network-activated admin bar*

Configuring the Network

Go to Settings ➤ Network Settings to begin configuring your network. This is a long screen with a lot of options. Figure 8-4 shows the first few sections. I'll go through each section one by one.

Network Settings

Operational Settings

Network Name	WordPressDev Sites
	What you would like to call this network.
Network Admin Email	steph@sillybean.net
	Registration and support emails will come from this address. An address such as support@wp is recom

Registration Settings

Allow new registrations	● Registration is disabled.
	○ User accounts may be registered.
	○ Logged in users may register new sites.
	○ Both sites and user accounts can be registered.
	If registration is disabled, please set NOBLOGREDIRECT in wp-config.php to a URL you will redirect visi
	visit a non-existent site.
Registration notification	☑ Send the network admin an email notification every time someone registers a site or user account.
Add New Users	☐ Allow site administrators to add new users to their site via the "Users → Add New" page.
Banned Names	www web root admin main invite administrator files
	Users are not allowed to register these sites. Separate names by spaces.
Limited Email Registrations	
	If you want to limit site registrations to certain domains. One domain per line.
Banned Email Domains	
	If you want to ban domains from site registrations. One domain per line.

Figure 8-4. *Network options (part 1 of 3)*

Operational Settings

The network name shown here should be the same as the network title you chose during the network setup. You can change it here.

The network admin e-mail address will be used as the sender for all the registration and support notifications sent to your network users.

Registration Settings

The registration settings (Figure 8-4) deal with the way users will be added to your network. If registration is disabled, no one can sign up for an account, and you will have to add site administrators manually. To allow people to sign up for accounts but not new sites, choose the second option. (This doesn't necessarily mean everyone in the world can register, as you'll see in a moment.) The third option allows the users you have added manually to create their own sites. The fourth option is the one to use if you want to create a blog network: allow users to register and create sites for themselves.

The next checkbox determines whether an e-mail notification will be sent to newly registered users. In a later section of this screen, you'll be able to customize the e-mails.

If you would then like the administrators to be able to add users to their network sites, you can check the next box as well.

The list of banned usernames exists to protect you from users who might launch phishing attempts from your site, especially if you have allowed administrators to invite users.

The next option, Limited Email Registrations, allows you to restrict user registration to specified domains. If you are building a site for users in a business or school, this options is the ideal way to limit your user pool.

On the flip side of that, there might be domains of users you don't want registering for your network, and you can specify those in the Banned Email Domains field.

New Site Settings

In this section (Figure 8-5), you can rewrite the welcome e-mail, which is sent when a user registers a new site, and the welcome user e-mail, which is sent when a new user is added without creating a site.

New Site Settings

Welcome Email	Dear User,
	Your new SITE_NAME site has been successfully set up at: BLOG_URL
	The welcome email sent to new site owners.
Welcome User Email	Dear User,
	Your new account is set up.
	You can log in with the following information:
	The welcome email sent to new users.
First Post	Welcome to <a href="SITE_URL">SITE_NAME</a>. This is your first post. Edit or delete it, then start blogging!

Figure 8-5. *Network options (part 2 of 3)*

You can also alter the first post, first page, first comment, first comment author, and first comment URL. Anything specified here will replace the "Hello, world!" post that appears when a new site is created.

Upload Settings

The upload settings (Figure 8-6) determine what files your users can upload, and how large they can be. The Site Upload Space option allows you to limit the size of each network site. You will have to determine how much space your hosting account allows you and how that should be divided among your network sites. The Max Upload File Size field allows you to limit the size of individual files added via the media uploader.

Upload Settings

Site upload space	☐ Limit total size of files uploaded to [100] MB
Upload file types	jpg jpeg png gif mp3 mov avi wmv midi mid pdf
Max upload file size	[1500] KB

Menu Settings

Enable administration menus	☐ Plugins

[Save Changes]

Figure 8-6. *Network options (part 3 of 3)*

Menu Settings

In this section, you may choose whether individual site administrators can access the plugin pages. If you do not check this box, they will not be able to activate or deactivate plugins for their sites.

Creating Additional Network Sites

To create your first new network site, go to Sites ➤ Add New. On this screen (Figure 8-7), you'll be able to add, edit, deactivate, or archive an entire network site. In the fields below the list of sites, enter the subdomain or subdirectory, the name of the new site, and the e-mail address of its administrator—for now, yours.

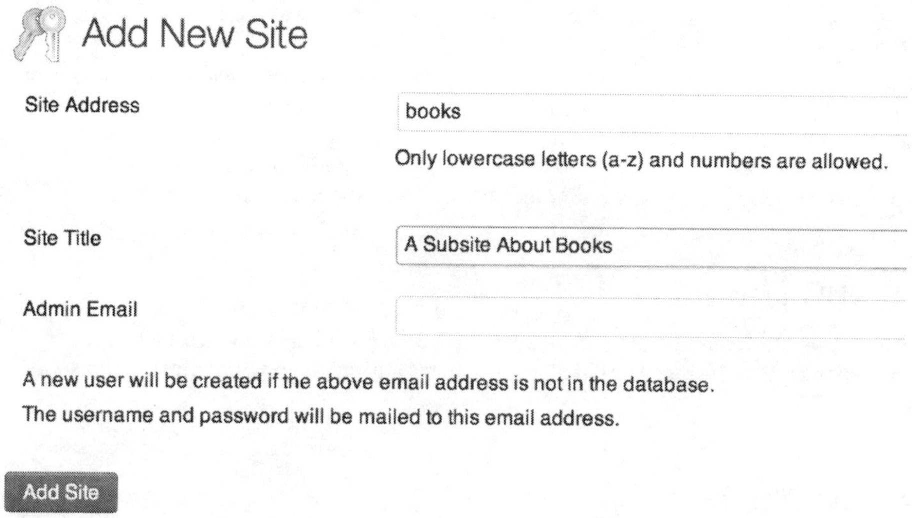

Add New Site

Site Address

> books
>
> Only lowercase letters (a-z) and numbers are allowed.

Site Title

> A Subsite About Books

Admin Email

A new user will be created if the above email address is not in the database.
The username and password will be mailed to this email address.

Add Site

Figure 8-7. *Adding a network site*

Click the "Dashboard" link below the site's subdomain in the list to visit its Dashboard. You should see a Dashboard that looks exactly like a new WordPress installation. The My Sites menu will still be visible in your admin bar, allowing you to switch back and forth between this site and the original one.

Network Users

Under Users, you can add more users to your network. They will not be added to any sites until individual site administrators add them or invite them to become users of their sites. Simply enter a username and e-mail address, and the person will be e-mailed a password.

To add a user to a subsite, go to the subsite's Dashboard, then to go Users ➤ Add New just as you did before. You'll have an option to enter an existing user's username (Figure 8-8). To invite the user, leave the checkbox blank and click "Add User." They'll receive a confirmation link allowing them to complete the registration process and fill in their account profile.

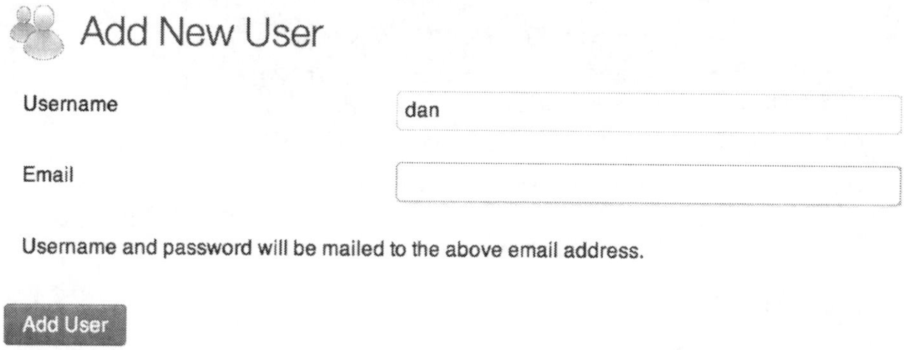

Add New User

Username

> dan

Email

Username and password will be mailed to the above email address.

Add User

Figure 8-8. *Adding a user to a network site*

Spam Users: Splogs

If you have chosen to allow people to sign up for sites on your network, you are about to discover a whole new kind of spam: splogs. Just as spammers will leave comments on random blogs and sign up for accounts on forums, they will sign up for blogs on your network and fill them with junk. In the list of sites under Sites, you can mark sites as spam. However, keeping up with splogs could soon consume more of your time than you're willing to spend.

There are a number of plugins that help prevent spam user registrations. See Appendix A for a partial list.

Network Plugins and Themes

Themes installed in your main site will not be available to the network sites until you activate them under Super Admin ➤ Themes, as shown in Figure 8-9. Individual sites' administrators may install themes, but those themes will be available only within that site.

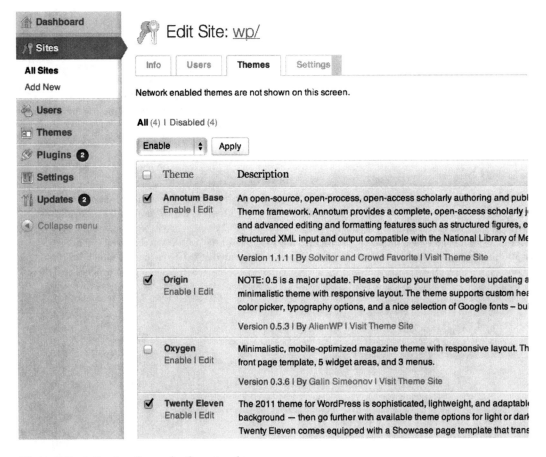

Figure 8-9. *Activating themes for the network*

When you install new plugins in Plugins ➤ Add New, you'll see a "Network Activate" link (Figure 8-10). This activates the plugin for every site on your network. Individual sites' administrators will not see network-activated plugins in their plugin lists, and they will not be able to deactivate them. Don't activate any plugins for the network if you want to give your site administrators a choice about using them.

Figure 8-10. *Activating a plugin for the network*

Plugin Settings and Network Activation

Many plugins install their default settings when you activate them. Network activation skips this step. If a plugin relies on its activation sequence, it will not work correctly when network-activated. You can work around this problem using the Proper Network Activation plugin. With this plugin in place, network activating a plugin will force WordPress to run its activation sequence on each site in the network. Beware, though: this does not scale well to large networks. If you have many sites in your network, you might run out of memory before your plugins finish activating.

Updating the Network

In a multisite installation, the Updates screen is located in the Network Dashboard. Updating a network is a two-step process. First, go to Update in your Network Dashboard and run the various updates as you normally would.

Once the main site has been upgraded, go Updates ➤ Network Update. Click the button there to upgrade all the network sites in turn, as shown in Figure 8-11.

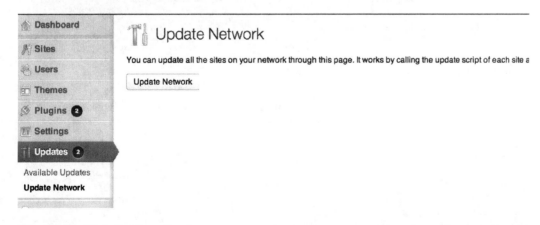

Figure 8-11. *Updating the network*

Mapping Domains

You can let your users map their own domains to their network sites using the WordPress MU Domain Mapping plugin (http://sleary.me/wp25)[1]. This creates an options page under Tools ➤ Domain Mapping where users can enter the domain(s) they want to use.

Once you have installed the plugin and enabled it for the network, go to Settings ➤ Domain Mapping in the Network Dashboard. You'll be asked to copy a file, sunrise.php, from the plugin's folder to wp-content. You'll also be asked to add define('SUNRISE', 'on'); to your wp-config.php file. Check the plugin's installation instructions to make sure everything is in the right place; this plugin's installation is a little more complicated than most.

Once the plugin is set up, the Domain Mapping screen will ask you to enter the IP address or CNAME of your server. Enter one of the two requested items, as shown in Figure 8-12.

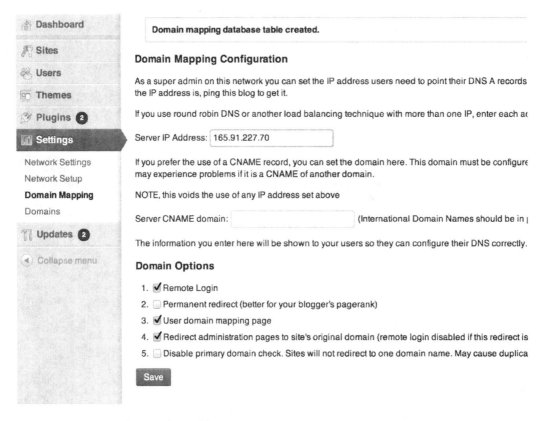

Figure 8-12. *Setting the server's IP address*

Now you can go back to Settings ➤ Domains, and you'll be able to enter domains for each of your subsites, as shown in Figure 8-13. Refer to the Sites ➤ All Sites screen to find each site's ID.

---

[1]http://wordpress.org/extend/plugins/wordpress-mu-domain-mapping

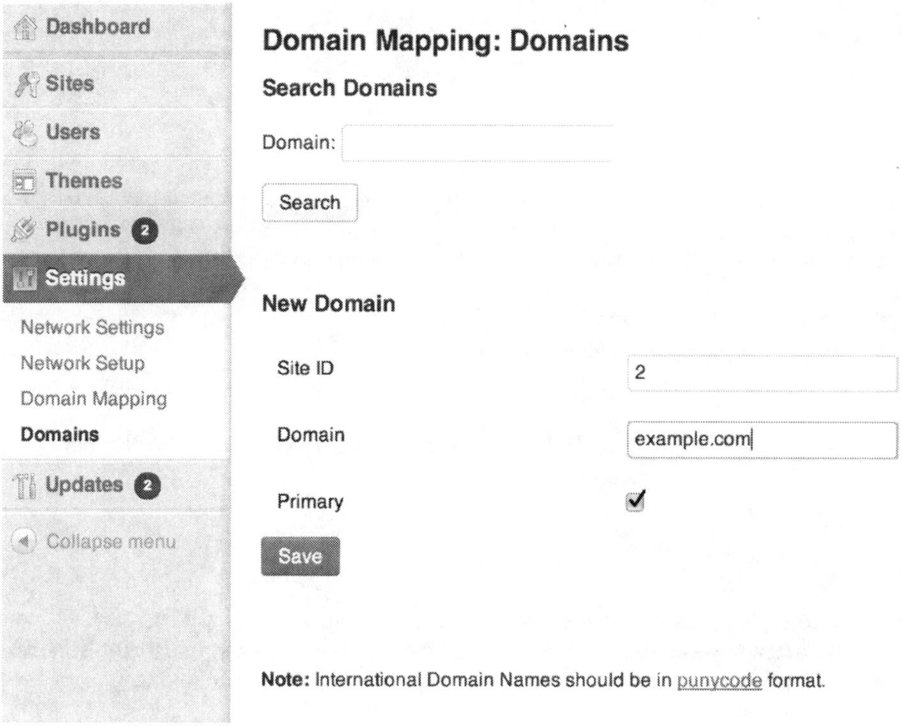

Domain Mapping: Domains

Search Domains

Domain: _____

[Search]

New Domain

Site ID	`2`
Domain	`example.com|`
Primary	✓

[Save]

Note: International Domain Names should be in punycode format.

Figure 8-13. *Mapping a domain*

You can enter multiple aliases and set one as the primary domain for the site. However, you can't use this plugin to add aliases for your main site.

Reverting to a Single Site

If you've decided that multisite is not for you, it's easy to reverse the process—in part. Simply switch the MULTISITE constant from true to false in wp-config.php (Listing 8-3). If you don't want the Network Setup option to appear in the Tools section of your Dashboard menu, you should also delete the WP_ALLOW_MULTISITE definition or switch it to false. You may also delete the rest of the multisite constants you added when you activated the network, although leaving them alone will save you a step if you decide to reactivate multisite mode later.

Listing 8-3. Turning Off Multisite

```
define( 'MULTISITE', false );
define( 'WP_ALLOW_MULTISITE', false );
```

This won't remove the extra network tables from your database; you'll have to drop them yourself from phpMyAdmin (or whatever MySQL administration interface you prefer). The multisite-specific tables are as follows:

- `wp_blogs`
- `wp_blog_versions`
- `wp_registration_log`

- wp_signups
- wp_site
- wp_sitecategories
- wp_sitemeta

There are also tables for each of the new sites you added (if any); they will begin with your table prefix followed by an underscore and a number. The first site will begin with wp_1_, and so on. All of these tables may be deleted. If you had allowed other people to create sites on your network, be sure to back up their data somehow.

■ **Note** Keep in mind that your table prefix can be something other than wp_!

Dropping these tables will not affect your original site. Still, as a general rule, you should make a backup before you drop any tables.

Summary

In this chapter, you've learned how to apply your knowledge of WordPress to create an entire network of WordPress-based sites. You've learned how to set up the network features, how to install and enable plugins and themes for the network, and how to manage network sites and users. You've seen how to set up domain mapping for your network users and how to block spambots from signing up for accounts.

In the next chapter, you'll learn how to secure your WordPress installation.

■ ■ ■

CHAPTER 9

Performance and Security

WordPress is database-driven, so it's not quite as fast at serving up individual pages as a CMS that writes static files to the server. However, there are a number of things you can do to improve its performance, starting with caching dynamic output to static pages. I'll explain how caching works and show you how to set it up. I'll also show you some ways to identify performance problems in your installation.

The downside of being the most popular CMS in the world is that WordPress attracts a lot of attention from would-be hackers. The development team does a great job of responding to newly discovered vulnerabilities quickly, so staying up to date with the latest release is the most important thing you can do to protect yourself from attacks. However, there are a number of other little things you can do, and I'll walk you through them in the second half of this chapter.

Backing Up the Database and Files

Keeping regular backups of your database is essential if you want to be able to restore your site after something has gone wrong. Your hosting provider might do this for you, but it's still a good idea to keep your own copies in case something catastrophic happens.

There are several plugins you can use to back up your database right from the WordPress administration screens. I'll show you the Better WP Security plugin, which you'll see again later in this chapter. Figure 9-1 shows the plugin's backup tools.

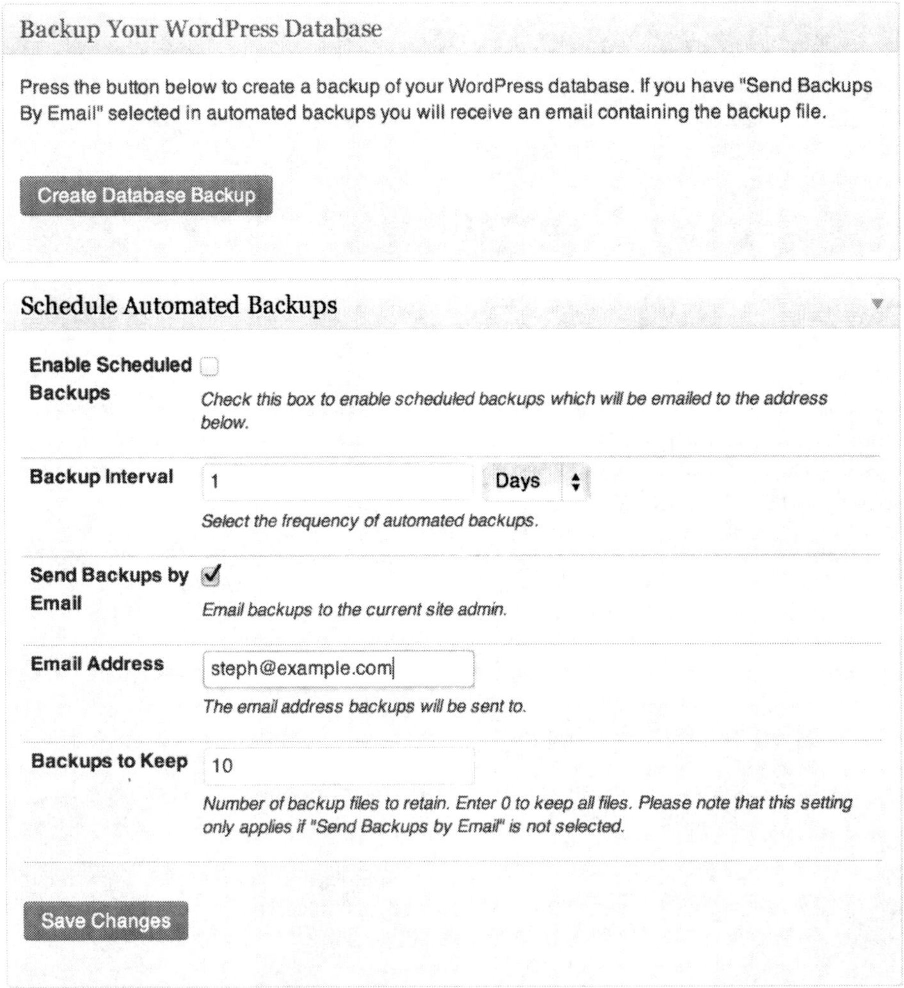

Backup Your WordPress Database

Press the button below to create a backup of your WordPress database. If you have "Send Backups By Email" selected in automated backups you will receive an email containing the backup file.

Create Database Backup

Schedule Automated Backups ▼

Enable Scheduled Backups ☐
Check this box to enable scheduled backups which will be emailed to the address below.

Backup Interval | 1 | Days ▲▼
Select the frequency of automated backups.

Send Backups by Email ☑
Email backups to the current site admin.

Email Address | steph@example.com |
The email address backups will be sent to.

Backups to Keep | 10 |
Number of backup files to retain. Enter 0 to keep all files. Please note that this setting only applies if "Send Backups by Email" is not selected.

Save Changes

Figure 9-1. *Backing up the database and scheduling regular backups with the Better WP Security plugin*

The lower half of the plugin's option screen (Figure 9-1) lets you schedule regular backups. Make sure the email account you enter here can handle a lot of attachments (unless you're diligent about deleting old copies when the new one comes in.) The compressed file is not all that large, but over time the size will add up.

To restore from one of these backups, you'll need some sort of interface to your MySQL database other than WordPress itself. If your host offers PHPMyAdmin, for example, you could go to the Import tab and upload your backup file. Check your host's documentation to see how you can import SQL files into your database.

Don't forget to back up your files, too. Your uploaded media files probably wouldn't be very easy to replace, and if you've made any changes to your theme, you'll need copies of those, too. In general, it's a good idea to keep backups of your entire wp-content directory. There are several plugins that can handle this for you; I just use my FTP client's synchronize feature to download an updated copy every time I log in to make a change.

Changing the Database Table Prefix

Now that you've backed up your database, it's a good time to consider changing the table prefix if you chose the default wp_ during installation. Since the default table prefix is well known, changing it is a good step toward protecting your site from basic SQL injection attacks. If you installed WordPress with your host's one-click installer (like Fantastico), you might not have had a choice about the prefix; otherwise, the prefix is an option you chose when you filled in your database username and password.

Better WP Security and WP Security Scan let you change the prefix to a randomly-chosen string (Figure 9-2). If you'd like to use a less arbitrary prefix, you'll need to modify the MySQL tables directly in a number of places and update your wp-config.php file. How to accomplish this depends on what sort of database access your host allows you. I'll demonstrate using PHPMyAdmin, the most popular interface.

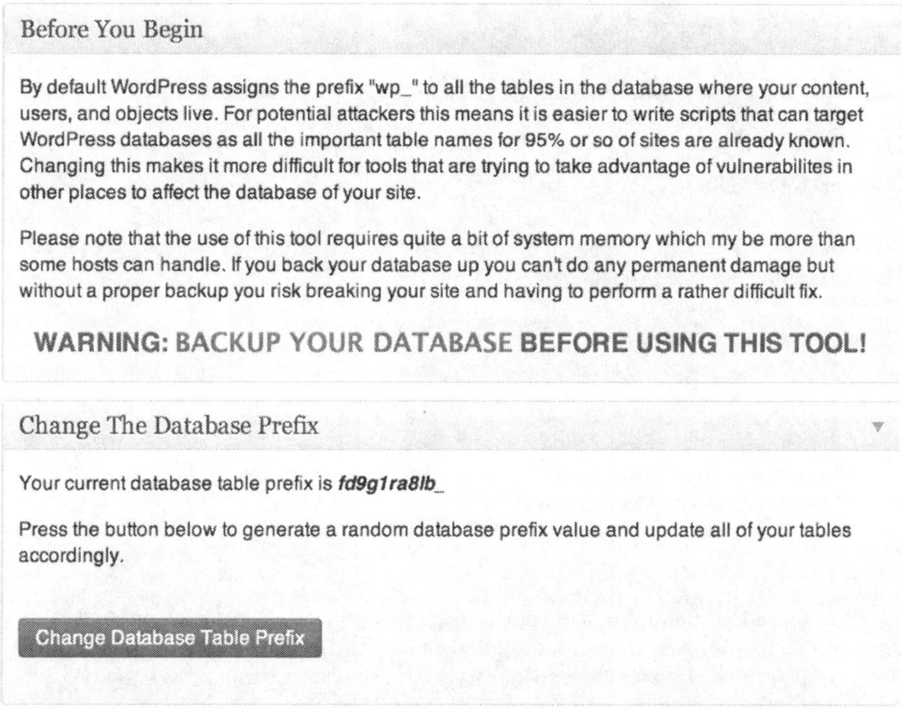

Before You Begin

By default WordPress assigns the prefix "wp_" to all the tables in the database where your content, users, and objects live. For potential attackers this means it is easier to write scripts that can target WordPress databases as all the important table names for 95% or so of sites are already known. Changing this makes it more difficult for tools that are trying to take advantage of vulnerabilites in other places to affect the database of your site.

Please note that the use of this tool requires quite a bit of system memory which my be more than some hosts can handle. If you back your database up you can't do any permanent damage but without a proper backup you risk breaking your site and having to perform a rather difficult fix.

WARNING: BACKUP YOUR DATABASE BEFORE USING THIS TOOL!

Change The Database Prefix ▼

Your current database table prefix is *fd9g1ra8lb_*

Press the button below to generate a random database prefix value and update all of your tables accordingly.

[Change Database Table Prefix]

Figure 9-2. *Changing database prefix in Better WP Security*

For each table in the database, click either the Browse or Structure icon, then choose Operations from the row of tabs across the top of the screen. You'll see a screen like Figure 9-3. In the Table Options group, you'll see a field where you can rename the table. Replace wp with your new prefix and click the Go button. Repeat for each table in the database.

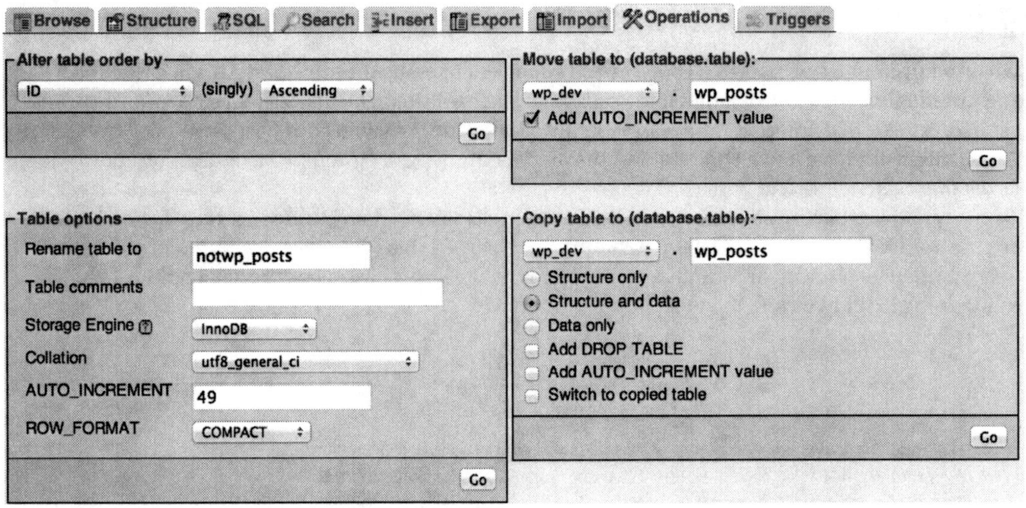

Figure 9-3. *Renaming a database table in PHPMyAdmin*

Once you've changed the tables, you'll need to update `wp-config.php` to reflect the change. The relevant portion of the configuration file is shown in Listing 9-1.

Listing 9-1. The Database Prefix Option in `wp-config.php`

```
/**
 * WordPress Database Table prefix.
 *
 * You can have multiple installations in one database if you give each a unique
 * prefix. Only numbers, letters, and underscores please!
 */
$table_prefix  = 'mysite_';
```

Now comes the tricky part: locating all the options that included the prefix. Look through your `wp_options` table (which now starts with something other than `wp_`) and change any option names that begin with your old prefix. If you are running a multisite installation, you'll have to repeat this step for each individual site's options table (`wp_1_options`, and so on). Last, go to the `wp_usermeta` table and rename any `meta_key` values that used the old prefix.

For all that work, changing the table prefix will not protect you from a determined hacker; it's basically security through obscurity. It will stop some SQL injection scripts that rely on the ubiquity of standard WordPress installations. Making yours just a little bit different from everyone else's helps. However, you should be prepared to restore your database from a clean backup if something does go wrong.

Caching

If you've ever seen a link go viral, only to visit the site and find a server error instead of the article you wanted, you've witnessed the consequences of insufficient caching. A dynamic site has to query the database several times to assemble each page a visitor requests. Queries for a typical WordPress page include the general settings (site title, description, language, theme stylesheet URL), the post or page title and contents, the comments, and the sidebar widgets. Servers can generally handle all those MySQL queries and PHP page-building functions for sites with low traffic, but when your site gets its 15 minutes of fame—or gets hit with a denial of service attack—your server will probably buckle under the sudden demand.

The solution is to cache the assembled pages—that is, to store copies as static files in a hidden directory and to redirect incoming visitors to those copies rather than allow them to continually hammer your dynamic site. Not only does this speed things up for your visitors, but if you're on a shared hosting server, it will prevent you from exceeding your allotted CPU usage. Some hosts are nice about helping you keep the site up and running when that happens; others will just shut down your site to protect the other users on the server.

WordPress does not come with built-in caching. (This is perhaps the biggest criticism leveled at the WordPress project by users of other open-source content management systems.) It *does* come with support for a number of different caching options, and it's up to you to decide which plugin best suits your needs and your hosting environment. Cache plugins available in the plugin repository include the following:

- WP Super Cache

- W3 Total Cache

- Batcache

- Hyper Cache

- WP Widget Cache

I'll walk through Super Cache, which is by far the most popular. First, though, take a look at your permalink settings. You *must* use a permalink structure other than the default in order for the caching plugins to work. Super Cache warns you if your permalink structure won't work, as shown in Figure 9-4. All of the cache plugins operate by using rewrite rules in your .htaccess file to redirect requests from your dynamic WordPress pages to static files saved in a hidden directory in your installation. If you aren't using permalinks, WordPress hasn't written any rewrite rules to .htaccess. If the rewrites never take place, your dynamic pages will be served up to your visitors even though you have installed and activated a caching plugin.

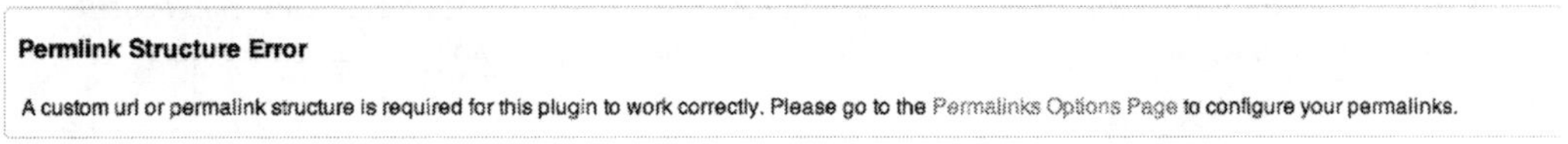

Permlink Structure Error

A custom url or permalink structure is required for this plugin to work correctly. Please go to the Permalinks Options Page to configure your permalinks.

Figure 9-4. *WP Super Cache warning message on permalink structures*

Setting Up Super Cache

Unlike most plugins, Super Cache doesn't start working as soon as you activate it. You have to configure it first. You'll see a red-outlined warning message on your plugin list until you set up caching or deactivate the plugin.

Basic Settings

Go to Settings ➤ Super Cache to configure the plugin (Figure 9-5). If you're in a hurry, you can just turn on caching, click Update Status, and move on to other things.

WP Super Cache Settings

| Easy | Advanced | CDN | Contents | Preload | Plugins | De |

Caching

● Caching On *(Recommended)*
○ Caching Off

Note: enables PHP caching, cache rebuild, and mobile support

Update Status »

Delete Cached Pages

Cached pages are stored on your server as html and PHP files. If you need to delete them use the button below.

Recommended Links and Plugins

Delete Cache » Caching is only one part of making a website faster. Here are some other plugins that will help:

Figure 9-5. *Main Super Cache settings*

If you have a minute, though, you should look through the advanced settings (Figure 9-6) to make things a little smoother for yourself and other content editors. First, you should probably turn on the option labeled *Don't cache pages for known users*. This will ensure that as you're making changes to the site, you can view them immediately without waiting for the cache to refresh.

WP Super Cache Settings

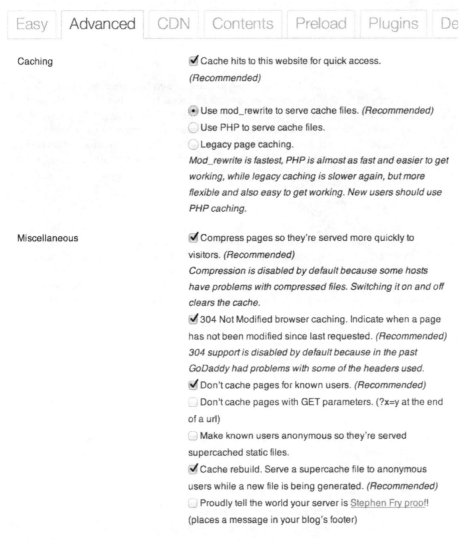

| Easy | Advanced | CDN | Contents | Preload | Plugins | De |

Caching ✓ Cache hits to this website for quick access.
(Recommended)

⦿ Use mod_rewrite to serve cache files. *(Recommended)*
○ Use PHP to serve cache files.
○ Legacy page caching.
Mod_rewrite is fastest, PHP is almost as fast and easier to get working, while legacy caching is slower again, but more flexible and also easy to get working. New users should use PHP caching.

Miscellaneous ✓ Compress pages so they're served more quickly to visitors. *(Recommended)*
Compression is disabled by default because some hosts have problems with compressed files. Switching it on and off clears the cache.
✓ 304 Not Modified browser caching. Indicate when a page has not been modified since last requested. *(Recommended)*
304 support is disabled by default because in the past GoDaddy had problems with some of the headers used.
✓ Don't cache pages for known users. *(Recommended)*
☐ Don't cache pages with GET parameters. (?x=y at the end of a url)
☐ Make known users anonymous so they're served supercached static files.
✓ Cache rebuild. Serve a supercache file to anonymous users while a new file is being generated. *(Recommended)*
☐ Proudly tell the world your server is <u>Stephen Fry proof</u>! (places a message in your blog's footer)

Figure 9-6. *Advanced Super Cache settings*

The *Cache rebuild* option will rebuild the cache when you add a post or page. This will ensure that your visitors will see the new content immediately, but it will also slow things down for you and your other users. Every time you publish something, the entire cache will have to be regenerated, and that can take a significant amount of processing power if you have a large site. My recommendation is to try writing a few posts with this option on and see how it goes. If your site becomes unusably slow, turn it off! Your visitors will just have to wait for the old cached pages to expire (within the time limit you'll set in just a moment) before they see your new posts.

Normally, a post's cached page will be rebuilt every time someone adds a comment. However, if you get so many comments that this would be counterproductive, you can turn on *Cache rebuild*. New files will still be generated, but if a new comment comes in while the page is being generated, the viewer will see the older copy.

The rest of the recommended settings work well on most servers. You might encounter problems with the compression option if your host is already compressing output; if you see garbage characters on your site with this setting on, simply turn it off.

Compression

The compression setting determines whether your cached files are stored in compressed (gzipped) format. Modern browsers are capable of unzipping pages after downloading them, so your server can send smaller files. Super Cache compression can cause problems if your server is already compressing output using mod_deflate (on Apache) or PHP compression (zlib). In this case, the doubly compressed files might appear as garbage characters to some users. You can turn off compression in Super Cache or adjust your server's settings. The plugin FAQ contains information on how to do this; if those instructions don't work, ask your hosting provider about your server's compression settings.

Garbage Collection

Under Expiry Time & Garbage Collection (Figure 9-7), you can choose how long your cached pages will last before they should be rebuilt. The default setting is 3600 seconds (one hour). You can lower this, but keep in mind that garbage collection requires server resources, just as rebuilding pages does. You should experiment with different settings to strike a balance between these two processes that doesn't overly tax your server. If your site is not updated hourly (including comments posted by users), you can set the timeout to 86400 seconds—a full day. This is also a good setting to use if your comments are handled by a separate service like Disqus, IntenseDebate, or Livefyre.

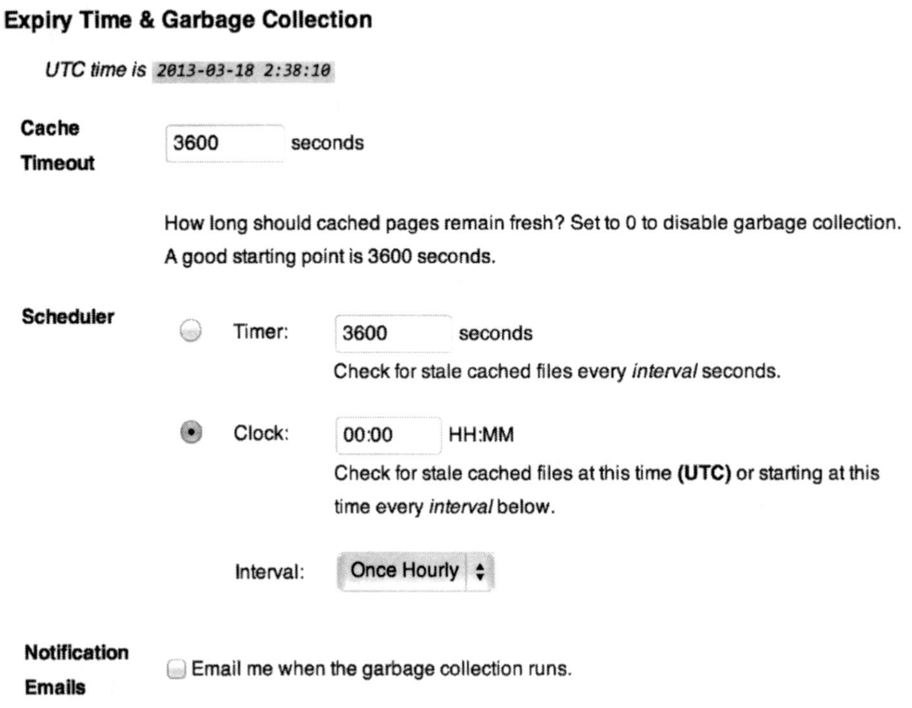

Expiry Time & Garbage Collection

UTC time is `2013-03-18 2:38:10`

Cache Timeout

`3600` seconds

How long should cached pages remain fresh? Set to 0 to disable garbage collection.
A good starting point is 3600 seconds.

Scheduler

○ Timer: `3600` seconds
Check for stale cached files every *interval* seconds.

◉ Clock: `00:00` HH:MM
Check for stale cached files at this time **(UTC)** or starting at this time every *interval* below.

Interval: Once Hourly ⬍

Notification Emails

☐ Email me when the garbage collection runs.

Figure 9-7. *Garbage collection in WP Super Cache*

Choosing What to Cache

In the Accepted Filenames and Rejected URIs section of the Super Cache settings (Figure 9-8), you can specify certain pages that should not be cached. Of these, I would recommend checking Feeds, to make sure your RSS subscribers always receive updated feeds. You can leave the rest of these settings on their default values in most cases.

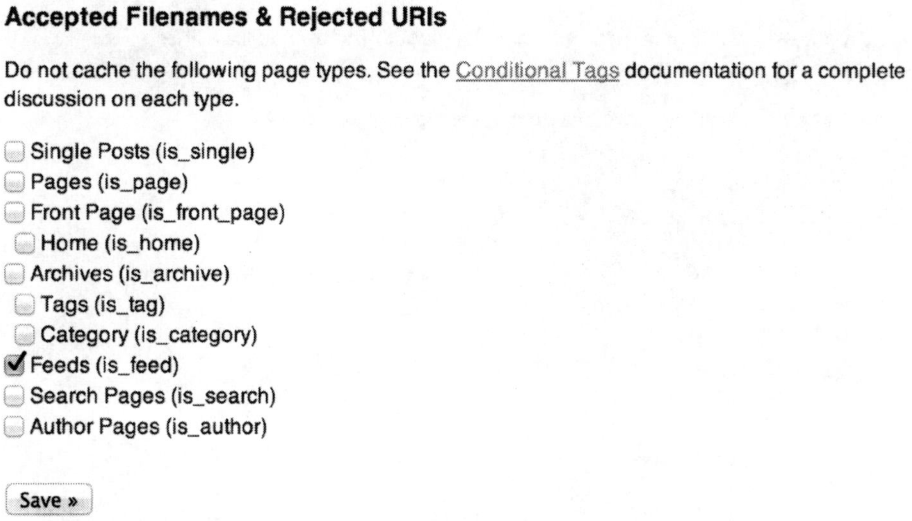

Accepted Filenames & Rejected URIs

Do not cache the following page types. See the Conditional Tags documentation for a complete discussion on each type.

☐ Single Posts (is_single)
☐ Pages (is_page)
☐ Front Page (is_front_page)
☐ Home (is_home)
☐ Archives (is_archive)
☐ Tags (is_tag)
☐ Category (is_category)
☑ Feeds (is_feed)
☐ Search Pages (is_search)
☐ Author Pages (is_author)

Save »

Figure 9-8. Choosing types of pages that should not be cached

At the bottom of the advanced settings screen, you'll have the option to directly cache a single file (Figure 9-9). If you write a post or a page that you know will bring in untold numbers of readers, you can head off the impending performance crisis by caching the page not in the usual hidden cache location, but right in your blog directory. How does this work? The WordPress rewrite rules—all of them, including Super Cache's—are set up to rewrite URLs only if the requested file or directory does not exist on the server. Therefore, if you create a cached page in the location that matches the permalink, the cached file will trump all rewrite rules. Since the server doesn't have to look through all those rewrites, it will be a little faster at serving up that particular file. And when you're looking at thousands of requests coming in, "a little faster" multiplies quickly into some significant performance.

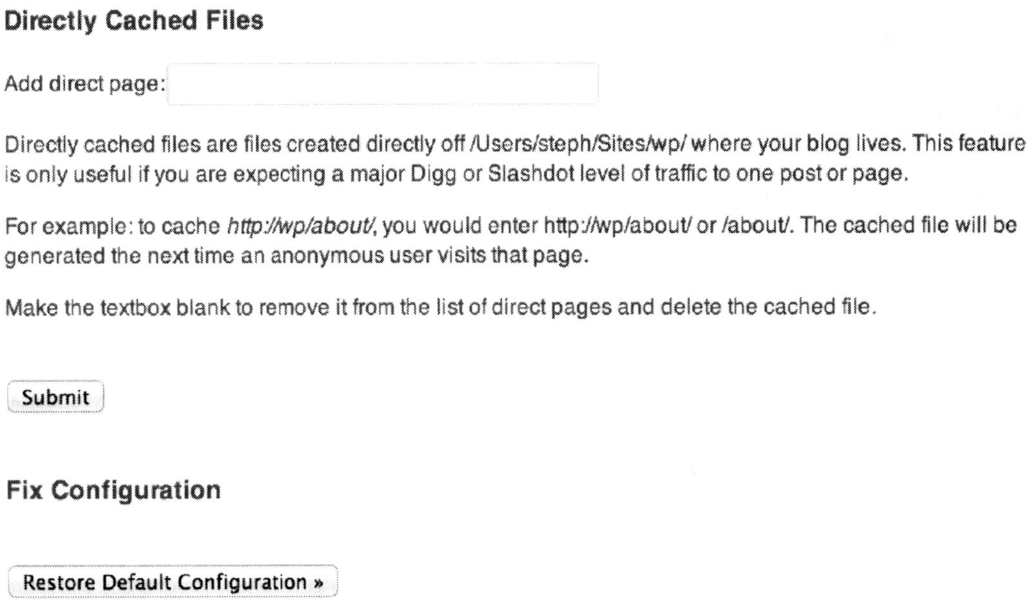

Directly Cached Files

Add direct page: [   ]

Directly cached files are files created directly off /Users/steph/Sites/wp/ where your blog lives. This feature is only useful if you are expecting a major Digg or Slashdot level of traffic to one post or page.

For example: to cache *http://wp/about/*, you would enter http://wp/about/ or /about/. The cached file will be generated the next time an anonymous user visits that page.

Make the textbox blank to remove it from the list of direct pages and delete the cached file.

[Submit]

Fix Configuration

[Restore Default Configuration »]

Figure 9-9. *Directly caching a popular file in WP Super Cache*

If you need to cache your entire site immediately, rather than waiting until someone visits each page, visit the Preload tab (Figure 9-10). Here you can have Super Cache handle all the pages at once.

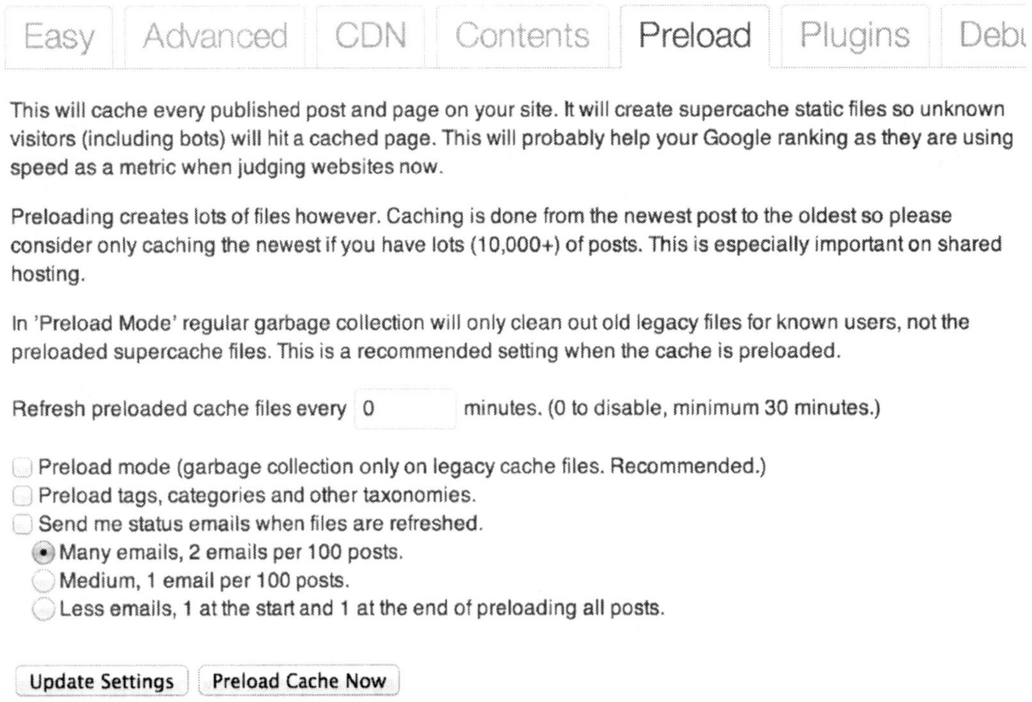

| Easy | Advanced | CDN | Contents | **Preload** | Plugins | Debu |

This will cache every published post and page on your site. It will create supercache static files so unknown visitors (including bots) will hit a cached page. This will probably help your Google ranking as they are using speed as a metric when judging websites now.

Preloading creates lots of files however. Caching is done from the newest post to the oldest so please consider only caching the newest if you have lots (10,000+) of posts. This is especially important on shared hosting.

In 'Preload Mode' regular garbage collection will only clean out old legacy files for known users, not the preloaded supercache files. This is a recommended setting when the cache is preloaded.

Refresh preloaded cache files every [0] minutes. (0 to disable, minimum 30 minutes.)

☐ Preload mode (garbage collection only on legacy cache files. Recommended.)
☐ Preload tags, categories and other taxonomies.
☐ Send me status emails when files are refreshed.
   ◉ Many emails, 2 emails per 100 posts.
   ○ Medium, 1 email per 100 posts.
   ○ Less emails, 1 at the start and 1 at the end of preloading all posts.

[Update Settings] [Preload Cache Now]

Figure 9-10. *Preloading the entire site into the cache*

Refreshing the Cache

Any time you change the Super Cache settings, you need to delete the cache so the cached pages will be rebuilt according to your new settings. Once you've saved your settings, go back to the main tab and press Delete Cache.

Securing Logins

In older versions of WordPress, the first user account was always named admin. This made it relatively easy for hackers to try to crack the password on the account. Since version 3.0, you have been able to choose your username during the installation process. This cuts down on the scale of the problem, but it doesn't mitigate it entirely. You might still want to lock down your login screens. For even more security, you could force the login process to take place over SSL, thus encrypting your password transmissions. You could even conduct all your administrative tasks over SSL.

Login Lockdown

Disabling the login function for a range of IP addresses after several failed attempts in a short period of time helps protect you from brute-force password attacks. The simplest plugin to solve this problem, Login Lockdown, is shown in Figure 9-11. (Using the default settings, it will lock you out for an hour after you've failed to enter the right password three times in five minutes.) If you're the sort of person who continually forgets your password, this might not be the plugin for you! However, since guessing at administrative passwords is a common method of breaking into WordPress sites, I recommend that you pick a password you can remember and install this plugin. Login Security Solution and Better WP Security also include this feature.

Figure 9-11. *An account locked out by the Login Lockdown plugin*

If your users have trouble remembering their passwords and they lock themselves out frequently once you start disabling logins after a few failed attempts, suggest that they try a password storage application. LastPass, 1Password, and KeePass will store (and generate) very secure passwords, which they can fill in by entering a single master password.

SSL

You have a few options when it comes to SSL. You can force WordPress to use SSL for logins only, or you can use SSL for all administrative sessions if your host supports it. If you're not sure, check with your host.

With the SSL login option, your username and password will be handled in a secure transaction. All your other traffic, including the authorization cookies you receive from WordPress, will be sent in the clear.

With SSL-only admin sessions, your username, password, and all your authorization cookies will be encrypted. While this is obviously somewhat more secure, it is slower. For most situations, SSL logins should be sufficient. The login option allows users to choose whether or not to use SSL for the entire admin session or just the login.

Listing 9-2 shows the two lines you may add to `wp-config.php` to enable SSL support. Choose just one of these!

Listing 9-2. SSL Settings in `wp-config.php`

```
// https for all admin sessions:
define('FORCE_SSL_ADMIN', true);

//https required for login; optional for the rest of the admin session:
define('FORCE_SSL_LOGIN', true);
```

Removing The Meta Generator Tag

One of the things `wp_head()` adds to a WordPress theme's header template is a meta generator tag showing which version of WordPress you're using. It helps the WordPress developers know how many WordPress sites there are in the world. However, it's also an advertisement to would-be hackers that your site runs on WordPress—especially if you haven't updated to the latest release. Now, you should always upgrade to the newest release as soon as possible, but of course there will be times when you just can't upgrade immediately. If that's the case, you wouldn't want to advertise to the world that you're running an older, potentially insecure version of WordPress. Several WordPress security plugins offer this feature, including Better WP Security and WP Security Scan.

File Permissions

All the files in your WordPress installation should list you as the owner. The files that WordPress needs to write to (e.g., `.htaccess`, `wp-content`) should belong to a group that contains the Web server user. For example, on a UNIX-based server running Apache, you would need to find out which user owns Apache's processes (usually it's www). On IIS, you need to know which user IIS runs as (SYSTEM). Then make sure that there's a group containing both you and the Web server user. That's the group your `wp-content` and `.htaccess` files should belong to. On most servers, that's done for you. However, to better secure your WordPress site, I recommend that you allow only `wp-content` to be group-writable, and make sure you're the only user who can write to `.htaccess`.

Securing `.htaccess` and `wp-config.php`

There are a number of ways hackers could use your `.htaccess` file maliciously. They could use rewrite rules to redirect your visitors to a site other than yours, but that's the sort of thing you'd notice immediately, and it doesn't happen very often. A subtle attack is more likely. One particularly nasty hack involves writing a file full of spam links to a writeable subdirectory deep in the WordPress package, then using PHP's auto_prepend_file or auto_append_file directives to include that file in your theme's index.php file. At first, it looks like someone has mauled your theme, but in fact the theme files haven't changed at all. This is the sort of attack that can leave you chasing your tail for hours, unless you realize that .htaccess is a big point of vulnerability in your installation.

WordPress needs write access to your .htaccess file only to make changes to your permalink structure. If you are using WP Super Cache, the plugin also requires write access to add the cache rewrite rules to the file. However, in both cases, if WordPress cannot write to the file, it will print the necessary rules on the screen and ask you to update the file manually. Therefore, I recommend that you adjust permissions on .htaccess so that your user account is the only one allowed to write to it. On UNIX-based operating systems, you can use the chmod 744 command to make sure you can write to it while everyone else can read only.

You can also modify the .htaccess file itself to secure your wp-config.php file. Normally, any visitor requesting your configuration file will just see a blank page, since the file doesn't echo anything to the screen. However, this addition to .htaccess prevents unwanted users from viewing your config file at all.

While .htaccess is not generally accessible through a browser, either, you can apply the same technique to give it a little extra protection, as shown in Listing 9-3. It looks a little recursive, but it works!

Listing 9-3. Securing wp-config.php and .htaccess using .htaccess

```
<Files wp-config.php>
order allow,deny
deny from all
</Files>

<Files .htaccess>
order allow,deny
deny from all
</Files>
```

For more security-related modifications to .htaccess, visit http://sleary.me/wp26[1], or see the .htaccess-related settings in the Better WP Security plugin.

Changing File Locations

It's possible to move wp-config.php and the wp-content folder. You can even put the WordPress files other than index.php in a separate subdirectory. All of these things will help minimize attacks that exploit writeable directories in predictable locations.

Moving wp-config.php

Your configuration file contains your database username and password, so it's important to keep this file secure. If you are installing WordPress in your web root directory (such as public_html), you can move your wp-config.php file to the parent directory—one that isn't readable from a browser—without changing any settings. WordPress will automatically recognize the file's new location.

---

[1]http://www.josiahcole.com/2007/07/11/almost-perfect-htaccess-file-for-wordpress-blogs

Giving WordPress Its Own Subdirectory

If you would prefer not to have WordPress's files cluttering up your site's root directory, or you would prefer a nonstandard location for your admin files as a security precaution, you can install WordPress in a subdirectory while keeping your site visible at the original location. For example, you can install WordPress at mydomain.com/wordpress but have the site appear at mydomain.com.

First, install WordPress *in the subdirectory* as you normally would. Then move the main index.php file and your .htaccess file from that subdirectory into the parent directory. In your example, you would install WordPress in the wordpress directory, then move index.php and .htaccess into the Web root directory.

Open index.php in a text editor and edit the path to wp-blog-header.php. Add your subdirectory to the file path. In this example, you're installing WordPress in the wordpress subdirectory, so your line would read require('./wordpress/wp-blog-header.php');. Of course, you can replace wordpress with anything you wish.

Now log in to the site at its new address: example.com/wordpress/wp-admin. Go to Settings General and change your WordPress address to the new one: example.com/wordpress. Leave the Blog address alone, and save your changes. See Figure 9-12 for an example.

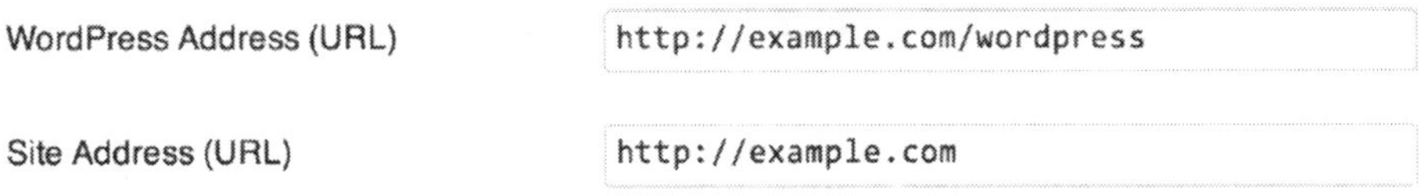

WordPress Address (URL)	http://example.com/wordpress
Site Address (URL)	http://example.com

Figure 9-12. *Changing the WordPress address without changing the blog address*

Once you've saved these options, you'll be logged out. You'll have to log back in at the new location (http://example.com/wordpress/wp-admin/).

Moving wp-content

You can move your wp-content folder elsewhere if you like or rename it to something else. However, there are a number of constants related to the wp-content and plugins directories. To make sure your plugins continue working correctly, you should define all of these constants in your wp-config.php file. Better WP Security can do this for you. If you prefer to do it by hand, add the constant definitions anywhere in the configuration file, as shown in Listing 9-4.

Listing 9-4. Renaming /wp-content to /files

```
define('WP_CONTENT_DIR', $_SERVER['DOCUMENT_ROOT'] . '/files');
define('WP_CONTENT_URL', 'http://example.com/files');
define('WP_PLUGIN_DIR', $_SERVER['DOCUMENT_ROOT'] . '/files/plugins');
define('WP_PLUGIN_URL', 'http://example.com/files/plugins');
define('PLUGINDIR', $_SERVER['DOCUMENT_ROOT'] . '/files/plugins');
```

Monitoring Security Problems

There are several plugins that will help you maintain a secure installation. Better WP Security is an incredibly comprehensive plugin that allows you to change your database prefix, your file locations and permissions, your users' minimum password strength, and more. It allows you to schedule database backups. It suggests changes to make your site more secure, and it offers one-click tools to make the suggested changes (after you back up your site, of course). You can use its "One-click protection" option to enable all the basic security precautions. Once you have done so, you'll see a System Status screen (Figure 9-13) with links to additional, optional settings you can handle one at a time.

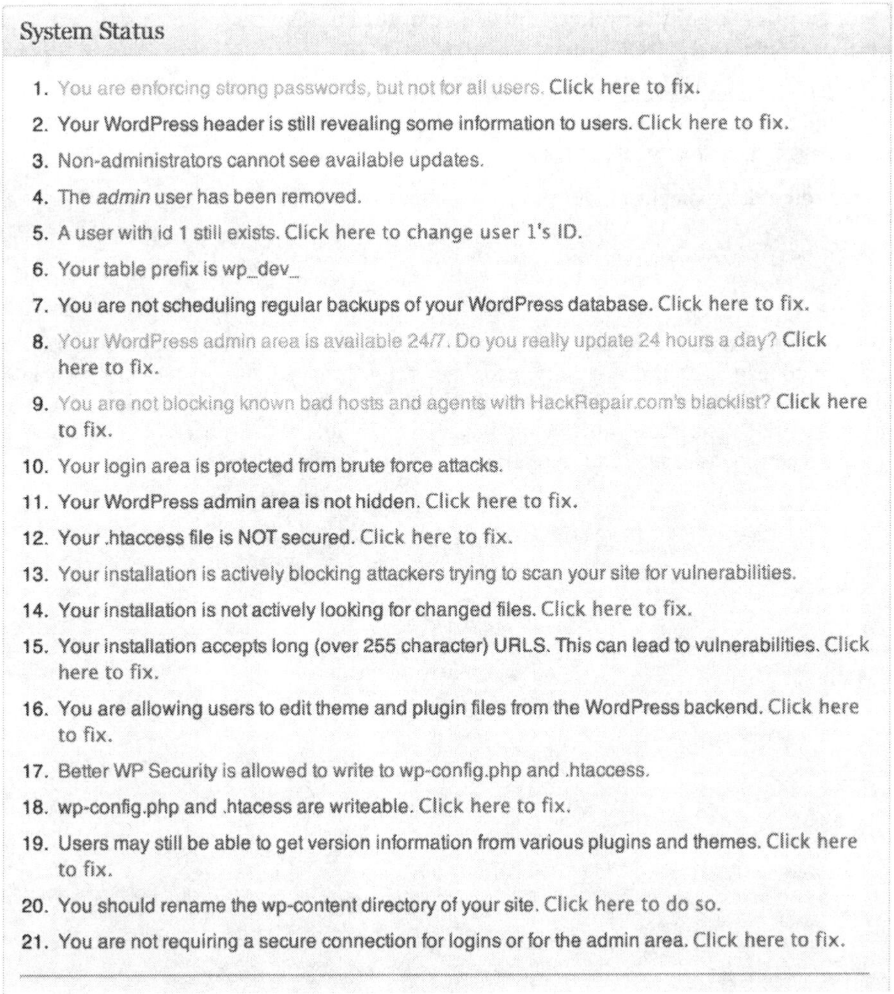

System Status

1. You are enforcing strong passwords, but not for all users. Click here to fix.
2. Your WordPress header is still revealing some information to users. Click here to fix.
3. Non-administrators cannot see available updates.
4. The *admin* user has been removed.
5. A user with id 1 still exists. Click here to change user 1's ID.
6. Your table prefix is wp_dev_
7. You are not scheduling regular backups of your WordPress database. Click here to fix.
8. Your WordPress admin area is available 24/7. Do you really update 24 hours a day? Click here to fix.
9. You are not blocking known bad hosts and agents with HackRepair.com's blacklist? Click here to fix.
10. Your login area is protected from brute force attacks.
11. Your WordPress admin area is not hidden. Click here to fix.
12. Your .htaccess file is NOT secured. Click here to fix.
13. Your installation is actively blocking attackers trying to scan your site for vulnerabilities.
14. Your installation is not actively looking for changed files. Click here to fix.
15. Your installation accepts long (over 255 character) URLS. This can lead to vulnerabilities. Click here to fix.
16. You are allowing users to edit theme and plugin files from the WordPress backend. Click here to fix.
17. Better WP Security is allowed to write to wp-config.php and .htaccess.
18. wp-config.php and .htacess are writeable. Click here to fix.
19. Users may still be able to get version information from various plugins and themes. Click here to fix.
20. You should rename the wp-content directory of your site. Click here to do so.
21. You are not requiring a secure connection for logins or for the admin area. Click here to fix.

Figure 9-13. System status in Better WP Security

Take a look at these other security-related plugins as well:

- WP Security Scan checks your file permissions, passwords, database security, and more. It provides tools to fix most of the problems it identifies.

- WordPress Firewall 2 monitors HTTP requests for blacklisted phrases and can email you when it finds something suspicious. However, I've found that its blacklist includes phrases related to many CMSs other than WordPress, which means you'll get a lot of false alerts in your inbox.

- Exploit Scanner searches your files and database for any suspicious entries, like files full of spam links.

- Audit Trail is also useful for letting you know who's been attempting to log in and what they changed.

- Sucuri, a plugin written by the security consulting firm of the same name, includes a comprehensive malware scanner and some one-click fixes.

- CloudFlare is perhaps better known as a content delivery network that serves cached files for better performance, but they also offer security services that can be tightened in the event of an attack and relaxed again once the threat has passed.

See Appendix A for more security-related plugins.

Summary

In this chapter, I've shown you how to speed up your WordPress site with WP Super Cache. To secure your site, I've talked about barring users from multiple login attempts, using SSL for logins and/or full admin sessions, and securing both your files and your database. Last, I've shown you a handful of plugins that help you keep an eye on your installation. Now that you know what to look for, these tools should help you maintain a fast, healthy WordPress site.

In the next chapter, you'll learn how to move sites between servers and import content from other sites.

■ ■ ■

CHAPTER 10

Importing Content and Migrating Sites

If you're switching to WordPress from some other platform, you probably need to import some content. There is a plethora of WordPress plugins to import content from other blogging and content management systems. In addition, the WordPress API makes it relatively easy to import content from any MySQL-based content management system.

In this chapter I'll look at the import tool for wordpress.com, one of the most commonly used import plugins. This tool can import blog posts, pages, comments, menus, images, categories, and tags. I'll also show you lesser-known import plugins, including a CSV importer that can be used to import content from other CMSs and a general script template that can be modified to suit other MySQL databases. I'll walk you through my own HTML Import plugin, which can be used to import static files as posts or pages.

Last, I'll go over the issues involved with moving a WordPress site from one server to another, including domain changes.

Before Importing

Importing can be tricky, and it doesn't always go well the first time. Therefore, it's important to install a backup plugin before you begin, and to make sure you know how to restore your site from the backup. You saw a few backup plugins in the previous chapter. If you haven't already, install one of them now, or use the WP DB Backup plugin, which is one of the simplest backup plugins to use.

Be sure to back up your media files as well (in wp-content/uploads, unless you have moved the files to another directory). Some buggy importers can create hundreds of duplicate image files; you might find that you need to start over without these extra copies.

If you're importing content into a WordPress site that already contains content, back up your database and put the site into maintenance mode before you begin importing, just as you would if you were upgrading (see Chapter 2).

If you've installed a plugin that crossposts your content to another site (like Facebook or Tumblr) or automatically notifies another site of your new posts (like Twitter), be sure to deactivate those plugins before you begin; otherwise, you'll flood your social network with your imported posts.

Installing Import Tools

You'll find a list of available importers under Tools ➤ Import (Figure 10-1):

- Blogger
- LiveJournal (and all sites based on the underlying software, such as DeadJournal)
- Movable Type/Typepad
- Tumblr
- WordPress
- RSS

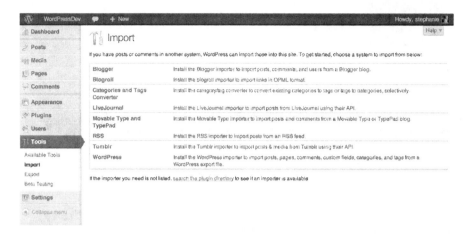

Figure 10-1. *Import tools listed in WordPress*

In addition to the various blog importers, the Import screen also lists tools for importing a blogroll (a list of links in the OPML format) and converting categories and tags.

These are by no means the only importers available for WordPress! See the Codex's article on Importing Content (`http://sleary.me/wp27`)[1] for a long list of import plugins for other content management systems, including Drupal, Joomla, Plone, Ning (using BuddyPress), and even photo gallery systems Zenphoto and Gallery2.

The importers listed under Tools ➤ Import used to be included with WordPress. Now, however, all the importers are maintained as separate plugins. (This allows the developers to update the importers as needed, independent of the WordPress core development cycle.) When you choose one from the Import screen, you'll be prompted to install the plugin (Figure 10-2).

Figure 10-2. *Installing the WordPress importer*

---

[1] `http://codex.wordpress.org/Importing_Content`

Importing from Other WordPress Sites

To import content from a `wordpress.com` blog or another self-hosted WordPress site, first you need to export it. Log in to your other site and go to the Dashboard of the site you want to move. Under the Tools menu, choose Export. You can choose to export all your content, or a subset: either posts or pages, optionally limited to a category, status, or date range. If your blog has multiple authors, you'll have the option to export just one person's posts.

You'll be prompted to save the XML file containing your posts, as shown in Figure 10-3.

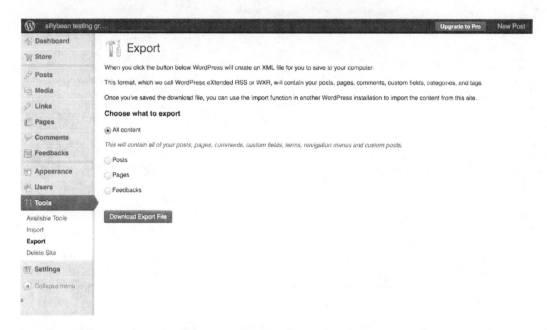

Figure 10-3. *Exporting from* `wordpress.com`

Once you have the XML file, log in to your new WordPress site and go to Tools ➤ Import. Choose WordPress from the list of importers. On the following screen (Figure 10-4), upload the XML file you saved from `wordpress.com`. Here, it's also referred to as a WXR file. WXR is a WordPress-specific variant of XML.

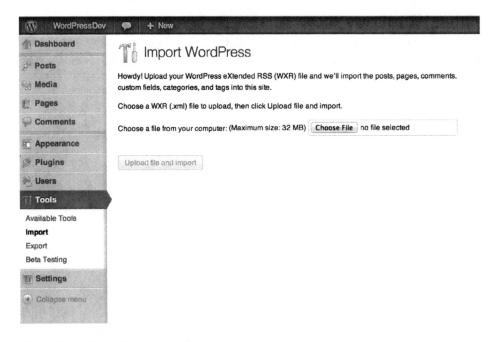

Figure 10-4. *Importing from* `wordpress.com`

WordPress will then ask you to map the authors of the `wordpress.com` posts to the users in your new site or to create a new user for the imported posts (Figure 10-5). You'll also need to choose whether or not to import the media files uploaded to your old posts. If your old posts included images, you should import them. Otherwise, your imported posts will contain links to the image's URLs on your old site.

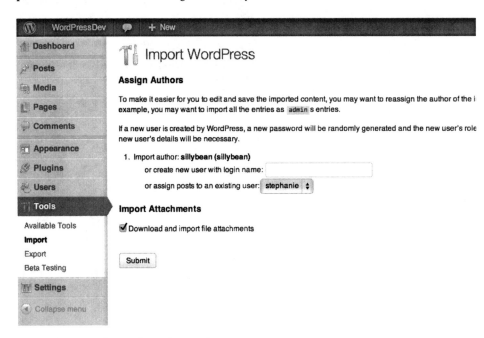

Figure 10-5. *Author and attachment choices*

Once you've made those decisions, click Submit. WordPress will process the files and present you with a log when it's finished.

Importing Other Database-Driven Sites

To import content from a database-driven site (MySQL or otherwise) that isn't represented on the official importer list, you have a few options. If you are a developer and you like to get your hands dirty, you can try using a simple PHP script to select values from your old database and insert them into the new one. Developer Joost de Valk has written a tutorial on importing content from another MySQL database into WordPress. The article (`http://sleary.me/wp28`)[2] contains a PHP script (broken into sections) that you can adapt to your own situation. The Codex article on the `wp_insert_post()` function, at `http://sleary.me/wp29`,[3] lists all the possible fields you can insert into the database. Using this script is not too difficult—it's a matter of filling in database values. You might also need to set up a second, temporary database for the migration process.

If, however, you are not comfortable modifying and running scripts like Joost's, you can try one of the CSV or XML import plugins.

CSV and XML Importers

Almost every database system has an option to export tables to CSV or XML files. There are two excellent plugins that will allow you to import posts these exported files: the CSV Importer plugin, and WP All Import, which can also accept XML files. A third plugin, Import Users from CSV, will let you migrate your users as well as your posts. These are the Swiss Army knives of importers; you can use them in almost any situation where a more specific import plugin does not work or is not available.

▦ **Note**   WP All Import is free, but more advanced features like custom post type and custom field support are available only in the commercial upgrade. CSV Importer lacks the easy drag-and-drop user interface, but supports all post types and fields.

The CSV Importer plugin expects that each row in the CSV file represents a post, and each column represents a post field—the title, the content, the date, and so forth. You'll need to create a header row to let the importer know what to do with each column. They can be in any order. The headings for the basic post fields are shown in Listing 10-1.

Listing 10-1. Sample CSV Importer Header Row

```
"csv_post_title","csv_post_post","csv_post_type","csv_post_excerpt","csv_post_categories",
"csv_post_tags","csv_post_date","custom_field_1","custom_field_2"
```

It can also handle custom fields and taxonomies, and includes sample CSV files demonstrating both. It can also import comments from a separate CSV file using different headers.

WordPress normally expects dates in the MySQL datetime format (`Y-m-d H:i:s` in PHP; see `http://php.net/date` for details), but the importer will attempt to convert other date formats using PHP's `strtotime()` function. If your dates are not imported correctly, check the `strtotime()` documentation (`http://php.net/strtotime`) to see how your dates were interpreted, and to find a more compatible date format.

---

[2]`http://yoast.com/importing-from-another-mysql-into-wordpress`
[3]`http://codex.wordpress.org/Function_Reference/wp_insert_post`

Importing HTML Files

I created the HTML Import plugin because the most common migration scenario I encounter is moving a site that was originally built using Dreamweaver templates into WordPress. I got very tired of copying and pasting! Since then, however, I've also heard from a number of people who have used it to import content from other CMSs, using either static files generated by the old CMS or a static copy of the site created using a content scraper. If you need to import content from another CMS and you don't have access to its database or administration screens, this might be your last resort.

The plugin works by reading in HTML as XML and copying the specified tags' contents into various WordPress fields. It therefore works best on well-formed HTML. Your files don't necessarily have to validate according to the W3C specification, but they should at least contain tags that are properly nested. They should also reside on the same server as your WordPress installation.

This is a complicated plugin with a lot of options—many more than you'll see in most importers. Because it doesn't use a fixed import format, it has to be very flexible. I'll go through all the tabs on the settings screen.

You'll find the HTML Import settings screen under the Settings menu. The first thing you'll be asked to fill in is the path to the directory of files you want to import. Find the absolute path—not a site- or file-relative one—to this directory. The plugin will provide you the absolute path to your WordPress installation for reference; you can use this to figure out the appropriate path to your HTML files. On a Windows machine, the path will begin with a drive letter (e.g., C:\sites\import). On a UNIX-based server (including Macs), the path will begin with a slash (e.g., /users/username/home/public_html or /Library/WebServer/mysite). Enter the path into the first field on the importer's options page, as shown in Figure 10-6.

HTML Import Settings

Welcome to HTML Import! This is a complicated importer with many options. Please look through all the tabs on this page before running your import.

| Files | Content | Title & Metadata | Custom Fields | Categories & Tags | Tools |

Directory to import

/Users/steph/Sites/html-site

The absolute path to the files you want to import.
Hint: the absolute path to this WordPress installation is: `/Users/steph/Sites/wp`

Old site URL

http://example.com

This will be used only to generate accurate `.htaccess` *redirects. The importer will not search for files here.*

Default file

index.html, default.htm

Enter the name of the default file (index.html, default.htm) for directories on this server.

File extensions to include

html,htm,shtml

File extensions, without periods, separated by commas. All other file types will be ignored.

Directories to exclude

images,includes,Templates

Directory names, without slashes, separated by commas. All files in these directories will be ignored.

Preserve file names

☑ Use the file's name as the imported page's slug

The slug will not include the file extension. To completely mimic your old URLs, add the extension to your permalink structure.

***Figure 10-6.** HTML Import: specifying directories, file types, and URLs*

The importer will ask for the old site's URL. If you enter a URL here, the importer will use it to update links to media files. The importer will not search for files at this address.

Next, identify the types of files you want to import and list the file extensions, separated by commas. If there are any directories the importer should skip, like image or script directories, specify those as well.

Selecting Content to Import

To select the part of the file that contains the main content—what will become the post or page content in WordPress—you can specify an HTML tag or a Dreamweaver template region. If your pages are based on Dreamweaver templates, select the Dreamweaver option and enter the name of the content area (e.g., "Main Content") into the template region field. If you're using a tag without attributes, or where the attributes don't matter, simply enter the tag (without brackets) in the tag field, and leave the attribute and value fields blank. If your tag does have an attribute that makes it unique, enter the attribute name (like `class` or `id`) in the attribute field and the value in the value field. For example, if your content is contained in the `<td id="main-content">` tag, your import setting would look like Figure 10-7.

HTML Import Settings

Welcome to HTML Import! This is a complicated importer with many options. Please look through all the tabs on this page before running your import.

| Files | Content | Title & Metadata | Custom Fields | Categories & Tags | Tools |

Select content by   ⦿ HTML tag   ○ Dreamweaver template region   ○ Import entire file

Tag	Attribute	= Value
div	id	content
The HTML tag, without brackets	*Leave blank to use a tag without an attribute, or when the attributes don't matter, such as `<body>`*	*Enter the attribute's value (such as width, ID, or class name) without quotes*

More content options

☑ Import linked images

☐ Import linked documents

☑ Update internal links

☑ Use meta description as excerpt

☑ Convert special characters (accents and symbols)

☐ Clean up bad (Word, Frontpage) HTML

Figure 10-7. *Content settings in HTML Import*

If you're not sure which HTML tag and attribute to use, open up one of the pages in a browser and use its developer tools to inspect your page. In Firefox, go to Tools ➤ Web Developer ➤ Inspect, or use the Firebug extension. In Chrome, go to View ➤ Developer ➤ Developer Tools. In Safari, first you must check *Show Develop menu in menu bar* in your Advanced preferences; then go to Develop ➤ Show Web Inspector. Once the inspector is active, hover over the part of your page you want to import. The inspector will show you the tag corresponding to the most specific thing you're looking at—probably a paragraph, link, or heading. Move upward or outward until you find the tag that encompasses the entire section you want to import. Figure 10-8 shows a page's highlighted content in Safari's inspector.

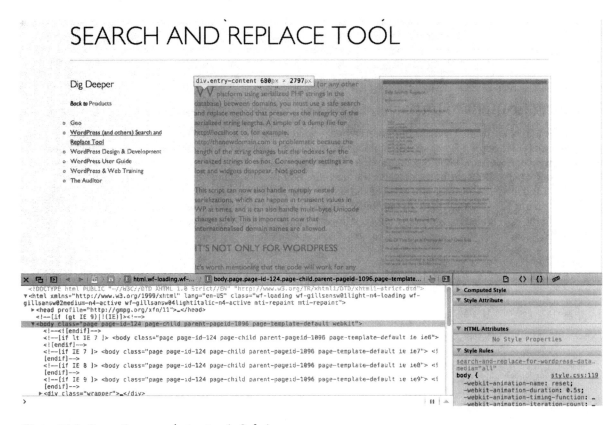

Figure 10-8. *Inspecting a page's structure in Safari*

Any tag that is unique will work. If your site wasn't designed using IDs, you can select your content using another attribute. For very old sites designed in tables, you can import a table cell using td as the tag, width as the attribute, and the width number for the value, as long as there are no other table cells with the same width.

You can have the importer clean up any unneeded HTML within the content you're importing. For example, if your files came from Microsoft Word or FrontPage, they're probably littered with extraneous div tags, smart tags, and class attributes. To clean them up, check the *Clean up bad (Word, FrontPage) HTML* option, then specify the HTML tags and attributes that should be allowed. Any tags and attributes not in these lists will be removed. A list of suggested tags and attributes is provided, along with an extra set that you should include if your content contains data tables.

Selecting the Title and Metadata

You can select the title tag the same way you chose your content area, as shown in Figure 10-9. You can have the importer remove common words or phrases from your titles. If your site title part of your HTML files' <title> tags, for example, you'll need to remove it now to avoid duplication on your WordPress site, where the <title> tag will include the site title automatically.

If your page titles come from an HTML tag that's within the main content area you specified in the content section, you can choose to remove the title from the imported content.

The metadata section (also shown in Figure 10-9) is where you can specify all the little details: whether you want to import the files as posts or pages, which user should be listed as the author, and what the categories and tags (for posts) or page parent (for pages) should be. You can also choose whether to use the meta description tag's contents as excerpts.

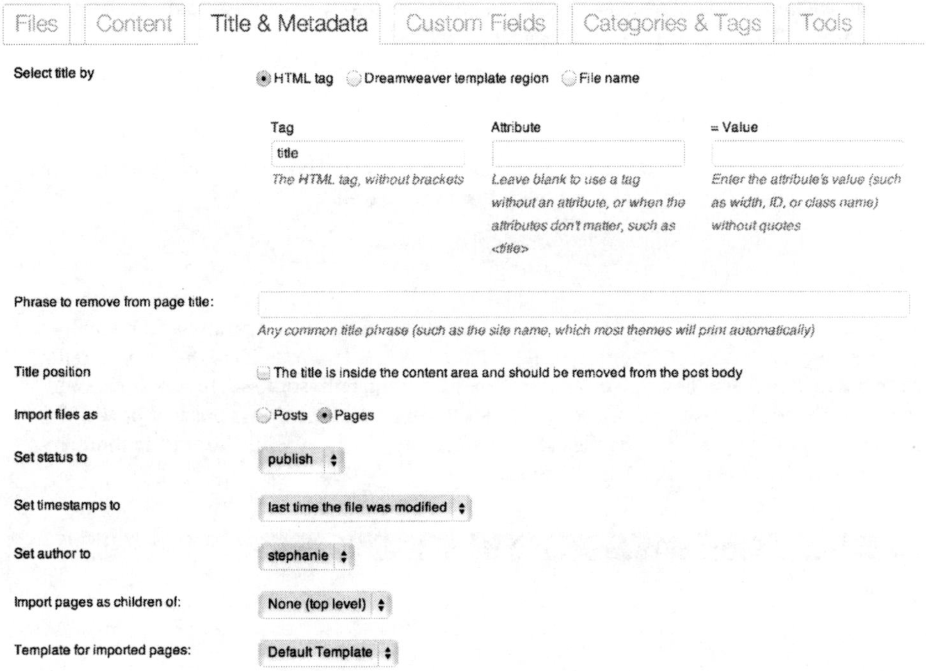

| Files | Content | Title & Metadata | Custom Fields | Categories & Tags | Tools |

Select title by   ◉ HTML tag   ○ Dreamweaver template region   ○ File name

Tag	Attribute	= Value
title		
The HTML tag, without brackets	*Leave blank to use a tag without an attribute, or when the attributes don't matter, such as `<title>`*	*Enter the attribute's value (such as width, ID, or class name) without quotes*

Phrase to remove from page title:

Any common title phrase (such as the site name, which most themes will print automatically)

Title position   ☐ The title is inside the content area and should be removed from the post body

Import files as   ○ Posts   ◉ Pages

Set status to   `publish ⬍`

Set timestamps to   `last time the file was modified ⬍`

Set author to   `stephanie ⬍`

Import pages as children of: `None (top level) ⬍`

Template for imported pages: `Default Template ⬍`

Figure 10-9. Choosing the title and metadata to import

To set the date of the imported posts or pages, you can use the current date or the date the file was last modified, or you can select the date from the file's contents using a custom field, which you'll specify in the next section.

Selecting Custom Fields

In this section (Figure 10-10), you can choose the HTML tags or Dreamweaver regions containing the date and any other custom fields you would like to import.

| Files | Content | Title & Metadata | Custom Fields | Categories & Tags | Tools |

Select date by   ◉ HTML tag   ○ Dreamweaver template region

Tag	Attribute	= Value
div	id	date

Custom fields

Custom field name

post_tag

[×]

Select field by: ◉ HTML tag   ○ Dreamweaver template region

Tag	Attribute	= Value
div	class	tags

[Add a custom field]

Figure 10-10. Importing custom fields

If your files contain a comma-separated list of terms you'd like to import as tags, you can use `post_tag` for the custom field name, and the importer will tag the imported posts accordingly.

Setting Categories, Tags, and Custom Taxonomies

In this section, you can choose categories and/or tags that will be applied to *all* the posts or pages you are importing. If you have created custom taxonomies for your site, you'll see fields for those as well.

Running the Importer

Once you've filled in all that information, press the Import button at the bottom of the page and sit back! If you have many files, this might take a minute or two. When the importer has finished, it will display a list of the imported files (Figure 10-11) with any errors noted. It will also give you a set of rewrite rules that, with some slight modifications, you can use in your `.htaccess` file to redirect visitors from your old files to your new WordPress posts or pages. The original paths won't be exact, especially if you moved the files into a temporary directory while importing them, but you should be able to correct them with a simple search and replace.

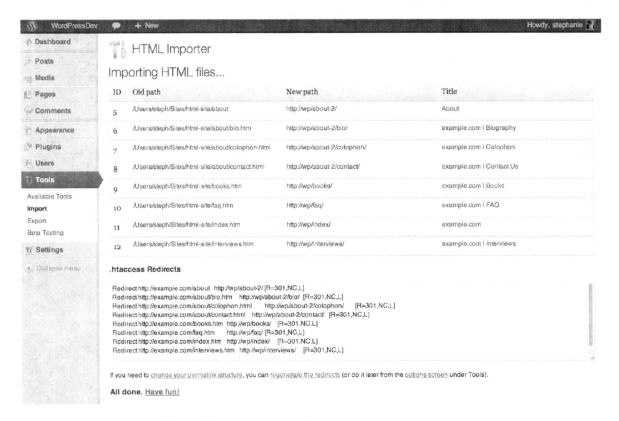

Figure 10-11. *The imported files and* `.htaccess` *rewrite rules*

If the site you're importing has a news section, keep in mind that you could import those files as posts, then remove them from your import directory, and import the rest of the files as pages. Or, having run the importer on the entire site, you could use the Post Type Switcher or Convert Post Type plugins to change the pages in the news section to posts. (You'll see these plugins again in Chapter 14: Custom Post Types, Taxonomies, and Fields.)

Migrating Sites between Servers

While the WordPress importer is very good at moving content from one installation to another, it does leave out some important information: settings. If you've built a complicated site, and you don't want to have to redo all your widgets and your plugin settings, you'll need to move your database and files instead of relying on the importer.

Moving Files

You can simply move all your files, including the WordPress core files, from one server to another. If you have already installed WordPress on your new server, you'll need to copy the files and directories in Listing 10-2 from your old installation, overwriting the files on the new server:

Listing 10-2. Files to Copy When Migrating WordPress Installations

```
wp-config.php
wp-content/
```

If your database name, username, or password is different on the new server, you'll need to update wp-config.php.

If you are changing your site's URL, you can add the lines in Listing 10-3 to wp-config.php to temporarily override the site and blog URLs stored in the database:

Listing 10-3. URL Constants in wp-config.php

```
define('WP_SITEURL', 'http://example.com/wordpress');
define('WP_HOME', 'http://example.com/wordpress');
```

Moving the Database

You'll also need to export your old database and import it on your new server. This is exactly like backing up and restoring the database. First, export all the tables from the old server to an SQL file. On the new server, drop any tables that are already in the new database, then import the SQL file.

Logging In and Resetting the Site

You should now be able to log in on your new site. If so, visit the Permalinks Settings page and save your options. This will regenerate the rewrite rules in your .htaccess or web.config file. Next, visit the administration pages of any caching and security plugins you have installed. Since most of them have server-specific settings, you'll need to update those. Then visit a few pages on your site—a single post, a monthly archive, a category archive, a page—and make sure everything is working.

Once you're comfortable with your new installation, you should edit your database's options table to reflect your new URL. Change the siteurl and home options to match the definitions you added to wp-config.php. Once you have saved these changes, you can remove the WP_SITEURL and WP_HOME definitions from your wp-config.php file.

After Importing or Migrating: Fixing What's Broken

No matter which import tool you used, there's a good chance you'll see some errors in your newly imported content. If you've switched domains, you'll need to change all your internal links and media file paths. There's also a common (and particularly nasty) problem with posts that are garbled or cut off mid-sentence after importing.

Updating Internal Links

If the site you imported lived on another domain, your content is probably full of internal links that contain the old URL. You'll need to search and replace the URL in your old posts and pages. There are a number of search and replace plugins available (Frank Bültge's is one of the best), but none of them can handle URLs embedded in serialized arrays—which is how many WordPress plugins store their options.

To do a thorough search and replace that includes serialized arrays, download the Safe Search Replace script at `http://sleary.me/wp30.`[4] Allow it to populate its settings from your WordPress config file, then select your database tables. On the search and replace screen, enter your old and new URLs. See Figure 10-12 for an example.

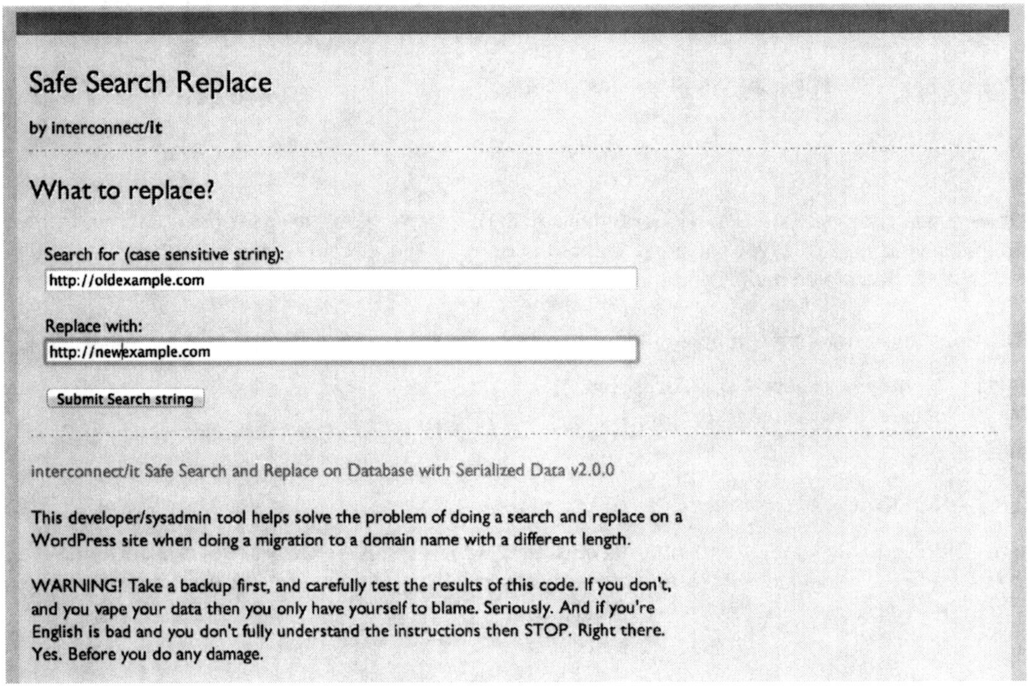

Figure 10-12. *Replacing using the Safe Search Replace script*

■ **Caution** Once you've finished your search and replace, delete the search and replace script file! Its auto-populate feature makes it easy to use, but it also creates a huge security vulnerability as long as the file remains on your server.

Paths to Linked Files

Most of the importers will copy the contents of your posts verbatim. That means that if you have any files linked within your old content (images, MP3s, documents), those links won't change. In addition to changing the domain, if necessary, you'll need to update the paths to your files. I like to use the Search & Replace plugin for this task. It has a

---

[4]http://interconnectit.com/124/search-and-replace-for-wordpress-databases

test mode (the top pair of input fields, shown in Figure 10-13) that you can use to determine which tables you need to search. Then you can use the lower half of the plugin's screen to perform the replacements in your chosen tables.

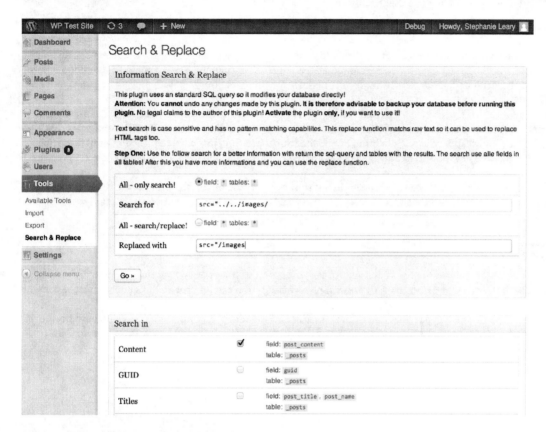

Figure 10-13. *The Search & Replace plugin*

If all your links were root-relative (`/images/photo.jpg`), it should be easy to perform a search and replace to accommodate any changes in your directory structure, or to simply copy your old files to your new site with the directory structure intact. If, however, you had file-relative links (`../../images/photo.jpg`), you'll have to do a couple of passes to change them all. Do yourself a favor and take this opportunity to make them absolute or root-relative!

You can try using the Add Linked Images plugin, which will search your posts for image tags, import the linked files into your media library, and update the URLs in your posts. However, it works only for posts—not pages—and it does not check for duplicates. If you have a single image file referenced in many posts, you'll end up with multiple copies in your media library. This plugin can be very helpful, but use it with caution.

Truncated or Garbled Content

After importing from another site, you might find that some of your posts or pages are filled with garbage characters or inexplicably cut off. What happened?

The key to the problem is the character set specified in your `wp-config.php` file (Listing 10-4).

Listing 10-4. The Config File's Character Set Definition

```
define('DB_CHARSET', 'utf8');
```

Most likely, your old database used a different character set than your new one. Garbage characters can appear when the import script incorrectly translates the character sets. Your posts might also be truncated at the point where an unrecognized character appeared: a curly quote, an em dash, anything that might have been stored as text and not an encoded HTML equivalent.

There's no easy way to fix this once it's happened. If you don't think the truncation problem is widespread, find one of the truncated articles and take a look at the original version from your old database. Find the character that's causing the problem, and search your old site for it. For all the results you find, just copy the remainder of the article by hand. WordPress does know how to handle special characters, and will encode them correctly once you save your post or page.

If the problem *is* widespread, there's nothing to do but start over. Try to convert the original database's character set to the same one your WordPress database is using. (Make a backup first!) Then run your import again.

Summary

In this chapter you've learned how to import content from `wordpress.com`, other MySQL-based CMSs, other databases via CSV files, and static HTML files. I've also shown you how to clean up broken links and truncated content in your imported data.

Now that you have moved all your old content into WordPress, it's time to dig into some code and learn how to create custom themes and plugins for your new site. In the next chapter, you'll learn how WordPress development works for both themes and plugins.

■ ■ ■

CHAPTER 11

Beginning Theme and Plugin Development

There's a lot of overlap between theme and plugin development in WordPress. Both themes and plugins rely on core functions and APIs, especially the Options API. In this chapter, you'll learn about these common functions and development concepts, and how WordPress theme and plugin files are organized.

If you're curious about WordPress development, you probably opened the files of a theme or plugin before you bought this book, or perhaps you started reading the WordPress core code itself. You probably saw a lot of functions that confused you, like __() and do_action(). This doesn't look like any PHP you've seen before. What is all this stuff?

You won't need to write any code as you read through this chapter, although you will see a number of examples. For now, you just need to become familiar with the way WordPress handles theme and plugin functions, settings, data validation, and translations. All you need to do in this chapter is learn to recognize these functions. For example, if a function in a theme file begins with an underscore, like __() or _e(), it probably has something to do with translations.

In the next three chapters, you'll see all these functions in context, and you'll begin to use them yourself as you create your own themes and plugins.

PHP You'll Need to Know

From this point on, you'll need some basic knowledge of programming in general, and preferably PHP in particular, in order to follow the code examples. PHP's syntax for functions, variables, strings, arrays, for/foreach/while loops, if/else statements, and comparison operators are essential. Knowing switch statements and classes would be helpful, as would knowing what comments look like.

Here are a few sites and books to help you get up to speed:

- PHP the Right Way, http://sleary.me/wp31[1]

- *PHP Solutions: Dynamic Web Design Made Easy*, by David Powers

- *PHP Cookbook*, by David Sklar and Adam Trachtenberg

PHP code can be embedded in HTML, but is always enclosed in <?php ... ?> tags. (The shorthand version, <? ... ?>, should never be used in themes or plugins, as it does not work reliably on all servers.) I've omitted them in most of the code examples in this chapter for brevity. Unless stated otherwise, assume that the code given is PHP without any surrounding HTML, and should be placed in the opening and closing tags in your own files.

---

[1] www.phptherightway.com/pages/The-Basics.html

Theme and Plugin Files

If you haven't already, look in your `wp-content` directory. You should see at least four subdirectories:

- `plugins`
- `themes`
- `updates`
- `uploads`

If you're running a multisite installation, or if you've installed a caching plugin, you might see a few more things. For now, all I'm interested in are the themes and plugin directories.

In your themes directory, you should see one directory per theme. You can't have loose files in the themes directory (other than `index.php`, which is present in all WordPress directories to prevent misconfigured servers from allowing people to list the directory's contents by entering its address into a browser). All theme files must be contained in a subdirectory. Most themes must contain at least two files: `index.php` and `style.css`. Child themes, which are just modifications of other themes, might contain only the stylesheet. However, this must be kept separate from the parent theme, so a subdirectory is still required.

Your plugins directory might be a little messier. Most plugins have more than one file and will therefore have their own subdirectories. A few very simple plugins consist of just one PHP file, like Hello Dolly, which you'll find in `wp-content/plugins/hello.php`—no subdirectory.

Theme Functions vs. Plugins

Themes can contain a file, `functions.php`, that is not displayed directly on the site, but instead houses functions that are used throughout the theme. The `functions.php` file is in effect a set of miniature plugins; the difference is they don't require separate activation. All the functions in the file will run every time the site is loaded (including the administration screens) as long as the theme is active.

Many WordPress tutorials on the web instruct you to place their example code into your theme's `functions.php` file. This requires less explanation than creating a new plugin, and makes for simpler tutorials. However, it's not always the right choice, especially for widgets, custom taxonomies, custom fields, and custom post types. All of these features involve storing new information in the WordPress database. If the user switches to another theme, she will be left with no way to work with the custom theme's data. It's still in the database, but it's effectively lost to her.

Ask yourself: does this code create a feature that a user would want to keep if she changed themes? Then it should be a plugin, not part of a theme's `functions.php`. Creating a new plugin is no more difficult than creating a theme, as you'll see in Chapter 13.

Using a Starter Theme for Experimentation

The Underscores theme (_s) was built by the `wordpress.com` theme group, and is intended to be modified. You can download it (`http://underscores.me`), pick it apart to see how it works, and use it to build a new custom theme.

There are several other starter themes available, including:

- Bones (`http://sleary.me/wp32`[2])

- Starkers (`http://sleary.me/wp33`[3])

- Toolbox (`http://sleary.me/wp34`[4])

Any of these themes will be helpful when you're starting to learn WordPress development. Once you understand how things work, you can build your own from scratch.

Never Edit Core Files

Never edit WordPress core files!

If you find that a function doesn't work quite the way you want it to, by all means, do look it up in the core files and read its code to find out how it works. Do *not* edit the core file to change the function. The next time you upgrade WordPress, your edits will be overwritten—and you must upgrade WordPress in order to keep your site secure. Never put off upgrading because you want to preserve changes you've made to core files.

Instead of editing the files, look for hooks that will let you achieve your goals in your own theme or plugin code.

Working with Hooks

Hooks are not functions. They are places where functions can be inserted into to WordPress's procedures without modifying core files. They are the reason WordPress is so extensible. Hooks are scattered throughout the WordPress code. A hook says, "Now, theme/plugin developers, do you have anything to add to what I've just done?"

There are two kinds of hooks in WordPress: filters and actions. Filters are called with `apply_filters()`. Actions are called with `do_action()`. Each hook has a name. To run your own code, you would find the name of the hook corresponding to the thing you want to do, write your function, then add your function to the hook by calling `add_action()` or `add_filter()` with two arguments: the hook name followed by your function's name.

For a complete list of available actions and filters, visit `http://sleary.me/wp103`[5] and `http://sleary.me/wp104`[6].

Actions

Actions allow you to add your own functions in predetermined locations. For example, you could send an e-mail notification to all users when a new post is published.

Action hooks are like empty paper cups in the giant Rube Goldberg machine that is WordPress. Imagine a gumball being dropped into the top of your page. This is your page request, and it's going to pass through a number of gizmos before it reaches the bottom. Some of those gizmos include paper cups that will tip over when the gumball

---

[2]`http://themble.com/bones`
[3]`http://viewportindustries.com/products/starkers`
[4]`http://wordpress.org/extend/themes/toolbox`
[5]`http://codex.wordpress.org/Plugin_API/Action_Reference`
[6]`http://codex.wordpress.org/Plugin_API/Filter_Reference`

falls into them. Adding your own functions to action hooks is like dropping pennies into those paper cups before you let the gumball go. Not only will the gumball fall out and continue on its path when the cup tips over, but your pennies will, too.

Notable actions include:

- `init`: one of the first things done on every page, both front end and administration

- `admin_init`: the first thing done on every administration page

- `wp_head`: the last thing done in the theme `<head>` section

- `admin_head`: the last thing done in the administration page's `<head>` section

- `admin_head-$filename`: the same, but for a specific administration page

- `admin_menu`: constructs the navigation menu in the administration pages

- `template_redirect`: occurs just before the theme template file is chosen, allowing you to override that choice

- `wp_enqueue_scripts`: printing the list of scripts in the theme header

- `wp_print_styles`: printing the list of stylesheets in the theme header

- `widgets_init`: constructing the list of active widgets

- `wp_footer`: the last thing done before the theme's closing `</body>` tag

Each `add_action()` function required two arguments: the name of the action hook and the name of your custom function. Listing 11-1 shows a simple example of a comment placed near the closing `</body>` tag using the `wp_footer` action.

Listing 11-1. Adding a Footer Comment with `wp_footer`

```
add_action( 'wp_footer', 'say_hello' );

function say_hello() {
        echo '<!-- Hello, curious theme developer! -->';
}
```

Filters

Filters allow you to modify or replace the output existing functions. Filters usually modify strings or arrays. For example, you could append ads or a copyright notice to content in feeds, or search and replace a word or phrase in your post/page content.

The filter function will pass you some piece of content to work with. You can filter many of WordPress's built-in strings: author names, links, post titles and content, category names, and so on; and you can filter things like arrays of pages and categories. Your filter function will take the original variable as its argument, and it will return the altered variable. You could append or prepend something, or perform a search and replace on a string.

Some of the filters you'll see often include:

- `wp_title`: allows the `<title>` tag to be altered or replaced

- `the_title`: allows the title of the post or page to be altered or replaced

- `the_content`: alters the content of the post or page

- `wp_autop`: automatically turns line breaks into paragraph tags

- do_shortcodes: processes shortcodes

- the_excerpt_length: determines the length (in characters) of excerpts

- the_excerpt_more: determines what's shown at the end of excerpts

- wp_list_pages: allows the list of pages to be modified

Listing 11-2 demonstrates how to use the the_excerpt_more filter to change the text that's appended to excerpts (by default, '[…]').

Listing 11-2. Using the the_excerpt_more Filter

```
add_filter( 'the_excerpt_more', 'no_ellipses' );

function no_ellipses( $more ) {
        return ' (Continue reading) ';
}
```

Removing Hooked Functions

It's possible to remove actions or filters that were added by another plugin. For example, if a plugin adds a Dashboard widget that you don't want, you can add a few lines to your plugin or theme functions.php file to get rid of it. Look through the offending plugin's code and find its add_action() function with the wp_dashboard_setup hook, as shown in Listing 11-3. Then simply reverse the process by calling remove_action() with the same hook and function names in your own code.

Listing 11-3. Removing a Hooked Function

```
// original plugin's code:
add_action('wp_dashboard_setup', 'unwanted_dashboard_widget');

// your theme functions file or plugin:
remove_action('wp_dashboard_setup', 'unwanted_dashboard_widget');
```

For filters, you can use the remove_filter() function the same way.

Avoiding Recursive Actions

It's possible to create a recursive action—that is, a function hooked to an action that calls itself. This creates an infinite loop: your function will never finish, and it will just continue to run, using up memory, until it reaches PHP's memory limit or execution time limit—or crashes the server.

For example, let's say you wanted all posts in the category with the ID 8 to have the 'private' post status. You could create the following function and add it to the save_post hook (Listing 11-4).

Listing 11-4. Creating an Infinite Loop When Setting the Post Status According to Category

```
add_action( 'save_post', 'set_category_eight_to_private' );

function set_category_eight_to_private( $postid ) {
        if ( in_category( 8 ) {
                wp_update_post( array( 'ID' => $postid, 'post_status' => 'private' ) );
        }
}
```

However, the `wp_update_post()` function includes the save_post action, which means your function would run indefinitely. To prevent this from happening, you should remove your hooked function, run `wp_update_post()`, and then add it back, as shown in Listing 11-5.

Listing 11-5. Creating the Private Category Without an Infinite Loop

```
add_action( 'save_post', 'set_category_eight_to_private' );

function set_category_eight_to_private( $postid ) {
        if ( in_category( 8 ) {
                // unhook this function so it doesn't loop infinitely
                remove_action( 'save_post', 'set_category_eight_to_private' );

                //update the post
                wp_update_post( array( 'ID' => $postid, 'post_status' => 'private' ) );

                // re-hook this function
                add_action( 'save_post', 'set_category_eight_to_private' );
        }
}
```

Prioritizing and Troubleshooting Actions and Filters

Both actions and filters can take an optional third argument: the priority. If left out, this argument will default to 10, and your hooked functions will occur after all the built-in ones have completed. However, you can set the priority to any number at all. Set it to a lower number if you need your function to operate before the built-in actions and filters.

If you have installed plugins that use filters, or you've written your own filter, it can be hard to tell where the original content ends and the filtered addition begins. Sometimes it's also not clear when certain actions take place. The Hooks & Filters Flow plugin (`http://sleary.me/wp35`[7]) lists all the actions and filters that are operating on your content. Unlike most plugins, this one must be placed in your WordPress root directory or `wp-admin`. You have to enter its URL into your browser, because there is no link to it from your admin menu.

Figure 11-1 shows the plugin's report on my test installation. It's not very pretty, but Hooks & Filters Flow is a great way to see if your plugin is interfering with another filter, or if you need to adjust its priority.

---

[7]`http://planetozh.com/blog/my-projects/wordpress-hooks-filter-flow/`

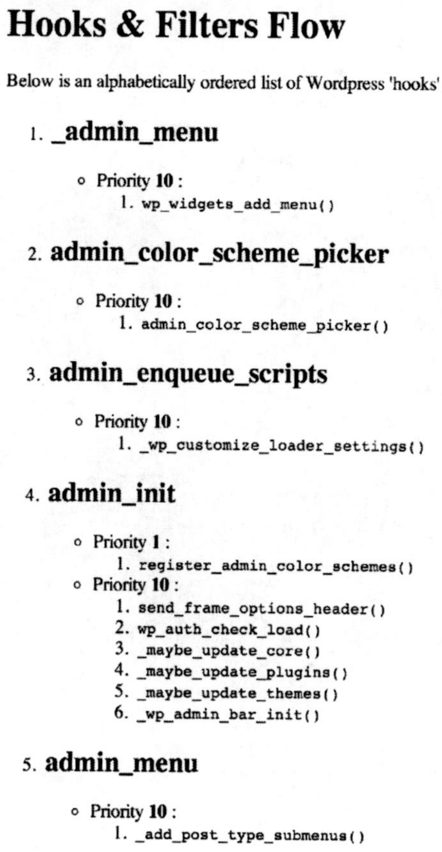

Hooks & Filters Flow

Below is an alphabetically ordered list of Wordpress 'hooks' and their associated filters / actions (i.e. PHP functions) on this Wordpress install.

1. **_admin_menu**

    ○ Priority **10** :
      1. `wp_widgets_add_menu()`

2. **admin_color_scheme_picker**

    ○ Priority **10** :
      1. `admin_color_scheme_picker()`

3. **admin_enqueue_scripts**

    ○ Priority **10** :
      1. `_wp_customize_loader_settings()`

4. **admin_init**

    ○ Priority **1** :
      1. `register_admin_color_schemes()`
    ○ Priority **10** :
      1. `send_frame_options_header()`
      2. `wp_auth_check_load()`
      3. `_maybe_update_core()`
      4. `_maybe_update_plugins()`
      5. `_maybe_update_themes()`
      6. `_wp_admin_bar_init()`

5. **admin_menu**

    ○ Priority **10** :
      1. `_add_post_type_submenus()`

Figure 11-1. *The Hooks & Filters Flow plugin*

Using the Options and Settings APIs

WordPress provides a complete framework for setting, updating, and deleting plugin and theme options in the database. The words "options" and "settings" are often used interchangeably to refer to these stored values, but there are two distinct APIs you'll use to handle them. The Options API does most of the work of saving options to the database. All you have to do is register the options you plan to use, so WordPress knows which ones it should handle. The Settings API is the group of functions you'll use to add form fields for your options to the WordPress administration pages.

The Options API Codex page (http://sleary.me/wp68[8]) lists all the options-related functions. For more information on the Settings API, visit its Codex page at http:sleary.me/wp36.[9]

---

[8]http://codex.wordpress.org/Options_API
[9]http://codex.wordpress.org/Settings_API

Adding an Options Page

Almost every WordPress plugin involves some sort of option, and that means you'll need to create the form that lets users manage those options. To add an options page to the main navigation menu, you need two functions. One will display the content of the options page, and the other hooks the add_options_page() function into the admin menu. Last, you'll need to add your container function to the admin_menu() hook using add_action().

Listing 11-6 shows the bare minimum that's required to add an options page.

Listing 11-6. An Empty Options Page

```
function scl_simple_options_page() {
?>
<div class="wrap">
        <form method="post" id="scl_simple_options" action="options.php">

                <h2><?php _e('Sample Options' ); ?></h2>

                <p class="submit">
                <input type="submit" value="<?php esc_attr_e('Update Options'); ?>"
class="button-primary" />
                </p>

        </form>
</div>
<?php
}

add_action('admin_menu', 'scl_simple_options_add_pages');

function scl_simple_options_add_pages() {
        add_options_page('Sample Options', 'Sample Options', 'manage_options', ↵
'simple-options-example', 'scl_simple_options_page');
}
```

The wrapper element (`<div class="wrap">`) is essential to the layout of all WordPress admin pages, so you must include it in your options forms. The form tags should go inside the wrapper. The id attribute is optional. Your form method should be post and the action should always be options.php (the file that processes all WordPress options).

The results of Listing 11-6 are shown in Figure 11-2.

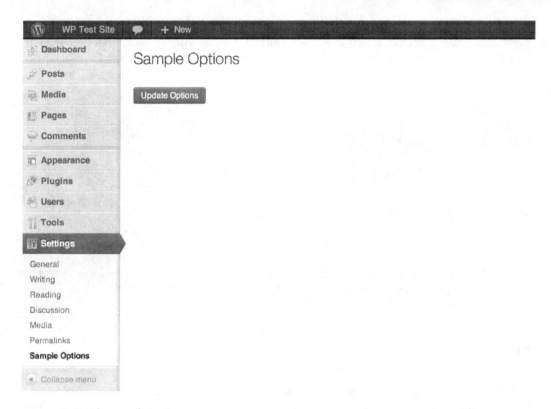

Figure 11-2. *The sample options page*

Now that you have an options page in place, it's time to add some fields to the form.

Registering Settings and Creating Defaults

Prior to version 2.7, you could create options without registering them with WordPress, but then you had to do a lot of manual security checks and updates. With the Settings API, all of that is much easier, but you *must* register your settings in order for them to work.

You may register a separate setting for each variable you need to store, but it's impolite to take up lots of database rows with your plugin's options. Instead, group your variables into arrays, each of which can be stored in a single database row. Listing 11-7 shows the code required to register a single setting. The first argument is the setting's name; the second is the name of the group in which it appears. In this case, you'll have just one group, so the names are the same.

Listing 11-7. Modifying the add_pages Function to Register a Setting

```
add_action('admin_menu', 'scl_simple_options_add_pages');
function scl_simple_options_add_pages() {
        add_options_page('Sample Options', 'Sample Options', 'manage_options', ↪
'simple-options-example', 'scl_simple_options_page');
register_setting( 'scl_simple_options', 'scl_simple_options' );
}
```

Registering the setting lets WordPress know that you plan to use it, but it doesn't do anything about setting default values. You'll have to do that yourself. Listing 11-8 shows a function that sets default option values, stored in a single array, when the plugin is activated. Later in this chapter, you'll see a slightly different way of doing this.

Listing 11-8. Setting Default Options on Activation

```
function scl_simple_options_defaults() {
        // set defaults
        $defaults = array(
                        'shortlink'             => 1,
                        'google_meta_key'       => '',
        );

        add_option( 'scl_simple_options', $defaults, '', 'yes' );
}
register_activation_hook( __FILE__, 'scl_simple_options_defaults');
```

The code here is fairly simple; it's just an array in which each element contains the default values for one of the options. Note the use of the add_option() function to save the options array to the database. The add_option() function requires four arguments:

- The name of the option to be saved

- Its value

- An empty string (a deprecated argument kept for backward compatibility)

- The $autoload variable. This last argument determines whether your options should be loaded into WordPress's object cache on each page load. If you'll be using these options on the front end, this value should be 'yes'.

That's it! You've set the default values, and now it's time to build the form that will let you change those values.

Creating the Options Form

In Listing 11-6, you saw the basic outline of the options page. Now you need to create the individual form fields that will allow users to change the plugin settings.

First, you need to tell WordPress that this form will be using the option you registered earlier, using the settings_field() function. You'll also go ahead and load the stored options into a variable using get_option() so you can use them throughout the form. Listing 11-9 shows these changes to the basic form.

Listing 11-9. Setting Up Options for Use in the Form

```
function scl_simple_options_page() {
?>
<div class="wrap">
        <form method="post" id="scl_simple_options" action="options.php">
                <?php
                settings_fields('scl_simple_options');
                $options = get_option( 'scl_simple_options' );
                ?>
                <h2><?php _e('Sample Options' ); ?></h2>
```

```
        <table class="form-table">
                <tr>
                        <th scope="row"><?php _e('Short Links' ); ?></th>
                        <td colspan="3">
                        <p>   <label>
                                        <input name="scl_simple_options[shortlink]"
type="checkbox" value="1" <?php checked($options['shortlink'], 1); ?>/>
                                        <?php _e('Display a short URL on all posts and
pages'); ?>

                                </label></p>
                        </td>
                </tr>

                <tr>
                        <th scope="row"><?php _e('Google Verification' ); ?></th>
                        <td colspan="3">
                        <input type="text" id="google_meta_key"
name="scl_simple_options[google_meta_key]" value="<?php echo esc_attr($options['google_meta_key']); ?>" />
                                <br /><span class="description"><?php _e('Enter the ↵
verification key for the Google meta tag.' ); ?></span>
                        </td>
                </tr>
        </table>

        <p class="submit">
                <input type="submit" value="<?php echo esc_attr_e('Update Options'); ?>"
class="button-primary" />
                </p>
        </form>
</div>
<?php
}
```

For each of the fields, I've used some escaping and translation functions, which you'll see later in this chapter, to display the stored value.

All of this results in the options form shown in Figure 11-3.

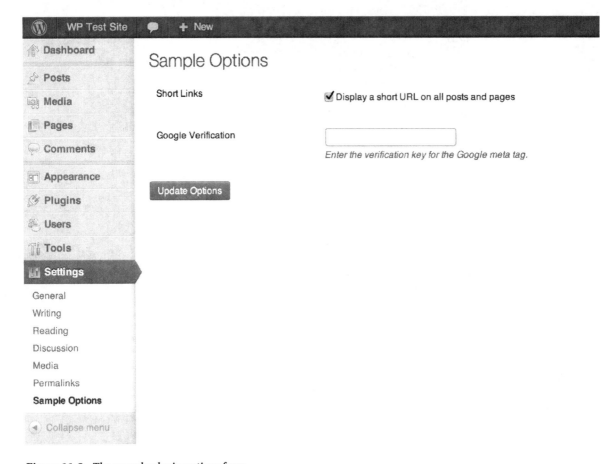

Figure 11-3. *The sample plugin options form*

Updating Options

If you've registered your options and called `settings_fields()` in your form, WordPress updates the options for you when you click the "Update Options" button.

No, really. That's all. We're done.

Well, that's not *really* all. For added security, you should validate the user's input before saving it to the database. I'll get to that in a moment.

If you need to make additional changes to the option's value elsewhere in your plugin, you can update the options manually as shown in Listing 11-10.

Listing 11-10. Updating an Option Manually

```
function change_options() {
        $options = get_option('my_option');
        // do something with $options here
        update_option('my_option', $options);
}
```

Deleting Options

It's a good practice to remove your plugin's options from the database when the user uninstalls it by deleting it from the Plugins screen. It's very easy to do, as you can see in Listing 11-11.

Listing 11-11. Removing the Sample Plugin Options on Deletion

```
register_uninstall_hook( __FILE__, 'scl_delete_simple_options' );

function scl_delete_simple_options() {
        delete_option('scl_simple_options');
}
```

That's all there is to it! Be a good citizen and add uninstall functions like this to your WordPress plugins. Your users will thank you for not cluttering up their database options tables with unneeded rows.

You can, while you're testing your plugin, remove the option on deactivation instead (Listing 11-12). This is helpful when you need to wipe out your previous values and test new defaults. However, once you've finished your plugin, you should comment out this line and switch back to deleting the options on deletion. Users might deactivate plugins during manual upgrades or while debugging other themes and plugins, and they shouldn't lose their data when doing so.

Listing 11-12. Removing the Sample Plugin Options on Deactivation

```
// during testing, delete options on deactivation instead
register_deactivation_hook( __FILE__, 'scl_delete_simple_options' );
// register_uninstall_hook( __FILE__, 'scl_delete_simple_options' );
```

Writing Secure Themes and Plugins

Writing themes and plugins often involves creating a form to collect input from the user and save it to the database. It's crucial that you make sure data is safe before storing it in the database (sanitizing input), and that you check it again before echoing it to the screen (escaping output). Failing to do so can open up your WordPress installation to hackers—and, if you're distributing your theme or plugin to the community, you'll have created a vulnerability in every site where your code is installed.

Imagine that your user, unaware that your options form expected plain text, enters an HTML heading tag. When the user saves the form, WordPress displays it again with the user's data as the input field's default value. In this case, the browser will print part of the heading tag and then stop. Some of your user's data has been lost. Figure 11-4 shows the result of such an error.

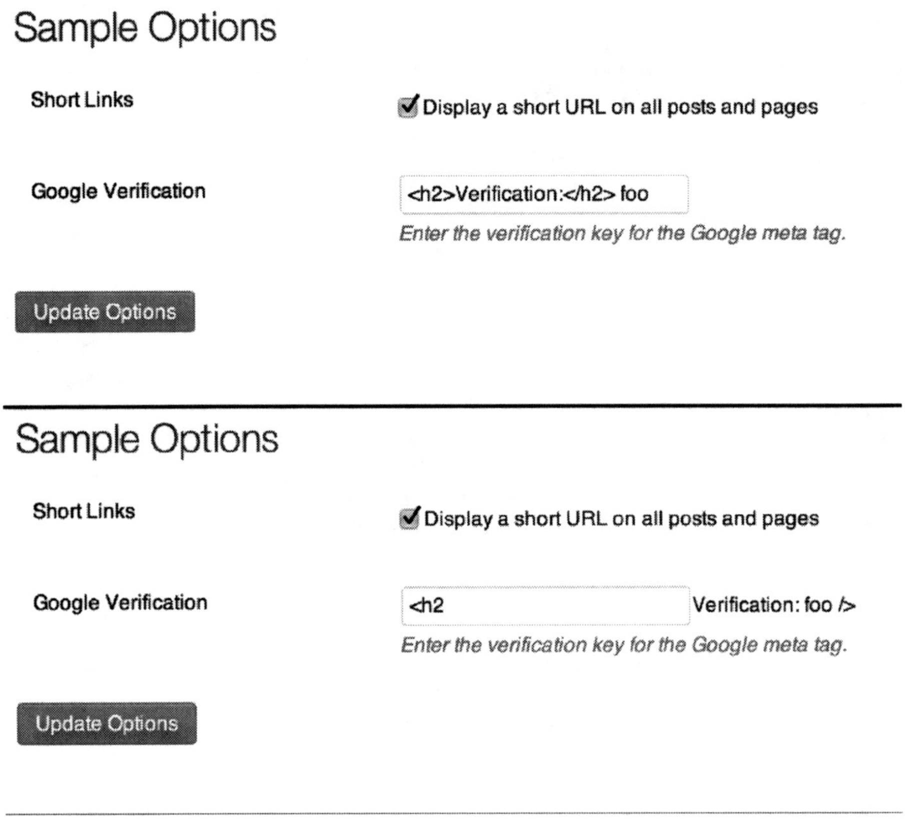

Sample Options

Short Links   ☑ Display a short URL on all posts and pages

Google Verification

<h2>Verification:</h2> foo

Enter the verification key for the Google meta tag.

Update Options

Sample Options

Short Links   ☑ Display a short URL on all posts and pages

Google Verification

<h2   Verification: foo />

Enter the verification key for the Google meta tag.

Update Options

Figure 11-4. *The result of an improperly escaped input field with an HTML tag entered*

This user's input was perfectly safe for storing in the database, but it caused problems when printed back to the screen. In this situation, the output needs to be escaped. In this example, you can use the esc_attr() function to escape the input tag's value attribute (Listing 11-13).

Listing 11-13. Escaping an Input Tag's Value Attribute

```
<input type="text" id="google_meta_key" name="scl_simple_options[google_meta_key]" value=" ↵
<?php echo esc_attr($options['google_meta_key']); ?>" />
```

This example is relatively innocuous—the form simply doesn't work as expected. However, the underlying problem is much more serious: this form makes the site vulnerable to attack. Cross-site scripting attacks like the one shown in Listing 11-14 take advantage of unescaped HTML and URLs to inject JavaScript commands into form fields.

Listing 11-14. JavaScript Breaks Out of the Improperly Escaped Value Attribute and Runs in the Browser

```
<input type="text" id="google_meta_key" name="scl_simple_options[google_meta_key]" value=" ↵
<?php echo 'foo" onchange="alert(\"Gotcha!\")"' ?>" />
```

See the Codex articles on Data Validation (`http://sleary.me/wp37`[10]) for a list of all the sanitization and escape functions. I'll cover the most common ones.

Sanitizing and Validating Input

Before you store a user's text in the database, you need to make sure that it doesn't include wording that, either accidentally or maliciously, would cause problems when WordPress runs the INSERT query on the database. "Drop table wp_posts," for example, could delete the database table if it were incorrectly enclosed in quotation marks. (This is one of the reasons you should use a nonstandard table prefix, as you saw in Chapter 10.)

In addition to simply cleaning up potentially malicious code from your users' input, you should check that they entered the sort of data you expected. If you asked for a US ZIP code, for example, and you expected only five digits, what happens to your code if the user includes the four-digit extension? What if they didn't enter numbers at all, but got confused about which field was which and entered their city name instead? Checking that the user entered the right kind of data is called validation, and WordPress has a few functions to help you validate text, HTML, and e-mail addresses.

To validate more specific kinds of input, you'll need to specify your own validation function when you register a new setting. You'll see examples of this in Chapter 13.

Text and HTML

The `sanitize_text_field()` function removes HTML tags and whitespace, including line breaks. Use this function when saving text entered from a form's input field (Listing 11-15).

Listing 11-15. Sanitizing Data from Text Input Fields

```
$option = sanitize_text_field($_POST['google_meta_key']);
```

In many cases, you do want to allow HTML tags, but perhaps only a subset of allowed tags. WordPress has three functions for this: `wp_kses_post()`, which allows the same tags that you can use in posts' content (Listing 11-16); `wp_kses_data()`, which allows the same tags readers can use when writing comments, and `wp_kses()`, which requires you to specify the list of tags that will be allowed.

Listing 11-16. Sanitizing HTML Input with `kses`

```
$option = wp_kses_post($_POST['post_content']);
```

Email Addresses

The `is_email()` function makes sure that the address entered is more than three characters long and contains the @ symbol, and that the domain includes at least one period. It does not check whether the address actually exists and can receive mail! Simply use this function (Listing 11-17) when assigning e-mail addresses to a variable; it will return the e-mail address given if it's valid, and `false` otherwise.

Listing 11-17. Sanitizing E-mail Addresses

```
$option = is_email($_POST['user_email']);
```

---

[10]`http://codex.wordpress.org/Data_Validation`

Numbers

For the most part, you can rely on the following PHP functions to handle numbers:

> is_numeric() checks whether the user entered a number of any kind
>
> is_int() checks whether the user entered a whole number
>
> is_float() checks whether the user entered a decimal number
>
> intval() treats the input as a whole number, regardless of what was entered (Listing 11-18)
>
> floatval() treats the input as a decimal number, regardless of what was entered

Listing 11-18. Sanitizing Integers

```
$my_integer = intval($_POST['zip_code']);
```

Escaping Output

Even if you've been careful about sanitizing input from your forms, you need to escape output as well. The data you're working with might have come from another source, or your saved option might have been modified by someone else's plugin or theme.

WordPress provides several functions for escaping various kinds of output. In most cases, using these functions is very similar to using PHP's htmlspecialchars() function. However, the WordPress functions include filters, allowing developers to customize them. They're also shorter and more readable, and can be modified in the future to prevent new kinds of attacks. Use WordPress's escape functions instead of PHP's whenever possible.

Most of WordPress's template tags, like the_title(), already include escaping functions. Writing something like the code in Listing 11-19 would be unnecessary.

Listing 11-19. Redundant Use of Escaping Functions

```
<?php
// this is redundant
esc_html( the_title() );
?>
```

HTML and Attributes

Escaping the value of a form's input field is probably the most common escaping scenario in WordPress. You can use esc_attr(), as you saw in the previous examples. You also saw esc_attr_e(), which both escapes and translates. You'll see more translation functions later in this chapter.

Class names have their own function: sanitize_html_class(). There's also a special function for printing post titles as attributes, often used in permalinks: the_title_attribute().

Listing 11-20 demonstrates esc_attr(), sanitize_html_class() and the_title_attribute().

Listing 11-20. Sanitized Class and Title Attributes

```
<?php
// The post title is "She's a <em>maniac</em>!"

$class = sanitize_html_class( get_the_title() );
?>
```

```
<h2 class="<?php echo esc_attr( $class ); ?>"><a href="<?php the_permalink(); ?>" title=" ↵
<?php the_title_attribute(); ?>"><?php the_title(); ?></a></h2>
```

The result is shown in listing 11-21. The class attribute is not what you probably expected, as it includes the letters in the HTML tags but not the angle brackets!

Listing 11-21. The Resulting Class Name, Title Attribute, and Title Contents

```
<h2 class="Shesaemmaniacem"><a title="She's a maniac!" href="http://wp/?p=6">She's a
<em>maniac</em>!</a></h2>
```

The esc_html() function is similar to esc_attr(). It can be used to echo any generic data that might contain < or > characters, which need to be escaped so the browser doesn't try to interpret them as HTML tags (Listing 11-22).

Listing 11-22. Escaping HTML

```
$html = '<h2> She's a <em>maniac</em>!</h2>';
echo esc_html( $html );
```

Figure 11-5 shows the results of Listing 11-21, followed by the escaped HTML of Listing 11-22.

She's a *maniac*!

<h2>She's a maniac!</h2>

Figure 11-5. The title heading, followed by the escaped HTML equivalent

Textareas have their own function: esc_textarea(). You can use it as shown in Listing 11-23 to print the contents of a textarea, like a comment form, for the user to edit.

Listing 11-23. Escaping a Textarea's Contents

```
<textarea><?php echo esc_textarea( $option['text'] ); ?></textarea>
```

JavaScript

When an attribute contains JavaScript, like a link's onclick, you should use esc_js() (Listing 11-24). In addition to the usual attribute cleanup, it fixes potential problems with line endings and provides a filter, js_escape.

Listing 11-24. Escaping a Variable for Use in Inline JavaScript

```
<input name="my_option" value="<?php echo esc_attr( $my_option ); ?>" onfocus="if ↵
( this.value == '' ) { this.value = '<?php echo esc_js( $my_option ); ?>'; }" />
```

URLs

The esc_url() function removes unsafe characters from URLs, like JavaScript functions that would do something the user didn't expect. Use esc_url() when echoing a URL to the screen (see Listing 11-25). If you need to sanitize a URL before saving it in the database, use esc_url_raw(), which does not encode special characters (like ampersands) as HTML entities.

Listing 11-25. Escaping the Administrator's Profile URL Field

```php
<?php $user = get_userdata(1); ?>
<a href="<?php echo esc_url( $user->user_url ); ?>">Administrator's Home Page</a>
```

Escaping MySQL Queries

You can use the wpdb class to run generic queries on your database instead of relying on WordPress's functions. However, if your query contains variables, you should wrap your queries in the $wpdb->prepare() method, which uses a syntax similar to PHP's sprintf() function. Preparing your query escapes its values before the query runs on the database. This helps protect your site from MySQL injection attacks. Listing 11-26 shows an unsafe version of a generic query, followed by the correct version.

Listing 11-26. Escaping MySQL Queries with $wpdb->prepare()

```php
// not safe!
$wpdb->query(
        "INSERT INTO $wpdb->postmeta
                ( post_id, meta_key, meta_value )
                VALUES ( 1, $metakey, $metavalue )"
        );

// safe!
$wpdb->query( $wpdb->prepare(
        "INSERT INTO $wpdb->postmeta
                ( post_id, meta_key, meta_value )
                VALUES ( %d, %s, %s )",
    1,
        $metakey,
        $metavalue
) );
```

See the Codex page on the wpdb class (http://sleary.me/wp38[11]) for more information on preparing queries (and the wpdb class in general).

■ **Caution**   You should omit $wpdb->prepare *only* if your query contains no variables. All queries containing variables should be escaped. See http://sleary.me/wp100[12] for more information on using $wpdb->prepare and escaping queries correctly.

Checking Capabilities

Any time you save information to the database or echo it back to the screen, you need to make sure that the current user is allowed to save things or to see what you're showing them.

---

[11]http://codex.wordpress.org/Class_Reference/wpdb
[12]http://make.wordpress.org/core/2012/12/12/php-warning-missing-argument-2-for-wpdb-prepare/

You learned about WordPress roles and capabilities in Chapter 7. Here's a quick review:

Administrators can do anything in the WordPress administration area: write, edit, and delete posts, pages, links, and comments; upload media files of any type; import content; manage the Dashboard; create, edit, and delete other users; enable and configure plugins and themes; change the site's theme; and manage all the available options.

Editors can publish, edit, and delete posts and pages written by any user. They can upload some kinds of files, and they can write HTML without restrictions. They can manage links and categories, and they can moderate comments. Editors and administrators are also the only users allowed to read private posts and pages.

Authors can publish, edit, and delete their own posts. They cannot write pages. They can upload some kinds of media files, and they are allowed to use only a limited set of HTML tags.

Contributors can write their own posts, but may not publish or delete them. Their HTML will be limited to a few HTML tags (see Listing 10-1), and they cannot upload media files.

Subscribers can manage their own profiles, but can do virtually nothing else in the administration area.

Visit the Codex page on roles and capabilities (http://sleary.me/wp39[13]) for a detailed list of all the capabilities assigned to each role.

The function that you'll use to check for your user's capabilities is current_user_can(). This function takes one argument: the capability you want to check.

Listing 11-27 shows the options form you saw earlier in the chapter. This time, the form fields are displayed only if the current user can manage options.

Listing 11-27. Wrapping Options Form Fields with current_user_can()

```
function scl_simple_options_page() {
?>
<div class="wrap">
        <form method="post" id="scl_simple_options" action="options.php">
                <?php
                settings_fields('scl_simple_options');
                $options = scl_simple_get_options();

                if ( current_user_can('manage_options') ) {
                ?>
        <h2><?php _e('Sample Options'); ?></h2>

                <table class="form-table">
                        <tr>
                                <th scope="row"><?php _e('Short Links'); ?></th>
                                <td colspan="3">
                                <p>    <label>
                                                <input name="scl_simple_options[shortlink]"
type="checkbox" value="1" <?php checked($options['shortlink'], 1); ?>/>
                                                <?php _e('Display a short URL on all posts and pages'); ?>
```

---

[13]http://codex.wordpress.org/Roles_and_Capabilities

```
                                                </label></p>
                                </td>
                        </tr>

                        <tr>
                                <th scope="row"><?php _e('Google Verification'); ?></th>
                                <td colspan="3">
                                <input type="text" id="google_meta_key"
name="scl_simple_options[google_meta_key]" value="<?php echo 'foo" onchange="alert(\"Gotcha!\")"' ?>" />
                                        <br /><span class="description"><?php _e('Enter the ↵
verification key for the Google meta tag.' ); ?></span>
                                </td>
                        </tr>
                </table>

                <p class="submit">
                <input type="submit" value="<?php esc_attr_e('Update Options'); ?>"
class="button-primary" />
                </p>

                <?php } // if current_user_can() ?>
        </form>
</div>
<?php
}
```

Checking Nonces and Referrers

A nonce is, in programming parlance[14], a "number used once." It's a unique identifier that's embedded in settings screens or URLs, and it's used to ensure that, when a user requests something from WordPress, the request came from a WordPress screen (not some other web site), and that it was made recently (not from a screen that was left open in a browser a week ago).

There are several ways to use nonces in WordPress, but the simplest is to add a hidden field to a form with the wp_nonce_field() function. The function's four arguments are as follows:

- $action: a unique name, providing context about the form

- $name: the name of the form field, defaulting to _wpnonce

- $referer: whether to include a second hidden field named _wp_http_referer

- $echo: whether to display the hidden field or return it for use in a PHP function

Listing 11-28 shows a form with the wp_nonce_field() function added, as well as a validation function that checks the nonce before saving the form input.

---

[14]Whoever coined the term among programmers was probably unaware that it has a completely different (and very derogatory) meaning in British slang. I apologize to my friends across the pond for the number of times you'll see the word in the following chapters and throughout the WordPress code.

Listing 11-28. A Simple Form with a Nonce and a Validation Function

```
<form method="post" id="scl_simple_options" action="/">

<?php wp_nonce_field(); ?>

<label><?php _e('Enter a number:'); ?>
<input type="text" id="number" name="number" value="<?php echo esc_attr($number); ?>" />
</label>

<input type="submit" value="<?php esc_attr_e('Update Options'); ?>" class="button-primary"/>

</form>

function scl_simple_options_validate($input) {

        if ( empty($input) || !wp_verify_nonce() )
        {
            echo 'You are not allowed to save this form.';
            exit;
        }

        $input['number'] = intval($input['number']);

        return $input;
}
```

Nonces can also be generated as URL parameters for use in links. For example, if you were creating a link from a category archive page directly to the Edit screen for that category, you would include a nonce to ensure that the user came from the category archive page and not some other web site, and that the link was clicked within the last 24 hours.

You'll see more examples of nonces in the following chapters. See the Codex page on nonces (http://sleary.me/wp40[15]) for a list of all the nonce and referrer functions in WordPress.

Translations: Localization and Internationalization

WordPress uses standard PHP gettext functions to allow string translations. To make your plugin available for translation, you have to localize all your strings.

The process of localizing strings is simple, but tedious. Each string must be wrapped in one of two functions. Echoed strings should be wrapped with _e(), while strings passed as arguments to other functions should be wrapped in __(). Additionally, each wrapper function must have a second argument, the text domain of your plugin. Most plugin authors use the directory name as the text domain. Last, you need to generate a separate file containing all those wrapped strings, which translators will use as a template.

■ **Note** Because *internationalization* is a 20-letter word that takes a while to type, it's often abbreviated as *i18n*, with the middle 18 letters omitted. Similar abbreviations include *l10n* (*localization*) and *a11y* (*accessibility*).

---

[15]http://codex.wordpress.org/WordPress_Nonces

Wrapping Strings in Gettext Calls

Listing 11-29 shows two page headings. The first is hard-coded and will not be available to translators. The second has been wrapped in the translate-and-echo function, and can be translated. The surrounding HTML tags do not need to be translated, and should not be included in the text passed to the translation functions.

Listing 11-29. Text Hard-Coded and with Translation Wrappers

```
<h2>Page Options</h2>
<h2><?php _e('Page Options'); ?></h2>
```

Adding the Gettext Domain

Each theme and plugin has its own gettext domain—that is, a unique slug that's used to identify the translation files that should be used for the theme or plugin's text. Many developers use their directory names for the domain. Each translation function should have the domain added as a second argument. For the example in Listing 11-30, we'll use 'my-plugin' as the domain.

Listing 11-30. A Translation Function with the Text Domain Argument

```
<?php _e('Page Options', 'my-plugin'); ?>
```

If you plan to release your plugin on wordpress.org, you can leave out the domain until you've submitted your plugin, then use the developer tools to automatically add the domain to all your translation functions.

There are several other translation functions: _n(), which returns a singular or plural form based on the number of items given, and _x(), _ex(), and nx(), which are context-aware versions of the three basic functions. See the Codex page on localization (http://sleary.me/wp41[16]) for documentation on all six functions. There are also a handful of functions that combine escaping and translating; see the Codex page on data validation (http://sleary.me/wp37[17]) for a complete list.

Other APIs

In this chapter, you've seen the Plugin API (hooks), the Options API, and the Settings API. As you can see, "API" is really a fancy way of saying that there are sets of functions designed to make it easier for developers to interact with WordPress core data. Each API is just a group of functions surrounding a specific task.

There are lots more APIs in WordPress (http://sleary.me/wp42[18]). They are:

- Dashboard Widgets
- Database
- Heartbeat
- HTTP
- File Header (used for reading titles, authors, and descriptions from plugin and theme headers)
- Filesystem

---

[16]http://codex.wordpress.org/L10n
[17]http://codex.wordpress.org/Data_Validation
[18]http://codex.wordpress.org/WordPress_APIs

- Metadata (for WordPress's internal use only)

- Quicktags (the toolbar buttons in the Text editing view)

- Rewrite (permalinks)

- Shortcode

- Theme Modification

- Theme Customization

- Transients (for storing temporary data)

- Widgets

- XML-RPC

You'll see more details on the Dashboard Widgets, Database, Shortcode, Theme Customization, Transients, and Widgets APIs in the chapters that follow, as you begin to create your own themes and plugins.

Developing in Debug Mode

Way back in Chapter 2, you saw how using debug mode—that is, setting the WP_DEBUG constant to true in your wp-config.php file (Listing 11-31)—can help you find problems in your themes and plugins. You can also debug scripts and queries with the SCRIPT_DEBUG and SAVEQUERIES definitions, respectively. The other definitions in Listing 11-31 will turn on error logging rather than displaying the error messages on the screen.

Listing 11-31. Debugging with wp-config.php (Partial)

```
define( 'WP_DEBUG', true );
define( 'SCRIPT_DEBUG', true );
define( 'SAVEQUERIES', true );
define( 'WP_DEBUG_LOG', true );
define( 'WP_DEBUG_DISPLAY', false );
```

Leave debug mode on while you're developing your themes and plugins. It'll help you catch small errors. Keep in mind that everyone has a slightly different server configuration, and that includes the level of errors that are displayed to the screen. While you might not see low-level errors like notices and warnings, your users might.

Sometimes, WordPress's error messages report that an error has occurred in a core file, like pluggable.php, when the problem clearly comes from a plugin. In these situations, PHP's debug_backtrace() and debug_print_backtrace() functions can help you figure out the real origin of the problem.

Plugins for Debugging

There are also a number of plugins that can help you track down errors. Debug Bar is probably the most helpful. Figure 11-6 shows the information that Debug Bar provides.

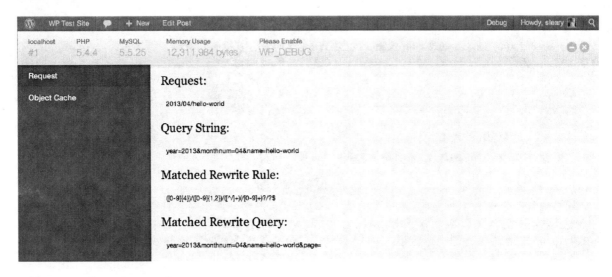

Figure 11-6. *The Debug Bar plugin*

There are several extensions for Debug Bar, like Debug Bar Extender, that display specialized information for cron jobs, transients, post meta data, and more; search the plugin repository (`http://sleary.me/wp43`[19]) for "Debug Bar" to find them all.

Summary

You've learned a lot in this chapter! You know where themes and plugins are stored and how the files work. You learned all about the Plugins and Options APIs. You've seen how data validation and escaping works, and you know how to check nonces and user capabilities so your themes and plugins will be secure.

Now you can at least recognize and understand the unfamiliar functions you've seen in theme and plugin files. You now have the foundation to begin writing new themes and plugins. In the next chapter, you'll create a complete theme of your own.

---

[19]`http://wordpress.org/extend/plugins`

CHAPTER 12

■ ■ ■

Creating a Theme

Now that you've configured your site and created some content, it's time to make it look good! First, you'll create a basic custom theme, starting with a standard HTML file. I'll walk you through the various WordPress template files you can use to make parts of your site look different based on context.

Once you've learned the basics of themes, you'll learn how to add options to your theme using the theme customizer. I'll show you child themes—a powerful way to customize existing WordPress themes while keeping the original code intact. You'll see how to create complete frameworks of your own. I'll also show you a few ways to handle responsive design in WordPress themes.

Last, you'll see the requirements for themes submitted to wordpress.org.

You'll also learn how to style pages that aren't part of themes: the database error page and the maintenance page.

This is by far the longest chapter in this book—about 60 pages of themes and nothing but themes. Are you ready? Let's theme!

Before You Begin

You can muddle along in WordPress using other people's themes and plugins if you don't know HTML and CSS. But if you're going to write your own custom theme, that won't do. You need to understand HTML in its entirety, more or less, and enough CSS to construct a page layout. You also need a little PHP knowledge. If you've ever taken a computer science course, it's freshman-level stuff. Of course, the more you learn, the better your themes will be.

HTML and CSS

The recent default themes (Twenty Eleven, Twenty Twelve, and Twenty Thirteen) all take advantage of new features in HTML5 and CSS3. If you haven't brushed up on your HTML and CSS skills lately, grab copies of the excellent short guides from A Book Apart (http://abookapart.com): *HTML5 for Web Designers*, by Jeremy Keith, and *CSS3 for Web Designers*, by Dan Cederholm. These books assume you know your way around HTML and CSS in general, and you just need to pick up the new features in the latest versions.

If you're completely new to web design, a more in-depth guide would be a better choice. Try the tutorials at HTML Dog (http://htmldog.com) or pick up a copy of *HTML and CSS: Design and Build Websites*, by Jon Duckett, or the *HTML5 and CSS3 Visual QuickStart Guide* by Elizabeth Castro and Bruce Hyslop.

PHP

As I mentioned in the previous chapter, you'll need to be familiar with the following aspects of PHP programming in order to build a theme:

- variable and function syntax

- string and array manipulation

- if/else statements and conditional operators

- for, foreach, and while loops

In this chapter, you'll see ways of interacting with WordPress's built-in features, like the theme customizer, that require working with classes and objects. While you don't need to know how to create your own, you're going to see how to work with existing ones.

If you're new to PHP, the following books and tutorials should help you get up to speed:

- *PHP Solutions, Second Edition*, by David Powers

- *PHP for Absolute Beginners*, by Jason Lengstorf

- *PHP Cookbook*, Adam Trachtenberg and David Sklar

- PHP Fundamentals series by Tuts+ (http://sleary.me/wp101[1])

Some of the newer features in WordPress rely on PHP functions introduced in version 5.2 (November 2006). If you're referring to another book or tutorial, make sure it's no older than that. (And if your web host *still* hasn't updated to 5.2, you probably need to find a new host.)

PHP is similar to other C-based languages. If you're already familiar with one of them, you could just refer to the manual at http://php.net to check each function's arguments and return values.

■ **Tip**   To look up a PHP function in the online manual, just type http://php.net/function_name—for example, http://php.net/in_array will take you to the manual page for in_array(), where you can check the order in which the function expects its two arguments.

Building the First Theme Files

WordPress theme files are basically HTML pages with some strategically placed, WordPress-specific PHP functions. While some PHP developers criticize the mingling of languages, preferring a strict separation of logic and layout, the WordPress system is flexible and easy to learn, once you figure out the Loop, which I'll go over in a bit.

A theme is a collection of files in a directory, which will be stored in wp-content/themes in the WordPress directory (unless you have changed this location in wp-config.php). The directory must contain at least two files: style.css, with a header containing some information about the theme, and index.php—unless you are creating a child theme, as you'll learn to do later in this chapter, in which case only the stylesheet is required. There are a number of other optional files that can be used to vary the site's appearance throughout its various sections: archives, pages, search results, and so on. I'll go over all the individual theme files, also called templates, in the "Template Files" section of this chapter.

---

[1]https://tutsplus.com/course/php-fundamentals/

About the Sample Theme

Throughout this chapter, I'll show you how to build a theme for a university department. The University theme will be similar to one you would build for a business, a nonprofit, or even a personal site with more structure than a simple blog. Figure 12-1 shows the finished theme you'll work toward. You can download the theme in a zipped file at http://sleary.me/theme.

Figure 12-1. *The University demo theme*

I'll start with the stylesheet file, which contains the comment block that defines the theme's name and other attributes.

Stylesheet

The `style.css` is a required file in any WordPress theme. You're free to include additional CSS files in your theme, but there must be one with this filename.

Not only is the file required, but it should also begin with a comment block containing the theme's name, URL, description, author name, and version number. Listing 12-1 shows the University theme's header, containing all the relevant information.

Listing 12-1. The University Theme Stylesheet Header

```
/*
Theme Name: The University
Theme URI: http://stephanieleary.com/code/themes/edu/
Description: Sample theme for the WordPress for Web Developers book.
Version: 1.0
License: GNU General Public License v2 or later
License URI: http://www.gnu.org/licenses/gpl-2.0.html
Author: Stephanie Leary
Author URI: http://stephanieleary.com
Tags: blue, two-columns, right-sidebar, flexible-width, custom-header, custom-menu, editor-style,
featured-images, microformats, post-formats, translation-ready, responsive
Text Domain: edu
*/
```

This comment block is not absolutely required; your theme will be recognized and listed under Appearance ➤ Themes without it, with the directory name used for the theme name.

The tag list is useful only for themes that will be distributed through `wordpress.org`, where the tags allow users to browse themes by feature or color. The text domain is also used for themes on `wordpress.org`; it's used to locate the translation of the theme description. See the section on Distributing Themes at the end of this chapter for more information on translating themes.

Recommended Styles

If you're working with a design that wasn't created for WordPress, you need to add a number of styles to your CSS files to account for things that might not have been in the original design, like comments, avatars, and tag and category links for each post. It can be tricky to account for all these elements if your site doesn't yet contain content! The WordPress developers have provided a sample content set for designers. You can download it at `http://sleary.me/wp44`[2], import it into a test site, and use it to make sure your theme contains all the styles it needs.

Styling your theme is almost entirely up to you, but every theme should include the styles required to make image alignment work as expected. You might recall from Chapter 4 that when you upload an image, you're offered four alignment choices: left, right, centered, or none. When you insert the image into your post or page, WordPress assigns classes to the image based on your selection. Of course, by themselves, those classes don't actually do anything. You'll need to insert the styles in Listing 12-2 (or something similar to them) in your theme's stylesheet.

---

[2]http://codex.wordpress.org/Theme_Development_Checklist#Theme_Unit_Test

Listing 12-2. Basic Styles Necessary to Support Aligned Images

```
.alignright { float:right; margin:0 0 1em 1em; }
.alignleft { float:left; margin:0 1em 1em 0; }
.aligncenter { display: block; margin-left: auto; margin-right: auto; }
```

The rest of the styles are your choice. Do you like to start with Eric Meyer's reset.css (http://sleary.me/wp45[3])? Paste it just under the comment block. Is the Less responsive framework (http://sleary.me/wp46[4]) your thing? Paste its media queries near the bottom. WordPress doesn't impose limits on what you can do with your site's design.

Near the end of this chapter, I'll talk about a few issues you might encounter when implementing responsive or adaptive layouts with WordPress.

Creating the Index Template

The best way to demonstrate how a theme file works is to start with a familiar HTML page and show you the tags required to transform it into a WordPress theme file. Listing 12-3 shows the simple HTML template you'll turn into the theme's main template file, index.php.

Listing 12-3. A Basic HTML File

```
<!DOCTYPE html>
<html lang="en">
<head>
<meta charset="utf-8" />
<title>The University</title>

<meta name="description" content="A description of the site" />
<meta name="viewport" content="width = device-width, initial-scale = 1.0">

<link rel="stylesheet" href="style.css" type="text/css" media="screen,projection" />
</head>

<body>
<div id="wrapper">

        <div id="header" class="section">
                <h1 class="header"> <a href="/">The University</a> </h1>
        </div>

        <div id="nav-top">
                <ul class="nav">
                        <li><a href="http://wp/about/">About</a></li>
                        <li><a href="http://wp/courses/">Courses</a></li>
                        <li><a href="http://wp/faculty/">Faculty</a>
                                <ul class='children'>
                                        <li><a href="http://wp/faculty/adjunct-faculty/"> ↩
Adjunct Faculty</a></li>

                                        <li><a href="http://wp/faculty/literature/"> ↩
Literature</a></li>
```

---

[3]http://meyerweb.com/eric/tools/css/reset
[4]http://lessframework.com

```
                              <li><a href="http://wp/faculty/rhetoric/">Rhetoric</a></li>
                    </ul>
                </li>
                <li><a href="http://wp/hours-and-location/">Hours and Location</a></li>
        </ul>
    </div>

<div id="content" class="section">

        <div <?php post_class(); ?> id="post-<?php the_ID(); ?>">

            <h2><a href="#" >Post Title</a></h2>
                <p class="postmetadata before">Posted by <a href="#">Stephanie</a></p>

                <p>This would be the post content.</p>

        </div> <!-- #post-n -->

</div> <!-- #content -->

<div id="sidebar" class="section">
        <div class="widget">
                <h3>Sidebar</h3>
                <p>Some useful ancillary information goes here.</p>
        </div>
</div>

<div id="footer" class="section">
        <p class="copyright">&copy; 2013 The University</p>
        <div class="contact"><p>P.O. Box 1111, College Town, MD</p></div>
</div>

</body>
</html>
```

The changes are noted in bold in Listing 12-4. This file would be saved as index.php, and could serve as the only file other than the stylesheet for a very simplistic theme.

Listing 12-4. The WordPress Equivalent, index.php

```
<!DOCTYPE html>
<html lang="en">
<head>
<meta charset="<?php bloginfo('charset'); ?>" />
<title>
        <?php wp_title('|', true, 'right'); ?>
        <?php bloginfo('name'); if ( is_home() ) echo ' | The University'; ?>
</title>
<meta name="description" content="<?php bloginfo('description'); ?>" />
<meta name="viewport" content="width = device-width, initial-scale = 1.0">

<link rel="stylesheet" href="<?php echo get_stylesheet_uri(); ?>" type="text/css" ↪
 media="screen,projection" />
```

```php
<?php wp_head(); ?>

</head>

<body <?php body_class( ); ?>>
<div id="wrapper">

        <div id="header" class="section">
                <h1 class="header"> <a href="/"><?php bloginfo('name'); ?></a> </h1>
        </div>

        <div id="nav-top">
                <?php wp_nav_menu(); ?>
        </div>

<div id="content" class="section">

        <?php if (have_posts()) : while (have_posts()) : the_post(); ?>

        <div <?php post_class(); ?> id="post-<?php the_ID(); ?>">

            <h2><a href="<?php the_permalink() ?>" rel="bookmark" title="Permanent Link to ➥
<?php the_title_attribute(); ?>"><?php the_title(); ?></a></h2>

                <?php the_content('Read more...'); ?>

                <?php comments_template(); ?>
        </div> <!-- #post-n -->

        <?php endwhile; else: ?>
                <p><?php _e('Sorry, no posts matched your criteria.'); ?></p>
        <?php endif; ?>

</div> <!-- #content -->


<div id="sidebar" class="section">
                <?php if ( !function_exists('dynamic_sidebar') || !dynamic_sidebar('Primary ➥
Sidebar') ) : endif; ?>
</div>


<div id="footer" class="section">

        <p class="copyright"><?php echo '&copy; ' . date( ' Y ' ) . get_bloginfo( 'name' ); ?></p>
        <div class="contact"><?php echo get_theme_mod( 'edu_footer_text', '' ); ?></div>

</div>
<?php wp_footer(); ?>
</body>
</html>
```

In the next few sections of this chapter, I'll show you how to break up this page into modular files that will become a more complete WordPress theme. Along the way, I'll go over all the places where I've replaced text from the original HTML file with WordPress template tags, and I'll explain what each template tag does.

Including Common Files

If you've ever built a site without a CMS, you know that the last thing you want to do is repeat common code like headers, footers, and navigation in every individual file, because every time there's a change, you have to edit dozens or hundreds of files. The sensible thing to do is to create a single header file, a single footer, and maybe a single sidebar. Then you can simply include those files in each page using PHP or Server Side Includes.

WordPress supports this design pattern. It lets you use the get_header(), get_sidebar(), and get_footer() functions to include these portions of each page. There's also a get_template_part() function to help you include other, less standard files. Figure 12-2 shows a diagram of the various include files that will make up the sample University theme. This pattern is common to almost all WordPress themes.

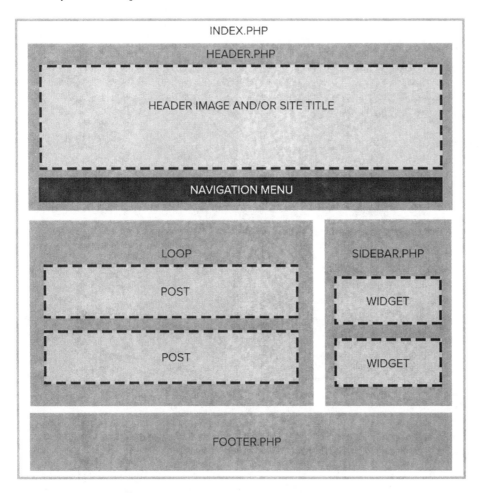

Figure 12-2. A diagram of include files in a WordPress theme

I'll go over each section in turn.

Header

Since the header will be consistent on every page of the site, I'll move it (doctype, <head>, and body content through the navigation section) into header.php, as shown in Listing 12-5. Then I can simply use <?php get_header(); ?> at the top of all my template files to include header.php.

Listing 12-5. The header.php File

```
<!DOCTYPE html>
<html <?php language_attributes(); ?>>
<head>
<meta charset="<?php bloginfo('charset'); ?>" />
<title>
        <?php wp_title('|', true, 'right'); ?>
        <?php bloginfo('name'); if ( is_home() ) echo ' | The University'; ?>
</title>
<meta name="description" content="<?php bloginfo('description'); ?>" />
<meta name="viewport" content="width = device-width, initial-scale = 1.0">

<link rel="stylesheet" href="<?php echo get_stylesheet_uri(); ?>" type="text/css" ↵
media="screen,projection" />

<?php wp_head(); ?>

</head>

<body <?php body_class( ); ?>>
<div id="wrapper">

        <div id="header" class="section">
                <h1 class="header"> <a href="/"><?php bloginfo('name'); ?></a> </h1>
        </div>

        <div id="nav-top">
                <?php wp_nav_menu(); ?>
        </div>
```

Site Header Template Tags

The doctype in WordPress looks a little different than the original HTML file. Rather than specifying a single language, you use the language_attributes() function to print the language code corresponding to the setting in your wp-config.php file (US English, unless you changed it). This allows WordPress to update the language code in the doctype to match the language in which the user is writing.

In the <title> tag, always start with wp_title(). Its output changes based on the page context. It prints first the title—which could be the title of a post or page, category, or date archive, depending on where this file is used—followed by the name of the site. This is a good practice for search engine optimization (SEO), but can be refined further with plugins like WordPress SEO (http://sleary.me/wp99[5]). Like many SEO plugins, WordPress SEO modifies the output of wp_title(). If this function is not present in the <title> tag, the plugin won't work correctly.

For the character set, again you should use the blog's setting rather than specifying one. Like the language, the character set is specified in the wp-config.php file.

The meta description tag is filled in here with the blog description you entered under Settings ➤ General ("Just another WordPress blog," unless you changed it). Again, this can be modified using SEO plugins. I'll show you how to generate a unique meta description for every page of your site in the "Search Engine Optimization" section of this chapter.

In the next line, `bloginfo('stylesheet_url')` prints the URL of the current theme's stylesheet. As you'll see in the "Parent and Child Theme Paths" section, there's a similar bit of code you can use to link to other files in the theme directory.

The `wp_head()` function should appear just before the closing `</head>` tag. It's a hook, which means that it does not print anything directly, but serves as a placeholder function. As you saw in Chapter 11, developers can add their own code to this hook when they need to insert something—an extra stylesheet or script, for example—to the page header. There are a few built-in functions that hook into `wp_head()`, mostly to call JavaScript files. Do not remove this; WordPress relies on it.

Body Classes

The `body_class()` function prints a series of class names based on the content of the page being viewed. Listings 12-6 through 12-9 show a few examples of the function's output in various contexts.

Listing 12-6. The Classes on a Single Post

```
<body class="single postid-63">
```

This tells you that you're looking at a single post, specifically post ID 63.

Listing 12-7. The Classes on a Page

```
<body class="page page-id-1952 page-parent page-child parent-pageid-1086 page-template ➥
page-template-default logged-in">
```

This tells you that:

- You're looking at a page, specifically page 1952.

- It's a parent of another page.

- It's a child of another page, specifically page 1086.

- It's using a page template, specifically the default template.

- The viewer is logged in.

Listing 12-8. The Classes on Page 2 of a Category Archive

```
<body class="archive paged category category-news paged-2 category-paged-2">
```

---

[5]`http://wordpress.org/extend/plugins/wordpress-seo`

This tells you that:

- You're looking at an archive page.
- It's a category archive, specifically the news category.
- The archive has more than one page, and you're looking at page 2.

Listing 12-9. Adding Classes to the body_class() Function

```
<body <?php body_class('main extra-class'); ?>>
// output:
<body class="single postid-63 main extra-class">
```

To add your own classes to the list, provide them as an argument of the body_class() function, as shown in Listing 12-9. They will be appended to the list of automatically generated classes.

Site Title, Tagline, and Header Image

Aside from all the under-the-hood stuff that goes into the <head> tag, the most important part of header.php is the site header: the site's title, its description, and the user-uploaded header image, if there is one.

The first two items are displayed using the bloginfo() function, which can also be used to print lots of other information about the site. You've already seen it used to print the language codes; you could use it to show the administrator's email address, the version of WordPress you're running, and a long list of useful URLs.

Listing 12-10 shows the title and description surrounded by appropriate HTML heading tags. If you wanted to store the title or description in a variable for use in some other PHP function, you could use get_bloginfo() instead of bloginfo().

Listing 12-10. Printing the Site Title and Description

```
<h1 class="header"> <a href="/"><?php bloginfo('name'); ?></a> </h1>
<h2 class="description"> <?php bloginfo('description'); ?> </h2>
```

To let your users upload custom header images, add the image tag in Listing 12-11 to header.php. You'll also need to turn on theme support for custom headers in your functions.php file; see the "Theme Functions" section later in this chapter.

Listing 12-11. Custom Header Image Tag

```
<img src="<?php header_image(); ?>" height="<?php echo get_custom_header()->height; ?>" ↵
width="<?php echo get_custom_header()->width; ?>" alt="" />
```

Sidebar

If you haven't already, grab the sidebar section from the original index.php file and paste it into sidebar.php. The sidebar is another one of those reusable sections of the theme, and you should use the get_sidebar() function to include it in your other templates. This one is even more flexible than the header, though, as you'll see in a minute.

The code in Listing 12-12 provides a basic sidebar with one widget area. If you wish, you can check whether any widgets are registered and provide some default sidebar content if they are not. Here, if there are no widgets defined, the viewer will see a search form and a list of archives.

Listing 12-12. The Widget Area in `sidebar.php`

```
<div id="sidebar" class="widget-area">
<?php if ( !dynamic_sidebar('first-widget-area') ) : // the ID of the sidebar ?>
        <div id="search" class="widget-container widget_search">
        <?php get_search_form(); ?>
        </div>

        <div id="archives" class="widget-container">
                <h3 class="widget-title"><?php _e( 'Archives'); ?></h3>
                <ul>
                <?php wp_get_archives('type=monthly'); ?>
                </ul>
        </div>

<?php endif; // end primary widget area ?>
</div><!-- first .widget-area -->
```

Note that widgets do not have to be placed on the side of the page. While that's their traditional location, widgets can be placed anywhere on the page. In WordPress, the word "sidebar" really means "widget area," regardless of its location on the screen. (In responsive layouts, the location will probably change depending on the user's screen size.) The new Twenty Thirteen default theme has widget areas in the footer instead of the sidebar. Many themes have multiple widget areas, often on the side of the page and in the footer.

You can define multiple sidebar files in your theme by giving them unique names. In addition to `sidebar.php`, you might have `sidebar-page.php` and `sidebar-author.php`. You can call these sidebars in your theme files using the `get_sidebar()` function, as shown in Listing 12-13. This feature might be most useful when you're customizing the appearance of various archive types. Later in this chapter, you'll see all the archive types that are possible in the WordPress theme hierarchy.

Listing 12-13. Including Multiple Sidebar Files

```
<?php get_sidebar(); ?>              // sidebar.php
<?php get_sidebar('page'); ?>        // sidebar-page.php
<?php get_sidebar('author'); ?>      // sidebar-author.php
```

Footer

As you did with the header and sidebar, you should copy the footer portion of `index.php` into `footer.php` and replace it with `get_footer()`. You'll reuse this footer in all your templates. Listing 12-14 shows the University theme's footer. The `get_theme_mod()` function will allow your users to edit the text (in this case, the address) that's displayed in the footer. I'll show you how this function works with the theme customizer feature in that section of this chapter.

Listing 12-14. The University Theme's Footer File

```
<div id="footer" class="section">

<p class="copyright"><?php echo '&copy; ' . date( 'Y' ) . get_bloginfo( 'name' ); ?></p>
<div class="contact"><?php echo get_theme_mod( 'edu_footer_text', '' ); ?></div>

</div>
<?php wp_footer(); ?>
</body>
</html>
```

The contents of your footer are entirely up to you, except for one thing: the `wp_footer()` function must be present, preferably just before the closing `</body>` tag. This is a hook. It might display nothing in a basic installation, but plugins may use it to add code to the theme file. For example, several Google Analytics plugins use `wp_footer()` to add the Analytics script to the bottom of the page. The `wp_footer()` hook is used internally to print scripts and stylesheets that the developer has set to load in the footer rather than the header.

■ **Tip**   If your site includes a copyright notice, use `<?php echo date('Y'); ?>` to display the year in your footer. It always displays the current year, so you don't have to remember to change it over the holidays.

Post Content: The Loop

The Loop makes up the main part of a WordPress template. It is essentially a PHP loop wrapped in an `if/else` statement. It says: if I have posts, then while there are posts, print some information about each one. If I don't have any posts, print an error message.

What's confusing is that you never see where the posts come from. WordPress performs a database query based on the context—that is, which page you're looking at—and the choices you made in Settings ➤ Reading regarding the number of posts to display. For example, if you're looking at a category archive page, WordPress understands (based on the URL) that it needs to display the most recent posts from that category, and it queries the database accordingly. This query is stored in the $query global variable, and the resulting posts are stored in $posts.

Inside the Loop, the global $post holds the information about each post. All the functions that call a particular piece of information—`the_title()`, `the_content()`, and so on—refer to this post, unless otherwise specified. These functions are meant to be used inside the Loop, and generally do not work correctly outside the Loop unless you do a bit of extra work to set up the post data. See the "Accessing Post Data Outside the Loop" section later in this chapter for details.

In most templates, you'll never need to interact directly with $query, $post, or any of the other global variables that define the page; you just need to work with the results. Just as the body classes did, the contents of the Loop will change depending on which page is being viewed. On the home page, either your most recent posts or a single page will be displayed, depending on your choices in the Settings. On a category archive page, the most recent posts in that category appear. Even the search page depends on an invisible database query. See the "Modifying the Loop: An Introduction to the Query" section later in this chapter for a few tips on viewing the query's contents for debugging purposes.

The next several sections of this chapter discuss all the post-specific template tags. Most of these are intended to be used only within the Loop. I'll show you how to access individual posts' information outside the Loop as well.

Post Template Tags

There is a template tag for every piece of information you can enter into a post or page. Figure 12-3 shows the tags that can be used to display the information from the Posts ➤ Edit screen. Listing 12-15 shows how to use some of these tags in a standard Loop.

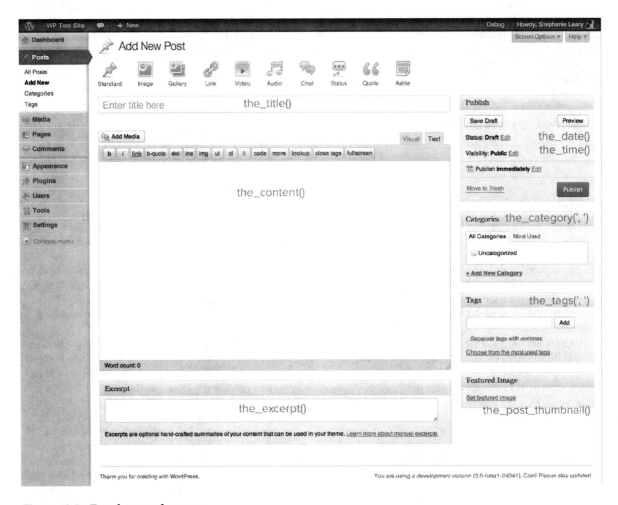

Figure 12-3. Template tags for a post

As you'll see throughout this chapter, there are a vast number of template tags you can use to customize your theme. I'll go over most of the essentials, but please visit http://sleary.me/wp47[6] for a complete list of available tags plus detailed documentation about each one.

■ **Note** The same template tags are used for both posts and pages (as well as custom post types, which you'll see in Chapter 14). Throughout this section, anything labeled "post" also applies to pages unless otherwise noted.

---

[6]http://codex.wordpress.org/Template_Tags

Listing 12-15. The Loop, Displaying the Post or Page Content

```php
<?php if (have_posts()) : while (have_posts()) : the_post(); ?>

        <div <?php post_class(); ?> id="post-<?php the_ID(); ?>">

            <h2><a href="<?php the_permalink() ?>" rel="bookmark" title="Permanent Link to ↦
 <?php the_title_attribute(); ?>"><?php the_title(); ?></a></h2>
<p class="postmetadata before"><?php _e('Posted by '); ?><a href="<?php ↦
get_the_author_link(); ?>"><?php the_author(); ?></a></p>

        <?php the_content('Read more...'); ?>

                <div class="navigation">
                <?php posts_nav_link(); ?>
                </div><!-- .navigation -->

        <?php comments_template(); ?>
        </div> <!-- #post-n -->

<?php endwhile; else: ?>
        <p><?php _e('Sorry, no posts matched your criteria.'); ?></p>
<?php endif; ?>
```

Let's break down the Loop a little.

The first line is a bit complicated; it contains both the conditional (if I have posts) and the beginning of the Loop itself (while I have posts, do something with them). From there to the endwhile() statement, you're inside the Loop, and you can use all the post-specific template tags (or functions). Here you use the_title(), the_content(), and comments_template(). This prints a very minimal amount of information about each post. For a complete list of template tags, visit http://sleary.me/wp47.[7]

After the Loop has ended, but before you're completely done with your posts, you need to print some navigation tags. The posts_nav_link() function provides links to older posts (and newer ones if you're viewing an archive page). Note that this tag works only for posts.

Figure 12-4 shows the simple Loop from Listing 12-15. As it iterates over five recent posts on the university department site, it prints the basic information about the post using the template tags I specified: the title, the post author, the content (truncated with the "read more" link), and an edit link that's visible only to the post author, a site editor, or a site administrator. In the "Multiple Loops" section of this chapter, you'll see how to create multiple loops on a single page, like the home page, to create more complex layouts.

---

[7]http://codex.wordpress.org/Template_Tags

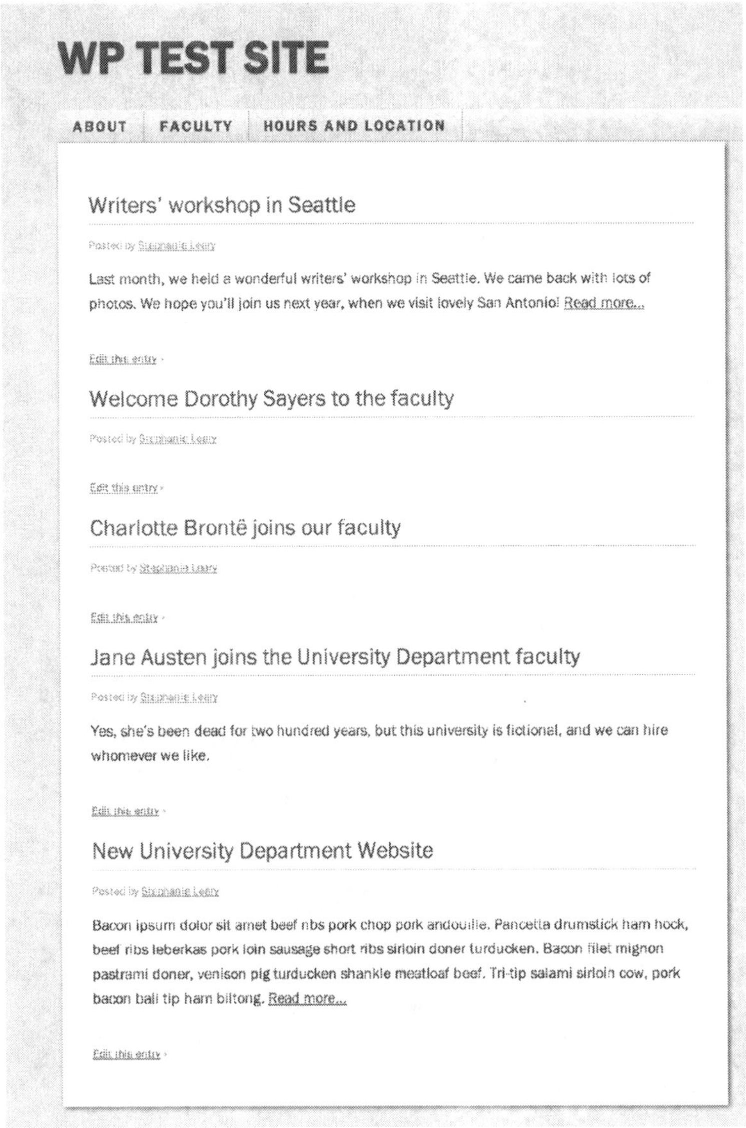

Figure 12-4. *The Loop iterates over each recent post, displaying the template tags you have specified*

There are a couple of arguments you can use to modify the way `the_content()` displays your content. The most commonly used is the "Read more" text string—that is, the text that will be displayed if you have used the `<!--more-->` tag to break up your post (see Chapter 4). Listing 12-16 shows how to modify the text.

Listing 12-16. Changing the "Read More" Link Text

```php
<?php the_content("Continue reading..."); ?>
```

Post Classes

The post_class() function, shown attached to the <h2> tag in Listing 12-17, works exactly like the body_class() function. It prints attributes about the individual post, including a microformat-specific class (hentry) that lets search engines know that this bit of content on the page is a blog entry. (See http://microformats.org for more on microformats.)

Listing 12-17. Sample Output of the post_class() Function

```
<h2 class="post-188 post type-post hentry category-cat-a category-cat-b category-cat-c
  category-uncategorized category-aciform tag-tag1 tag-tag2 tag-tag3">
```

Listing 12-17 shows the post classes printed for a sticky post with an ID of 188, several tags (tag1, tag2, tag3) and categories (cat-a, cat-b, cat-c, uncategorized, aciform).

As you can see, these styles offer many opportunities to style posts differently based on their categories, tags, and sticky status. I encourage you to set your sticky posts apart somehow; you could give them a slightly different background color, for example. The rest of the classes are there if you need them.

Post Date and Time Template Tags

The date and time tags, the_date() and the_time(), are based on PHP's date() function. If they are called without arguments, they use the date and time formats you chose under Settings ➤ General.

These two tags work exactly the same way, except for one thing: when the_date() appears inside the Loop, it will print the date only once for each set of posts that fall on that date. This behavior makes sense when you're using dates as headers, but it doesn't work so well when you have the date listed alongside the post's other metadata (author, categories, tags, etc.). In the latter case, you need to use the_time() and specify the date format you want. For example, the_time("F j, Y"); will print the month, day, and year in the common American format: May 1, 2010. To use the date format you chose in Settings ➤ General, use the get_option() function as shown in Listing 12-18.

Listing 12-18. the_date() and the_time() in the Loop

```
<?php if (have_posts()) : while (have_posts()) : the_post(); ?>
<h3 class="date"><?php the_date(); // prints once per day ?></h3>
        <h2 id="post-<?php the_ID(); ?>" class="<?php post_class(); ?>">
        <a href="<?php the_permalink() ?>" rel="bookmark" title="Permanent link
to <?php the_title(); ?>"><?php the_title(); ?></a>
</h2>
        <?php the_content(); ?>
        <?php wp_link_pages(); ?>
<p class="postmeta">Posted on
<?php
// these dates and times will print for every post
the_time(get_option("date_format")); // uses date format instead of time
?>
at <?php the_time(); // uses time format by default ?>
</p>
        <div class="commentblock">
                <?php comments_template(); ?>
        </div><!--commentblock-->
         <?php endwhile; ?>
```

```
    <div class="navigation">
        <?php posts_nav_link(); ?>
    </div><!-- .navigation -->
<?php endif; ?>
```

Post Permalink and Shortlink Template Tags

In some of the preceding code listings, you've seen the tag the_permalink(), which prints a link to an individual post or page view. The actual URL printed here depends on the permalink structure you chose in Settings ➤ Permalinks back in Chapter 2.

In that chapter, I mentioned that the default link format, http://example.com/?p=123, always works. You can use this as a short URL, if your permalink structure generates something very long (which is easy to do when you have several pages in a parent/child hierarchy). Use the_shortlink() to print the short version of the URL.

The shortlink function is filtered, which means that it's very easy to alter its output. There are many plugins that do just that, acting as a site-specific version of URL shorteners like bit.ly or tinyurl.com. The Jetpack plugin includes the wordpress.com link shortening service, wp.me.

If you need to fetch the full or short URLs without echoing them to the screen immediately, use get_permalink() or wp_get_shortlink().

Building Separate Loop Template Files

WordPress has a special template file include function, get_template_part(). This function can take two arguments. With one argument, the slug, the function will include a filename matching that slug. If a second argument, the specific name, is included, WordPress will first look for slug-name.php, and if it doesn't exist, it will substitute the more generic slug.php file. Listing 12-19 shows two common uses of this function: moving the Loop into its own include file.

Listing 12-19. Using the get_template_part() Function

```
get_template_part('loop');            // loop.php
get_template_part('loop', 'index');   // loop-index.php
```

With the get_template_part() function, you can create your own hierarchy of included files that works just like the sidebars. In this case, moving the Loop into its own file allows you to reuse the same Loop in multiple templates without duplicating the code. If you want to change your Loop in every template, you can simply edit the loop.php file. Or, if you want a full-content Loop for your home page and an excerpt Loop for your archives and search results, you can create just two files and include them in the appropriate templates.

Breaking up a template into several include files might seem needlessly complicated, but it's very helpful if you're creating a theme that's intended to be used as the parent for child themes. When a parent theme uses a separate Loop file, the child theme can modify the Loop portion of the page layout without changing the surrounding templates. You'll learn more about child themes later in this chapter.

Navigation

If you want to have a navigation bar at the top of your site, the menu tag should be placed in header.php. Prior to version 3.0, most themes used either page or category lists as menus. Of course, you can still create menus this way. This method is less flexible than the navigation menu, but does have one big advantage: unlike navigation menus, page and category lists update themselves automatically.

I'll go through all three of the common methods of creating menus: the page menu tag, page lists, and category lists. There are widgets corresponding to each of these functions. You can use either the widget or the template tag, whichever is most appropriate for your theme and users. The template tag can appear in header.php, sidebar.php, or any other template file, as your design requires.

Navigation Menu Tag

The wp_nav_menu() tag prints one of the menus you created in Appearance ➤ Menus. By default, the class on the surrounding <div> tag will be "menu", but you can change this in the function parameters. In fact, you can change the <div> tag to something else entirely, as shown in Listing 12-20. You can specify arguments in a string or as an array.

Listing 12-20. Using the wp_nav_menu() Function

```php
<?php
// argument style
wp_nav_menu( 'sort_column=menu_order&format=ul&menu_class=nav' );
// array style equivalent
wp_nav_menu(array('sort_column' => 'menu_order', 'format' => 'ul', 'menu_class' => 'nav'));
?>
```

There are several fallback functions that will be used when the user has not yet created a menu. If wp_nav_menu() is called but there are no menus defined, wp_page_menu() is substituted. If you would prefer another substitute, such as wp_list_categories(), you can add the name of your preferred function using the fallback_cb() parameter, as shown in Listing 12-21.

Listing 12-21. Changing the wp_nav_menu() Fallback Function

```php
<?php wp_nav_menu( 'sort_column=menu_order&fallback_cb=wp_list_categories' ); ?>
```

Page Lists and Page Menus

The wp_list_pages() function supports several parameters that allow you to change the way pages are listed. By default, all pages will be listed in alphabetical order. Listing 12-22 shows several alternatives. See the Codex page for wp_list_pages() (http://sleary.me/wp98[8]) for the full list of available parameters and their default settings.

Listing 12-22. Using the wp_list_pages() Function

```html
<!-- all pages in alphabetical order -->
<ul> <?php wp_list_pages(); ?> </ul>
<!-- all pages in menu order -->
<ul> <?php wp_list_pages('sort_column=menu_order'); ?> </ul>
<!-- to exclude a single page (in this case, the one with an ID of 12) -->
<ul> <?php wp_list_pages('sort_column=menu_order&exclude=12'); ?> </ul>
```

There's a second function that you can use for a few extra options in your page lists: wp_page_menu(). This is essentially a clone of wp_list_pages() that has just a few extra features. It includes the <ul> tags, so you don't have to specify those separately. It includes a menu_class parameter so you can still style the list using your own class names. This function also adds a "Home" link to the page list, as shown in Listing 12-23.

---

[8]http://codex.wordpress.org/Template_Tags/wp_list_pages

Listing 12-23. Using the `wp_page_menu()` Function

```
<!-- all pages in menu order, then alphabetically by page title -->
<?php wp_page_menu(); ?>
<!-- the above, plus a 'home' link, with a different class on the <ul> -->
<?php wp_page_menu('show_home=true&menu_class=nav'); ?>
```

These parameters give you a great deal of flexibility in creating your navigation menus, but you will quickly discover that WordPress's page management features are a little lacking when it comes to creating the navigation for a complicated site. Changing the page order, choosing which pages are included or excluded, and linking to external sites are all much harder to accomplish with page lists than with the navigation menus.

Category Lists

Much like `wp_list_pages()`, `wp_list_categories()` lets you customize the category list in a number of ways. By default, it lists all your categories in alphabetical order. A few of the function's optional parameters are shown in Listing 12-24.

Listing 12-24. Using the `wp_list_categories()` Function

```
<!-- all categories in alphabetical order -->
<ul> <?php wp_list_categories(); ?> </ul>
<!-- all categores in menu order: My Category Order plugin required -->
<ul> <?php wp_list_pages('sort_column=menu_order'); ?> </ul>
<!-- show only parent categories -->
<ul> <?php wp_list_categories('depth=1'); ?> </ul>
```

Unlike pages, categories don't have a menu order. You can add this feature with the My Category Order plugin.

Once you have chosen your navigation method and put the appropriate template tag in place, you can save `header.php`. It's time to return to `index.php` and work with the page content.

Comments

The `comments_template()` function works like an `include()` statement, but it's specific to one file: `comments.php`. (Some older themes might instead use `comments-popup.php`, which opened comments in a pop-up window.) On the home page or an archive list, it doesn't print anything. On a single post or page, it will display the list of comments and trackbacks (if there are any) and the comment form (if comments are allowed).

Comments can be displayed using the `wp_list_comments()` tag. Listing 12-25 shows a simple list of comments. (This is just a small part of the `comments.php` file.) This tag displays all the comments on a single post or page according to the options under Settings ➤ Discussion.

Listing 12-25. The Comment List

```
<h3 id="comments"><?php comments_number('No Comments', 'One Comment', '% Comments' );?> to
&#8220;<?php the_title(); ?>&#8221;</h3>

<div class="navigation">
        <div class="alignleft"><?php previous_comments_link() ?></div>
        <div class="alignright"><?php next_comments_link() ?></div>
</div>
```

```
<ol class="commentlist">
<?php wp_list_comments(); ?>
</ol>

<div class="navigation">
        <div class="alignleft"><?php previous_comments_link() ?></div>
        <div class="alignright"><?php next_comments_link() ?></div>
</div>
```

Listing comments is simple; it takes just one function. The comments template file, however, is complicated. That's because it needs to check for a lot of different conditions: whether comments are allowed, whether they've been closed, whether there are any comments, whether the user is logged in, and so forth.

Listing 12-26 shows the comments.php file from the University theme, which is almost identical to the default themes' corresponding files.

Listing 12-26. The University Theme's comments.php Template

```php
<?php
if ( post_password_required() )
        return;
?>

<div id="comments" class="comments-area">

        <?php if ( have_comments() ) : ?>
                <h2 class="comments-title">
                        <?php
                        printf( _nx( 'One thought on &ldquo;%2$s&rdquo;', '%1$s thoughts on
&ldquo;%2$s&rdquo;', get_comments_number(), 'comments title', 'twentythirteen' ),
number_format_i18n( get_comments_number() ), '<span>' . get_the_title() . '</span>' );
                        ?>
                </h2>

                <ol class="comment-list">
                        <?php
                                wp_list_comments( array(
                                        'style'       => 'ol',
                                        'format'      => 'html5',
                                        'short_ping'  => true,
                                        'avatar_size' => 50,
                                ) );
                        ?>
                </ol><!-- .comment-list -->

                <?php
                        // Are there comments to navigate through?
                        if ( get_comment_pages_count() > 1 && get_option( 'page_comments' ) ) :
                ?>
                <nav class="navigation comment-navigation" role="navigation">
                        <h1 class="screen-reader-text section-heading"><?php _e( 'Comment navigation',
'twentythirteen' ); ?></h1>
```

```
                    <div class="nav-previous"><?php previous_comments_link( __( '&larr;↪
Older Comments', 'twentythirteen' ) ); ?></div>
                    <div class="nav-next"><?php next_comments_link( __( 'Newer Comments &rarr;',
'twentythirteen' ) ); ?></div>
            </nav><!-- .comment-navigation -->
            <?php endif; // Check for comment navigation ?>

            <?php if ( ! comments_open() && get_comments_number() ) : ?>
            <p class="no-comments"><?php _e( 'Comments are closed.' , 'twentythirteen' ); ?></p>
            <?php endif; ?>

        <?php endif; // have_comments() ?>

        <?php comment_form( array( 'format' => 'html5' ) ); ?>

</div><!-- #comments -->
```

There's a lot going on here, so I'll take it one piece at a time.

First, if the post is password protected and the reader has not already entered the password, you have to prevent them from seeing the comments. This if statement prints an error message to the reader and exits without printing any comments.

Once that's out of the way, you begin a comment Loop. You do the usual check to see if there are any comments before you print anything, but if there are, you print a header containing the number of comments. This is done with PHP's sprintf() function, which has an odd syntax. You don't need to change this section, so I won't go into detail here, but you can always refer to the documentation at php.net/sprintf if necessary.

The next section checks to see if there's more than one page of comments. This depends entirely on the settings you chose back in Settings ➤ Discussion. If you chose not to split comments into multiple pages, nothing will happen here. If you did, however, this section prints the page navigation. This block of code will be repeated below the comments list as well.

Last, you display the comments themselves. Here, you see the wp_list_comments() function. Some older themes use a loop to display comments. You can do this if you wish, but wp_list_comments() makes it much easier to support threading, paging, avatars, and the other options in the Settings ➤ Discussion screen.

Once you print the navigation again, you're done with the if (have_comments()) portion of this Loop, but you're not done yet! You could print something in the event that there are no comments yet, but in this case you've chosen to just leave the comment area blank. However, next you need to print a message if comments have been closed. This is the message your readers will see if you turned off comments on an individual post after allowing them for a while, or if you chose to automatically close comments on older posts.

Once you have taken care of all that, you can print the comment form. The comment_form() function prints out a standard form and performs all the necessary checks to see whether comments are open. You could instead use a handcrafted form, as all themes did prior to version 3.0, but I recommend using the comment_form() tag with whatever styles you need to make its appearance match your theme.

Page Templates

If you've been following along and creating theme files as I go, your new theme now has six files:

- comments.php

- footer.php

- header.php

- index.php
- sidebar.php
- style.css

This is a great start. However, there's a lot more you can do to distinguish posts from pages, archives from single posts, and more.

To give you a taste of the different template files you're about to see, I'll create a new file, page.php, and copy the contents of index.php into it. Now I can make changes to the way pages are displayed without affecting posts. For example, on the University site, I don't want pages to display the author's byline. I'll remove that paragraph from page.php. I also don't want to accept comments on pages. Since I do want them on blog posts, I won't turn them off altogether in the settings; I'll just remove the comments section from page.php. Listing 12-27 shows my new page template. Save this file and view a page in your site. The author byline and comment form should be gone.

Listing 12-27. The University Theme's Page Template

```php
<?php if (have_posts()) : while (have_posts()) : the_post(); ?>

<div <?php post_class(); ?> id="post-<?php the_ID(); ?>">

    <h2><a href="<?php the_permalink() ?>" rel="bookmark" title="Permanent Link to
<?php the_title_attribute(); ?>"><?php the_title(); ?></a></h2>

        <p><?php the_content('Read more...'); ?></p>

        <p class="postmetadata after">
        <?php edit_post_link(__('Edit this entry' ), '<br /><span class="edit_link">',
' &raquo;</span>'); ?>
        </p>
</div> <!-- #post-n -->

<?php endwhile; else: ?>
        <p><?php _e('Sorry, no posts matched your criteria.'); ?></p>
<?php endif; ?>
```

These are just a few of the changes you can make based on the context of your content. To do more, you'll need to learn your way around the other template files you can use, and the hierarchy WordPress uses to determine which one is used to display each page in your site.

Template Files

I've shown you sample index.php and page.php files, and your theme now has several other files as well: header.php, footer.php, sidebar.php, and comments.php, not to mention the style.css file. However, as I mentioned earlier, there are many other theme files you can use to customize various portions of your site. A few, like header.php and searchform.php, do not represent a complete page view, but rather only a portion of a page. These are include files that are meant to be used within the other templates.

The template files are:

404.php	archive.php
archive-**type**.php	attachment.php
author.php	author-**id**.php
author-**nickname**.php	category.php
category-**id**.php	category-**slug**.php
comments.php (Include)	date.php
footer.php (Include)	front-page.php
functions.php	header.php (Include)
home.php	index.php (Required)
links.php	page.php
page-**id**.php	page-**name**.php
screenshot.png	search.php
searchform.php (Include)	sidebar.php (Include)
sidebar-**name**.php (Include)	single.php
single-**type**.php (including single-attachment.php)	style.css (Required)
tag.php	tag-**id**.php
tag-**slug**.php	taxonomy.php
taxonomy-**name**.php	taxonomy-**name**-**term**.php

It is also possible to have template files whose names correspond to attachments' MIME types. For example, image.php would be used for any image/* file type: image/jpeg, image/png, and so forth. I'll look more closely at attachment template files later in this chapter. See "Attachment Pages" for details.

Figuring out which file is used to display a page requires an understanding of the template hierarchy.

■ **Tip** You can use the Show Template plugin to identify the theme file that was used to generate a page. It adds a comment in the footer, using wp_footer(), giving the full path to the active template file.

Template Hierarchy

As you've seen, WordPress can use different template files to display posts and pages. In fact, there are dozens of possible template files for different contexts: category archives, author archives, even attachment pages for each type of uploaded file. All the template files exist in a hierarchy. The most specific possibility is used if it exists. If not, the next most specific file is used. In all cases, index.php serves as the fallback. That is, if a more specific template is not present, index.php will be used.

I'll show you the entire hierarchy, as of version 3.6. New types of templates are sometimes added to support new features. See http://sleary.me/wp48[9] for up-to-date information about the theme file hierarchy.

---

[9]http://codex.wordpress.org/Template_Hierarchy

The Home Page and Front Page

For your site's home page, the `front-page.php` template will be used, if it exists. This file will be used no matter what you have set as your home page display under Reading ➤ Settings; it is used either to display recent posts or a static page.

If you have chosen a static page as your home page, and you have designated a blog page to contain your most recent posts, `home.php` will be used to display that blog page.

If you have chosen to show your most recent posts on your home page and `front-page.php` does not exist, `home.php` will be used.

If neither `front-page.php` nor `home.php` exists, `index.php` will be used. It's also possible to use `index.php` as a unique home page template if your theme contains all the other possible archive templates, so that `index.php` is never used for any other page display. I don't recommend relying on this, though. New template files are added to the hierarchy as new features are introduced—tag-**id**.php and archive-**type**.php were both added in recent versions of WordPress, for example. While you might have all your bases covered for now, new scenarios requiring new templates will arise as WordPress gains new features.

Single Posts

For individual posts, WordPress will use `single.php`, if it exists. If not, `index.php` will be used.

There is no `single-id.php` or `single-slug.php` file. However, you can still style individual posts using body and post classes and conditional tags. Later in this chapter, you'll see how to style posts differently based on context.

Pages

The most specific page template is the one you chose in the Page Template drop-down option on the Edit Page screen. If you haven't chosen a template, WordPress will first look for page-**slug**.php, where `slug` is the page's slug. For example, `page-about.php` would be used for your About page.

If page-**slug**.php does not exist, WordPress will move on to page-**id**.php, where `id` is the ID of the page. For example, if you did not remove the Sample Page that was installed with WordPress, its template would be `page-2.php`.

Failing all of that, WordPress will use the generic page template, `page.php`. If that does not exist, `index.php` will be used instead.

Custom Post Types

To display individual views of custom post types, if you have any, WordPress will look for a file called single-**type**.php, where `type` is the slug of the custom post type. For example, if you created a post type called Movies with the slug `movies`, the specific theme file for that type would be (ungrammatically) `single-movies.php`.

If there is no theme file specific to the content type, `single.php` will be used, with `index.php` as the fallback.

For archives of custom post types, WordPress uses archive-**type**.php. If that does not exist, it falls back to `archive.php` and then `index.php`. The post type must have its `has_archive` argument set to `true`; otherwise the archive address (site name / post type slug, e.g. `http://example.com/`**type**`/`) will return a 404 "Not Found" error.

In Chapter 14, you'll learn how to create custom post types and their archives.

■ **Note** If a page exists with the same name as the post type, it will be displayed instead of the post type archive.

Category Archives

Much like page archives, WordPress will look first for the slug, then the ID, then a generic category template, and last archive.php and index.php.

1. category-**slug**.php

2. category-**id**.php

3. category.php

4. archive.php

5. index.php

Category archives have a little quirk: if you're looking at a category that has subcategories, posts from those subcategories will be mixed in with the posts from the parent category. Listing 12-28 shows a category archive template that first lists the child categories, then shows the posts assigned only to the parent category using the in_category() conditional.

Listing 12-28. Listing Subcategories and Limiting the Loop to the Parent Category

```
<h2 class="pagetitle"><?php single_cat_title(); ?></h2>
<?php
        $catid = get_query_var('cat');
?>
<ul class="subcategories">
        <?php $cats = get_categories('order=desc&title_li=&child_of='.$catid);
            foreach ($cats as $cat) { ?>
            <li>
            <h4><a href="<?php echo get_category_link( $cat->cat_ID ); ?>" rel="bookmark"↪
title="<?php echo $cat->cat_name; ?>"><?php echo $cat->cat_name; ?></a></h4>
        </li>
            <?php } ?>
</ul>
<?php if (have_posts()) : while (have_posts()) : the_post(); ?>
<?php if (in_category($catid) ) : ?>
    <h2 <?php post_class(); ?>><a href="<?php the_permalink() ?>" rel="bookmark"↪
title="Permanent Link to <?php the_title_attribute(); ?>"><?php the_title(); ?></a></h2>
    <?php the_content(); ?>
<?php endif; endwhile; ?>
```

Here, you use the get_query_var() function to find out which category you're looking at. You can use this function to retrieve any of the variables that make up the invisible Loop query, but since you know you're working with a category archive, it's the category ID you're interested in.

Once you have the ID, you can use get_categories() to print a list of all the current category's subcategories. Then you can go into your typical Loop, but you've added a conditional tag (which is discussed under "Conditional Tags" in this chapter) that will print the title and content only if the post is in the parent category, not any of its subcategories.

Tag Archives

Tags work much like categories: slug, then ID, then tag, then `archive.php`, and last, `index.php`.

1. `tag-`**`slug`**`.php`

2. `tag-`**`id`**`.php`

3. `tag.php`

4. `archive.php`

5. `index.php`

Taxonomy Archives

A "taxonomy" is a geeky way of saying "a new group of categories or tags." It's a way of separating pools of tags. For example, if you were writing about movies, you would probably tag them with the names of actors, directors, and genres. Creating custom taxonomies lets you separate those tags into logical groups, rather than having them together in one long and confusing list. I'll show you how to create custom taxonomies in Chapter 14.

WordPress will first look for a `taxonomy-`**`taxonomy-term`**`.php` file. To use Actors as an example, the taxonomy is actors and the slug for Will Smith's tag might be `will-smith`. WordPress would look for `taxonomy-people-will-smith.php`. If an archive specifically for Will doesn't exist, WordPress will look for a generic actors archive, `taxonomy-actors.php`. If that doesn't exist, it will try `taxonomy.php`, then `archive.php`, and last, `index.php`.

Post Format Archives

WordPress has three built-in taxonomies: categories, tags, and post formats. While categories and tags have their own template files, as you have seen, WordPress relies on the generic taxonomy templates for post format archives.

The post format taxonomy name is `post-format`. The slug for each format is `post-format-`**`name`**. For example, the video format's slug is `post-format-video`. Its archive template file would therefore be the redundant-sounding `post-format-post-format-video.php`.

Author Archives

It's possible to create a different archive template for every individual author. WordPress will look for `author-`**`nickname`**`.php` first. If your username is Joe, your ID is 3, and your nickname is joe, `author-joe.php` is the most specific theme file for your archives. If that file does not exist, WordPress will then look for `author-`**`id`**`.php`, making `author-3.php` the file for Joe's archives.

If neither of those files exists, WordPress will use the generic author template, `author.php`. Failing that, it will use `archive.php`, and then `index.php` as a last resort.

In an author template, you might use a special sidebar to display a short bio of the author in question. You saw how to access the author profile information directly in Chapter 10; in Chapter 13, you'll learn how to add new fields to author profiles.

Listing 12-29 shows how an extra sidebar might be included in an `author.php` template to contain the user's bio and any other author-specific information you'd like to display.

Listing 12-29. Including a Sidebar File with Author Information

```php
<?php get_sidebar(); ?>          // sidebar.php
<?php get_sidebar('author'); ?> // sidebar-author.php
```

Date-Based Archives

There is just one date-specific archive file, `date.php`. There are no individual template files for month, year, or day displays, but you can customize this file to display different things for each context using conditional tags, which you will see in the "Conditional Tags" section of this chapter.

If `date.php` does not exist, `archive.php` or `index.php` will be used.

Search Results

If it exists, the `search.php` file will display your search results. Otherwise, `index.php` will be used.

Make sure your `search.php` file contains the `posts_nav_link()` function. Otherwise, your visitors will have no way to reach any pages of search results other than the first!

If your search results use the same loop as your home page, your visitors will see the full text of your posts and pages in the list of results. That might be a lot of text! Instead, consider using `the_excerpt()`.

Pages don't have excerpts, so this will require a little setup. Remember that posts and pages share the same database table, which means they really have all the same fields, even if you don't see them in the edit screens. The PJW Page Excerpt plugin adds the excerpt box to the Page ➤ Edit screen. With this in place, you can write brief summaries of your pages for the search results list.

In your `search.php` file, replace `the_content()` with `the_excerpt()`. You should see a much shorter, more user-friendly search results page.

Error 404 (File Not Found) Page

There is just one file, `404.php`, that is used to display a "File not found" error message. If this file does not exist, the contents of the `else()` statement of the other files' Loops will be displayed, as shown in Listing 12-30.

Listing 12-30. Displaying the "Not Found" Error Message in Theme Files Other Than `404.php`

```
<?php if (have_posts()) : while (have_posts()) : the_post(); ?>
      <h2 id="post-<?php the_ID(); ?>">
      <a href="<?php the_permalink() ?>" rel="bookmark" title="Permanent link ↪
to <?php the_title(); ?>"><?php the_title(); ?></a>
</h2>
      <?php the_content(); ?>
      <?php wp_link_pages(); ?>
      <div class="commentblock">
      <?php comments_template(); ?>
      </div><!--commentblock-->
      <?php  endwhile; ?>

   <div class="navigation">
       <div class="alignleft"><?php posts_nav_link(); ?></div>
       <div class="clear"><!-- --></div>
   </div><!-- .navigation -->
<?php else: ?>
      <h2>Not Found</h2>
      <p>The posts you were looking for could not be found.</p>
<?php endif; ?>
```

Attachment Pages

When you upload media files, you have the option of linking them to a post page rather than the file URL. Attachment pages are shown when files are linked to post pages.

You can create different attachment pages for different media types. The name of the MIME type will be the name of your file; you could have `image.php`, `video.php`, `audio.php`, and `application.php` as well as a generic `attachment.php` file.

If no attachment page file exists, `single.php` will be used, and as a last resort, `index.php`.

Screenshots and Other Image Files

Other than `style.css` and the various PHP template files, the only file that must match the naming convention is `screenshot.png`. This is the thumbnail preview of your theme that's used in the Appearance ➤ Themes screen. The screenshot should be in PNG format, and should be 300 pixels wide by 225 tall.

Screenshots are not required, but they are recommended if other people will manage the themes on your site. A screenshot is required if you intend to distribute your theme on `wordpress.org`. Furthermore, `wordpress.org` requires that the image be an actual screenshot of a site using your theme, not a logo or other graphic you have designed to represent your theme's branding.

For all images used in the theme itself, you may use whatever formats and file names you like. I recommend grouping them into a subdirectory, but this is not required.

Conditional Tags

You've already seen how the body and post class functions can be used to apply different styles based on which content is being viewed. However, sometimes styling isn't enough. WordPress provides a number of conditional tags you can use to modify the content itself based on the context.

Conditional tags can be used in any template, but they're especially useful in the include files—the header, sidebar, and footer—where using conditional tags let you handle alternatives without creating separate files. Table 12-1 lists the conditional tags and their arguments. In the next few sections, you'll see several ways of using these conditional tags.

Table 12-1. *Arguments Accepted by the Conditional Tags*

Conditional	ID	Slug	Title	Array	Other
is_single	X	X	X	X	
is_singular					Post type
post_type_exists					Post type
is_post_type_hierarchical					Post type
is_post_type_archive					Post type
is_sticky	X				
is_page	X	X			
is_page_template					File name
is_category	X	X	X	X	
in_category	X				

(*continued*)

Table 12-1. (*continued*)

Conditional	ID	Slug	Title	Array	Other
is_tag		X	X	X	
has_tag		X	X	X	
is_tax		X	X	X	
taxonomy_exists		X			
has_term		X	X		
is_author	X	Username	Nickname	X	
has_excerpt	X				
has_nav_menu					Menu location
is_active_sidebar	X	X			Number
is_main_site	X				
is_super_admin	X				
is_plugin_active					Subdirectory
current_theme_supports		X			

There are four groups of conditionals: is*, in*, has*, and *open. Is_sticky() and is_paged() refer to properties of individual posts or pages. All the other is* functions are true if the currently viewed page is of that type. For example, is_single() returns true if it appears in a single post archive template. The is_front_page() function returns true if you're viewing the site's home page, whether you've set the Reading options to display blog posts or a single page, whereas is_home() is true only on the main blog posts page, whether that's your site home page or some other page. To accommodate both your users' possible choices, you should use both conditional tags in most cases, as shown in Listing 12-31.

Listing 12-31. Checking Whether the User Is Viewing the Home Page of Posts or the Front Page (Either a Static Page or the First Page of Posts)

```
if ( is_home() || is_front_page() ) {
        // this code runs only on the home/front page
}
```

The in*, has*, and *open functions refer to properties. For example, comments_open() is true if displayed on the archive page for a post that allows comments. The in_category() function is true only if a post has been assigned directly to the category in question; the function does not check subcategories.

Like all WordPress template tags, conditionals are really just functions. Most of these functions can be used inside the Loop or in a specific archive template without arguments. Outside the Loop—that is, in an advanced theme function like you'll see in Chapter 13, or in a plugin—you need to provide some identifying information about the post, page, author, tag, category, or taxonomy term you're interested in. Table 12-1 lists the various arguments that each function accepts.

The following conditional tags do not accept arguments; they are true if the corresponding archive template is being used to display the current page.

```
is_home
is_admin
is_search
```

```
is_feed
is_404
is_comments_popup
is_front_page
is_attachment
is_archive
is_preview
is_trackback
is_new_day
is_day
is_date
is_year
is_time
is_month
```

The following conditional tags do not accept arguments at all. They return `true` or `false` based on information about the currently viewed page or the site in general.

```
comments_open
pings_open
is_paged
is_active_sidebar
is_multi_author
is_multisite
```

Creating Contextual Sidebars with Conditional Tags

Most themes use separate files to display posts and pages rather than using `index.php` for both. There are simple changes, like removing the category and tag listings from the page display or moving the date tag (or removing it altogether). There are many other changes you could make, though. For example, you could use the conditional tags `if_page()` and `if_single()` in your sidebar to display different sidebars for posts and pages. That way, you can display post-related things like archives, categories, and tag clouds only on your post archives and use the page sidebars to list the page's children (if it has any) or media attachments. Listing 12-32 shows a `sidebar.php` file that includes various sidebars depending on the type of page being viewed.

Listing 12-32. A `sidebar.php` File That Calls Other Sidebar Files Conditionally

```
<div id="sidebar">
<?php
if ( is_page() )
      get_sidebar( 'page' );
else
      get_sidebar();
?>
</div>
```

Theme Functions

You've probably realized by now that PHP functions can be placed in any theme file. That means you can create functions right in your template; however, if it's something you'll want to reuse in other templates, it's best to put it in the theme functions file, `functions.php`. This file doesn't correspond to any particular page view and is never loaded by itself. Instead, it acts as a container for functions that should be available to every other template in the theme. The functions in this file act like miniature plugins, except they don't require activation.

■ **Tip**   If your function is something you would want to reuse when you change themes, you should create a plugin for it instead of placing it in `functions.php`. See Chapter 13 for details.

The theme functions file is used to register widget areas, enable support for features like custom header images and post featured images, and to apply any theme-specific filters to template tags like the_excerpt(). I'll show you some of the most common uses of the theme functions file.

Enabling Widgets

The functions.php file was added to the theme hierarchy in order to support the widget feature in WordPress 1.5. For each widget area you want in your theme, you need to register an array telling WordPress what the area should be called and what code should be displayed before and after the widget block and title.

I'll show you an example. The code in Listing 12-33 defines two widget areas. The results are shown in Figure 12-5.

Listing 12-33. Defining Two Widget Areas

```
if ( function_exists('register_sidebar') ) {
        register_sidebar(array(
          'name' => 'Primary Sidebar',
          'id' => 'primary-sidebar',
          'description' => 'Side column, left.',
          'before_widget' => '<div id="%1$s" class="widget clearfloat %2$s">',
          'after_widget' => '</div>',
          'before_title' => '<h2 class="widgettitle">',
          'after_title' => '</h2>',
    ));
        register_sidebar(array(
          'name' => 'Home Page Slideshow',
          'id' => 'home-slideshow-sidebar',
          'description' => 'Above the main content.',
          'before_widget' => '<div id="%1$s" class="widget clearfloat %2$s">',
          'after_widget' => '</div>',
          'before_title' => '<h2 class="widgettitle">',
          'after_title' => '</h2>',
    ));
}
```

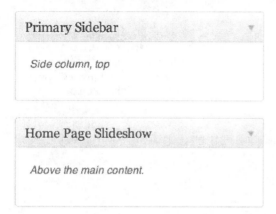

Figure 12-5. *The widget areas defined by Listing 12-31*

The classes and IDs in the widget code follow the PHP sprintf() syntax and allow each widget to have a unique ID and a class based on the widget type. For example, a text widget placed third in a widget area, after two other widgets, would open with the list item tag shown in Listing 12-34.

Listing 12-34. A Text Widget Generated by Listing 12-33

```
<li id="text-3" class="widget-container widget_text">
        <h3 class="widgettitle">This is a widget</h3>
        <div class="textwidget">
                <p>And this is its text!</p>
        </div>
</li>
```

You can define as many widget areas as you like. They don't have to appear in the sidebar; many themes have widget areas in the footer, and some have them in the header (usually intended to contain navigation menu widgets or the search form).

Enabling Menus

If you want to support custom menus in your new theme, you'll need to add the code in Listing 12-35 to your theme files.

Listing 12-35. Enabling Navigation Menus

```
// in functions.php:
add_theme_support('nav-menus');
```

Without this line in your theme file, the Appearance ➤ Menu screen will not let you create menus. Instead, it will display a message that the current theme does not support the menu feature.

Enabling Featured Images

If you don't see a Featured Image box on your Edit Posts screen, you can enable one by adding the code in Listing 12-36 to your functions.php file. Featured images were known as post thumbnails prior to version 3.0, and the theme functions still use the old terminology. Once you've added this line to your functions file, refresh your post editing screen. You should now see the Featured Image meta box (Figure 12-6) near the bottom of the right column.

Listing 12-36. Enabling Featured Images

```
add_theme_support( 'post-thumbnails' );
```

Figure 12-6. *The featured image meta box in the Post ➤ Edit screen*

Enabling Custom Backgrounds and Headers

It's very easy to enable custom backgrounds for your theme. Just add the line in Listing 12-37 to your theme's functions.php file.

Listing 12-37. Enabling Custom Backgrounds in functions.php

```
add_theme_support('custom-background');
```

That's all! Once you save this change, you'll see a new menu item under Appearance—Custom Background—and you can go choose your background image. You don't have to add anything to your stylesheet. The styles in Listing 12-1 (at the beginning of this chapter) are automatically added via wp_head().

Adding support for custom headers is a bit more complicated. You will probably need to define some defaults: an image to be shown if the user hasn't yet chosen one, the image dimensions, and whether the text (site title and description) should be displayed in addition to the image. Listing 12-38 shows everything you need to add to your functions.php file

Listing 12-38. Enabling Custom Headers in functions.php

```
$defaults = array(
        'default-image'          => '',
```

```
            'random-default'           => false,
            'width'                     => 0,
            'height'                    => 0,
            'flex-height'               => false,
            'flex-width'                => false,
            'default-text-color'        => '',
            'header-text'               => true,
            'uploads'                   => true,
            'wp-head-callback'          => '',
            'admin-head-callback'       => '',
            'admin-preview-callback'    => '',
);
add_theme_support( 'custom-header', $defaults );
```

The styles function will include a few CSS rules in the page header. Since they will be inserted at the wp_head() hook, after the theme stylesheet link, they'll override its values.

Changing Excerpt Length and Ellipsis

Listing 12-39 shows two optional filters that help customize the display of excerpts in your theme. The first set of functions changes the excerpt length simply by returning the desired number of words as an integer. The second set replaces the default text appended to auto-generated excerpts ('[...]') with a link to the complete post.

Listing 12-39. Changing Excerpt Length and Adding "Read More" Link

```
// Control excerpt length
function my_excerpt_length( $length ) {
        return 100;
}
add_filter( 'excerpt_length', 'my _excerpt_length' );

// Make a nice read more link on excerpts
function my_excerpt_more($more) {
        return '&hellip; <a href="'. get_permalink() . '">' . 'More &rarr;' . '</a>';
}
add_filter( 'excerpt_more', 'my_excerpt_more' );
```

Figures 12-7 and 12-8 show the same excerpt first without and then with the two filters in Listing 12-39.

New University Department Website

Posted by Stephanie Leary

Bacon ipsum dolor sit amet beef ribs pork chop pork andouille. Pancetta drumstick ham hock, beef ribs leberkas pork loin sausage short ribs sirloin doner turducken. Bacon filet mignon pastrami doner, venison pig turducken shankle meatloaf beef. Tri-tip salami sirloin cow, pork bacon ball tip ham biltong. Tri-tip pork belly ribeye short loin pancetta t-bone... (Continue reading)

Filed under News
Edit this entry »

Figure 12-7. *The unfiltered excerpt*

New University Department Website

Posted by Stephanie Leary

Bacon ipsum dolor sit amet beef ribs pork chop pork andouille. Pancetta drumstick ham hock, beef ribs leberkas pork loin sausage short ribs sirloin doner turducken. Bacon filet mignon pastrami doner, venison pig turducken shankle meatloaf beef. Tri-tip salami sirloin cow, pork bacon ball tip ham biltong. Tri-tip pork belly ribeye short loin pancetta t-bone shoulder pork loin bresaola turducken pastrami tongue pig bacon chicken. Kielbasa shank shankle pastrami andouille beef ribeye pig fatback corned beef shoulder. Doner pork turducken, ball tip tongue bresaola fatback capicola beef pastrami shankle turkey spare ribs. Strip steak prosciutto frankfurter, cow chuck andouille pork... More →

Filed under News
Edit this entry ›

Figure 12-8. *The filtered excerpt*

Visual Editor Styles

If you've used any of the recent default themes, from Twenty Ten through Twenty Thirteen, you might have noticed that the text you add to the Visual editor looks almost exactly like the published page, whereas with most other themes, what you see in the Visual editor is somewhat different.

The default themes accomplish this by including a second stylesheet specifically for the Visual editor, `editor-style.css`. It's optional, but it's a fantastic feature for your users.

This stylesheet should include any styles that affect text, including headings, links, block quotes, ordered and unordered lists, and images and captions. If the content area in your theme includes a background color, include that. Check your work in the Visual editor until your editor stylesheet is as close as possible to the published page.

To add your editor stylesheet, you don't have to go through the usual enqueueing business. Simply add `add_editor_style();` to your `functions.php` file. One line and you're done!

Listing Child Pages

Often, as you arrange your pages into a hierarchy, you'll find that you want to automatically list a page's child pages in the content. We can do this using a filter, `the_content`.

Listing 12-40 shows how to create the child pages filter. In this case, you'll assume that the filter should operate only on single pages; if the page content is shown as part of a Loop, you probably don't want to clutter the Loop display with a bunch of page lists.

Listing 12-40. Appending Child Pages Using a Filter

```
function append_child_pages( $content ) {
        if ( is_page() )
            return $content.'<ul>'.wp_list_pages('title_li=&child_of='.get_the_ID()).'</ul>';
        return $content;
}
add_filter( 'the_content', 'append_child_pages' );
```

The filter passes the original post content to our function as the $content variable. Here, I've checked to see if the user is looking at a page with the `is_page()` conditional. If so, I'll return the original content with the list of child pages appended. Since `wp_list_pages()` prints list items without the surrounding list tags, you have to add those manually.

I've used get_the_ID() to find the ID of the current page so I can include that in my arguments as the parent ID of the pages we want. Last, at the end of the function, I'll return the original $content. I could have prefaced this with else, but it's not necessary; this line will execute only if nothing was returned above it.

You could easily alter this function to print the child pages only if the parent page's content is empty, as shown in Listing 12-41.

Listing 12-41. *Appending Child Pages Only if the Parent Page Is Empty*

```
function append_child_pages( $content ) {
        if ( is_page() && empty( $content ) )
            return $content.'<ul>'.wp_list_pages( 'title_li=&child_of='.get_the_ID()).'</ul>';
        return $content;
}
add_filter( 'the_content', 'append_child_pages' );
```

Modifying Themes the Right Way: Child Themes

Child themes are also useful if you've downloaded a theme from the repository and you want to keep up with any updates the author releases, but you need to customize it for your own site.

Child themes are modifications of other themes. They have their own directories and you upload them just like a separate theme, but they depend on their parent themes, and they won't work if the parent is not installed. All your modifications to the original theme will take place in the child theme, so the parent theme remains untouched—and you can update it without wiping out your changes.

Child themes must include at least a style.css file. All other files are optional, even index.php. If a required file is not present in the child theme directory, WordPress will look for the file in the parent theme directory. In other words, you need to create files only when you want to override the parent theme's display. Figure 12-9 illustrates how a parent and child theme are combined to display a site.

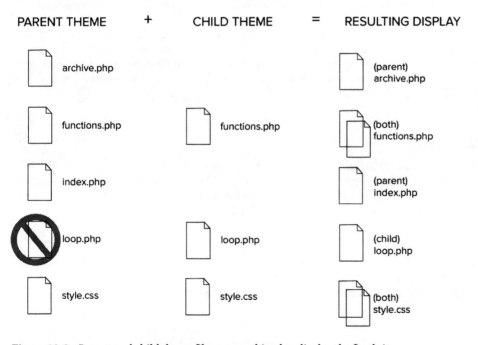

Figure 12-9. *Parent and child theme files are combined to display the final site*

A typical child theme might contain three files: `style.css`, `loop.php`, and `functions.php`. The style and functions files from both themes are used. The loop file in the child theme replaces the parent theme's loop file. All the other files not present in the child theme are filled in using the files from the parent theme.

Stylesheets

The child theme's comment block requires one additional line: the Template. This should be the name of the directory containing your parent theme, as shown in Listing 12-42.

Listing 12-42. Importing the Parent Theme Styles

```
/*
Theme Name: Sophomoric
Description: Child theme for the university department's faculty
Version: 1.0
Author: Stephanie Leary
Author URI: http://stephanieleary.com
Template: university
*/

@import url(../university/style.css);
```

Child themes' stylesheets take advantage of the cascade feature of CSS. In short, stylesheet files added to a page with a `<link>` tag override styles added via the `@import` rule. You can override individual styles from the imported file by adding the same selectors, or more specific ones, in your linked stylesheet. In your child theme, therefore, you'll import the parent theme's stylesheet first, then add new styles of your own.

The first line of your child theme, after the required comment block, should import the parent theme's stylesheet. If the parent theme contains multiple stylesheets, you should include them all, unless you plan to replace them with your own.

If you want to replace the parent theme's styles entirely, or you plan to use just a handful of them, you may omit the `@import` statement and simply copy and paste the styles you want to use from the parent theme. This will be more efficient than loading the parent stylesheet file only to override all its styles in the child theme. The `@import` statement is optional; as long as the parent theme's directory name appears in the `Template` line of the comment block, the child theme will work correctly.

Child Theme Functions

Be careful with the theme functions file! If you include one in the child theme, *both* `functions.php` files will be executed, so be careful not to duplicate any functions from the parent theme, or you'll see fatal errors. If the functions in the parent theme have been wrapped in `if (function_exists(...))` statements, as shown in Listing 12-43, you can safely replace them with your own, since your theme functions file will be called first.

Listing 12-43. Replacing a Parent Theme's Functions

```
// parent theme function:
if ( !function_exists( 'edu_simple_slideshow' ) )
        function edu_simple_slideshow( $parent ) {
        // ...
        }
```

```
// child theme function will be used instead
// because it exists before parent theme's functions are called
function edu_simple_slideshow( $parent ) {
//...
}
```

Child themes can also override their parents by removing hooked functions and/or adding their own. To change the excerpt example you saw earlier in Listing 12-39, you could remove the parent theme's hooked excerpt filter and add a new one, as shown in Listing 12-44.

Listing 12-44. Removing a Parent Theme's Filter and Adding a New One in a Child Theme Functions File

```
remove_filter( 'excerpt_length', 'edu_excerpt_length' );
add_filter( 'excerpt_length', 'sophomoric_excerpt_length' );
function sophomoric_excerpt_length( $length ) {
    return 40;
}
```

Parent and Child Theme Paths

WordPress offers six functions that will print URLs to the two theme directories or stylesheet files (Listing 12-45). These are helpful when you want to reference background images, include or import other CSS files, or enqueue scripts.

In these functions, stylesheet refers to the child theme, and template refers to its parent.

Listing 12-45. Getting URLs for Parent and Child Theme Stylesheets and Directories

```
<?php
echo get_stylesheet_uri();              // Child theme style.css URL
echo get_stylesheet_directory_uri();    // Child theme directory URL
echo get_stylesheet_directory();        // Child theme directory file path, for use in PHP
echo get_template_uri();                // Parent theme style.css URL
echo get_template_directory_uri();      // Parent theme directory URL
echo get_template_directory;            // Parent theme directory file path, for use in PHP
?>
```

Modifying the Loop: An Introduction to the Query

Normally, the Loop generates a list of posts based on the context of the page being viewed (e.g., home page, archive, search results) and your Reading settings. To modify what the Loop displays, you need to change the invisible database query that defines your Loop.

Every query—you can have more than one per page, in some cases—is an instance of the WP_Query class. This class has a huge set of parameters, as shown below:

- post_type
- post_status
- offset
- showposts [deprecated; use posts_per_page]
- posts_per_page

- posts_per_archive_page [overrides posts_per_page on archives and search results]
- nopaging [boolean; disables pagination if true]
- paged
- perm [readable or editable; returns posts for which the user has the specified capability]
- ignore_sticky_posts [excludes stickies if true]
- post_parent
- order
- orderby
- year
- monthnum
- w [week number, 0-53]
- day
- hour
- minute
- second
- post__in [array]
- post__not_in [array]
- p [post ID]
- name
- page_id
- pagename
- author
- author_name
- cat
- category_name
- category__in [array]
- category__not_in [array]
- category__and [array]
- tag
- tag_id
- tag__and [array]
- tag__in [array]
- tag_slug__and [array]

- tag_slug__in [array]
- tax_query [array, containing:]
  - taxonomy
  - field
  - terms [ID, string, or array of either]
  - include_children [boolean]
  - operator [IN, NOT IN, or AND]
- meta_key
- meta_value
- meta_value_num
- meta_compare [operator]
- meta_query [array, containing:]
  - taxonomy
  - field
  - terms [ID, string, or array of either]
  - include_children [boolean]
  - operator [IN, NOT IN, or AND]
- fields [id or id=>parent; specifies which fields to return. Defaults to all.]
- no_found_rows [boolean; disables SQL_CALC_FOUND_ROWS if true]
- cache_results [boolean]
- update_post_term_cache [boolean]
- update_post_meta_cache [boolean]

The tax_query array allows you to specify more than one set of taxonomy parameters, which means (using our earlier movie example) you can query posts that have both an particular actor and genre, or posts that have one actor but not another. The meta_query array does the same thing for custom fields. For more information about WP_Query and all its possible parameters, see its Codex page (http://sleary.me/wp92[10]).

When WordPress runs a query, it caches the results for a while so it can serve up the results more quickly if the same query is run again. The various cache-related parameters allow you to disable this caching. See Thomas Griffin's article on optimizing WordPress queries (http://sleary.me/wp49[11]) for more information.

You can combine most of these parameters to further customize your Loops. I'll demonstrate a handful of the most common Loop modifications. I hope these examples will give you the foundation you need to create your own custom Loops.

---

[10]http://codex.wordpress.org/Class_Reference/WP_Query
[11]http://thomasgriffinmedia.com/blog/2012/10/optimize-wordpress-queries

Viewing the Query

The hardest part of working with the query is that you can't see it! Or can you?

The Debug Bar Extender plugin, which you saw briefly in Chapter 11, lets you inspect the query object on every page view (Figure 12-10). Note that in order to use Debug Bar Extender, you must first install Debug Bar.

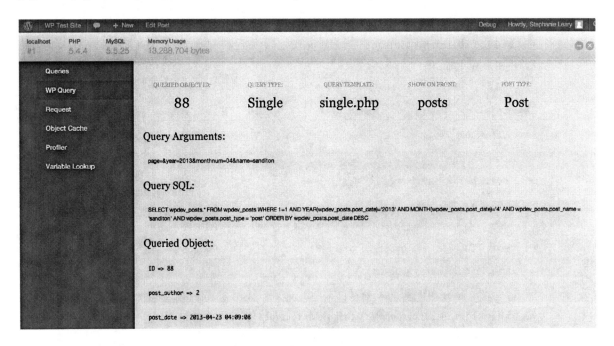

Figure 12-10. Debug Bar Extender's view of the query object

You can also dump the query to the screen, but be warned: it's very long, with about 200 items for a single post or page. Among other things, you'll be able to see the actual MySQL query that was run in order to get the results you're seeing. The query object also contains the complete HTML content of every post in the Loop, so you'll want to view source in your browser to inspect the object rather than relying on what's displayed; some things might be hidden by the HTML tags in the content. Listing 12-46 shows how to dump the query to the screen. You could place this code anywhere in a single archive template, or somewhere near the Loop in an index or archive template. Listing 12-47 shows the first few lines of the query object that's returned for a single post page.

Listing 12-46. Dumping the Query to the Screen

```
global $wp_query;
var_dump( $wp_query );
```

Listing 12-47. A Single Post's $wp_query Object (Partial)

```
object(WP_Query)#124 (47) {
  ["query"]=> array(4) {
    ["page"]=>  string(0) ""
    ["year"]=>  string(4) "2013"
    ["monthnum"]=>  string(2) "04"
    ["name"]=>  string(10) "test-audio"
  }
```

```
  ["query_vars"]=> array(59) {
  ...
}
```

Debug Bar Extender makes it much easier to inspect your query, but I encourage you to use the var_dump() method at least a few times to get a feel for what's included.

Modifying the Query

Modifying the Loop display involves changing the query parameters, preferably before it runs, to avoid duplicating queries and slowing down your site. To do that, we use the pre_get_posts action. Listing 12-48 shows a simple example of a function hooked to pre_get_posts that prevents a single category from displaying on the home page using the is_home() conditional tag. This code should be placed in your functions.php file.

Listing 12-48. Removing a Single Category from the Loop on the Home Page

```php
add_action( 'pre_get_posts', 'scl_exclude_category_seven' );

function scl_exclude_category_seven( $query ) {
        if ( is_home() ) {
                $query->set( 'cat', -7 );
        }

        return $query;
}
```

Looping Through All Children of a Page

This query (Listing 12-49) illustrates how to combine several arguments. Here, you want to list pages instead of posts, so use post_type to grab those. You don't want all the pages, just the children of the current page, so use the post_parent attribute with get_the_ID(). Then you need to sort them by menu_order, an attribute unique to pages, and list them in ascending order, rather than the default descending. Last, to make sure you get all the children of the current page without bumping into the per-page limit set in the Reading Settings screen, set posts_per_page to -1. Setting posts_per_page to a negative value removes the per-page limit, thus showing all the posts at once.

Listing 12-49. A Page Template File with a Second Loop Showing Children of the Current Page, with Thumbnails

```php
<?php
/*
Template Name: Page with Child Page List
*/
?>
<?php get_header(); ?>

<div id="main">

<?php if (have_posts()) : while (have_posts()) : the_post(); ?>
<div class="post" id="<?php echo $post->post_name; ?>">
        <h2><a href="<?php the_permalink(); ?>"
title="<?php the_title_attribute(); ?>"><?php the_title(); ?></a>
</h2>
```

```php
<?php the_content(); ?>

        <?php
        // LOOP 2: children of the current page, with thumbnails
        $loop2 = new WP_Query( array(
                            'posts_per_page' => -1,
                            'child_of' => get_the_ID(),
                            'order' => ASC,
                            'orderby' => 'menu_order'
                            ) );
        while ($loop2->have_posts()) : $loop2->the_post(); ?>
        <li <?php post_class(); ?> id="post-<?php the_ID(); ?>">
         <h3><a href="<?php the_permalink() ?>" rel="bookmark" title="Permanent Link
to <?php the_title_attribute(); ?>"><?php the_title(); ?></a></h3>
                    <?php the_post_thumbnail(); ?>
      </li>
        <?php endwhile; ?>

</div><!-- .post -->
<?php endwhile; ?>
<?php else: ?>
    <p>Sorry, these posts could not be found.</p>
<?php endif; ?>
</div><!-- #main -->

<?php get_sidebar(); ?>
<?php get_footer(); ?>
```

Listing Attached Files

You can display all the attached files of a post without going to the trouble of inserting each one into the post content. The required code looks very much like a second Loop, as shown in Listing 12-50. This could be placed inside the main Loop, perhaps just after the_content().

Listing 12-50. Listing a Post's Attached Files Inside the Loop

```php
<?php
    $attachments = get_children(array(
            'post_type' => 'attachment',
            'posts_per_page' => -1,
            'post_status' => 'inherit',
            'post_parent' => get_the_ID()
            ));
    if ($attachments) { ?>
        <ul class="attachments">         <?php
            foreach ($attachments as $attachment) {
                    if (substr($attachment->post_mime_type, 0, 5) != 'image') {
                        $type = sanitize_html_class($attachment->post_mime_type);
                        echo '<li class='.esc_attr($type).'>';
                        the_attachment_link($attachment->ID, false);
```

```
                                echo '</li>';
                        }
                }
        ?> </ul>
<?php } ?>
```

The get_children() function can also be used to display child pages, but here you've used the post_type parameter to limit the list to attachments. Setting the posts_per_page parameter to -1 ensures that you get all attachments, and the post_parent parameter is set to the current post's ID so that you get only those attachments that were uploaded to this particular post.

As you loop through the returned attachment objects, you need to skip over the images, since those will work better with the [gallery] shortcode shown in Chapter 4. (You could use a similar if() statement to exclude any other type of file.) For the rest of the attached files, you need to clean up the MIME type a little bit for use with CSS. You use the attachment's MIME type as the list item class, which allows you to style each link with a file icon background image. In order to get a valid class name, however, you replace the slash in the original MIME type (e.g., application/pdf) with a hyphen using PHP's str_replace() function.

You separate the_attachment_link() instead of placing it in the echo statement because it echoes by default.

Listing 12-51 provides a few examples of the CSS you might use to style the attachment links, using the same set of icons WordPress uses in the media manager (they're located in /wp-includes/images/crystal). The end result is shown in Figure 12-11.

Listing 12-51. CSS for Listing 12-6

```
ul.attachments li {
        list-style: none;
}
ul.attachments li a {
        display: block;
        padding-left: 50px;
        line-height: 60px;
        min-height: 60px;
        background-position-top: 0;
        background-position-left: 0;
        background-repeat: no-repeat;
        background-image: url(/wp-includes/images/crystal/archive.png);  /* default */
}
ul.attachments li.audiompeg a {
        background-image: url(/wp-includes/images/crystal/audio.png);
}
ul.attachments li.applicationvndms-excel a {
        background-image: url(/wp-includes/images/crystal/spreadsheet.png);
}
```

loin venison fatback. Capicola rump tenderloin, ground round pastrami chuck chicken turducken prosciutto corned beef ham hock shankle shank pork loin spare ribs. Capicola filet mignon t-bone pork chop kielbasa tail.

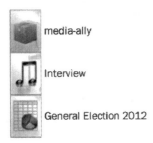

media-ally

Interview

General Election 2012

Edit this entry »

Figure 12-11. *The styled list of post attachments*

Multiple Loops

Now that you know how to create specialized Loops, the next logical step is to display several of these loops on your home page. Showing multiple, modified Loops is the key to "magazine" layouts, which treat categories like departments or columns in magazines and newspapers. Each category gets its own section of the page. The demo theme does this to some extent, and I'll demonstrate how its three category-specific loops work.

Resetting the Query

All the multiple query examples you've seen so far have used a second WP_Query object. Once you've modified a Loop query, it stays modified! Therefore, before you start a new Loop, you need to reset the query. Otherwise, your new modifications will operate on the posts already returned by your first query—and that leads to some very unpredictable results. Fortunately, resetting the query takes just one line of code, as shown in Listing 12-52.

Listing 12-52. Resetting the Query

```
<?php wp_reset_query(); ?>
```

That's it! Remember to reset the query in between each of your Loops to avoid strange errors in your advanced layouts.

A Loop for Each Category

Now that you've reset your query, it's time to create that magazine layout. There are various ways to accomplish this, depending on how you've set up your content. Perhaps you've created a hierarchy of pages, and you want to show those instead. For the moment, however, let's assume that you're using categories to segregate your posts into different departments, since this is the most common scenario. Once you see how this works, you should be able to adapt this code to your needs using some of the other Loop examples in this chapter.

You could use get_all_category_ids() to fetch an array of IDs, and then loop through each one. However, this is not a very flexible solution. If you have a deep hierarchy of categories, it's unlikely that you actually want to loop through every one of them on your home page. More likely, you really want a box for every top-level category, as illustrated in Figure 12-12.

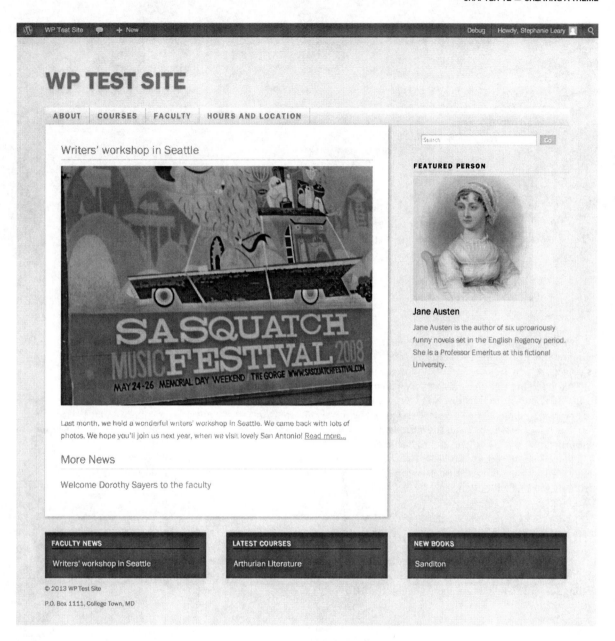

Figure 12-12. *Each dark gray box represents a separate Loop showing the most recent post in a category*

In order to better control which categories you'll work with, use the `get_categories()` function instead, as shown in Listing 12-53. This will require a bit more code, since this function returns an array of category objects rather than simple IDs, but that's OK. You can make use of that object data, and if you really need to pass the ID as a parameter to some other function, hey, that's part of the object, too.

Listing 12-53. Creating a Loop for Each Top-Level Category

```
<?php
$categories = get_categories();

foreach ($categories as $cat) : ?>
        <div class="category_box">
                <?php
                $loop2 = new WP_Query( array(
                                    'posts_per_page' => 1,
                                    'cat' => $cat->ID,
                                    ) );
                while ( $loop2->have_posts()) : $loop2->the_post(); ?>
                        <li <?php post_class(); ?> id="post-<?php the_ID(); ?>">
                                <h3><a href="<?php the_permalink() ?>" rel="bookmark" ↵
 title="Permanent Link to <?php the_title_attribute(); ?>"><?php the_title(); ?></a></h3>
                                <?php the_content('Continue reading...'); ?>
                        </li>
                <?php endwhile; ?>
        </div> <!-- .category_box -->
<?php endforeach; ?>
```

In this example, you use get_categories() to retrieve a list of all the categories. This function can take a number of arguments to limit the list it returns, but in this case you want the complete list. The function returns the categories as objects, so you use the object notation (object -> property) to get the category IDs for the query function.

As you loop through each category, call another Loop with the query set to show only posts in that category. Inside this Loop, print the title and excerpt of the first post only. Then you perform yet another query to get the next four posts, skipping the first. (Note that it might be more efficient to get all five posts in one query and use a true/false flag to determine whether the surrounding markup is a paragraph or a list item, but for now, the multiple query demonstration is more important than efficiency.)

You could, of course, modify the above code to create a Loop for all the children of a certain category, or any other scenario you can think of. See http://sleary.me/wp50[12] for all the possible arguments of the get_categories() function.

Showing the Author's Other Recent Posts

In the Twenty Ten theme, there's a footer in single.php that displays the author's Gravatar and bio, and a link to all their posts. You can enhance this to show a list of the author's most recent posts using the code shown in Listing 12-54. The results are shown in Figure 12-13.

---

[12]http://codex.wordpress.org/Function_Reference/get_categories

Listing 12-54. Displaying the Post Author's Four Most Recent Other Posts Inside the Loop

```php
<?php if ( is_single() && get_the_author_meta( 'description' ) ) :
// If a user has filled out their description, show a bio on their entries  ?>
        <div id="entry-author-info">
                <div id="author-avatar">
                        <?php echo get_avatar( get_the_author_meta( 'user_email' ), ➥
 apply_filters( 'twentyten_author_bio_avatar_size', 60 ) ); ?>
                </div><!-- #author-avatar -->
                <div id="author-description">
                        <h2><?php printf( __( 'About %s', 'twentyten' ), get_the_author() ); ?></h2>
                        <?php the_author_meta( 'description' ); ?>
                        <h4>More Posts:</h4>
                        <ul class="authorposts">
                                <?php
                                $authorloop = new WP_Query( array(
                                                'posts_per_page' => 4,
                                                'author' => $post->post_author,
                                        ) );
                                while ( $authorloop->have_posts()) :
                                                                        $authorloop->the_post(); ?>
                                <li><a href="<?php the_permalink() ?>" rel="bookmark" title="'Permanent
link to <?php the_title_attribute(); ?>">
                                        <?php the_title(); ?></a></li>
                                        <?php endwhile; ?>
                        </ul>
                        <div id="author-link">
                        <a href="<?php echo get_author_posts_url( get_the_author_meta('ID') ➥
 ); ?>" rel="author">
                                <?php printf( __( 'View all posts by %s <span class="meta ➥
-nav">&rarr;</span>', 'twentyten' ), get_the_author() ); ?>
                        </a>
                        </div><!-- #author-link -->
                </div><!-- #author-description -->
        </div><!-- #entry-author-info -->
<?php endif; ?>
```

Figure 12-13. Listing the author's most recent posts in Twenty Ten

Accessing Post Information Outside the Loop

Most of the post-related template tags seen in the previous chapter (the_title(), the_content(), and so on) are available only inside the Loop. So what do you do when you need to access information outside the Loop? Use global variables! WordPress has a number of globals that store information about the current state of the application: the current post or page, user, database, and more. All these variables are available to you in your own functions and theme files.

You can access post data using the $post global. Listing 12-53 shows how to get the post's ID, which is often needed as an argument for various functions, outside the Loop. Here, I'll use the ID to retrieve a custom field. If all you need is the ID, though, there's a shorter method: use the get_the_ID() function. Listing 12-55 shows both methods.

Listing 12-55. Getting a Post's Custom Field Outside the Loop

```php
<?php
// method #1:
$custom = get_post_meta( get_the_ID(), 'my_custom_field_name', true);

// method #2:
global $post;
$custom = get_post_meta( $post->ID, 'my_custom_field_name', true);
?>
```

If you aren't sure whether you're inside the Loop or not, you can use the in_the_loop() conditional tag to check. If you are inside the Loop, this function will return true, as shown in Listing 12-56.

Listing 12-56. Checking Whether You're Inside the Loop

```
<p>Am I inside the Loop? <?php if (in_the_loop()) echo "yes"; else echo "no"; ?></p>
```

Search Engine Optimization (SEO)

Because the CSS-based theme system encourages standards-based design, and because most themes use proper HTML heading tags for post and page titles, WordPress sites tend to do well in search engine rankings. Of course, there are improvements you can make to your own themes. In this section I'll go over three common concerns: title tags, meta descriptions, and meta keywords.

Improving the Title Tag

In many WordPress themes, the title tag looks something like Listing 12-57.

Listing 12-57. The Usual Title Tag and Its Output

```
<title><?php wp_title(); ?><?php bloginfo('name'); ?></title>

<title>example.com &raquo; Howdy, stranger.</title>
```

Good SEO dictates that the more specific information—the post title—should come first, followed by the site name. You can switch the order (and in the process, change the style and position of the separator) using the code in Listing 12-58 instead.

Listing 12-58. The Revised Title Tag and Its Output

```
<title><?php wp_title('|', true, 'right'); ?><?php bloginfo('name'); ?></title>

<title>Howdy, stranger. | example.com</title>
```

The wp_title() function prints various things depending on the context. For posts and pages, it prints the title. For categories and tags, it prints the name. On the 404 error page, it prints "Page not found."

Titles can be altered using the filter wp_title.

Using Categories and Tags as Keywords

If you need to add meta keywords to your single post archive template, you have all the data you need: your categories and tags. All you have to do is get a combined list, separated by commas.

In this example, you first use a conditional tag to make sure this code is used only on single post archives. (Pages don't have categories or tags, and the get_the_tags() and get_the_category() functions won't work correctly on archive pages containing multiple posts.) Then, for each tag and category, you force the name to all lowercase and add it to an array of keywords. As you print the <meta> tag, you remove duplicates from the array with array_unique() and convert the array to a comma-separated string using implode().

Listing 12-59 shows how to build the array of keywords and print it as the content of the <meta> tag.

Listing 12-59. Creating Meta Keywords Tag from Post Categories and Tags in header.php

```php
<?php if (is_single()) {
  foreach((get_the_tags()) as $tag) {
    $keywords[] = strtolower($tag->name);
  }
  foreach((get_the_category()) as $category) {
    $keywords[] = strtolower($category->cat_name);
  }
?>
<meta name="keywords" content="<?php echo implode(", ", array_unique($keywords)); ?>" />
<?php } ?>
```

Using the Excerpt As a Description

Listing 12-60 shows how to use the excerpt as the meta description tag for single posts and pages. Since the_excerpt() prints directly to the screen and can't be passed to other PHP functions, you can't wrap it in the esc_attr() function, as you normally would when using a template tag as an HTML attribute. Instead, you use the_excerpt_rss(). This function formats the excerpt for RSS feeds, but in this case it will work equally well in your description attribute, since excerpts can't contain HTML.

Listing 12-60. Using the_excerpt As a Meta Description

```php
<?php
if (is_singular()):
global $post;
setup_postdata($post);
?>
<meta name="description" content="<?php the_excerpt_rss(); ?>" />
<?php endif; ?>
```

Adding Scripts and Stylesheets

WordPress includes several popular JavaScript libraries, including jQuery. It's easy to integrate plugins for these libraries, as long as you're careful to avoid conflicts. You also need to use the built-in functions to add scripts and stylesheets to your themes rather than simply hard-coding the <script> and <style> tags in your header file.

Using JavaScript Libraries

WordPress includes a number of JavaScript libraries because it uses them in the administration screens. They're available for you to use in your themes and plugins as well. The libraries include jQuery, Backbone, SWFUpload, and Thickbox. See http://sleary.me/wp51[13] for a complete list of the scripts available, along with their handles.

---

[13]http://codex.wordpress.org/Function_Reference/wp_enqueue_script

Listing 12-61 shows how to add the built-in jQuery and UI core libraries to your theme.

Listing 12-61. Including jQuery

```php
<?php
function add_jquery() {
        wp_enqueue_script('jquery');
        wp_enqueue_script('jquery-ui-core');
}
add_action('wp_head', 'add_jquery');
?>
```

Using jQuery in WordPress is a bit tricky. Most jQuery scripts rely on a dollar sign function. For example, `$("div.main").addClass("wide");` would add the `wide` class to a div that already had the `main` class. However, several other libraries, including Prototype, use this same convention. Because WordPress also uses Prototype, the jQuery library is loaded in "no conflict" mode (`http://sleary.me/wp52`[14]).

You have two options. You can use `jQuery` in place of the dollar sign function (`$`) throughout your script, or you can wrap your script in an extra function. Both methods are shown in Listing 12-62.

Listing 12-62. Using jQuery in WordPress

```js
// without wrappers, in no-conflict mode
jQuery("div.main").addClass("wide");

// with wrappers
jQuery(document).ready(function($) {
        $("div.main").addClass("wide");
});
```

Adding Your Own Scripts

When you need to add a JavaScript file to your theme, it's tempting to simply paste the `<script>` tag into `header.php`, dust off your hands, and move on to your next task. However, this is the wrong way to add scripts to a WordPress theme. You might recall from Chapter 3 that you can specify the location of the `wp-content` directory. If someone who has moved `wp-content` tries to use this theme, the scripts will never load.

Adding the `<script>` tags via the `wp_head` action, as shown in Listing 12-63, is also not a good idea.

Listing 12-63. How Not to Link Scripts

```php
function slider_scripts() { ?>
        <script type="text/javascript" src="<?php bloginfo('url'); ?>/wp-content/themes/test ➥
-theme/jquery.js"></script>
        <script type="text/javascript" src="<?php bloginfo('url'); ?>/wp-content/themes/test ➥
-theme/jquery-slider.js"></script>
<?php }
add_action('wp_head', 'slider_scripts');
```

This will get the job done, but it's inefficient. You might have a plugin that has already called the jQuery library; now it will be included twice. It's also a bad idea to hard-code the path to the theme directory.

---

[14]`http://docs.jquery.com/Using_jQuery_with_Other_Libraries`

The correct way to add scripts is to use the `wp_enqueue_script()` function. This function adds your script to the header using the `wp_enqueue_scripts` hook. (Note the one-letter difference between the function name and the hook name!) Listing 12-64 shows how to enqueue a script in the header using a small function and an action hook in `functions.php`.

Listing 12-64. Enqueueing Scripts

```
function add_header_scripts() {
        wp_enqueue_script('header-script', <?php get_stylesheet_directory_uri(); ?>'/js/ ↵
header-script.js', array('jquery'), '1.0', false);
}
add_action('wp_enqueue_scripts', 'add_header_scripts');
```

The `wp_enqueue_script()` function requires several arguments. First, you need to give your script a unique handle, or name. This allows you to refer to it later and ensures that only one script of that name will be included in the page. Next, you need to provide the URL to your script file. Third, if your script relies on any libraries (like jQuery), you need to provide the handles of those dependencies in an array. Fourth, if you need to call a specific version, provide its number. (To use the most recent version, use an empty string for this argument.) Last, you need to tell WordPress whether the script should be loaded in the footer via `wp_footer()`. In this case, you want to load the script in the header, so this argument should be false (or blank).

Conditionally Adding Scripts

The `wp_enqueue_script()` function will add your script to every page on your site *and* the Dashboard screens. To prevent your script from loading on every Dashboard screen, possibly creating conflicts with core scripts and/or slowing down your site, you should wrap your code in an `if` statement using a conditional tag. In Listing 12-65, I've added my script to the page only if it is not an admin screen. You could be even more specific, using other conditionals to add the script only to a single page or type of archive.

Listing 12-65. Conditionally Enqueueing Scripts

```
function add_header_scripts() {
        if ( !is_admin() )
                wp_enqueue_script(
                'header-script',
                get_stylesheet_directory_uri().'/js/header-script.js', array('jquery'),
                '1.0',
                false
                );
}
add_action('wp_enqueue_scripts', 'add_header_scripts');
```

Adding Stylesheets

If you need to add stylesheets other than your theme's main `style.css` file, enqueuing is the proper method for many of the same reasons you'd use it for conditionally adding scripts. The `wp_enqueue_style()` function is shown in Listing 12-66. Note that it's very similar to the one you used for scripts.

Listing 12-66. Enqueuing Styles

```
function add_header_styles() {
        wp_enqueue_style(
        'print-styles',
        get_stylesheet_directory_uri().'/css/print.css',
        false,
        false,
        'print'
        );
}
add_action('wp_head', 'add_header_styles');
```

The arguments for the function are: a handle for the stylesheet, the file's URL, any dependencies, the version number, and the media type for which this stylesheet should be added. In this case, there are no dependencies or version numbers, so you used false for both arguments.

Creating Theme Options

Some themes include options allowing the user to select layouts, color schemes, or other alternatives to the theme's default settings. Prior to WordPress 3.5, this was done by adding a Theme Options page to the Dashboard menu in the Appearance section. This page would work just like plugin options, using the Settings API (http://sleary.me/wp36[15]) to store the user's choices in the database. All the code for this options page would be part of the functions.php file, or a secondary file referenced in functions.php using PHP's require_once() function. You saw a similar example in Chapter 11; the only difference is that, instead of add_options_page(), you would use add_theme_page() to place your options screen in the Appearance section of the menu.

While you can still create theme options pages, 3.5 introduced a more elegant solution: the theme customizer, which includes a live preview of the user's changes. You saw this back in Chapter 4, when you adjusted the site's title and description.

Since you have already seen an example of an options page, and will see another in Chapter 13, I'll show you how to integrate your theme options into the customizer instead. The sample theme download includes both methods, though. If you prefer to work with the traditional options page, open the theme functions file and change the commented include lines, as shown in Listing 12-67.

Listing 12-67. Using Traditional Theme Options Instead of the Customizer in the Sample Theme

```
include_once('theme-options.php');
//include_once('theme-customizer.php');
```

Creating Customizer Options

Adding options to the customizer involves using *methods*—functions that are part of the customizer class to modify the $wp_customize object. The add_section(), add_setting(), and add_control() functions can't be called without the $wp_customize object to give them context. If that sounds daunting, don't worry; I'll go through it all step by step.

First, if you need a whole new section to contain your options, you need to create it and give it a name. If you prefer, you could add your option to one of the built-in sections. See the Codex page on the Customizer API (http://sleary.me/wp53[16]) to get a list of their names.

---

[15]http://codex.wordpress.org/Settings_API
[16]http://codex.wordpress.org/Theme_Customization_API

Next, you need to define each of your settings with a name. Optionally, you can include a default value, the name of a sanitization function, and the transport argument. If you leave transport out or set it to its default value, refresh, the user will need to click the blue Save button at the top of the customizer in order to see her changes in the live preview. You can change transport to postMessage if you want to add your own JavaScript function to update the preview in real time. I'll show you how to enable live updates later in this section.

Last, you need to add a control to display your setting within the customizer section. The first argument should match the name of your setting. Within the array of arguments, you'll define your form field's label and input type, and tell the customizer which section this field goes in.

To add more options within your new group, simply add more settings and controls using the same section name.

All three of these methods—that is, these class-specific functions—get wrapped up in a function of your own, so you can hook it into place using the customize_register action. You need all three before you'll see anything in the customizer, so Listing 12-68 shows it in one big chunk. This is the contents of the theme-customizer.php file I have called using include_once() in the sample University theme's functions.php. You could place this code directly in your functions.php file if you prefer. I'll talk about each piece in turn.

Listing 12-68. Adding a Section, Option, and Control to the Theme Customizer

```
add_action( 'customize_register', 'edu_customizer_sections' );
function edu_customizer_sections( $wp_customize ) {

        $wp_customize->add_section( 'edu_footer', array(
                'title' => 'Footer',
                'priority' => 105,
                'capability' => 'edit_pages',
        ) );

        $wp_customize->add_setting( 'edu_footer_text', array(
                'default' => 'P.O. Box 1111, College Town, MD',
                'sanitize_callback' => 'edu_sanitize_footer_text',
                'transport' => 'refresh',
        ) );

        $wp_customize->add_control( 'edu_footer_text', array(
                'label' => 'Footer contact info',
                'section' => 'edu_footer',
                'type' => 'text',
        ) );

}
```

Here, I've defined a section called "Footer" using $wp_customize->add_section(). I've assigned it an internal name (like a slug), edu_footer, and have specified that anyone with the edit_pages capability (i.e., editors and administrators, using the default set of roles) may edit this option. The priority argument determines where this section falls in the customizer; you can increase its value to move it down, or decrease it to move it up.

Next, I've defined the setting itself using $wp_customize->add_setting(). Its name (slug) is edu_footer_text. This setting has a sanitization function, and its transport is set to refresh. I'll return to all three of those items in just a minute.

Last, I've defined the form field, using $wp_customize->add_control(), where the user will actually enter a value for this option. It has the same name as the setting itself; this is how WordPress knows which control to use for which setting. Its section argument must also match the section name; otherwise WordPress won't know where to put it. This setting is a text field, so its type is text and I've given it a label.

Paste this code into your theme's `functions.php` file and go to Appearance ➤ Customize. You should see a Footer section, as shown in Figure 12-14.

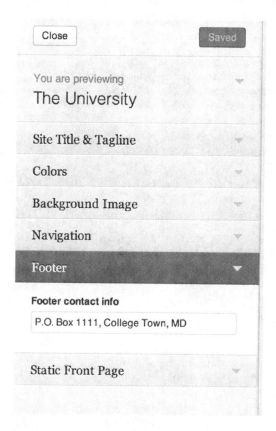

Figure 12-14. *The new Footer section of the theme customizer*

Sanitizing Customizer Options

When I defined the setting above, I gave it the name of a sanitization function. We need to add that function now (Listing 12-69).

Listing 12-69. The Customizer Option's Sanitization Function

```
function edu_sanitize_footer_text( $input ) {
    return wp_kses_post( force_balance_tags( $input ) );
}
```

This should look very similar to the options sanitization functions you saw in the Chapter 11. It accepts the user's input and runs it through two functions: here, I'm forcing any open tags to close and stripping out tags that aren't allowed in posts. Then I return the cleaned-up data to WordPress to save in the database.

Try editing your footer text! You should be able to save simple HTML—since I used `wp_post_kses()` as the sanitization function, you can use any tags that are allowed in the post editor.

If you prefer, you can sanitize several customizer settings at once rather than specifying a callback function for each one. See http://sleary.me/wp54[17] for an example of a group validation function.

Enabling Live Updates

It would be nice to see the footer text update itself in real time as we type things into the input field, wouldn't it? Let's set that up. First, go back to your $wp_customize->add_setting() function and change the setting's transport argument to postMessage, as shown in Listing 12-70. Then, add the edu_customizer_live_preview() function and hook it using customize_preview_init, which ensures that the script is loaded only on the live preview screen.

Listing 12-70. The Customizer Functions, Modified to Use postMessage for the Setting Transport, Plus the Enqueued Script Function

```
add_action( 'customize_register', 'edu_customizer_sections' );
function edu_customizer_sections( $wp_customize ) {

        $wp_customize->add_section( 'edu_footer', array(
                'title' => 'Footer',
                'priority' => 105,
                'capability' => 'edit_pages',
        ) );

        $wp_customize->add_setting( 'edu_footer_text', array(
                'default' => 'P.O. Box 1111, College Town, MD',
                'sanitize_callback' => 'edu_sanitize_footer_text',
                'transport' => 'postMessage',
        ) );

        $wp_customize->add_control( 'edu_footer_text', array(
                'label' => 'Footer contact info',
                'section' => 'edu_footer',
                'type' => 'text',
        ) );

}
function edu_sanitize_footer_text( $input ) {
    return wp_kses_post( force_balance_tags( $input ) );
}

add_action( 'customize_preview_init', 'edu_customizer_live_preview' );

function edu_customizer_live_preview() {
        wp_enqueue_script( 'edu-theme-customizer', get_template_directory_uri().'/js/theme-customizer.js', array( 'jquery','customize-preview' ), '', true );
}
```

This is the final version of the code we'll paste into functions.php, although you're not quite done yet. We still need to write the JavaScript file. Create a new subdirectory in your theme, js, and create a file called theme-customizer.js inside it. This file will contain the code in Listing 12-71.

[17]http://themeshaper.com/2013/04/29/validation-sanitization-in-customizer/

Listing 12-71. The Theme Customizer JavaScript File

```
jQuery(document).ready(function($) {
        wp.customize('edu_footer_text', function( value ) {
                        value.bind(function(to) {
                                        $('#footer .contact').html( to );
                        });
        });
});
```

Translation: get the value of the edu_footer_text option and place it inside the #footer .contact element (which, in our theme's footer.php file, is a div).

Save both the theme-customizer.js and your functions.php file and refresh the customizer page. You should now be able to see updates live as you type things into the Footer Text field.

▨ **Caution** Be sure your theme works correctly with the default options! Many users will activate the theme and go on their merry way without ever using the customizer.

Further Reading on the Theme Customizer

The customizer settings you've seen so far represent only a small fraction of the things you can do. I could write a whole mini-book on the customizer, but instead I'll refer you to four guides on the web.

The Codex page on the Customizer API (http://sleary.me/wp53[18]) includes a complete overview, but does not cover the different types of controls you can use. It does include an example theme customizer class, which you can use if you prefer a more object-oriented approach than the one I've shown here.

The WordPress Theme Customizer: A Comprehensive Developer's Guide, by Alex Mansfield (http://sleary.me/wp55[19]), is exactly that. It includes a thorough discussion of the other supported control types: radio buttons, checkboxes, select lists (drop-downs), page lists, color pickers, and file or image uploads. He includes with sanitization examples for each. I highly recommend this guide.

Developer Simon "Otto" Wood has written several excellent guides to the customizer, including one on creating a custom control (http://sleary.me/wp56[20]). It involves extending the WP_Customize_Control class to use a new render_control() function containing the HTML markup of your new control. Otto demonstrates using a simple textarea. If extending a class is new to you, just read along and use the examples. You'll extend classes again in Chapter 13 when we create custom widgets.

Last, German developer Frank Bültge—the author of the excellent Search and Replace plugin you saw in Chapter 10—has posted several sample custom classes on GitHub (http://sleary.me/wp57[21]), including select lists for users, categories and other taxonomy terms, posts, pages, and menus. There's also a date picker, a layout picker, and even a rich text editor using the standard TinyMCE toolbar. Once you've read Otto's tutorial, you'll see exactly how to make use of these examples.

Keep in mind that the theme customizer, for all its benefits, might not be the right place for your theme options. Its layout is cramped, and its live preview shows only your site's home page. If you need more room, or you have a setting that doesn't lend itself to the live preview, you can always create a traditional theme options page using the sample code for the University theme, as you saw in Chapter 11.

---

[18]http://codex.wordpress.org/Theme_Customization_API
[19]http://themefoundation.com/wordpress-theme-customizer
[20]http://ottopress.com/2012/making-a-custom-control-for-the-theme-customizer
[21]https://github.com/bueltge/Wordpress-Theme-Customizer-Custom-Controls

Creating Theme Frameworks for Large Sites

In Chapter 11, you saw some examples of theme frameworks—advanced WordPress themes that allow users to build very customized layouts by choosing options rather than writing code. These theme frameworks are all different, but they have a few things in common:

> They use theme options pages to make choices simpler for users.

> They take advantage of the template file hierarchy to create rich context in archives.

> They include their own widgets or even full plugins using the theme functions file.

> They are designed to be parent themes.

If you are designing a theme for a large organization with many divisions and corresponding subsites, you could create a parent theme framework containing all your organization's branding and any page templates, widgets, and other theme functions that would be used on all the subsites. You could then create child themes for each division. The child theme would contain any modifications to the parent organizations' branding as well as any functions or page layouts that are specific to that division.

When combined with the multisite feature, child themes allow you to create a cohesive website for a large organization while retaining enough flexibility to meet the needs of its divisions. With one installation—one set of plugins, one set of themes—you can be sure that everyone always has the most up-to-date version of the code, without worrying about rogue divisions maintaining different, outdated versions of their themes.

To build your own framework, start with a solid parent theme that's as modular as possible. It should definitely use a separate file for the Loop as well as the header, sidebar, and footer; it might even use an include file for the navigation as well. Build in any theme functions you think child themes might need—the functions for listing child pages are among my favorites—but wrap them in `if (function_exists())` statements so child theme developers can write their own versions. Last, add hooks of your own. This is as simple as including `do_action('action_name')` or adding a filter to some text; WordPress will recognize and execute any functions hooked to that name. For example, adding an action hook after the site description in the University theme would allow child themes to add a search form to the header.

If you need to build your own theme framework, take a look at existing ones like Genesis or Hybrid to see how they work. However I don't recommend using one of them as the basis for your organization's theme framework. WordPress doesn't support "grandchild" themes. That is, you can have one parent theme, but not two. You can always import multiple stylesheets, of course, but the functions files and templates won't be inherited more than one level down.

If your framework is itself a child theme, you'll have a lot of trouble customizing it further for your various divisions. Imitate the big theme frameworks, but don't start with them if you know you'll need child themes of your child theme.

Outside the Theme Hierarchy: Database Errors and Maintenance Messages

There are also two extra files that live outside the theme directory, but that still affect how your site looks at times. For example, you can create a file called `db-error.php` in your `wp-content` directory and use it to style your database connection error message, as shown in Listing 12-72.

Listing 12-72. Basic `db-error.php` File

```
<html>
<head>
<title>Database Error | MySite.com</title>
</head>
```

```
<body>
<h1>Database Error</h1>
<p>The database is not responding, and this site is unavailable.
We're sorry! Please try again later.
If you have an urgent question, call us at (111) 555-1234.</p>
</body>
</html>
```

You can dress this up to match the rest of your site by copying the contents of your theme's header.php, sidebar.php, and footer.php files into the appropriate locations, but remember to remove any WordPress-specific functions, since they won't work if the database is unavailable. You can also link directly to the stylesheet in your theme directory; just remember to change the path if you switch themes.

You can also customize your maintenance mode file, .maintenance (Listing 12-73). This is also located in your wp-content directory and is shown to your visitors while you're upgrading WordPress core files or plugins.

Listing 12-73. Maintenance Mode File

```
<?php
$protocol = $_SERVER["SERVER_PROTOCOL"];
if ( 'HTTP/1.1' != $protocol && 'HTTP/1.0' != $protocol )
        $protocol = 'HTTP/1.0';
header("$protocol 503 Service Unavailable", true, 503 );
header('Content-Type: text/html; charset=utf-8' );
?>
<html>
<head>
<title>Down for Maintenance | MySite.com</title>
</head>
<body>
<h1>Down for Maintenance</h1>
<p>This site is temporarily unavailable due to scheduled maintenance.
Please try again later.</p>
</body>
</html>
<?php die(); ?>
```

■ **Note** .maintenance is a hidden file on UNIX-based operating systems, including Macs, so you might have trouble seeing it in some applications unless you turn on the option to view hidden files (if there is one). You can use the Finder's options to turn on hidden files, or just use your FTP client's local file viewer.

Responsive Design and WordPress

Responsive Web Design, as described by Ethan Marcotte in his groundbreaking article on A List Apart (http://sleary.me/wp58[22]), uses three techniques to adjust a page's layout in response to the size of the user's browser: media queries, fluid grids, and scalable media.

---

[22]http://alistapart.com/article/responsive-web-design

Implementing responsive design in WordPress is, for the most part, just like implementing it anywhere else. Most of the magic happens in the stylesheet, where you'll create your media queries and fluid layouts. For more information on the CSS involved, see Marcotte's original article, or his book of the same name (http://sleary.me/wp59[23]).

I'll look at four issues you'll encounter in responsive WordPress themes: adding the meta viewport tag to a theme that didn't originally include it, scaling media files embedded in post content, duplicating elements in your theme's source code in order to reposition them in different layouts, and adapting responsive frameworks to WordPress.

The Viewport and Child Themes

One of the first things you need to do in order to make your site responsive is to add the viewport `<meta>` tag to your document's `<head>`. This is what tells the browser to scale itself to its native resolution rather than displaying a zoomed-out, desktop-sized version of the site (as iPhones and iPads do). Here, I've set only the initial scale. You can set a minimum and maximum scale value as well (see http://sleary.me/wp102[24]), but this can prevent users from zooming in to read small text, and I generally don't recommend setting these values.

If you're writing a new theme, you can simply include the tag in your `header.php` file. If you're creating a child theme, and the parent theme did not include the viewport, you can insert it using the `wp_head()` function/hook, as shown in Listing 12-74.

Listing 12-74. Adding the Meta Viewport Tag via `wp_head()`

```
function my_child_theme_viewport() {
        echo '<meta name="viewport" content="width=device-width, initial-scale=1" />';
}

add_action( 'wp_head', 'my_child_theme_viewport' );
```

Now that your layout is resizing according to the user's screen size, you have some work to do on your images and other embedded media.

Fluid Images and Videos

One of the primary principles of responsive design is making images, videos, and other embedded media stretch to fill (and fit) their containers. Almost all images and videos have inherent width and heights set in pixels. Most of the time, according to conventional wisdom, simply adding Listing 12-75 to your stylesheet solves your fixed-width media problems by making them all fluid.

Listing 12-75. Fluid Images

```
img, video, object, embed { max-width: 100%; }
```

However, this assumes that the image tags do not have hard-coded width and height attributes. WordPress's images do, when inserted via the media manager, and it's not realistic to expect your users to strip these attributes by hand.

The most recent default themes include some extra styles (Listing 12-76) to make WordPress's embedded images work with responsive layouts.

---

[23]http://abookapart.com/products/responsive-web-design
[24]http://developer.mozilla.org/en-US/docs/Mozilla/Mobile/Viewport_meta_tag

Listing 12-76. Styles for Responsive Images in WordPress

```
/*
 * Responsive images
 *
 * Fluid images for posts, comments, and widgets
 */
.entry-content img,
.entry-summary img,
.comment-content img,
.widget img,
.wp-caption {
      max-width: 100%;
}

/* Make sure images with WordPress-added height and width attributes are scaled correctly. */
.entry-content img,
.entry-summary img,
.comment-content img[height],
img[class*="align"],
img[class*="wp-image-"],
img[class*="attachment-"] {
      height: auto;
}

img.size-full,
img.size-large,
img.wp-post-image {
      height: auto;
      max-width: 100%;
}

/* Make sure videos and embeds fit their containers. */
embed,
iframe,
object,
video {
      max-width: 100%;
}
```

If you are creating a responsive layout, these styles should be a good starting point, if not a complete solution, for your design.

You might encounter image quality problems when your users embed scaled-down versions of images, which are then enlarged to fill their containers in your responsive layout. In order to resolve the problem, you could simply remove the downsized images from the list of user choices. The image_size_names_choose filter allows you to edit the array of image sizes before it's turned into the user's select list. Listing 12-77 shows how to remove the "thumbnail" and "small" sizes from the user's choices.

Listing 12-77. Removing "thumbnail" and "small" from the User's Image Insertion Choices

```
add_filter('image_size_names_choose', 'my_responsive_image_sizes');
function my_responsive_image_sizes( $sizes ) {
        unset( $sizes['thumbnail'] );
        unset( $sizes['small'] );
        return $sizes;
}
```

Figure 12-15 shows the resulting options in the insert media screen.

Figure 12-15. *The filtered list of image sizes available for users to insert*

This means that your users will always be dealing with large embedded images in the editor's Visual mode. To compensate for this, you might add some constraints in your `editor.css` file.

These are by no means the only methods of dealing with scaled media. See Tim Kadlec's book, *Implementing Responsive Design,* for more ideas.

Duplicating Content

Another common trick of responsive layouts is to position elements like navigation in a sidebar—after the page content—for desktops, but move it to a collapsed menu in the header on mobile-sized layouts. You can accomplish this by including the menu twice and hiding one or the other using `display: none;` in your stylesheet, but that's a confusing solution for the user who has to drag the menu into two different theme locations. Widgets are also tricky to duplicate—and there's no easy way for a user to duplicate the post content or other basic fields at all.

You can handle this in your theme, though, using the `wp_is_mobile()` conditional tag. Listing 12-78 shows a simplified example of a menu that displays at the top in mobile views and on the side in desktop layouts.

Listing 12-78. Duplicating Menus with `wp_is_mobile()`

```
if ( wp_is_mobile() )
        wp_nav_menu( array( 'menu' => 'main-menu' ) );

/* ... page content ...   */

if ( !wp_is_mobile() )
        wp_nav_menu( array( 'menu' => 'main-menu' ) );
```

The `wp_is_mobile()` function relies on user agent strings to determine whether the browser is on a mobile device, and it returns `true` for both tablet and phone sizes. Use it carefully.

Responsive Frameworks

A word of caution about responsive frameworks like Bootstrap: while WordPress gives you great control over your markup in most cases, some things are not as fine-grained as they could be. When you don't have complete control over HTML or class names, it can be difficult to integrate frameworks that come with their own. Case in point: menus.

The `wp_nav_menu()` tag usually prints something like the markup in Listing 12-79. As you can see, it's nothing like Bootstrap's nav markup, in Listing 12-80.

Listing 12-79. Typical `wp_nav_menu()` Output

```
<div class="nav">
<ul>
<li class="page_item page-item-26"><a href="http://wp/page-one/">Page One</a></li>
<li class="page_item page-item-28 current_page_item"><a href="http://wp/page-two/"> ↪
Page Two</a></li>
<li class="page_item page-item-2"><a href="http://wp/sample-page/">Sample Page</a></li>
</ul>
</div>
```

Listing 12-80. A Bootstrap Navigation Menu

```
<div class="navbar">
<div class="navbar-inner">
<a class="brand" href="#">Title</a>
<ul class="nav">
<li class="active"><a href="#">Home</a></li>
<li><a href="#">Link</a></li>
<li><a href="#">Link</a></li>
</ul>
</div>
</div>
```

While you can adjust the classes and wrapping elements to some extent, you can't emulate Bootstrap's markup through `wp_nav_menu()` arguments alone. The solution is to change WordPress's output for the template tag altogether. To do this, you would write a custom walker class for the navigation menus. This is a big undertaking, but it's essential if you need complete control over the attributes and contents of individual list items. You can also write custom walkers for page and category lists.

If you need to integrate a responsive framework into your design, I recommend Stephen Harris's tutorial on the walker class at `http://sleary.me/wp60`.[25]

Distributing Themes

If you want to publish your theme on the official theme repository at WordPress Extend, you need to make sure your theme meets a long list of requirements (see the link to the checklist in the "Theme Review" section hereafter). You also need to localize your theme so it can be translated. You saw the basics of localization and internationalization in Chapter 11. The rest of the process of localizing themes is very similar.

First, you need to wrap text in translation functions like `__()` and `_e()`, using a text domain slug as the second argument. Refer back to Chapter 11, or see the Codex's Localization page (`http://sleary.me/wp41`[26]), for more on this step.

Second, create a `/languages` subdirectory in your theme's files. In the functions file, call the `load_theme_textdomain()` function with the path to the subdirectory, as shown in Listing 12-81.

Listing 12-81. Using `load_theme_textdomain()`

```
add_action('after_setup_theme', 'setup_my_theme');
function setup_my_theme () {
        load_theme_textdomain( 'mytheme', get_template_directory() . '/languages' );
}
```

Third, add your text domain to your stylesheet's comment block, as you saw in Listing 12-15 at the beginning of this chapter.

Last, you need to create a POT, a file containing a bare list of all the translation-ready phrases in your theme files, a `.po` file containing the English version, and a `.mo` file—a machine-readable version of the `.po` file. There are many different applications to help you generate these files, some web-based and some for the desktop, and each of them have slightly different procedures. See `http://sleary.me/wp61`[27] for a list of the applications and instructions for each. Once you have the three files, place them in the `/languages` subdirectory you created. As you receive additional translations from other developers, place them in the `/languages` subdirectory as well.

Theme Review

The Codex contains the list of theme review guidelines (`http://sleary.me/wp62`[28]) used by the team that approves themes for inclusion in the directory at `wordpress.org`. If you don't plan to distribute your theme to the public, don't sweat over each and every one of the items on the checklist! Just glance at it to make sure you haven't overlooked anything essential. If, however, you want your theme to be available on `wordpress.org`, you'll need to follow all the guidelines carefully.

---

[25]`http://wp.tutsplus.com/tutorials/creative-coding/understanding-the-walker-class`
[26]`http://codex.wordpress.org/L10n`
[27]`http://codex.wordpress.org/Translating_WordPress`
[28]`http://codex.wordpress.org/Theme_Review`

Further Reading

You're already seen some additional resources on the theme customizer. For more information on developing themes in general, see:

The wordpress.com Theme Developer guidelines http://sleary.me/wp63[29]

The wordpress.org Theme Review guidelines http://sleary.me/wp62[30]

Themeshaper's Theme Tutorial (Second Edition) http://sleary.me/wp64[31]

CodePoet articles http://sleary.me/wp65[32]

Web Designer's Guide to WordPress: Plan, Theme, Build, Launch, by Jesse Friedman

Summary

In this chapter, you've learned all the essential steps to creating a theme, from a simple blog layout all the way to a complete framework. You've learned about the files that make up a theme, the theme's stylesheet and the WordPress-specific styles that should be included in it, and the template tags (including conditional tags) that are used to display your site's information in the theme files. You've created sidebars and widget areas, navigation menus, and customized header images and backgrounds.

I've shown you how to modify the Loop and run multiple Loops per page. You've learned how to access post information outside the Loop, which is especially useful in your sidebars (and widgets, in Chapter 13). I've discussed the proper way to include scripts and extra stylesheets in your themes, including how to use the built-in jQuery library. Last, you've learned to add sections and settings to the theme customizer.

Take a deep breath. The longest chapter is behind you! In the next chapter, you'll learn how to create a custom plugin, including widgets and Dashboard widgets. Then, in the last chapter of this book, you'll put together everything you've learned about themes and plugins to create a custom post type and display it on your site.

---

[29]http://developer.wordpress.com/themes/
[30]http://codex.wordpress.org/Theme_Review
[31]http://themeshaper.com/2012/10/22/the-themeshaper-wordpress-theme-tutorial-2nd-edition/
[32]http://build.codepoet.com/asset/articles/

CHAPTER 13

■ ■ ■

Creating Plugins

While theme functions are quite powerful, they aren't very portable. If you ever want to switch themes, you'll have to copy all your essential functions from one theme to another. There's another option: many of the theme functions you've seen throughout this book could become plugins. Plugins offer much better control over functions, since you can activate and deactivate them as needed. The plugin manager also provides some safeguards, since plugins containing errors will fail to activate, whereas errors in a theme functions file will affect your site immediately. You can do any number of things with plugins: modify or replace existing functions (filters), add your functions in predetermined locations (actions), create new template tags and shortcodes, and more.

As you add features to WordPress, you'll find that many of them are just variations on things WordPress already does—listing posts, for example, or creating a form field on an administration page. When your new feature is similar to an old feature, look through the core WordPress files—that is, the ones that came in the zipped file you downloaded when you installed the software; this is usually everything but the wp-content directory. If you're working with the user profile, as you will in this chapter, open up wp-admin/user-edit.php and see how the profile page is built. Look for the hooks, named in the do_action() and apply_filters() functions. See how WordPress does that thing you want to do, and emulate the core functions and user interface as closely as you can. Not only will this provide a consistent experience for users, but it helps ensure that your code will continue to work in future versions. The very best plugins don't require constant updates, because they use the same hooks and functions as WordPress itself.

Getting Started

In this chapter, you'll learn how to build a staff directory for our fictitious university department. The administrative assistants have been updating a table of names, titles, e-mail addresses, and phone numbers for years, and they're understandably tired of it. Faculty members also have individual pages showing their photo and biography, and they're clamoring to have their Twitter accounts linked in the directory. What's more, all of these pages tend to be out of date, since the staff seldom remembers to update them when people retire or are reassigned to other divisions.

You're going to improve the situation by extending the user profiles to include titles and phone numbers, so everyone in the department can log in to the website and update their own contact information. Then you'll build a template tag and shortcode to display a directory of this user data on the site. You'll also create a custom widget that shows a random user profile as the featured staff member of the day, and a Dashboard widget for administrators that will show them a list of users whose profiles are incomplete. Last, you'll create an options page, complete with a validation function, like the one you saw in Chapter 11.

The first step is to create your plugin files. While you can create a plugin that's just one file—like the Hello, Dolly plugin included in the WordPress download package—most plugins contain multiple files (even if it's just one PHP file and a readme.txt), so it's a good idea to start by creating a directory for your plugin. It should go inside your /wp-content/plugins directory.

To begin the Sample User Directory project, I created the /wp-content/plugins/sample-user-directory/ user-directory.php file. There is no official naming convention for plugin files, but giving the primary PHP file the same name as the directory is the most common approach. The first thing that goes into this file is the header comment block, as shown in Listing 13-1. The title and description will appear in your list of plugins. If you provide a URL in addition to your name as the author, your name will be linked to that URL. You may also provide a URL for the plugin, if it has its own page on your website. You should also include a license, either as a single line (as shown) or as a separate comment block (if, for example, you are including the standard GNU Public License header).

Listing 13-1. The Sample User Directory Plugin Header Comment Block

```php
<?php
/*
Plugin Name: Sample User Directory
Plugin URI: http://stephanieleary.com/wordpress/plugins/sample-user-directory/
Description: Creates a directory of the site's users.
Version: 1.0
License: GPLv2
Author: Stephanie Leary
Author URI: http://stephanieleary.com/
*/
```

There are a few additional requirements for plugins distributed through the official repository. If you intend to submit your plugin, you'll need to include a `readme.txt` file, some screenshots (optional), and a few extra functions that will allow your plugin to be translated into other languages (also optional, but preferred). These steps are detailed at the end of this chapter.

Extending User Profiles

WordPress user profiles include two contact fields: an e-mail address and a URL. If you installed WordPress prior to version 3.6, your user profiles also include three instant messenger account fields: AIM, Yahoo!, and Google Talk (or Jabber). You can change or add to these fields with just a few lines of code.

Changing Contact Fields

I'll start by adding job titles, Twitter usernames, and phone numbers to the users' profiles. WordPress has a filter function that allows you to change the fields that appear in the Contact Info section. The code is fairly simple, as shown in Listing 13-2. Place it in your new plugin file, below the comment block.

Listing 13-2. Changing User Profile Contact Fields

```php
// change user contact fields
function edu_contact_methods( $contactmethods ) {
        // Add some fields
        $contactmethods['title'] = 'Title';
        $contactmethods['phone'] = 'Phone Number';
        $contactmethods['twitter'] = 'Twitter Name (no @)';
        // Remove AIM, Yahoo IM, Google Talk/Jabber if they're present
        unset($contactmethods['aim']);
        unset($contactmethods['yim']);
        unset($contactmethods['jabber']);
        // make it go!
        return $contactmethods;
}
add_filter( 'user_contactmethods', 'edu_contact_methods', 10, 1 );
```

This function accepts an associative array of contact fields. You've added three new fields, where the array key is a short name for the field and the value is the label that will appear in the form. Then you've removed the array items containing the fields you no longer want—all three instant messenger accounts, in this case. The e-mail and URL fields cannot be removed, but that's all right; you'll use them in the directory.

Last, you need to call the filter. The add_filter() function takes four arguments: the name of the built-in filter (user_contactmethods), the name of the custom function (edu_contact_methods), a priority (10, which in this case means the filter has a low priority and will be called after most other filters), and the number of arguments the custom function requires (in this case, just one). In this example, the priority and the number of arguments could have been omitted, since you're using the default values for both.

Save your tiny plugin. Go to Plugins in the Dashboard and activate Sample User Directory. Once it's activated, visit your own profile page. You'll see the new contact fields displayed, as shown in Figure 13-1.

| Display name publicly as | sleary ⭥ |

Contact Info

E-mail *(required)*	steph@example.com
Website	http://stephanieleary.com
Title	Author
Phone Number	555-1234
Twitter Name (no @)	sleary

About Yourself

| Biographical Info | |

Figure 13-1. *The new contact fields in the user profile*

Listing All Users' Information

WordPress provides an archive template that displays all posts, but there is no template that displays a list of all users. You will create a template tag, a shortcode, and a widget to display various users, but first, you need to retrieve the list of users.

In this example, you will get all user IDs of your blog with the get_users() function. Then, because this function doesn't allow sorting by the user's last name, you'll use the PHP usort() function to alphabetize the array of objects returned by get_users(). If you wanted to sort users by display name or username, you could skip this step. Listing 13-3 shows this portion of the plugin.

Listing 13-3. Getting a Sorted Array of User Objects

```
function edu_get_users() {
        $blogusers = get_users(array(
                                'fields' => 'all_with_meta',
                                'order' => 'ASC',
                                'orderby' => 'nicename',
                        ));
```

```
        usort($blogusers, 'edu_user_sort');

        return $blogusers;
}

function edu_user_sort( $a, $b ) {
        return strcmp( $a->last_name, $b->last_name );
}
```

Creating Template Tags

By now, you've probably realized that template tags in WordPress are just plain old PHP functions. Some take arguments; some don't. Some echo their results by default; others return the results for use in other functions. Creating a new template tag for your plugin is as simple as deciding what sort of function you need to write and whether it should return a value or echo it to the screen.

The edu_get_users() function returns the array of users, but it doesn't print anything yet. To create a table of users and their contact information, you need a third function, as shown in Listing 13-4. This loops through all the users in the array, printing a table row for each. I have wrapped all the HTML in a variable, because in a few minutes I'm going to want the option not to echo the output immediately. To that end, I've included a single argument for the function, echo, which defaults to true. At the end of the function, I echo the output if this is the case, and return it otherwise.

Listing 13-4. Printing the User Array As a Table

```
function edu_users_table( $echo = true ) {
        $users = edu_get_users();
        $output = '<table cellspacing="1" id="user-directory">
                    <thead>
                    <tr>
                    <th>'.__('Name', 'sample-user-directory' ).'</th>';
        $output .= '<th>'.__('Title', 'sample-user-directory' ).'</th>';
        $output .= '<th>'.__('Phone', 'sample-user-directory' ).'</th>';
        $output .= '<th>'.__('Email', 'sample-user-directory' ).'</th>';
        $output .= '<th>'.__('Twitter', 'sample-user-directory' ).'</th>';
    $output .= '</tr>
            </thead>
            <tbody>';

        foreach ($users as $user) {

            $name = join( ', ', array( $user->last_name, $user->first_name ) );
            if ( !empty( $user->user_url ) )
                $name = '<a href="'.esc_url( $user->user_url ).'">'.esc_html( $name ).'</a>';

            $output .= '<tr class="vcard" id="' . esc_attr( $user->user_nicename ) .'">';
            $output .= '<td class="fn uid">'.$name.'</td>';
            $output .= '<td class="title">' . esc_html($user->title) .'</td>';
            $output .= '<td class="tell">' . esc_html($user->phone) .'</td>';
```

---

[1]http://microformats.org/wiki/hcard
[2]http://h2vx.com/vcf/

```
        $output .= '<td class="email">';
        $output .= '<a href="mailto:' . esc_attr($user->user_email) .'">';
        $output .=  esc_html($user->user_email) .'</a></td>';
        $output .= '<td class="twitter">';
        if ( !empty( $user->twitter ) )
            $output .= '<a href="http://twitter.com/'.esc_attr($user->twitter).'">@' ↪
. esc_html($user->twitter) . '</a>';
        $output .= '</td>';
        $output .= '</tr>';
    }
    $output .= '</tbody>
    </table>';

    if ($echo) {
            echo $output;
            return;
    }

    return $output;
}
```

The vcard class on the row, the row ID, and the extra classes on the table cells are all part of the hCard microformat (http://sleary.me/wp65[1]). This extra markup lets visitors with the right browser tools download the users' information into their address books. You could use the IDs to create vCard download links in each user's row with the hCard-to-vCard conversion service (http://sleary.me/wpp66[2]), but I've omitted that here for brevity. See the sample plugin download file for the full markup, including the vCard download links.

You've just created a template tag! Now, how are you going to use this in your site? You have a few options:

- Use a hook to print this table somewhere automatically.

- Create a theme template, like page-staff.php, and include `<?php edu_users_table(); ?>` in place of the Loop. Then select this file as a page's template in the Edit screen.

- Create a shortcode for this template tag and enter it into a page's content.

The hook option is attractive, but there's a good chance the table would end up displayed somewhere you didn't intend. Since it's a sizeable chunk of HTML, you want to avoid that. In this case, it's probably better to confine the use of this template tag to a single page. The choice between page template and shortcode is up to you. I'll demonstrate how to create a shortcode for this template tag.

■ **Caution**   While developers love to litter their themes and plugins with shortcodes, it's likely that the average content editor won't remember what shortcodes are or how to use them. Use them sparingly!

Creating Shortcodes

Creating shortcodes in WordPress is a matter of creating the function that prints out what you want, and then registering a shortcode for it. If you've been working with images in your posts and pages, you've probably seen at least two examples of shortcodes: image captions and galleries.

Creating a simple shortcode that will display the users table is very easy (Listing 13-5).

Listing 13-5. The Users Shortcode

```
function edu_users_table_shortlink( $atts = null, $content = null ) {
        $content .= edu_users_table( false );
        return $content;
}
add_shortcode( 'users', 'edu_users_table_shortlink' );
```

Of course, shortcodes can be far more complicated than this. They can accept arguments, and you can have opening and closing shortcodes that surround a bit of text.

For more information on shortcodes and examples of shortcodes with arguments and content, see the Codex page at http://sleary.me/wp67.[3]

Now that users have an easy way to place the users table where they want it, try adding it to a page. If you have at least a few users, the output should look something like Figure 13-2.

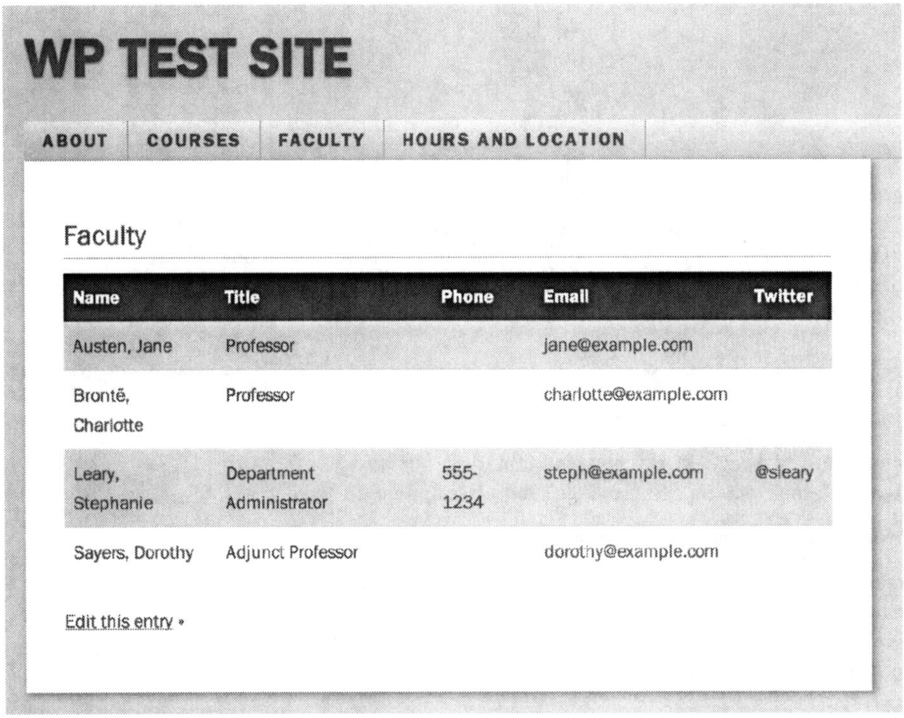

Figure 13-2. The completed user directory

---

[3]http://codex.wordpress.org/Shortcode_API

Creating Settings Screens

WordPress provides a complete framework, the Options API, for setting, updating, and deleting plugin and theme options in the database. The Settings API provides a secure way for users to manage those options through forms in administration screens. The Settings API handles a lot of security issues for you, although there are still things for you to check. All you have to do is register the settings you plan to use, so WordPress knows which ones it should handle. For more information on the Settings API, visit the Codex page at `http://sleary.me/wp36`.[4] For information on the Options API, which does the work of adding, updating, and removing items from the options table in the database, see `http://sleary.me/wp68`.[5]

Now that you have both a template tag and a shortcode at your disposal, it's time to reexamine the final output of the users table. Will you need every column in every context where you might display this table? Perhaps you don't want to display the phone number or Twitter handles to the general public, but you have a private version of the page, accessible only to logged-in users, where you do want to display all the available information. There are several ways you could approach this problem, but the most flexible solution is to create a settings screen where the site administrators can select which fields are public and which are private.

Registering the Setting

As you saw in Chapter 11, it's possible to store several options in a single database row by grouping them into an array. Listing 13-6 shows the code required to register a single setting. The first argument is the setting's name; the second is the name of the group in which it appears.

Listing 13-6. Registering a Setting

```
add_action('admin_menu', 'edu_add_pages');
function edu_add_pages() {
        add_options_page( 'User Profile Visibility', 'User Profile Visibility',↩
'manage_options', 'edu_settings', 'edu_settings_screen' );
        register_setting( 'edu_settings', 'edu_settings_group', 'edu_settings_validate');
}
```

Next, think about default settings. You can use an activation hook to store your options in the database when the plugin is activated. However, do you need to? As I mentioned in Chapter 8, network-activating a plugin in a multisite installation does not automatically run the plugin's activation routine on every site. Also, there's no point in taking up a row in the database with nonessential information. If you don't really need an activation routine, don't create one!

The sample options page I showed you in Chapter 11 did include an activation routine. Here, you can do without it. As you modify the `edu_users_table()` function to check the new options, you will assume that the contact information is public if no option is set.

■ **Tip** When you store several variables as an array in a single option, the database entry for that option will be serialized. This can make it more difficult to read and debug. Use the Online PHP Unserializer (`http://sleary.me/wp69`[6]) to see the serialized values in a more readable format.

---

[4]`http://codex.wordpress.org/Settings_API`
[5]`http://codex.wordpress.org/Options_API`
[6]`http://blog.tanist.co.uk/files/unserialize/index.php`

Creating the Options Form

Now you need to create the individual form fields that will allow users to change the plugin settings. First, you need to tell WordPress that this form will be using the options group you registered earlier. You'll also go ahead and load the stored options into a variable so you can use them throughout the form. If there is no stored option, load some default settings. Listing 13-7 shows these changes to the basic form.

Listing 13-7. Setting Up Options for Use in the Form

```php
function edu_settings_screen() {
?>
<div class="wrap">
        <form method="post" id="sample_user_directory" action="options.php">
                <?php
                settings_fields('edu_settings_group');
                $options = get_option('edu_settings');
                if (empty($options))
                        $options = array(
                                'user_email' => '1',
                                'user_url' => '1',
                                'title' => '1',
                                'phone' => '1',
                                'twitter' => '1',
                        );
                if ( current_user_can( 'manage_options' ) ) {
                ?>
        <h2><?php _e('User Profile Visibility' ); ?></h2>

        <p><?php _e('Please choose which profile fields should be visible in the user ↪
directory.'); ?></p>

        <!--form fields will go here -->

        <p class="submit">
        <input type="submit" value="<?php esc_attr_e( 'Update Options' ); ?>" class="↪
button-primary" />
        </p>

        <?php } // if current_user_can() ?>
        </form>
</div>
<?php
}
```

Now that you have your options, you can use them to print the default values for each form field. Listing 13-8 shows the form fields for the Next Page options. This should look fairly similar to the settings screen you saw in Chapter 11. You may lay out your plugin options pages however you wish, but the table layout shown here is the one used throughout the core WordPress settings screens. It is required if you are adding options to an existing page, as you'll see later in this chapter.

Listing 13-8. Adding the Options Fields

```php
function edu_settings_screen() {
?>
<div class="wrap">
        <form method="post" id="sample_user_directory" action="options.php">
                <?php
                settings_fields('edu_settings_group');
                $options = get_option('edu_settings');
                if (empty($options))
                        $options = array(
                                'user_email' => '1',
                                'user_url' => '1',
                                'title' => '1',
                                'phone' => '1',
                                'twitter' => '1',
                        );
                if ( current_user_can( 'manage_options' ) ) {
                ?>
        <h2><?php _e('User Profile Visibility' ); ?></h2>

        <p><?php _e('Please choose which profile fields should be visible in the user ↪
  directory.'); ?></p>

    <table class="form-table">
        <tr>
        <th scope="row"><label for="edu_settings[user_firstname]"> <?php _e('First Name'); ?> </label></th>
        <td> <input name="edu_settings[user_firstname]" type="checkbox" value="1" checked="checked" ↪
disabled="disabled" /> </td>
        </tr>
        <tr>
        <th scope="row"><label for="edu_settings[user_lastname]"> <?php _e('Last Name'); ?> </label></th>
        <td> <input name="edu_settings[user_lastname]" type="checkbox" value="1" checked="checked" ↪
disabled="disabled" /> </td>
        </tr>
        <tr>
        <th scope="row"><label for="edu_settings[user_email]"> <?php _e('Email Address'); ?> </label></th>
        <td> <input name="edu_settings[user_email]" type="checkbox" value="1" <?php ↪
checked($options['user_email'], '1'); ?> /> </td>
        </tr>

        <tr>
        <th scope="row"><label for="edu_settings[user_url]"> <?php _e('Website Address'); ?> </label></th>
        <td> <input name="edu_settings[user_url]" type="checkbox" value="1" <?php ↪
checked($options['user_url'], '1'); ?> /> </td>
        </tr>

        <tr>
        <th scope="row"><label for="edu_settings[title]"><?php _e( 'Title' ); ?></label></th>
        <td> <input name="edu_settings[title]" type="checkbox" value="1" <?php ↪
checked($options['title'], '1'); ?> /> </td>
        </tr>
```

```
        <tr>
        <th scope="row"><label for="edu_settings[phone]"> <?php _e('Phone Number'); ?> </label></th>
        <td> <input name="edu_settings[phone]" type="checkbox" value="1" <?php ↩
checked($options['phone'], '1'); ?> /> </td>
        </tr>

        <tr>
        <th scope="row"><label for="edu_settings[twitter]"> <?php _e('Twitter Username'); ?> </label></th>
        <td> <input name="edu_settings[twitter]" type="checkbox" value="1" <?php ↩
checked($options['twitter'], '1'); ?> /> </td>
        </tr>
    </table>

        <p class="submit">
        <input type="submit" value="<?php esc_attr_e( 'Update Options' ); ?>" class="button-primary" />
        </p>

        <?php } // if current_user_can() ?>
        </form>
</div>
<?php
}
```

For each of the fields, you can use the `get_option()` function to retrieve the stored value. However, remember from Chapter 11 that you need to sanitize that value before you can display it as an attribute of an HTML tag, so here you've wrapped each one in the `esc_attr()` function.

Adding Scripts and Styles to Individual Settings Screens

You can add a stylesheet to the settings page without adding it to every Dashboard screen, which would be inefficient and might conflict with other plugins. You'll piggyback onto the function you used to add the settings page to the menu, and grab the resulting hook suffix. Then you'll append that value to the plugin-specific `admin_print_scripts-()` or `admin_print_style-()` hooks.

The sample plugin in this chapter doesn't use any scripts or styles on its settings screen, but Listing 13-9 shows how you would add script and stylesheet files from your plugin directory.

Listing 13-9. Adding a Stylesheet to This Options Page, but Not All the Admin Screens

```
add_action('admin_menu', 'edu_add_pages');
function edu_add_pages() {
        $page = add_options_page( 'User Profile Visibility', 'User Profile Visibility', ↩
'manage_options', 'edu_settings', 'edu_settings_screen' );
        register_setting( 'edu_settings', 'edu_settings_group', 'edu_settings_validate');
        add_action( 'admin_print_scripts-'.$page, 'edu_settings_js');
        add_action( 'admin_print_styles-'.$page, 'edu_settings_css' );
}
```

```
// add JS and CSS to settings page only
function edu_settings_js() {
        wp_enqueue_script( 'my-plugin-script', plugins_url( '/my-plugin-script.js' ) );
}

function edu_settings_css() {
        wp_enqueue_style( 'my-plugin-stylesheet', plugins_url( '/my-plugin-style.css' ) );
}
```

Deleting Options

To avoid cluttering the database with unneeded options, you should remove yours when the plugin is deactivated. It's very easy to do, as you can see in Listing 13-10.

Listing 13-10. Removing the Plugin Options on Deactivation

```
register_uninstall_hook( __FILE__, 'edu_delete_options' );

function edu_delete_options() {
        delete_option( 'edu_settings' );
}
```

Validating Options

When I registered the setting in Listing 13-9, I included the name of a validation function. Now I need to write that function, which will sanitize the user's input before it's saved to the database. The validation function is shown in Listing 13-11. This process is similar to the examples in Chapter 11.

Listing 13-11. The Validation Function

```
function edu_settings_validate( $input ) {
        // first and last name are required and disabled.
        // Remove any values that should not be here.
        unset( $input['user_firstname'] );
        unset( $input['user_lastname'] );
        // all others should be positive integers
        $input = array_walk( $input, 'absint' );
        return $input;
}
```

In your validation function, you will need to think about every option on the page, what data type its value *should* be, and what could go wrong if the user enters something else. In this case, I have two elements in the options array, user_firstname and user_lastname, that were disabled on the settings screen because I don't want them to be turned off under any circumstances. Therefore, those two should not be saved and can be removed from the options array using PHP's unset() function. Their values will be reset to the defaults on the settings screen.

The rest of the elements in the array, which appeared as checkboxes on the settings screen, should have values of either zero or one. I can use the absint() function to sanitize them, and since these are the only elements remaining in the array, I can use PHP's array_walk() function to apply absint() to every element in the array instead of writing out the function five times.

The Complete Settings Screen

Once you've completed all your functions, activate your plugin and try it out! Figure 13-3 shows the finished settings screen.

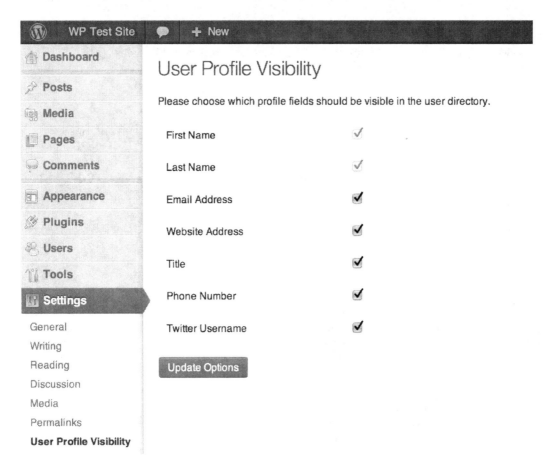

Figure 13-3. *The final settings screen*

Make sure there is no extra white space after your closing ?> tag, or WordPress will give an error on activation. In fact, you could omit that closing tag entirely as long as the file ends with PHP and not HTML.

Variations on Settings Screens

I've demonstrated how to add your settings screen to the Settings menu, which is the conventional location for plugin settings. You have several other choices available, though. You can add your page in another section of the navigation menu (e.g., Tools). You can create a top-level menu for your plugin, which is especially useful if your plugin requires more than one settings screen. You can even add your options to one of the existing pages rather than creating a whole new one. See http://sleary.me/wp70[7] for detailed documentation on the navigation menu. I'll go over a few of the most common scenarios.

---

[7]http://codex.wordpress.org/Administration_Menus

Adding Other Submenus

Most plugins' settings screens are placed in the Settings portion of the menu. However, if you feel that another section would be more appropriate for your plugin's page, you can simply change the add_options_page() function to one of the others shown in Listing 13-12.

Listing 13-12. Submenu Functions

```
//Settings
add_options_page(page_title, menu_title, capability, handle);
// Tools
add_management_page(page_title, menu_title, capability, handle);
// Appearance
add_theme_page(page_title, menu_title, capability, handle);
// Posts
add_posts_page(page_title, menu_title, capability, handle);
// Pages
add_pages_page(page_title, menu_title, capability, handle);
// Media
add_media_page(page_title, menu_title, capability, handle);
// Comments
add_comments_page(page_title, menu_title, capability, handle);
// Users
add_user_page(page_title, menu_title, capability, handle);
// Dashboard
add_dashboard_page(page_title, menu_title, capability, handle);
```

All the functions require the same arguments you saw in Listing 13-7; the only difference is the location of the resulting option page.

Adding a Top-Level Menu Item

Unless your plugin requires several options pages, it's best to add your options page under the Settings menu as shown in Listing 13-7. However, if you do have a number of separate pages, you can create a top-level menu item for your plugin as shown in Listing 13-13. This code would replace the first few lines of Listing 13-7.

Listing 13-13. Adding a Top-Level Menu Item

```
add_action('admin_menu', 'next_page_add_pages');

function next_page_add_pages() {
        add_menu_page( 'Top Level Section', 'Top Level Section', 'manage_options', ↪
'edu_settings', 'edu_settings_screen' );
}
```

This add_menu_page() function looks quite a bit like the add_options_page() function in Listing 13-7. The arguments for both functions are

- *Page title:* the <title> of your options page

- *Heading:* the heading shown above your options form

- *Capability:* the minimum user capability required to access the page (usually manage_options)

- *File handle:* an identifier for your plugin file (in this case, the file name)

- *Options form function:* the name of the function that displays the options <form>

- *Menu icon* (optional in add_menu_page()): you can specify the file location of an icon for your menu item

The results of Listing 13-13 are shown in Figure 13-4.

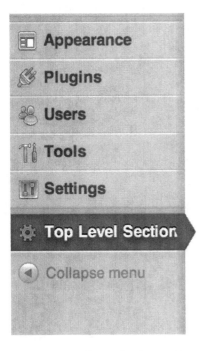

Figure 13-4. *The top-level menu item*

Adding a Section to an Existing Options Page

If you have just a few settings to work with and it would make sense to include them on an existing page rather than creating a whole new one, you can do so. For example, if you had an option related to privacy, you could use the code in Listing 13-14 to add your option to that page.

Listing 13-14. Adding an Option to the Media Page

```
function add_extra_media_options() {
    add_settings_field('extra_media', 'Extra Media Option', 'extra_media_options_fields', ↵
 'media', $section = 'default', $args = array());
    register_setting('media','extra_media');
}

add_action('admin_init', 'add_extra_media_options');
```

```
// displays the options page content
function extra_media_options_fields() { ?>
        <p> the form fields will go here </p>
<?php
}
```

Keep in mind that the standard WordPress options pages are laid out using tables. The contents of your display function will appear inside a table cell.

The results of Listing 13-14 are shown in Figure 13-5.

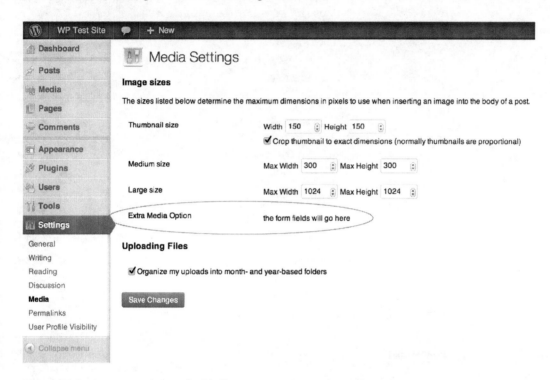

Figure 13-5. *An extra option on the Media page*

Creating Widgets

Widgets are the building blocks of WordPress sidebars. Widgets display a bit of content inside the widget areas you defined in your theme's functions.php file in Chapter 12. They can be created in a theme's functions file or in a plugin.

Basic Widgets

WordPress widgets are classes, which makes them easy to duplicate, even if you've never worked with object-oriented programming before. A class provides a blueprint for objects that will be reused in various ways. Creating a new widget is a matter of copying the basic widget class, then adjusting the enclosed functions to output the content you have in mind. The widget class contains four functions: one that registers the widget, one that prints the widget output, one that updates the widget options, and one that displays the options form.

Examining the Calendar Widget

Before I go into the details of custom widgets, take a look at the code for some of the built-in widgets. I'll show you one of the simplest, the calendar (Figure 13-6). The code (from wp-includes/default-widgets.php) is given in Listing 13-15. Things you would change in your own widget are in bold.

Figure 13-6. *The calendar widget in the widget manager area and the Twenty Twelve theme*

Listing 13-15. The Built-In Calendar Widget

```
class WP_Widget_Calendar extends WP_Widget {

        function __construct() {
                $widget_ops = array('classname' => 'widget_calendar', 'description' => ↪
__( 'A calendar of your site&#8217;s posts') );
                parent::__construct('calendar', __('Calendar'), $widget_ops);
        }

        function widget( $args, $instance ) {
                extract($args);
                $title = apply_filters('widget_title', empty($instance['title']) ? '' :
$instance['title'], $instance, $this->id_base);
                echo $before_widget;
                if ( $title )
                        echo $before_title . $title . $after_title;
                echo '<div id="calendar_wrap">';
                get_calendar();
```

```
                echo '</div>';
                echo $after_widget;
        }

        function update( $new_instance, $old_instance ) {
                $instance = $old_instance;
                $instance['title'] = strip_tags($new_instance['title']);

                return $instance;
        }

        function form( $instance ) {
                $instance = wp_parse_args( (array) $instance, array( 'title' => '' ) );
                $title = strip_tags($instance['title']);
?>
                <p><label for="<?php echo $this->get_field_id('title'); ?>">
                   <?php _e('Title:'); ?>
                   </label>
                <input class="widefat" id="<?php echo $this->get_field_id('title'); ?>" name="<?php
echo $this->get_field_name('title'); ?>" type="text" value="<?php echo esc_attr($title); ?>" /></p>
<?php
        }
}
```

Look how little you have to change! Now, this is one of the simplest widgets. Your widgets might have more options, and therefore a longer form and more fields to update. Still, this is going to be pretty easy, right?

Setting Up Your Widget

To create your own widget, you need to duplicate the widget class and add your own logic and form fields. Then you just need a few extra lines to register your widget and make it available on the widget manager screen.

First, you need to create your class and add it to WordPress's list of available widgets using `register_widget()`. Every new widget in WordPress extends the basic `WP_Widget` class. If you're not entirely comfortable with classes, that's all right. All you would need to change from Listing 13-15 would be the name of the class, `EduUserProfile`, in the class declaration, the constructor function, and the argument of the `register_widget()` function below.

Listing 13-16 shows the widget class with the required hooks. The four functions inside the class are empty for now. I'll show you each component of the widget class individually, then put it all together at the end of this section.

Listing 13-16. Starting the New Widget Class

```
class EduUserProfile extends WP_Widget {

        // constructor
        function EduUserProfile() {
        }

        // widget output
        function widget( $args, $instance ) {
        }
```

```
            // save options from widget administration screen
            function update( $new_instance, $old_instance ) {
            }

            // display form fields on widget administration screen
            function form( $instance ) {
            }
}

// register widget
function edu_profile_widget_init() {
        register_widget('EduUserProfile');
}

// hook registration function
add_action('widgets_init', 'edu_profile_widget_init');
```

The setup function, the constructor, is shown by itself in Listing 13-17. This is the first function in the class, and its name should match the class name. This function provides the information about the widget that WordPress needs to display on the widget manager screen.

Listing 13-17. The Widget Constructor

```
function EduUserProfile() {
        $widget_ops = array('classname' => 'edu_user_profile', 'description' => ↵
__( 'A random user profile') );
        $this->WP_Widget('EduUserProfile', __('Random User'), $widget_ops);
}
```

The classname and description are up to you; just make sure the classname is a valid name for a class in CSS (see http://sleary.me/wp71[8] for details, or escape your chosen name using the sanitize_html_class() function). When you call $this->WP_Widget, you need to pass it three arguments: the name of this widget (which should match this function's name), its title (for the widget manager screen), and the array of options you created in the previous line. You could accomplish all this in one line, but for readability, I've created an array containing the class name and description properties.

The Options Form

The form function defines what will appear in the widget manager under Appearance ➤ Widgets. Before you dive into the form, think about what this widget will display in the theme: a heading for the widget, followed by the user's avatar, name, and biography. The first option will be the heading—the title of the widget. For the avatar, it would be nice for the user to be able to choose the appropriate size, so I'll add a field for that. The rest will work without additional options. Were you generating a more complicated bit of code, you would need more options, and you would add those fields here in the form function.

Listing 13-18 shows the user profile widget's form function, with fields for the title and the avatar image dimensions.

---

[8]http://www.w3.org/TR/CSS21/syndata.html#characters

Listing 13-18. The Form Function

```php
function form( $instance ) {
                        //Defaults
                        $instance = wp_parse_args( (array) $instance, array(
                                'title' => __('Featured Person'),
                                'avatar_size' => 150,
                                ));
?>
        <p><label for="<?php echo $this->get_field_id('title'); ?>"><?php _e('Title:'); ?></label>
        <input class="widefat" id="<?php echo $this->get_field_id('title'); ?>" name="<?php ➥
echo $this->get_field_name('title'); ?>" type="text" value="<?php echo $instance['title'];?>" /></p>
        <p><label for="<?php echo $this->get_field_id('avatar_size'); ?>"><?php _e('Size of ➥
user picture (in square pixels):'); ?></label>
        <input class="widefat" id="<?php echo $this->get_field_id('avatar_size'); ?>" ➥
name="<?php echo $this->get_field_name('avatar_size'); ?>" type="text" value="<?php echo ➥
esc_attr($instance['avatar_size']); ?>" /></p>

<?php
}
```

In the first line of the form function, you parse the arguments passed in the $instance variable and merge it with a second array containing the default values for your options.

Now it's time to display the form fields. There's no need for a <form> tag; that will be taken care of for you. You just need to wrap the title in a <label> tag and provide an input field for each option. Note the $this->get_field_id() and $this->get_field_name() functions, which are methods of the Widget class designed to give your form fields the appropriate names which will be recognized by the update() function. For the values themselves, use the esc_attr function to sanitize the stored values for use in the HTML value attribute.

And you're done with the form! The submit button will be added automatically.

The Update Function

The first thing to do in any widget update function is to save the old values, in case any of them didn't change. Then, go through each of the fields from your form, do any required processing on them, and save them to the new form instance.

In this case, the only thing you need to do with your widget title is to strip any HTML tags. The avatar size should be a positive whole number, so you can use absint() to validate the user's input. Listing 13-19 shows the isolated update function.

Listing 13-19. The User Profile Widget's Update Function

```php
function update( $new_instance, $old_instance ) {
        $instance = $old_instance;
        $instance['title'] = strip_tags($new_instance['title']);
        $instance['avatar_size'] = intval($new_instance['avatar_size']);
        return $instance;
}
```

The Widget Output

The widget() function displays the HTML that makes up the interior of the widget as it is displayed in the sidebar.
Listing 13-20 shows the isolated widget() function for the user profile.

Listing 13-20. The Widget Function

```
function widget( $args, $instance ) {
        extract( $args );

        $title = apply_filters( 'widget_title', $instance['title'] );

        echo $before_widget;
        if ( !empty($title) )
                echo $before_title . $title . $after_title;

        // get random ID
        global $wpdb;
        $id = $wpdb->get_var( "SELECT ID FROM $wpdb->users ORDER BY RAND() LIMIT 1" );

        // get user
        $user = get_user_by( 'id', $id );

        // get instance option for gravatar size
        $size = $instance['avatar_size'];

        // display gravatar, user name linked to URL, and bio
        $output = get_avatar( $id, $size, '', $user->display_name );
        $output .= '<h3>' . esc_html( $user->display_name ) . '</h3>';
        $output .= wp_kses_post( $user->user_description );

        echo $output . $after_widget;
}
```

The $args variable passed to the widget function is an array of all the fields in the form. To make them easier to
work with, the first line extracts them into separate variables.

Now it's time to print the heart of the widget. In this case, you use just one template tag, edu_users_table().
Of course, you could do something much more complicated here. You could also echo everything immediately,
but in a minute I'm going to show you a variation on this function that makes it more sensible to save everything into
a variable and echo it once at the end.

Once you're finished with the widget output, you print $after_widget, and you're done. Figure 13-7 shows the
final widget.

Featured Person

Jane Austen

Jane Austen is the author of six up-
roariously funny novels set in the
English Regency period. She is a Pro-
fessor Emeritus at this fictional University.

Figure 13-7. *The finished profile widget*

That's almost all there is to widgets! The widget function could contain just about anything. Just keep in mind that widgets are (usually) outside the Loop, so you'll need to access post data accordingly or create your own Loop, as you saw in Chapter 12.

Caching Widget Output with the Transient API

Widgets are often the source of performance problems on WordPress sites. This is not surprising when you think about the way WordPress page views are constructed; there tend to be several widgets in every sidebar, and they're all querying the database, even if it's just to fetch their own options. If some of them query posts as well (or users, or data from an external site), then WordPress has to run all the widget queries in addition to the main Loop before the page can finish loading.

Therefore, unless it's essential that your widget displays up-to-the-second current information, I suggest caching your widget's output using transients. By storing the results of your query for a few hours, you'll reduce the number of queries on each page. The widget's queries will run only when the transient expires, at which point the output will be stored again for a little while.

Transients are just options that are stored temporarily. On many hosts, transients are stored in the database's options table. However, if your host uses an opcode cache like APC, WordPress will use that system instead, and you won't see transients in your options table. Each transient has a name, a value, and an expiration time. The Transient API functions follow the same pattern as the Settings API; they are `get_transient()`, `set_transient()`, and `delete_transient()`. To use them, you will

- Attempt to get the stored transient.

- Use the stored data, if it exists.

- Otherwise, generate your output as usual. Set the transient again with the new data.

Since the random user widget runs its own SQL query, it's ideal for caching in a transient. Listing 13-21 shows the modified widget() function incorporating the transient functions.

Listing 13-21. Caching the User Profile Widget's Output for a Day with a Transient

```
function widget( $args, $instance ) {
        extract( $args );

        $title = apply_filters( 'widget_title', $instance['title'] );

        echo $before_widget;
        if ( !empty($title) )
                echo $before_title . $title . $after_title;

        $output = get_transient( 'edu_random_user' );
        if ( !isset( $output ) ) {
                        // get random ID
                global $wpdb;
                $id = $wpdb->get_var("SELECT ID FROM $wpdb->users ORDER BY RAND() LIMIT 1");

                // get user
                $user = get_user_by( 'id', $id );

                // get instance option for gravatar size
                $size = $instance['avatar_size'];

                // display gravatar, user name linked to URL, and bio
                $output = get_avatar( $id, $size, '', $user->display_name );
                $output .= '<h3>' . esc_html( $user->display_name ) . '</h3>';
                $output .= wp_kses_post( $user->user_description );

                // cache this for a day
                set_transient( 'edu_random_user', $output, 60 * 60 * 1 );

        } // end if

        echo $output . $after_widget;
}
```

■ **Note** This query does not involve any variables. If yours does, you should use the `$wpdb->prepare()` method to sanitize the values before the query is run against the database. See Chapter 11 for information on sanitizing database queries.

In light of this change, you should also modify the update() function. It's fairly safe to assume that any time an administrator directly updates a widget's options, you should delete the old output stored in the transient. There's no need to go to the trouble of setting a new value now; that will happen automatically the next time someone views the widget. Listing 13-22 shows the revised update() function for the user profile widget.

Listing 13-22. Deleting the Transient When the Widget Options Are Updated

```php
function update( $new_instance, $old_instance ) {
        $instance = $old_instance;
        $instance['title'] = strip_tags($new_instance['title']);
        $instance['avatar_size'] = intval($new_instance['avatar_size']);
        delete_transient( 'edu_random_user' );
        return $instance;
}
```

The Complete Widget

Listing 13-23 shows the combined code for the complete Random User Profile widget.

Listing 13-23. The Complete User Profile Widget

```php
// Widget to display individual user profile
class EduUserProfile extends WP_Widget {

        // constructor
        function EduUserProfile() {
            $widget_ops = array('classname' => 'edu_user_profile', 'description' => ↪
__( 'A random user profile') );
            $this->WP_Widget('EduUserProfile', __('Random User'), $widget_ops);
        }

        // widget output
        function widget( $args, $instance ) {
                extract( $args );

                $title = apply_filters( 'widget_title', $instance['title'] );

                echo $before_widget;
                if ( !empty($title) )
                        echo $before_title . $title . $after_title;

                $output = get_transient( 'edu_random_user' );
                if ( !isset( $output ) ) {
                        // get random ID
                        global $wpdb;
                        $id = $wpdb->get_var( "SELECT ID FROM $wpdb->users ORDER BY RAND() LIMIT 1" );

                        // get user
                        $user = get_user_by( 'id', $id );

                        // get instance option for gravatar size
                        $size = $instance['avatar_size'];

                        // display gravatar, user name linked to URL, and bio
                        $output = get_avatar( $id, $size, '', $user->display_name );
                        $output .= '<h3>' . esc_html( $user->display_name ) . '</h3>';
                        $output .= wp_kses_post( $user->user_description );
```

269

```php
                        // cache this for a day
                        set_transient( 'edu_random_user', $output, 60 * 60 * 1 );

                } // end if

                echo $output . $after_widget;
        }

        // save options from widget administration screen
        function update( $new_instance, $old_instance ) {
                        $instance = $old_instance;
                        $instance['title'] = strip_tags($new_instance['title']);
                        $instance['avatar_size'] = intval($new_instance['avatar_size']);
                        delete_transient( 'edu_random_user' );
                        return $instance;
        }

        // display form fields on widget administration screen
        function form( $instance ) {
                        //Defaults
                        $instance = wp_parse_args( (array) $instance, array(
                                        'title' => __('Featured Person'),
                                        'avatar_size' => 150,
                                        ));
        ?>

        <p><label for="<?php echo $this->get_field_id('title'); ?>"><?php _e('Title:'); ?></label>
        <input class="widefat" id="<?php echo $this->get_field_id('title'); ?>" name="<?php⮐
echo $this->get_field_name('title'); ?>" type="text" value="<?php echo $instance['title'];?>" /></p>

        <p><label for="<?php echo $this->get_field_id('avatar_size'); ?>">
<?php _e('Size of user picture (in square pixels):'); ?></label>
        <input class="widefat" id="<?php echo $this->get_field_id('avatar_size'); ?>"
name="<?php echo $this->get_field_name('avatar_size'); ?>" type="text" value="<?php echo
esc_attr($instance['avatar_size']); ?>" /></p>

                <?php
        }
}

// register widget
function edu_profile_widget_init() {
        register_widget('EduUserProfile');
}

// hook registration function
add_action('widgets_init', 'edu_profile_widget_init');
```

Dashboard Widgets

Creating new Dashboard widgets is as easy as creating sidebar widgets. Updating their options, if they have any, is not quite as elegant. For a very basic Dashboard widget, you'll have two essential functions: the widget itself and the setup function. Last, you'll use the add_action() function to add your new widget to the Dashboard setup process using the wp_dashboard_setup() hook.

The Dashboard widget listing incomplete user profiles is outlined in Listing 13-24. I'll fill in each piece as I walk you through the code.

Listing 13-24. The Incomplete User Profiles Dashboard Widget Source Code (Partial)

```
function edu_dashboard_widget() {
        // echo widget contents here
}

function edu_dashboard_widget_control() {
        // update options with saved input; echo form fields here
}

function edu_dashboard_widget_setup() {
        wp_add_dashboard_widget( 'edu_dashboard_widget', __('Incomplete User Profiles'),
'edu_dashboard_widget', 'edu_dashboard_widget_control');
}

add_action('wp_dashboard_setup', 'edu_dashboard_widget_setup');
```

You are probably not surprised to find that you will create a setup function and hook it somewhere; in this case, the wp_dashboard_setup action. The function you are running on this hook calls wp_add_dashboard_widget() with four arguments: a slug for the widget, its translated title, the name of the function that prints its output, and the name of the function that contains its configuration form. This last is optional; if your widget does not require configuration, you can omit the last argument and the corresponding function.

The first function is where you'll echo something to the screen. In this case, I want to find all the users who haven't filled out the first and last name fields in their profiles. (I could check for all the other contact fields, but the code would be repetitive; this will give you the gist.) WordPress 3.5 introduced the nifty meta_query parameter to query classes, including WP_User_Query. This parameter lets you work with multiple meta fields in your query. It includes a NOT EXISTS comparison, which should let you find users who do *not* have the specified meta fields, but this is buggy as of this writing, so here I'm testing for empty fields instead. Listing 13-25 shows the completed edu_dashboard_widget() function, which queries the users for missing first or last names and prints them in an ordered list. The users' display names linked to their user profiles so the administrator can edit the missing fields. Figure 13-8 shows the Dashboard widget.

Incomplete User Profiles

1. Charlotte
2. Sayers
3. Austen

Figure 13-8. *The Incomplete User Profiles Dashboard widget*

Listing 13-25. The edu_dashboard_widget() Function (Dashboard Widget Output)

```
function edu_dashboard_widget() {
        $options = get_option( 'edu_dashboard' );
        if (!isset($options['limit_profiles']))
                $options['limit_profiles'] = 10;

        $args = array(
                'number' => $options['limit_profiles'],
                'meta_query' => array(
                        'relation' => 'OR',
                        array(
                                'key' => 'first_name',
                                'compare' => '=',
                                'value' => '',
                        ),
                        array(
                                'key' => 'last_name',
                                'compare' => '=',
                                'value' => '',
                        ),
                )
        );

        $users = new WP_User_Query( $args );

        if ( $users->total_users ) {
                echo '<ol class="incomplete-profiles">';

                foreach ( $users->results as $user ) {
                        echo '<li><a href="' . get_edit_user_link( $user->user_id ) .'">'
. $user->display_name . '</a></li>';
                }

                echo '</ol>';
        }
}
```

If you didn't want to include any configuration options for the widget, you could end here. Simply remove the first three lines referencing $options, set the number argument to 10 (or some other reasonable number), and you're done! You could refine it further of course; among other things, it might be prudent to wrap the output in an if statement with current_user_can(), checking to see if the current user can edit other users.

For the purposes of demonstration, I'll add a simple Dashboard widget control to let the user choose the number of users shown in the list.

Dashboard Widget Controls

The edu_dashboard_widget_control() function will do three things: get the existing options from the database, update any options if necessary, and print the form fields for each option. As with the sidebar widgets, you don't have to include the form tag or the submit button; those are taken care of automatically.

The control function has to be added to the widget setup function. The name of the control function is the last argument passed to wp_add_dashboard_widget(). If this argument is not present, the widget will not have a configuration screen. Listing 13-26 shows the control function for the Dashboard widget.

Listing 13-26. The Incomplete User Profiles Dashboard Widget Control

```
function edu_dashboard_widget_control() {
                if ( isset($_POST['edu_dashboard[limit_profiles]']) ) {
                        update_option( 'edu_dashboard', absint($_POST['edu_dashboard ↪
[limit_profiles]']) );
                }
                $options = get_option( 'edu_dashboard' );
                if (!isset($options['limit_profiles']))
                        $options['limit_profiles'] = 10;
        ?>
        <p>
        <label for="limit_profiles"><?php _e( 'Limit to the first ' ); ?>
        <input type="text" id="limit_profiles" name="edu_dashboard[limit_profiles]" value=" ↪
<?php echo esc_attr( $options['limit_profiles'] ); ?>" size="4" /> <?php _e(' profiles'); ?>
        </label>
        </p>
<?php
}
```

Unlike the other widgets you created (or, for that matter, any settings screen you've seen so far), here you are working directly with PHP's $_POST variable. It's especially important to sanitize the input here, as you're working without the usual safeguards of the Settings API. Since the option in question is just a number, I've sanitized it using absint(). I've also updated the option only if the value was set in the form input.

Next, I've set the limit to the default value if no option existed in the database—which would be the case the first time this Dashboard widget was used, at least.

Last, I've printed the input field for my option. Even though I have just one field, I'm using the array syntax for the field name. This will make life easier if I ever want to add a second field to the form.

Figure 13-9 shows the configuration screen I've just created. To reach this from your own Dashboard, hover your cursor over the widget title and look for the Configure link that appears on the right side of the title bar.

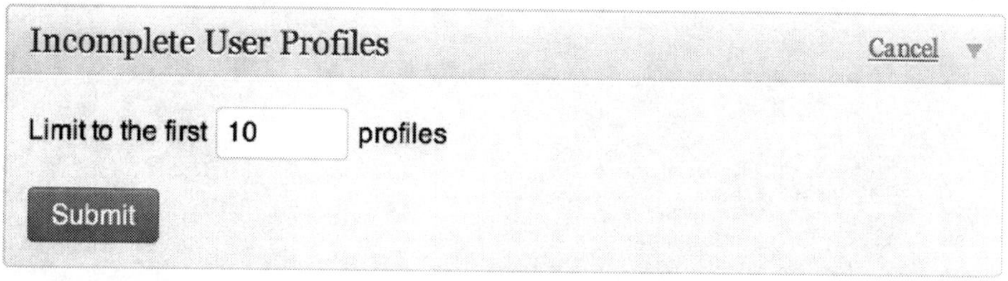

Figure 13-9. *The Incomplete User Profiles Dashboard widget configuration screen*

■ **Note** As with your plugin settings, you should use sensible defaults here. Many users overlook the Configure link on Dashboard widgets.

273

To see more examples of Dashboard widgets, open the `wp-admin/includes/dashboard.php` file in your WordPress installation. All the default Dashboard widgets are defined there.

Publishing a Plugin

If you've been using the examples in this book to develop your own theme or plugin, you probably have a bunch of files stashed in a directory somewhere. You could just zip them up and dump them onto your web server, but that's not an ideal solution. Will you maintain copies of the older versions as you develop new ones? How will you alert users when updates are available? What happens to your code if you decide to stop developing for WordPress?

The repository at WordPress Extend takes care of all those problems for you. To use it, you're going to have to get familiar with source control using Subversion. First, however, you need to create your readme file.

Readme Files and Screenshots

Along with the PHP file(s) containing your plugin's code, you are required to include a `readme.txt` file in plugins uploaded to WordPress Extend. Readme files use the Markdown syntax. Each main heading is surrounded by two equal signs—==— and will become a linked tab on the plugin page. Subheadings use fewer equal signs. Listing 13-27 shows an empty readme file with all the possible headings. If you prefer filling in form fields to dealing with Markdown, you can use the online readme file generator at `http://sleary.me/wp72`.[9]

Listing 13-27. A Sample `readme.txt` File

```
=== My Plugin ===

Plugin Name: My Plugin
Contributors: sillybean
Plugin URI: http://example.com
Author URI: http://example.com
Donate link: http://example.com
Requires at least: 2.8
Tested up to: 3.0
Stable tag: 1.0
Version: 1.0
Tags: posts, pages

== Description ==

Describe your plugin here.

[wpvideo fft9IGgw]

== Installation ==

1. Upload the plugin directory to `/wp-content/plugins/`
1. Activate the plugin through the 'Plugins' menu in WordPress
1. Go to Settings &rarr; My Plugin to set the options
```

---

[9]`http://sudarmuthu.com/wordpress/wp-readme`

```
== Upgrade Notice ==

You should upgrade to 1.0 immediately because there was a serious bug in 0.9.

== Screenshots ==

1. The caption for screenshot-1.png
1. The caption for screenshot-2.png

== Changelog ==

= 1.0 =
* New feature X
= 0.9 =
* Beta release for testers

== Frequently Asked Questions ==

= Question? =

Answer.

= Question 2? =

Answer 2.
```

On the Contributors line, list your username on wordpress.org along with the usernames of any collaborators you have. If you have a page on your own site for your plugin, give the URI in the Plugin URI line; otherwise you can omit the line or use the address of the plugin's Extend page. If you accept donations, use the Donate link line to provide the URI of the page where users can send you donations.

The Version line refers to the version of the plugin accompanying this copy of the readme file. You could upload an alpha version for testers, in which case the version would be something like 1.1-alpha while Stable tag remains 1.0. This way, your alpha version would be available under "Other versions" but end users would not be prompted to upgrade from the Plugins screen.

"Requires at least" and "Tested up to" refer to the versions of WordPress on which this plugin is known to work.

Note that numbered lists can use 1 for each list item. Markdown will correct the numbering so you don't have to renumber your entire list if you add a step in the middle. If you prefer, you can number your lists the usual way. You may also use HTML (including entities like →) if you wish.

See the sample readme file (http://sleary.me/wp73[10]) for a readme.txt file filled with dummy text. It has a number of Markdown syntax examples. See the Daring Fireball site (http://sleary.me/wp74[11]) for a complete guide to Markdown.

You may embed video files in your readme. If you have published a screencast to YouTube or Vimeo video, simply enter the video's URL. If your video is hosted on wordpress.tv, enter the video's ID, as shown earlier in the Description section.

---

[10]http://wordpress.org/extend/plugins/about/readme.txt
[11]http://daringfireball.net/projects/markdown

When you're finished with your readme file, you should run it through the validator (http://sleary.me/wp75[12]) to avoid unexpected formatting problems on your Extend page.

If your plugin includes an option page or generates some kind of output (a template tag, a JavaScript effect, etc.), you should take a screenshot or two and include them in your plugin directory. They should be named screenshot-1.png, screenshot-2.png, and so on. The dimensions are up to you.

Subversion

If you've never used Subversion (SVN) before, getting your plugin listed at WordPress Extend can be a little daunting. You'll have to become familiar with the Subversion source control system. (If you're already familiar with GitHub, you can continue using it for development; just push each release to the Extend Subversion repository when it's finished.) Fortunately, you'll use only a few of Subversion's many commands and options.

First, go to the Plugin Development Center (http://sleary.me/wp76[13]) and sign up to have your plugin added. You'll have to give it a name, a description, and a link to a .zip file containing a working copy of the plugin, which the review team will test. The name will be shortened to a slug for your plugin's address on Extend and cannot be changed later. You can take this step even if you haven't figured out Subversion yet, because it might take a while to get the plugin approved—anywhere from a few hours to a week, because a real person has to look at your submission and determine that it's not broken or malicious. Eventually, you'll receive an e-mail containing your repository URL. In the meantime, keep reading. I'll explain the basic concepts of Subversion and walk you through the whole process of submitting your plugin.

Basic Concepts

Subversion is a form of source control. Like CVS (Concurrent Versioning System, not the pharmacy chain) and Git, Subversion lets you keep track of all the changes you've made to your code. A Subversion repository is a web-accessible archive of those changes. Ever wished you could undo several days' worth of work and roll back to an earlier iteration? If you've kept your local copy in sync with your repository, you can. Furthermore, you can make all those versions—the current release as well as the whole history of the project—available to the public, as shown in Figure 13-10. WordPress plugins and themes are distributed using a Subversion repository, as is the core WordPress software.

---

[12]http://wordpress.org/extend/plugins/about/validator
[13]http://wordpress.org/extend/plugins/about

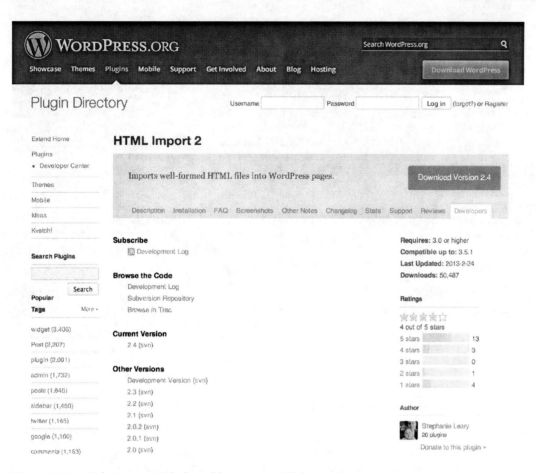

Figure 13-10. *A plugin page with the stable version and links to other versions*

Working with a repository breaks down into three common steps: checking out, updating, and committing. If you're new to Subversion, this will make more sense in the context of an established project, like WordPress itself, rather than the new one you're submitting. Let's say that you wanted to check out a nightly version of WordPress to use as the basis for your development. You'd go to wordpress.org/download/svn/ and locate the address of WordPress's trunk: core.svn.wordpress.org/trunk/. You'd enter this into your client and check out an initial copy. Then, let's say a week or so later, you realize that there have probably been some updates since you checked out your copy, and you'd like to stay in sync. You'd tell your client to update your copy, and it would download all the files that had changed since your initial checkout. If you had changed any of those files in your local copy, your client would alert you to the conflict and ask you what to do. Now, if you're reading this, I'm guessing that you are probably not a WordPress core developer. If you were, though, you'd be able to upload your changes to the repository, making them available to everyone, by committing your altered files.

That's how Subversion works for an existing project. When you first submit your plugin to Extend, you'll receive the address of your repository, and you'll check out an initial copy. This seems nonsensical, because you haven't submitted anything yet, so what is there to check out?

Branches, Tags, and Trunk

WordPress Extend conforms to the Subversion convention of splitting software projects (like plugins or themes) into three major subdirectories: branches, tags, and trunk. When you check out a copy of the code from the repository, these are the three directories you'll download. For a new project, like your plugin or theme, all the directories will be empty—just a framework to help you organize your files. To help illustrate this, Figure 13-11 shows the tag and trunk directories for my HTML Import plugin.

▶ ▦ 2.1	672,598	430,824	Aug 30, 2011 1:22 PM
▶ ▦ 2.2	672,598	630,513	Nov 26, 2012 9:47 PM
▶ ▦ 2.3	672,598	636,712	Dec 10, 2012 1:24 PM
▼ ▦ 2.4	672,599	672,599	Feb 24, 2013 11:16 AM
🗎 html-import-options.php	672,599	672,599	Feb 24, 2013 11:16 AM
🗎 html-import-styles.css	672,599	672,599	Feb 24, 2013 11:16 AM
🗎 html-import.php	672,601	672,601	Feb 24, 2013 11:23 AM
🗎 html-importer.php	672,599	672,599	Feb 24, 2013 11:16 AM
▶ ▦ js			
▶ ▦ languages			
🗎 readme.txt	672,599	672,599	Feb 24, 2013 11:16 AM
▼ ▦ trunk	672,599	672,599	Feb 24, 2013 11:16 AM
🗎 html-import-options.php	672,599	672,599	Feb 24, 2013 11:16 AM
🗎 html-import-styles.css	672,599	635,706	Dec 7, 2012 10:27 PM
🗎 html-import.php	672,601	672,601	Feb 24, 2013 11:23 AM
🗎 html-importer.php	672,599	672,599	Feb 24, 2013 11:16 AM
▶ ▦ js			
▶ ▦ languages	672,599	414,265	Jul 23, 2011 10:50 AM
🗎 readme.txt	672,599	672,599	Feb 24, 2013 11:16 AM

Figure 13-11. *Tag and trunk files for the HTML Import plugin*

The trunk directory is your working copy. On a public repository, like the one for WordPress itself, the nightly builds are snapshots of the trunk. This is the copy of the code that's in active development, so it's generally not considered stable, and it's not recommended for public use. It is useful for alpha and beta testers.

Branches are for major releases. For WordPress, these are the versions that get jazz nicknames and press releases: 3.0, 3.4, 3.5, 3.6. When you're ready to release a major version, create a new subdirectory under branches using the version number as the directory name. Copy the files from trunk into the branch directory and commit your changes.

The tags are the individual, minor version releases of your plugin or theme. For WordPress itself, these are the point releases containing bug fixes and security updates: 3.4.2, 3.5.1. For each minor version of your theme or plugin, you'll create a corresponding tag directory. When your trunk reaches a stable point, you'll copy the files into a new tag directory, update the readme file, and commit your changes. After that, leave the directory alone! You should maintain each release as an archival copy, not to be altered. If you want to release more changes, create a new tag.

Further Reading

Subversion is a big topic, and one I can't fully cover here. The Codex guide to releasing and maintaining plugins in Subversion (http://sleary.me/wp77[14]) is very good. It does rely on the command line; if you prefer a graphical user interface, you can download the trial versions of TortoiseSVN for Windows, or Versions or Cornerstone for Macs, and try the basic checkout/edit/tag/commit cycle in each application. Versions, for example, doesn't handle tagging and branching automatically; if you're uncomfortable tagging each release manually, it might not be the best choice for you.

---

[14]http://wordpress.org/extend/plugins/about/svn/

Localization and Internationalization

As you saw in Chapter 11, if you want to make your plugin available for translation, you need to localize your strings. Use the _e() function to translate and echo, and the __() function (note the double underscore) to translate and return the string for use in other functions. You'll also need to add the text domain of your plugin as the second argument in each wrapper function.

I'll walk you through the localization process for the sample plugin. First you'll wrap all the strings in the appropriate functions. Next, you'll add the text domain to each translation function. Last, you'll generate the template files for translators.

Wrapping Strings in Gettext Calls

If you haven't already, wrap all your strings in the appropriate translation functions. Each gettext call should have the text domain added as a second argument, as shown in Listing 13-28.

Listing 13-28. A Translated String with a Text Domain

```
_e( 'Name', 'sample-user-directory' )
```

Creating the .POT File

If you are submitting your plugin to wordpress.org, you can use the developer tools there to create the .POT (Portable Object Template) file. This is the file that will contain all the translatable strings for your future translators to work with.

Choose the trunk or the appropriate tag from the drop-down menu and click Get POT. The .POT file will be downloaded to your computer. Place it somewhere in your plugin directory. I like to create a subdirectory called languages to hold the .POT file and any translations, but this is entirely up to you.

If you are not submitting your plugin but would like to create the translation files anyway, you can generate the .POT file using Poedit (http://sleary.me/wp78[15]). See BetterWP.net's detailed tutorial (http://sleary.me/wp79[16]) for instructions on using the software.

Adding the i18n Function Block

The very last thing you need to do is to load the plugin's text domain. This is the function that makes the translation go; it passes all your gettext-wrapped strings through the language file (if it exists) matching the user's language as set in his or her configuration. The necessary code is shown in Listing 13-29.

Listing 13-29. The load_plugin_textdomain() Function

```
load_plugin_textdomain('sample-user-directory', '', plugin_dir_path(__FILE__).'/languages');
```

Here, you've called the load_plugin_textdomain() function, which requires three arguments: the domain (as chosen when you added the gettext calls), an empty argument that's present for backward compatibility, and the path to the language directory where your translation files will be stored.

Once you've made all your localization changes, increment your plugin's version number and commit the updates. Your plugin is now ready for translators!

---

[15]http://poedit.net
[16]http://betterwp.net/wordpress-tips/create-pot-file-using-poedit

There is not yet an automated process by which translators can submit their work to you for inclusion in the plugin. Be sure to provide an e-mail address in the plugin's readme file so translators can send you their files. For each language, they will generate a PO (Portable Object) and MO (Machine Object) file. The .po file is human-readable; the .mo file is a compressed binary for faster loading. When you receive them, add them to the same directory where you stored your .POT file. You can then update your plugin version with the new translations.

The Final Result

Listing 13-30 contains the complete code of the sample plugin, complete with gettext functions and text domain. This includes all the plugin components you built throughout the chapter: the new user contact fields, the template tag, the shortcode, the public widget, and the Dashboard widget.

This file is available for download on the book website (http://sleary.me/wpbook[17]).

Listing 13-30. The Finished Sample User Directory Plugin

```php
<?php
/*
Plugin Name: Sample User Directory
Plugin URI: http://stephanieleary.com/wordpress/plugins/sample-user-directory/
Description: Sample plugin that creates a directory of the site's users. Not intended to ↵
be used as-is; download and modify as needed.
Version: 1.0
License: GPLv2
Author: Stephanie Leary
Author URI: http://stephanieleary.com/
*/

function add_extra_media_options() {
    add_settings_field('extra_media', __('Extra Media Option', 'sample-user-directory' ), ↵
'extra_media_options_fields', 'media', $section = 'default', $args = array());
    register_setting('media','extra_media');
}

add_action('admin_init', 'add_extra_media_options');

// displays the options page content
function extra_media_options_fields() { ?>
        <p> the form fields will go here </p>
<?php
}

// change user contact fields
function edu_contact_methods( $contactmethods ) {
        // Add some fields
        $contactmethods['title'] = __('Title', 'sample-user-directory' );
        $contactmethods['phone'] = __('Phone Number', 'sample-user-directory' );
        $contactmethods['twitter'] = __('Twitter Name (no @)', 'sample-user-directory' );
```

[17]http://stephanieleary.com/books/wordpress-for-web-developers/

```
        // Remove AIM, Yahoo IM, Google Talk/Jabber if they're present
        unset($contactmethods['aim']);
        unset($contactmethods['yim']);
        unset($contactmethods['jabber']);
        // make it go!
        return $contactmethods;
}
add_filter( 'user_contactmethods', 'edu_contact_methods', 10, 1 );

// Retrieve list of users
function edu_get_users() {
        $blogusers = get_users(array(
                                'fields' => 'all_with_meta',
                                'order' => 'ASC',
                                'orderby' => 'nicename',
                                ));

        usort($blogusers, 'edu_user_sort');

        return $blogusers;
}

// Sort list of users
function edu_user_sort($a, $b) {
    return strcmp($a->last_name, $b->last_name);
}

// Table displaying user contact information. Echo or return.
function edu_users_table( $echo = true ) {
        $users = edu_get_users();

        $output = '<table id="user-directory">
                                <thead>
                                        <tr>
                        <th>'.__('Name', 'sample-user-directory' ).'</th>';
        $output .= '<th>'.__('Title', 'sample-user-directory' ).'</th>';
        $output .= '<th>'.__('Phone', 'sample-user-directory' ).'</th>';
        $output .= '<th>'.__('Email', 'sample-user-directory' ).'</th>';
        $output .= '</tr>
                </thead>
                <tbody>';

        foreach ($users as $user) {

                        $name = join( ', ', array( $user->last_name, $user->first_name ) );
                        if ( !empty( $user->user_url ) )
                                $name = '<a href="'.esc_url( $user->user_url ).'">' . esc_html( $name ) .'</a>';

        $output .= '<tr class="vcard" id="' . esc_attr( $user->user_nicename ).'">';
        $output .= '<td class="fn uid">'.$name.'</td>';
        $output .= '<td class="title">' . esc_html( $user->title ) .'</td>';
        $output .= '<td class="tell">' . esc_html( $user->phone ) .'</td>';
```

281

```php
            $output .= '<td class="email"><a href="mailto:' . esc_attr( $user->user_email ) .'">'.
esc_html($user->user_email) .'</td>';
                        $output .= '<td class="twitter">';
                        if ( !empty( $user->twitter ) )
                                $output .= '<a href="http://twitter.com/' . esc_attr( $user->↵
twitter ) .'">' . esc_html( $user->twitter ) . '</a>';
                        $output .= '</td>';
                        $output .= '</tr>';
        }
        $output .= '</tbody>
        </table>';

        if ($echo) {
                echo $output;
                return;
        }

        return $output;
}

// Create shortlink to display user info table
function edu_users_table_shortlink($atts = null, $content = null) {
        $content .= edu_users_table(false);
        return $content;
}
add_shortcode('users', 'edu_users_table_shortlink');

// Widget to display individual user profile
class EduUserProfile extends WP_Widget {

        // constructor
        function EduUserProfile() {
                $widget_ops = array('classname' => 'edu_user_profile', 'description' => ↵
__( 'A random user profile', 'sample-user-directory' ) );
                $this->WP_Widget('EduUserProfile', __('Random User', 'sample-user-↵
directory' ), $widget_ops);
        }

        // widget output
        function widget( $args, $instance ) {
                extract( $args );

                $title = apply_filters( 'widget_title', $instance['title'] );

                echo $before_widget;
                if ( !empty($title) )
                        echo $before_title . $title . $after_title;

                $output = get_transient( 'edu_random_user' );
                if ( !isset( $output ) ) {
```

```php
                // get random ID
                        global $wpdb;
                        $id = $wpdb->get_var( "SELECT ID FROM $wpdb->users ORDER BY RAND() LIMIT 1" );

                        // get user
                        $user = get_user_by( 'id', $id );

                        // get instance option for gravatar size
                        $size = $instance['avatar_size'];

                        // display gravatar, user name linked to URL, and bio
                        $output = get_avatar( $id, $size, '', $user->display_name );
                        $output .= '<h3>' . esc_html( $user->display_name ) . '</h3>';
                        $output .= wp_kses_post( $user->user_description );

                        // cache this for a day
                        set_transient( 'edu_random_user', $output, 60 * 60 * 1 );

                } // end if

                echo $output . $after_widget;
        }

        // save options from widget administration screen
        function update( $new_instance, $old_instance ) {
                        $instance = $old_instance;
                        $instance['title'] = strip_tags($new_instance['title']);
                        $instance['avatar_size'] = intval($new_instance['avatar_size']);
                        delete_transient( 'edu_random_user' );
                        return $instance;
        }

        // display form fields on widget administration screen
        function form( $instance ) {
                        //Defaults
                        $instance = wp_parse_args( (array) $instance, array(
                                'title' => __('Featured Person', 'sample-user-directory' ),
                                'avatar_size' => 150,
                                ));
        ?>

        <p><label for="<?php echo $this->get_field_id('title'); ?>"><?php _e('Title:', ↪
'sample-user-directory' ); ?></label>
        <input class="widefat" id="<?php echo $this->get_field_id('title'); ?>" name="<?php↪
echo $this->get_field_name('title'); ?>" type="text" value="<?php echo $instance['title'];?>" /></p>

        <p><label for="<?php echo $this->get_field_id('avatar_size'); ?>">
<?php _e('Size of user picture (in square pixels):', 'sample-user-directory' ); ?></label>
```

```php
        <input class="widefat" id="<?php echo $this->get_field_id('avatar_size'); ?>" name="<?php
echo $this->get_field_name('avatar_size'); ?>" type="text" value="<?php echo ➥
esc_attr($instance['avatar_size']); ?>" /></p>

            <?php
        }
}

// register widget
function edu_profile_widget_init() {
    register_widget('EduUserProfile');
}

// hook registration function
add_action('widgets_init', 'edu_profile_widget_init');

// Dashboard widget to list incomplete profiles
function edu_dashboard_widget() {
    $options = get_option( 'edu_dashboard' );
    if (!isset($options['limit_profiles']))
        $options['limit_profiles'] = 10;

    $args = array(
        'number' => $options['limit_profiles'],
        'meta_query' => array(
            'relation' => 'OR',
            array(
                'key' => 'first_name',
                'compare' => 'NOT EXISTS',
            ),
            array(
                'key' => 'last_name',
                'compare' => 'NOT EXISTS',
            ),
        )
    );

    $users = new WP_User_Query( $args );

    if ( $users->total_users ) {
        echo '<ol class="incomplete-profiles">';

        foreach ( $users->results as $user ) {
            echo '<li><a href="' . get_edit_user_link( $user->user_id ) .'">' . ➥
$user->display_name . '</a></li>';
        }

        echo '</ol>';
    }
}
```

```php
function edu_dashboard_widget_control() {
            if ( isset($_POST['edu_dashboard[limit_profiles]']) ) {
                    update_option( 'edu_dashboard', absint($_POST['edu_dashboard[limit_profiles]']) );
            }
            $options = get_option( 'edu_dashboard' );
            if (!isset($options['limit_profiles']))
                    $options['limit_profiles'] = 10;
    ?>
    <p>
    <label for="limit_profiles"><?php _e( 'Limit to the first ', 'sample-user-directory' ); ?>
            <input type="text" id="limit_profiles" name="edu_dashboard[limit_profiles]" ↵
value="<?php esc_attr_e( $options['limit_profiles'] ); ?>" size="4" />
<?php _e( ' profiles', 'sample-user-directory' ); ?></label>
    </p>
<?php
}

function edu_dashboard_widget_setup() {
        wp_add_dashboard_widget( 'edu_dashboard_widget', __('Incomplete User Profiles', ↵
'sample-user-directory' ), 'edu_dashboard_widget', 'edu_dashboard_widget_control');
}

add_action('wp_dashboard_setup', 'edu_dashboard_widget_setup');

// Register settings and add CSS to settings screen only
add_action('admin_menu', 'edu_add_pages');
function edu_add_pages() {
        $page = add_options_page( __('User Profile Visibility', 'sample-user-directory' ), ↵
__('User Profile Visibility', 'sample-user-directory' ), 'manage_options', 'edu_settings', ↵
 'edu_settings_screen' );
        register_setting( 'edu_settings', 'edu_settings_group', 'edu_settings_validate');
        // These lines are not used in this plugin, but have been left here for reference
        // add_action( 'admin_print_scripts-'.$page, 'edu_settings_js');
        // add_action( 'admin_print_styles-'.$page, 'edu_settings_css' );
}

// add JS and CSS to settings page only
// These functions are never called, unless you un-comment the add_action
// lines inside edu_add_pages()
function edu_settings_js() {
        wp_enqueue_script( 'my-plugin-script', plugins_url( '/my-plugin-script.js' ) );
}

function edu_settings_css() {
        wp_enqueue_style( 'my-plugin-stylesheet', plugins_url( '/my-plugin-style.css' ) );
}

// Settings screen
function edu_settings_screen() {
?>
<div class="wrap">
        <form method="post" id="sample_user_directory" action="options.php">
```

```php
<?php
settings_fields('edu_settings_group');
$options = get_option('edu_settings');
if (empty($options))
        $options = array(
                'user_email' => '1',
                'user_url' => '1',
                'title' => '1',
                'phone' => '1',
                'twitter' => '1',
        );
if ( current_user_can( 'manage_options' ) ) {
?>
<h2><?php _e('User Profile Visibility', 'sample-user-directory' ); ?></h2>

<p><?php _e('Please choose which profile fields should be visible in the user ↪
directory.', 'sample-user-directory' ); ?></p>

<table class="form-table">
<tr>
<th scope="row"><label for="edu_settings[user_firstname]"> <?php _e( 'First Name', ↪
'sample-user-directory' ); ?> </label></th>
<td> <input name="edu_settings[user_firstname]" type="checkbox" value="1" ↪
checked="checked" disabled="disabled" /> </td>
</tr>
<tr>
<th scope="row"><label for="edu_settings[user_lastname]"> <?php _e( 'Last Name', ↪
'sample-user-directory' ); ?> </label></th>
<td> <input name="edu_settings[user_lastname]" type="checkbox" value="1" ↪
checked="checked" disabled="disabled" /> </td>
</tr>
<tr>
<th scope="row"><label for="edu_settings[user_email]"> <?php _e( 'Email Address', ↪
'sample-user-directory' ); ?> </label></th>
<td> <input name="edu_settings[user_email]" type="checkbox" value="1" <?php ↪
checked($options['user_email'], '1'); ?> /> </td>
</tr>

<tr>
<th scope="row"><label for="edu_settings[user_url]"> <?php _e( 'Website Address', ↪
'sample-user-directory' ); ?> </label></th>
<td> <input name="edu_settings[user_url]" type="checkbox" value="1" <?php ↪
checked($options['user_url'], '1'); ?> /> </td>
</tr>

<tr>
<th scope="row"><label for="edu_settings[title]"> <?php _e( 'Title', 'sample-user-↪
directory' ); ?> </label></th>
<td> <input name="edu_settings[title]" type="checkbox" value="1" <?php ↪
checked($options['title'], '1'); ?> /> </td>
</tr>
```

```
        <tr>
        <th scope="row"><label for="edu_settings[phone]"> <?php _e( 'Phone Number', ↪
'sample-user-directory' ); ?> </label></th>
        <td> <input name="edu_settings[phone]" type="checkbox" value="1" <?php ↪
checked($options['phone'], '1'); ?> /> </td>
        </tr>

        <tr>
        <th scope="row"><label for="edu_settings[twitter]"> <?php _e( 'Twitter Username', ↪
'sample-user-directory' ); ?> </label></th>
        <td> <input name="edu_settings[twitter]" type="checkbox" value="1" <?php ↪
checked($options['twitter'], '1'); ?> /> </td>
        </tr>
        </table>

        <p class="submit">
        <input type="submit" value="<?php esc_attr_e( 'Update Options', 'sample-user-↪
directory' ); ?>" class="button-primary" />
        </p>

        <?php } // if current_user_can() ?>
        </form>
</div>
<?php
}

// Validation callback
function edu_settings_validate($input) {
        // first and last name are required and disabled
        unset( $input['user_firstname'] );
        unset( $input['user_lastname'] );
        // all others should be positive integers
        $input = array_walk( $input, 'absint' );
        return $input;
}

// when uninstalled, remove option
register_uninstall_hook( __FILE__, 'edu_delete_options' );

function edu_delete_options() {
        delete_option( 'edu_settings' );
}

// i18n
load_plugin_textdomain( 'sample-user-directory', '', plugin_dir_path(__FILE__) . ↪
'/languages' );
?>
```

Plugin Possibilities

Creating template tags, shortcodes, settings screens, and widgets are just a few of the things you can do in a plugin. The possibilities are quite literally endless! If you need inspiration, take a look at the WordPress Ideas forum (`http://sleary.me/wp80`[18]) for features WordPress users have requested.

Since I can't cover every possibility here, I've gathered a list of tutorials on some of the more common things you might want to do in a plugin.

The Custom List Table Example plugin (`http://sleary.me/wp81`[19]) demonstrates how to create a paged list of items similar to the post and page edit screens. The core code for these screens is quite complicated; this plugin offers a simpler version with plenty of helpful comments.

Adding custom bulk actions on the edit list tables is not as straightforward as you'd think, and invoves using jQuery to edit the Bulk Actions dropdown. There's a good overview at `http://sleary.me/wp82`.[20]

Adding links (and whole submenus) to the Admin Bar is easy to do; see `http://sleary.me/wp83`.[21]

Otto, the author of all those helpful tutorials on the theme customizer you saw in Chapter 12, has an excellent overview on adding a Help tab to your settings screen (`http://sleary.me/wp84`[22]).

Ajax in WordPress: the Codex page (`http://sleary.me/wp85`[23]) is fairly comprehensive. Ronald Huereca has written an entire book on the subject, which you can download for free (`http://sleary.me/wp86`[24]). Andrew Peters has written a guide to JSON requests in WordPress (`http://sleary.me/wp87`[25]).

Further Reading

For more general information on developing plugins, see:

- *Professional WordPress Plugin Development*, by Brad Williams, Ozh Richard, and Justin Tadlock

- WPCandy's unofficial UI guide for plugin and theme settings screens (`http://sleary.me/wp88`[26])

- Using classes in WP plugins (`http://sleary.me/wp89`[27])

- Plugin development best practices (`http://sleary.me/wp90`[28])

If you are interested in writing code for WordPress itself, and not just your own plugins, take a look at the Core Contributor Handbook (`http://sleary.me/wp91`[29]).

---

[18] `http://wordpress.org/extend/ideas/`
[19] `http://wordpress.org/extend/plugins/custom-list-table-example`
[20] `www.foxrunsoftware.net/articles/wordpress/add-custom-bulk-action`
[21] `http://wp-snippets.com/add-links-to-wordpress-3-3-new-toolbar`
[22] `http://ottopress.com/2011/new-in-wordpress-3-3-more-useful-help-screens`
[23] `http://codex.wordpress.org/AJAX_in_Plugins`
[24] `http://wpajax.com`
[25] `www.andrewmpeters.com/blog/how-to-make-jquery-ajax-json-requests-in-wordpress`
[26] `http://wpcandy.com/presents/wordpress-plugin-user-interface-guide`
[27] `http://jumping-duck.com/tutorial/wordpress-plugin-structure/`
[28] `http://wp.tutsplus.com/tutorials/7-simple-rules-wordpress-plugin-development-best-practices`
[29] `http://make.wordpress.org/core/handbook/`

Summary

In this chapter, I've shown you all the basics of WordPress plugin development: adding options forms, creating template tags and shortcodes, checking user capabilities, filtering content, and adding your own functions to action hooks. I've also gone over the process of publishing a plugin on WordPress Extend, including how to create a `readme.txt` file, localize your plugin, and upload it using Subversion.

While I have by no means shown you everything you will ever need to know about writing plugins for WordPress, I hope I have given you a solid foundation for further research. As always, the Codex should be your first stop when you need to find a function or look up an action hook. If the relevant Codex is incomplete—and I'm sorry to say the end-user documentation is far more complete than that for developers—try searching the forums, Google, the PHPdocs, and the Xref documentation.

I've also shown you very briefly how to check for users' capabilities in your plugins. In the next chapter, you'll learn all about the built-in roles and capabilities in WordPress. You'll also learn how to change them to suit your needs.

■ ■ ■

CHAPTER 14

Custom Post Types, Taxonomies, and Fields

In the preceding chapters, I've shown you how to bend posts, pages, categories, and tags to your needs. However, these types of content aren't always sufficient, and sometimes it's just not feasible to have several kinds of content jumbled together under Posts.

In this chapter, I'll show you how to use custom taxonomies to create separate groups of categories and tags for your existing content. Then I'll show you how to create whole new post types. Last, I'll show you how to extend post types (including posts and pages) with custom fields for even more flexibility. At the end of the chapter, you'll find a complete plugin that creates a new post type, several taxonomies, and a few custom fields. It also modifies the theme's queries when displaying the new post type.

Throughout this chapter, you'll see examples of the theme and plugin development concepts you learned in Chapters 11, 12, and 13: actions and filters, callback functions, the query object, and specific theme archive pages. If you haven't read those chapters yet, you might encounter some unfamiliar code here. Refer back to the earlier chapters if you encounter something you don't understand.

Custom Taxonomies

First, some terminology. A *taxonomy* is a group of labels, like tags. *Terms* are the individual labels in that group. For example, Post Tags is a taxonomy, and each tag is a term within that taxonomy. Likewise, Post Categories is a taxonomy, and each category is a term. Each taxonomy term has a label, a slug, and a description. You've seen this before when creating a new category.

Creating a new taxonomy requires just one function: `register_taxonomy()`. However, the arguments can get a little complicated. Listing 14-1 shows all the possible arguments for a new taxonomy, people, that can be used to tag people who are mentioned in a post.

Listing 14-1. Registering a New Taxonomy

```
register_taxonomy(
        'people',
        'post',
        array(
                'labels' => array(
                        'name'          => _x( 'People', 'taxonomy general name' ),
                        'singular_name' => _x( 'Person', 'taxonomy singular name' ),
                        'search_items'      => __( 'Search People' ),
                        'all_items'         => __( 'All People' ),
```

```
                    'edit_item'                => __( 'Edit Person' ),
                    'update_item'              => __( 'Update Person' ),
                    'add_new_item'             => __( 'Add New Person' ),
                    'new_item_name'            => __( 'New Person Name' ),
                    'menu_name'                => __( 'People' ),
                    'separate_items_with_commas' => __( 'Separate people with commas' ),
                    'add_or_remove_items'      => __( 'Add or remove people' ),
                    'choose_from_most_used' => __( 'Choose from the most used people' ),
                ),
            'show_admin_column' => true,
            'rewrite'           => true,
            'query_var'         => true,
            'show_ui'           => true,
            'show_tagcloud'     => true,
            'hierarchical'      => false,
            )
);
```

Let's break down these arguments:

- The first argument is the taxonomy name—an internal name for the new taxonomy.

- The second argument is the name of the post type that can use this taxonomy. This argument can be a string containing a single post type or it can be an array of several post types.

- The third argument is an array containing the optional arguments:

  - labels: an array containing the various translated forms of the taxonomy name. These provide the text for the Dashboard navigation menu item leading to the management page for this taxonomy, the title for the taxonomy's meta box on the Post ➤ Edit screen, and any other references in the Dashboard. (See Figure 14-1.) Specifying all the labels ensures that your instructions to users are grammatically correct (e.g., "Add a new person" instead of "Add a new people").

  - show_admin_column: whether this taxonomy's terms should appear in a column in the Edit Posts (or custom post type) list screens (see Figure 14-4). Defaults to false.

  - rewrite: Possible values are:

    - false: No permalink rules will be created for this taxonomy.

    - true: The permalink structure will be /?taxonomy=term in the default structure or /taxonomy/term using any other permalink structure. In this example, a person named Joe would have a taxonomy permalink of /people/joe.

    - Array containing a slug: The slug will be used in place of the taxonomy name. Here, you could set rewrite to 'person' to create permalinks like /person/joe.

  - query_var: possible values are:

    - false: This taxonomy will not be available in custom queries.

    - true: You can use the taxonomy name in queries. In this case, query_posts('people=joe'); would return any posts tagged with "Joe" in the people taxonomy.

    - string: The given string will be the query variable rather than the taxonomy name.

- `show_ui`: whether or not the management screens and meta boxes should be shown for this taxonomy. Defaults to `true`. You could set this to `false` if you were creating a hidden taxonomy that would be used in your plugin code, but never by users.

- `show_tagcloud`: whether this taxonomy should be an option in the tag cloud widget. (See Figure 14-3.) Defaults to the value of `show_ui`. Applies only to non-hierarchical taxonomies.

- `hierarchical`: whether this taxonomy should be hierarchical (category-like) or non-hierarchical (tag-like). Defaults to `false` (tag-like).

The resulting People taxonomy meta box is shown in Figure 14-1.

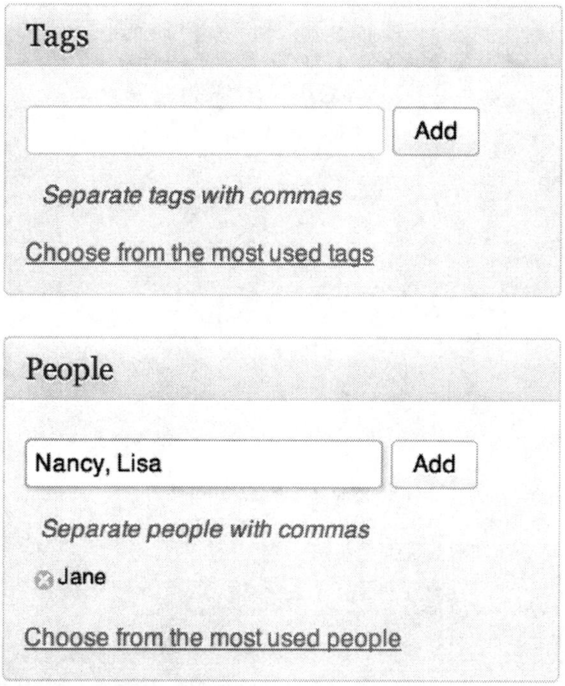

Figure 14-1. *The People taxonomy*

This code could be placed in a plugin file or in your theme's `functions.php` file. However, if the taxonomy is something you would want to continue using even if you switch themes, you should create a plugin for it, as shown in Listing 14-2.

You can register as many new taxonomies as you need. Taxonomies can be hierarchical, like categories, or non-hierarchical, like tags.

Non-hierarchical (Tag-like) Taxonomies

Non-hierarchical taxonomies don't have parent/child relationships. The meta box added to the Post ➤ Edit screen looks like the tag entry field: a single text input box with an autocomplete feature.

To illustrate, I'll create some taxonomies for the university department. Listing 14-2 shows the custom plugin you would write. Since there are three taxonomies, wrap them into a single function, which is called using the init() action hook. (This is exactly how the built-in tag and category taxonomies are created.)

Listing 14-2. Creating the Course Taxonomies

```php
<?php
/*
Plugin Name: Course Taxonomies
*/

add_action('init', 'create_course_tax');
register_activation_hook( __FILE__, 'activate_course_tax' );

function activate_course_tax() {
        create_course_tax();
        flush_rewrite_rules();
}

function create_course_tax() {
        register_taxonomy(
                'colleges',
                'post',
                array(
                    'labels' => array(
                        'name'                 => _x( 'Colleges', 'taxonomy general name' ),
                        'singular_name'        => _x( 'College', 'taxonomy singular name' ),
                        'search_items'         => __( 'Search Colleges' ),
                        'all_items'            => __( 'All Colleges' ),
                        'parent_item'          => __( 'Parent College' ),
                        'parent_item_colon'    => __( 'Parent College:' ),
                        'edit_item'            => __( 'Edit College' ),
                        'update_item'          => __( 'Update College' ),
                        'add_new_item'         => __( 'Add New College' ),
                        'new_item_name'        => __( 'New College Name' ),
                        'menu_name'            => __( 'Colleges' ),
                        'separate_items_with_commas' => __( 'Separate colleges with commas' ),
                        'add_or_remove_items' => __( 'Add or remove colleges' ),
                        'choose_from_most_used' => __( 'Choose from the most used colleges' ),
                    ),
                'hierarchical' => false,
                'show_admin_column' => true,
                )
        );

        register_taxonomy(
                'departments',
                'post',
```

```php
        array(
            'labels' => array(
                'name'                    => _x( 'Departments', 'taxonomy general name' ),
                'singular_name'           => _x( 'Department', 'taxonomy singular name' ),
                'search_items'            => __( 'Search Departments' ),
                'all_items'               => __( 'All Departments' ),
                'parent_item'             => __( 'Parent Department' ),
                'parent_item_colon'       => __( 'Parent Department:' ),
                'edit_item'               => __( 'Edit Department' ),
                'update_item'             => __( 'Update Department' ),
                'add_new_item'            => __( 'Add New Department' ),
                'new_item_name'           => __( 'New Department Name' ),
                'menu_name'               => __( 'Departments' ),
                'separate_items_with_commas' => __('Separate departments with commas'),
                'add_or_remove_items' => __( 'Add or remove departments' ),
                'choose_from_most_used' => __( 'Choose from most used departments' ),
                ),
            'hierarchical' => false,
            'show_admin_column' => true,
            )
    );

    register_taxonomy(
            'people',
            'post',
            array(
                'labels' => array(
                    'name'     => _x( 'People', 'taxonomy general name' ),
                    'singular_name' => _x( 'Person', 'taxonomy singular name' ),
                    'search_items'            => __( 'Search People' ),
                    'all_items'               => __( 'All People' ),
                    'edit_item'               => __( 'Edit Person' ),
                    'update_item'             => __( 'Update Person' ),
                    'add_new_item'            => __( 'Add New Person' ),
                    'new_item_name'           => __( 'New Person Name' ),
                    'menu_name'               => __( 'People' ),
                    'separate_items_with_commas' => __('Separate people with commas'),
                    'add_or_remove_items'   => __( 'Add or remove people' ),
                    'choose_from_most_used' => __('Choose from the most used people'),
                    ),
                'hierarchical'      => false,
                'show_admin_column' => true,
                )
        );
}
?>
```

In addition to creating the taxonomies themselves, you must flush the rewrite rules (which are cached) for the new permalinks to take effect. Since this needs to be done just once, wrap it up in a plugin activation function. This function calls create_course_tax() once to get all the new rewrite rules into place, then flushes the rewrite rules.

Figure 14-2 shows the resulting meta boxes on the Post ➤ Edit screen. Figure 14-3 shows the management page for one of the new taxonomies, and Figure 14-4 shows the Edit Posts screen once all three taxonomies have been added.

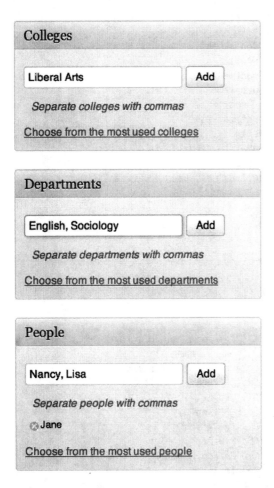

Figure 14-2. *The resulting taxonomy boxes, on the right side of the Edit Post screen*

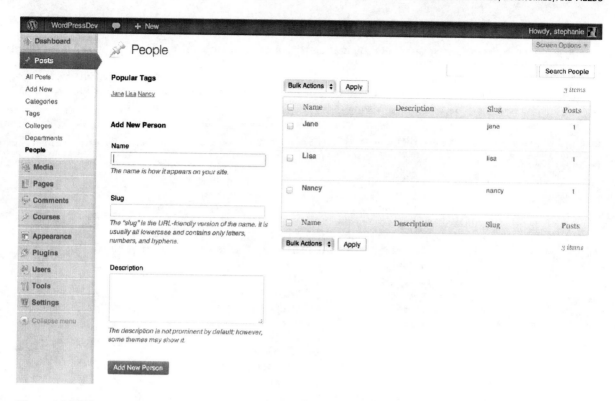

Figure 14-3. The management page for the new People taxonomy

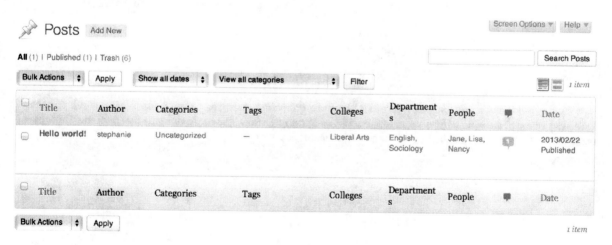

Figure 14-4. The Edit Posts screen with the new taxonomy columns

Hierarchical (Category-like) Taxonomies

Hierarchical taxonomies can have parents and children, and the meta box on the Post ➤ Edit screen looks just like the category box.

For the book series site, you might want your users to classify things in fine-grained subgenres, not just the major categories one would find in a bookstore. To do this, just change the hierarchical argument to true in the register_taxonomy() function, as shown in Listing 14-3.

Listing 14-3. Changing Colleges to a Hierarchical Taxonomy

```
register_taxonomy(
                'colleges',
                'post',
                array(
                    'labels' => array(
                        'name'                 => _x( 'Colleges', 'taxonomy general name' ),
                        'singular_name'        => _x( 'College', 'taxonomy singular name' ),
                        'search_items'         => __( 'Search Colleges' ),
                        'all_items'            => __( 'All Colleges' ),
                        'parent_item'          => __( 'Parent College' ),
                        'parent_item_colon'    => __( 'Parent College:' ),
                        'edit_item'            => __( 'Edit College' ),
                        'update_item'          => __( 'Update College' ),
                        'add_new_item'         => __( 'Add New College' ),
                        'new_item_name'        => __( 'New College Name' ),
                        'menu_name'            => __( 'Colleges' ),
                        'separate_items_with_commas' => __('Separate colleges with commas'),
                        'add_or_remove_items' => __( 'Add or remove colleges' ),
                        'choose_from_most_used' => __('Choose from the most used colleges'),
                        ),
                'hierarchical'      => true,
                'show_admin_column' => true,
                )
);
```

Figure 14-5 shows a post with the altered Colleges taxonomy meta box. The Categories meta box is still present; here, it's just out of view, near the bottom of the screen. Figure 14-6 shows the management screen for the Colleges taxonomy, which now looks just like the category management screen.

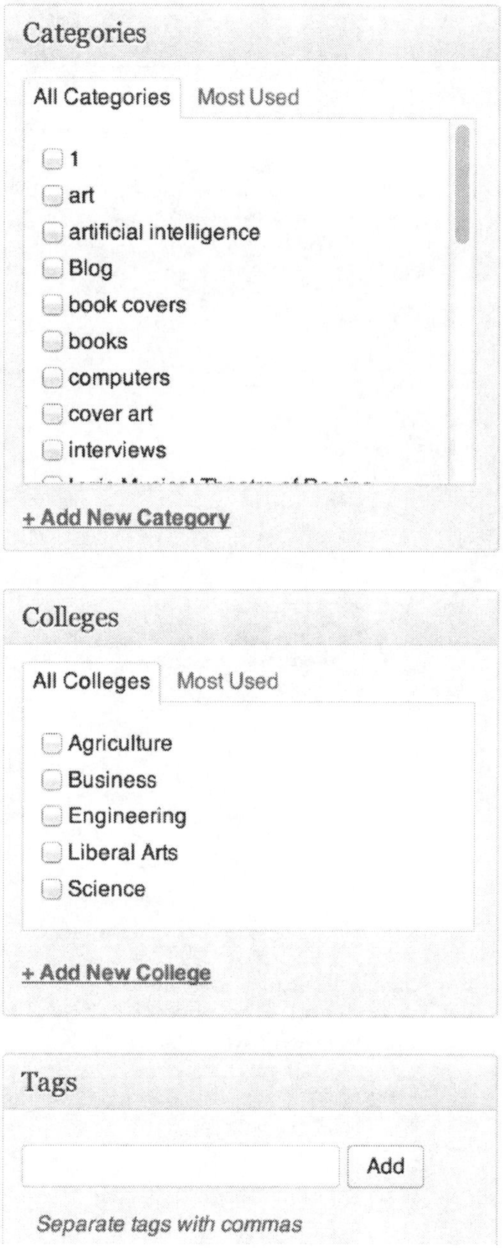

Categories

| All Categories | Most Used |

- ☐ 1
- ☐ art
- ☐ artificial intelligence
- ☐ Blog
- ☐ book covers
- ☐ books
- ☐ computers
- ☐ cover art
- ☐ interviews

+ Add New Category

Colleges

| All Colleges | Most Used |

- ☐ Agriculture
- ☐ Business
- ☐ Engineering
- ☐ Liberal Arts
- ☐ Science

+ Add New College

Tags

[   ] [Add]

Separate tags with commas

Figure 14-5. *A hierarchical Colleges taxonomy in Post ➤ Edit*

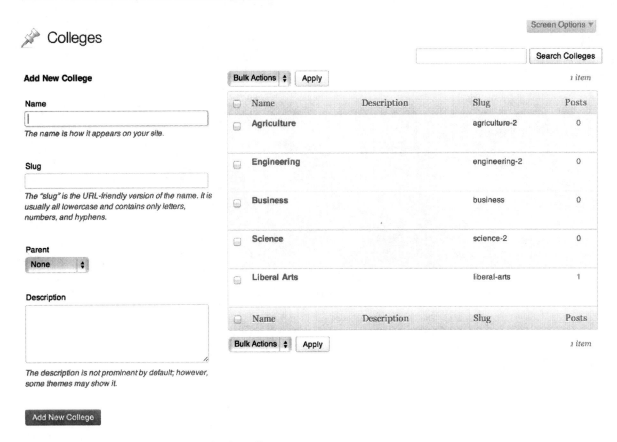

Figure 14-6. *The management screen for the Colleges taxonomy*

Using Custom Taxonomies

If you publish the post shown in Figure 14-2, you can then browse to your archive page using the permalink structure you created and one of the terms you assigned. In this case, /colleges/liberal-arts results in the archive page shown in Figure 14-7. If you weren't using a permalink structure, the URL would be /?taxonomy=colleges&term=liberal-arts.

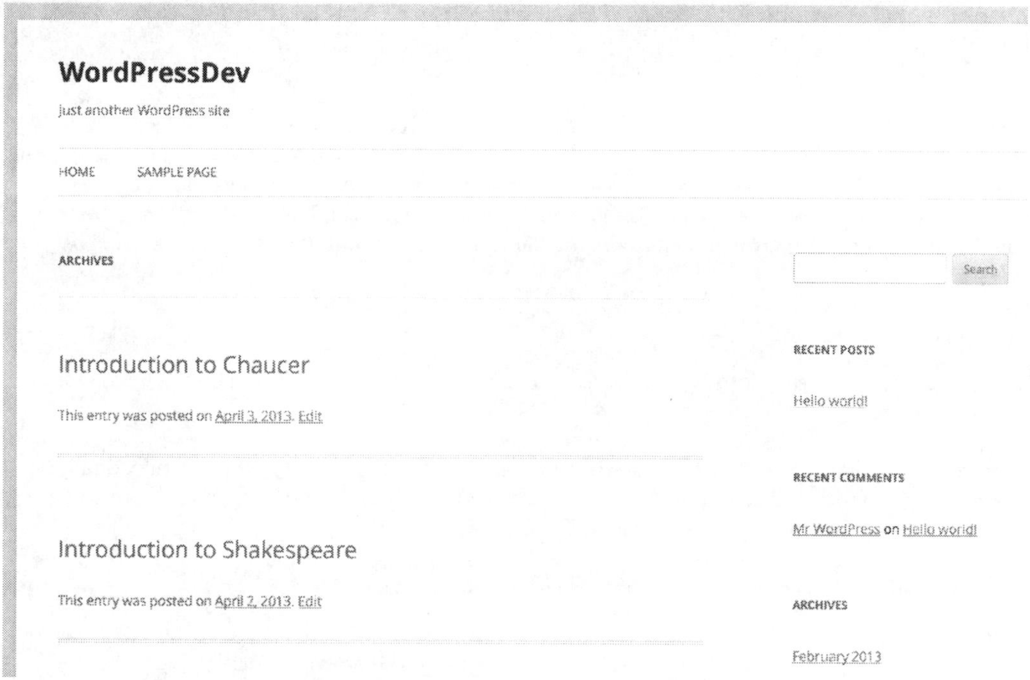

WordPressDev

Just another WordPress site

HOME   SAMPLE PAGE

ARCHIVES

Search

Introduction to Chaucer

This entry was posted on April 3, 2013. Edit

RECENT POSTS

Hello world!

RECENT COMMENTS

Mr WordPress on Hello world!

Introduction to Shakespeare

This entry was posted on April 2, 2013. Edit

ARCHIVES

February 2013

Figure 14-7. *The Liberal Arts college archive page*

As you can see, this archive page is a little generic. The default theme does not include a taxonomy archive template, so the title of the page is simply "Archives." To fix it up, you can either add a conditional statement checking `is_tax()` to your generic `archive.php` template, or you can create a `taxonomy.php` template. I'll use the latter option. Listing 14-4 shows a basic taxonomy template for Twenty Twelve. (You can use Twenty Thirteen if you prefer, but its color scheme doesn't print well in this book.)

Listing 14-4. A New `taxonomy.php` File for the Twenty Twelve Theme

```php
<?php get_header(); ?>
        <section id="primary" class="site-content">
                <div id="content" role="main">
                <?php if ( have_posts() ) : ?>
                        <header class="archive-header">
                                <h1 class="archive-title"><?php single_term_title(); ?></h1>
                        </header><!-- .archive-header -->
                        <?php
                        while ( have_posts() ) : the_post();
                                get_template_part( 'content', get_post_format() );
                        endwhile;
                        twentytwelve_content_nav( 'nav-below' );
                        ?>
                <?php else : ?>
                        <?php get_template_part( 'content', 'none' ); ?>
                <?php endif; ?>
                </div><!-- #content -->
```

```
        </section><!-- #primary -->
<?php get_sidebar(); ?>
<?php get_footer(); ?>
```

All that's changed from archive.php is that you've removed the date-based conditionals and replaced the standard title with a function, single_term_title(), that prints a title based on the name of the term being displayed.

It would also be nice to include the custom taxonomy terms in the post's metadata alongside the categories and post tags. You could use the_taxonomies(), but this function is indiscriminate and prints *all* the taxonomies, including the built-in ones. There's no way to limit it to a particular taxonomy. Its output for the Shakespeare post is shown in Listing 14-5.

Listing 14-5. Result of the_taxonomies()

Categories: News. Post Tags: drama, plays, revenge. Colleges: Liberal Arts. Departments: English. People: William Shakespeare.

To list just one taxonomy at a time with better control over the output, add them to the template individually, using get_the_term_list() as shown in Listing 14-6. This function won't print anything if there are no terms associated with the post, so you don't need to check first to see if it's empty.

Listing 14-6. Listing the Terms of a Particular Taxonomy Alongside Categories and Tags

```
<p>Posted in <?php the_category(',') ?>
<?php echo get_the_term_list( get_the_ID(), 'colleges', 'in the College of ', ', ', '' ); ↵
 ?></p>
<?php if ( the_tags('<p>Tagged with ', ', ', '</p>') ) ?>
```

There's no built-in page to display a list all the taxonomies. The get_taxonomies() function will display them, but it includes all the registered taxonomies, including the defaults, as shown in Listing 14-7.

Listing 14-7. Listing All Registered Taxonomies

```
<ul id="taxonomies">
<?php
        $taxes = get_taxonomies();
        foreach ($taxes as $tax) echo '<li>'.$tax.'</li>';
?>
</ul>
```

With our university taxonomies, the list will be:

- category
- post_tag
- nav_menu
- colleges
- departments
- people

To remove the built-in taxonomies from the list and show only the custom taxonomies you've created, use the taxonomies' _builtin argument. It's a private argument, intended for WordPress's internal use, to specify which taxonomies are built in. (Don't ever abuse it to create your own "built-in" taxonomy). You can use it to filter your taxonomy list, as shown in Listing 14-8.

Listing 14-8. Listing Only Custom Taxonomies

```
<ul id="taxonomies">
<?php
        $taxes = get_taxonomies(array('_builtin' => false));
        foreach ($taxes as $tax) echo '<li>'.$tax.'</li>';
?>
</ul>
```

Now the result is more useful:

- colleges
- departments
- people

If you want a page that lists your custom taxonomies this way, create a new page template with the code in Listing 14-8 in place of the loop.

Custom Post Types

While custom taxonomies provide a powerful way to organize posts, sometimes that organization just isn't enough. For a blogger, using posts for movie and book reviews as well as slice-of-life vignettes might suffice, but posts and pages can be too limiting a framework for more complex sites.

WordPress provides methods of creating whole new content types. New types can be hierarchical, like pages, or non-hierarchical, like posts. As you create the new types, you can choose which attributes (revisions, thumbnails, etc.) they support. And, of course, you can assign taxonomies to your custom types.

░ **Note** Custom post types are often confused with post formats. Post *formats* are intended to allow special formatting for the different kinds of posts that make up a blog: quotes, links, videos, and so forth. Post *types* are for cataloging things that are not posts or pages, like store products.

Consider the university department site you saw in the theme and plugin development chapters (12 and 13). The site needs to list specific courses as well as news updates (the blog) and informational pages (hours and location, a staff directory, etc.). Without custom content types, the choice for storing the course data lies between posts and pages. The office would like to keep the course information out of their news blog, and they'd like to publish a separate feed of all the courses available. Therefore, they have elected to use a custom post type to store the course information.

The register_post_type() function looks an awful lot like register_taxonomy(), and many of its attributes work the same way. Listing 14-9 shows a sample content type with all the possible arguments.

Listing 14-9. Creating a New Content Type

```
register_post_type(
        'mytype',
        array(
                'labels' => array(
                        'name' => __( 'My Types' ),
                        'singular_name' => __( 'My Type' ),
                ),
                'public' => true,
                'supports' => array(
                        'title',
                        'editor',
                        'author',
                        'excerpts',
                        'custom-fields',
                        'revisions',
                        'thumbnail')
                )
        );
register_taxonomy_for_object_type('category', 'mytype');
register_taxonomy_for_object_type('post-tag', 'mytype');
?>
```

As with taxonomies, the post types are created with a handle and an array of attributes. Here are all of the possible attributes:

- labels: an array containing the names of the content type in their plural ('name') and singular ('singular_name') forms.

- description: a short description of the content type. Empty by default.

- public: whether this content type should be shown in the admin screens. Set to false (hidden) by default.

- exclude_from_search: whether content of this post type should be excluded from search results. By default, inherits the value of public.

- publicly_queryable: whether queries can be performed using the post_type argument. By default, inherits the value of public.

- show_ui: whether Edit and Add New screens should be added for this post type. By default, inherits the value of public.

- has_archive: whether users will be able to view archive pages specific to this post type. Defaults to false.

- inherit_type: If you would like the new type to use the capabilities of an existing type, use this argument to set it.

- capability_type: content type for read_, edit_, and delete_ capabilities. The default type used is post if no other is specified. You can use this argument to create a whole new set of capabilities specific to the new content type (e.g., 'course').

- capabilities: an array of capabilities ('edit_post', 'delete_post', 'publish_posts'). If you created a new capability_type, these values will default to the standard post capabilities with the name of your content type substituted for 'post' (e.g., 'edit_course', 'delete_course', 'publish_courses').

- hierarchical: whether the post type is hierarchical (page-like). Defaults to false (post-like).

- supports: As a substitute for calling the add_post_type_support() function, lists supported features here. Defaults to none. The possible features are:

  - author: the user writing the custom entry

  - title: whether this content type includes a title

  - editor: whether the visual/HTML content textarea and media uploader should be used

  - excerpts: whether the excerpts field should be used

  - thumbnail: whether this content type should include image thumbnails

  - comments: whether comments will be accepted for this content type

  - trackbacks: whether trackbacks will be accepted for this content type

  - custom-fields: whether the Custom Fields box will be shown and custom fields automatically saved.

  - revisions: whether revisions will be stored and displayed.

  - page-attributes: the Page Attributes box, containing the parent, template, and menu order options.

- register_meta_box_cb: the name of a callback function that will set up any custom meta boxes for the edit screens. This function should contain any remove_meta_box() and add_meta_box() calls.

- taxonomies: an array of taxonomy names that will be used by the content type. Default is none. You can register taxonomies later with register_taxonomy() or register_taxonomy_for_object_type().

Note that public is true by default for taxonomies but is false by default for post types. The query_vars, rewrite, and show_ui attributes all inherit from public, so be sure to set public to true (or turn on each of those items individually).

The has_archive argument does *not* inherit from public and defaults to false, so be sure to set it to true if you want archives for your post type, and make sure you don't have a page whose slug is the same as your post type's rewrite argument (which is its name, by default).

Non-hierarchical (Post-like) Content Types

Next I'll start transforming the courses by creating a new post type for a university. Listing 14-10 shows a simple plugin that creates a new non-hierarchical post type—something very similar to posts. As with register_taxonomy(), you don't have to include arguments if you plan to use the default values.

Listing 14-10. Creating a Non-hierarchical Content Type for Courses

```
function post_type_courses() {
        register_post_type(
                'course',
                        array(
                        'labels' => array(
                                'name' => __( 'Courses' ),
                                'singular_name' => __( 'Course' ),
                                'add_new' => __('Add New'),
                                'add_new_item' => __('Add New Course'),
                                'edit_item' => __('Edit Course'),
                                'new_item' => __('New Course'),
                                'view_item' => __('View Course'),
                                'search_items' => __('Search Courses'),
                                'not_found' => __('No courses found'),
                                'not_found_in_trash' => __('No courses found in Trash'),
                                'menu_name' => __('Courses'),
                        ),
                        'capability_type' => 'post',
                        'description' => __('Individual course data'),
                        'public' => true,
                        'show_ui' => true,
                        'hierarchical' => false,
                        'supports' => array(
                                'title',
                                'editor',
                                'author',
                                'excerpt',
                                'custom-fields',
                                'revisions',
                        )
                )
        );
}
```

In this case, you've decided that the course type should not support comments or trackbacks.

If you activate this little plugin, your navigation menu will immediately gain a new section just below Comments: Courses, with options to edit, add a new course, or manage course taxonomies (Figure 14-8).

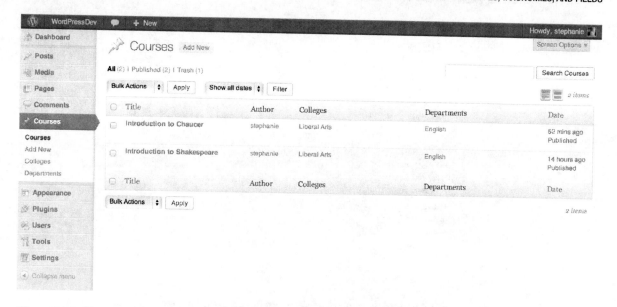

Figure 14-8. *New Courses menu section and management screen*

Hierarchical (Page-like) Post Types

A hierarchical post type can have children, just as pages do. If the department needed to create several related entries for each course—a general overview, a syllabus, and a reading list—it would make more sense to create the courses as hierarchical content types, like pages. To do so, you need to set the `hierarchical` argument to `true`, and add `page-attributes` to the list of things this content type supports (Listing 14-11).

Listing 14-11. *Creating a Non-hierarchical Post Type for Courses*

```
function post_type_courses() {
        register_post_type(
        'courses',
                array(
                'labels' => array(
                        'name' => 'Courses',
                        'singular_name' => 'Course',
                        'add_new' => 'Add New',
                        'add_new_item' => 'Add New Course',
                        'edit_item' => 'Edit Course',
                        'new_item' => 'New Course',
                        'all_items' => 'All Courses',
                        'view_item' => 'View Course',
                        'search_items' => 'Search Courses',
                        'not_found' =>  'No Courses found',
                        'not_found_in_trash' => 'No Courses found in Trash',
                        'parent_item_colon' => '',
                        'menu_name' => 'Courses'
                        ),
                'capability_type' => 'post',
                'map_meta_cap' => true,
```

```
                'description' => __('Individual Course data'),
                'public' => true,
                'show_ui' => true,
                'has_archive' => true,
                    'hierarchical' => true,
                'supports' => array(
                        'title',
                        'editor',
                        'author',
                        'excerpt',
                        'thumbnail',
                        'custom-fields',
                        'revisions',
                        'page-attributes',
                ),
                )
        );
}
```

Now your editing screen will look more like a page, as shown in Figure 14-9. And, since you now have the Attributes meta box, you can choose parents.

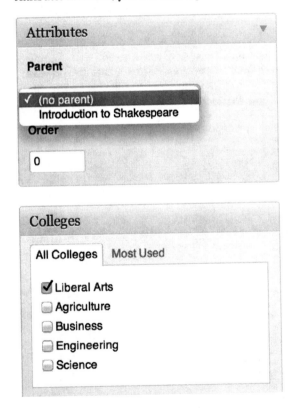

Figure 14-9. *Editing the hierarchical content type with attributes meta box*

Later in this chapter, you'll see how to work with queries to display the courses in your theme.

Changing Post Types

If you are working with a site that already has different types of content stored as posts, you now need to change your old posts to the new post type. All post types are stored in the wp_posts table, and the only difference at the database level is the post_type field.

You don't have to copy and paste all your old posts into the new type. There are two plugins you can use: Post Type Switcher and Convert Post Types.

Post Type Switcher is ideal for changing the type of one post at a time (Figure 14-10), or a selection of posts using Bulk Edit. Convert Post Types is better for changing hundreds of posts all at once. It lets you change the post type of all posts in a category, or all the children of a particular page. Figure 14-11 shows all the plugin's options.

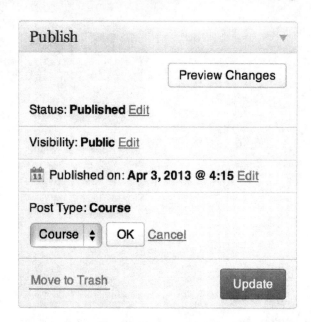

Figure 14-10. *Post Type Switcher adds a Post Type drop-down to the Publish meta box*

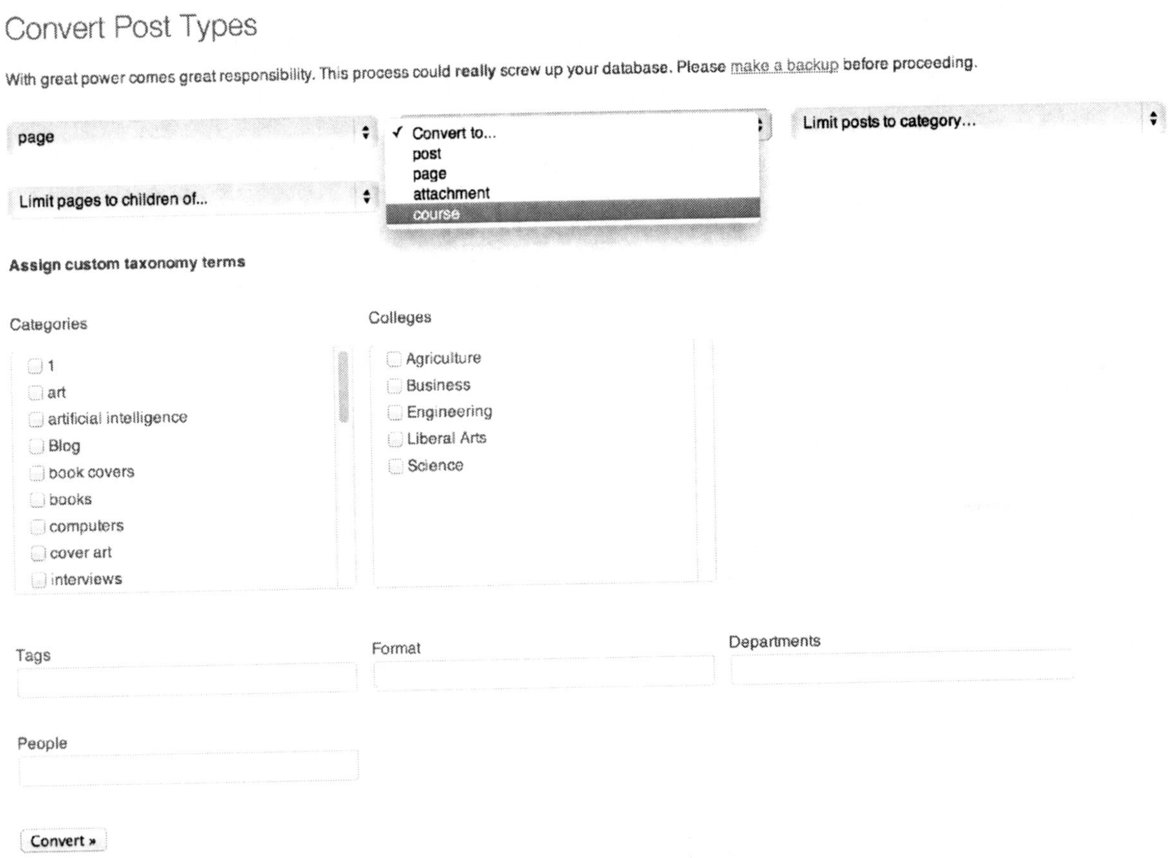

Convert Post Types

With great power comes great responsibility. This process could really screw up your database. Please make a backup before proceeding.

page ⬍	✓ Convert to...	Limit posts to category... ⬍
	post	
Limit pages to children of... ⬍	page	
	attachment	
	course	

Assign custom taxonomy terms

Categories

- [ ] 1
- [ ] art
- [ ] artificial intelligence
- [ ] Blog
- [ ] book covers
- [ ] books
- [ ] computers
- [ ] cover art
- [ ] interviews

Colleges

- [ ] Agriculture
- [ ] Business
- [ ] Engineering
- [ ] Liberal Arts
- [ ] Science

Tags

Format

Departments

People

[Convert »]

Figure 14-11. *Changing pages to courses with the Convert Post Types plugin*

Including Custom Post Types in Your Theme

As long as the has_archive argument was set to true when the post type was registered, displaying your custom post types in your theme is easy. To create a single archive page for a custom post type, all you have to do is create another file in your theme directory, single-**type**.php. To create an archive list page for the post type, create a file called archive-**type**.php.

For the courses, it would make sense to sort our custom posts by name instead of date. You can use the pre_get_posts filter to change the query's orderby parameter before WordPress queries the database. Listing 14-12 shows how to filter the queries to sort courses alphabetically by title. The resulting list is shown in Figure 14-12.

Listing 14-12. pre_get_posts Filters for Courses

```
add_filter( 'pre_get_posts', 'alphabetize_courses' );

function alphabetize_courses( $query ) {
        if ( is_post_type_archive('course') ) {
                $query->set( 'orderby', 'title' );
                $query->set( 'order', 'ASC' );
        }
        return $query;
}
```

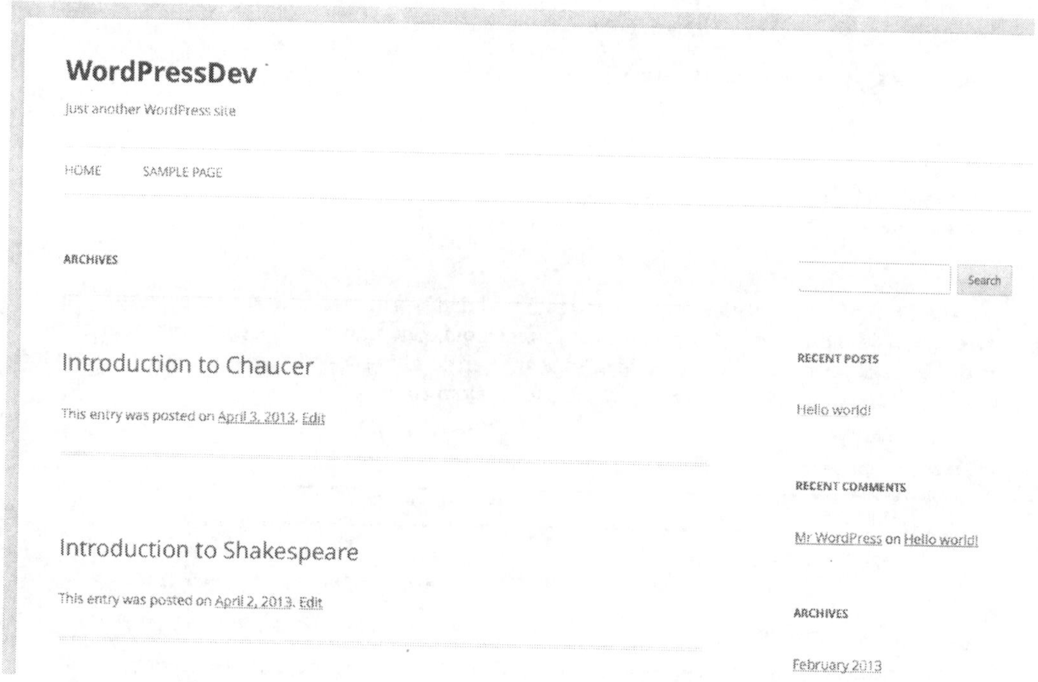

WordPressDev

Just another WordPress site

HOME   SAMPLE PAGE

ARCHIVES

Introduction to Chaucer

This entry was posted on April 3, 2013. Edit

Introduction to Shakespeare

This entry was posted on April 2, 2013. Edit

Search

RECENT POSTS

Hello world!

RECENT COMMENTS

Mr WordPress on Hello world!

ARCHIVES

February 2013

Figure 14-12. The course archive page, sorted by title

Custom post types will be included automatically in taxonomy archives (as long as the taxonomy is registered for the post type) and in search results. They will not be included in the main loop on your home page unless you add a filter specifying that they should be included. Listing 14-13 demonstrates how to include the course post type on the department's home page using the is_home() conditional. You could remove this to ensure that the courses are included everywhere.

Listing 14-13. Displaying Courses in the Main Loop on the Home Page

```
add_filter( 'pre_get_posts', 'my_get_posts' );

function my_get_posts( $query ) {
        if ( is_home() )
                $query->set( 'post_type', array( 'post', 'course' ) );
        return $query;
}
```

Feeds for Custom Content Types

You can use the pre_get_posts filter to include custom post types in feeds. The required code is shown in Listing 14-14, and looks almost identical to the home page code you saw in Listing 14-13.

Listing 14-14. Showing the Course Post Type Alongside Posts in the Site Feed

```
add_filter( 'pre_get_posts', 'my_get_posts' );

function my_get_posts( $query ) {
        if ( is_feed() )
                $query->set( 'post_type', array( 'post', 'course' ) );
        return $query;
}
```

As you saw in Chapter 4, there are many feeds that aren't publicized in WordPress. You can use a query string format similar to the one you used for searches to get feeds of your custom content types. The post_type parameter given should match the name of your custom content type. You can even combine content types using the parameters instead of filters. Table 14-1 lists some of the possible feed URLs for custom content types.

Table 14-1. Course Content Type Feeds in WordPress

Feed Type	Default URL	Clean URL
RSS 2.0 (default)	/?feed=rss2&post_type=course	/feed/?post_type=course /feed/rss2/?post_type=course
Atom 1.0	/?feed=atom&post_type=course	/feed/atom/?post_type=course
Combining content types	/?feed=rss2&post_type=course,post, professor	/feed/?post_type=course,post, professor

Custom Fields in Custom Content Types

Now that you've separated our courses from posts and pages, you can think about structuring the content of each course. The university office used to store three distinct pieces of information in the content textarea: the instructor's name, his or her e-mail address, and a brief description of the course. Furthermore, the title field contained the university's internal code (ENGL 412) as well as the actual course title. What if the office asks you to create a table of honors courses with the code and the title in separate, sortable columns? There's no good way to separate that data with the standard WordPress fields.

The course description can stay in the content field, but the course code, instructor name, and e-mail address would all be better off in separate custom fields. However, the built-in custom field interface is not very friendly, and the office's administrative assistant is not going to find it intuitive. You ought to provide a better interface for adding this information.

Creating the Custom Fields

First, you have to modify your post type function to add a callback. This is the name of the function that will add (and/or remove) custom meta boxes from the Edit screen. Listing 14-15 shows the change.

Listing 14-15. Updating the post_type_courses() Function to Include 'register_meta_box_cb' Argument

```
function post_type_courses() {
        register_post_type(
                'course',
                array(
```

```
                'labels' => array(
                        'name' => __( 'Courses' ),
                        'singular_name' => __( 'Course' ),
        ),
                        'description' => __('Individual course data'),
                        'public' => true,
                        'show_ui' => true,
                        'register_meta_box_cb' => 'course_meta_boxes',
                        'supports' => array(
                        'title',
                        'editor',
                        'author',
                        'excerpt',
                        'custom-fields',
                        'revisions',)
                )
        );
}
```

Then you need to add the course_meta_boxes() function, as shown in Listing 14-16. You'll add a whole new section to the Course Post Types plugin to handle the custom meta boxes, and this will be the first part of that section.

Listing 14-16. The Callback Function That Adds Meta Boxes

```
/* Custom Fields */

function course_meta_boxes() {
    add_meta_box( 'course_code_meta', __('Course Code'), 'course_code_meta_box', 'course',↪
'normal', 'high' );
    add_meta_box( 'instructor_meta', __('Instructor'), 'instructor_meta_box', 'course',↪
'normal', 'high' );
}
```

This function adds two meta boxes, one for the course code and one for the instructor information. The course code box will contain one text field for the code. The instructor box will contain two fields, the name and the e-mail. The arguments of add_meta_box() are:

- Handle: a unique name for this meta box, for your internal use

- Title: the title of the box

- Callback: the name of the function that will print the contents of the box

- Post type: the names of all the post types that will use this box. To have the box appear on a page as well as a course, you would have used array('course', 'page') here.

- Section: which part of the Edit screen this box will appear in by default (normal, advanced, or side)

- Priority: how high the box should appear within its section (high, normal, or low)

Next, create the callback functions that print the contents of each meta box, as shown in Listing 14-17.

Listing 14-17. Printing the Meta Boxes

```php
function course_code_meta_box() {
        if ( function_exists('wp_nonce_field') )
                wp_nonce_field('course_code_nonce', '_course_code_nonce');
?>
        <p><label for="_course_code">Course Code (e.g. ENGL 101)</label>
        <input type="text" name="_course_code"
        value="<?php echo esc_html( get_post_meta( get_the_ID(), '_course_code', true ), ↵
 1 ); ?>" /></p>

<?php
}

function instructor_meta_box() {
        global $post;
        if ( function_exists('wp_nonce_field') ) wp_nonce_field('instructor_nonce', ↵
 '_instructor_nonce');
?>
        <p><label for="_instructor_name">Name</label>
        <input type="text" name="_instructor_name"
            value="<?php echo esc_html( get_post_meta( get_the_ID(), '_instructor_name', ↵
 true ), 1 ); ?>" /></p>
        <p><label for="_instructor_email">Email</label>
        <input type="text" name="_instructor_email"
            value="<?php echo esc_html( get_post_meta( get_the_ID(), '_instructor_email', ↵
 true ), 1 ); ?>" /></p>
        <p><label for="_instructor_phone">Phone</label>
        <input type="text" name="_instructor_phone"
            value="<?php echo esc_html( get_post_meta( get_the_ID(), '_instructor_phone', ↵
 true ), 1 ); ?>" /></p>

<?php
}
```

Each function simply prints the form fields within each meta box. To make sure the field values are populated with any previously saved data, call get_post_meta(), which requires three arguments: the post ID, the meta key, and a true/false value determining whether the function should return a single value or all values stored with that key for the post.

The resulting Edit Course screen is shown in Figure 14-13.

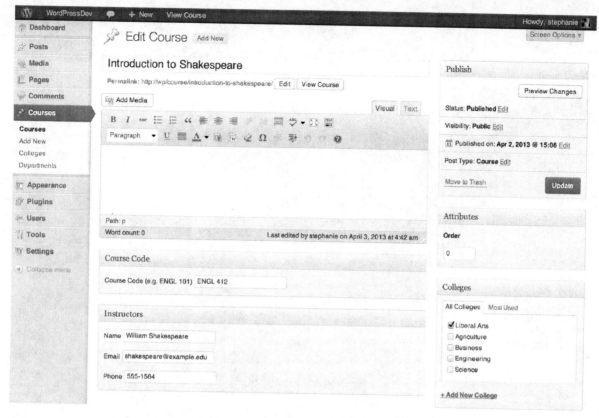

Figure 14-13. *The Edit Course screen with the new custom fields*

In this case, you use meta key names that begin with underscores. If you hadn't, you would see each of these three custom fields in the Custom Fields meta box in addition to your new meta boxes, as shown in Figure 14-14. WordPress will not print meta fields whose keys begin with underscores; they are considered hidden.

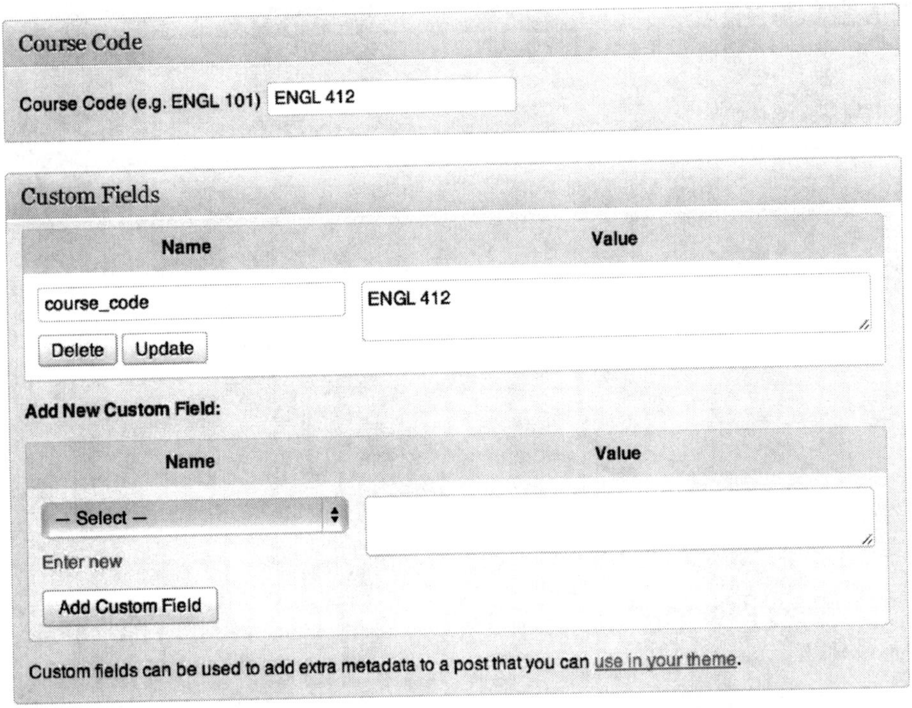

Figure 14-14. *Duplicated custom fields when keys do not begin with underscores*

Verifying and Saving User Input

You might have noticed that these form fields contain nonces (`http://sleary.me/wp40`[1]). A nonce is a number used once, and it's a security precaution you didn't have to take when you created plugins because you were using the settings API, which handled all that for you. Here, you aren't registering any settings. Instead, you are saving user input directly to the database, and you need to verify that the data in `$_POST` came from a valid source. To do that, you create a nonce for each box. The `wp_nonce_field()` function creates a hidden form field. It can take just one argument, a key you use to check the value later (`'course_code_nonce'`). If you were using just one nonce, you could leave it at that, and the field's name would be `_wp_nonce` by default. However, in this form you have two nonces, and you need to give each one a unique name, so you use a second argument to do so.

Last, you have to write a function to save your custom field data when the post is saved. You should first check the nonces you created in the meta boxes, and then check to make sure the user has permission to edit this post type. Anything in the built-in meta boxes would be handled automatically, but custom meta box fields must be updated manually, as shown in Listing 14-18. You need to make sure this function runs every time a post is saved, so use the `save_post()` action hook.

Listing 14-18. Saving the Meta Box Fields

```
function save_course_meta_data( $post_id ) {
        // ignore autosaves
        if ( defined( 'DOING_AUTOSAVE' ) && DOING_AUTOSAVE )
                return $post_id;
```

---

[1]`http://codex.wordpress.org/WordPress_Nonces`

```
// check post type
if ( 'course' != $_POST['post_type'] )
        return $post_id;

// check capabilites
if ( 'course' == $_POST['post_type'] && !current_user_can( 'edit_post', $post_id ) )
        return $post_id;

// check nonces
check_admin_referer( 'course_code_nonce', '_course_code_nonce' );
check_admin_referer( 'instructor_nonce', '_instructor_nonce' );

// Still here? Then save the fields
if ( empty( $_POST['_course_code'] ) ) {
    $storedcode = get_post_meta( $post_id, '_course_code', true );
    delete_post_meta( $post_id, '_course_code', $storedcode );
}
else
    update_post_meta( $post_id, '_course_code', $_POST['_course_code'] );

if ( empty( $_POST['_instructor_name'] ) ) {
    $storedname = get_post_meta( $post_id, '_instructor_name', true );
    delete_post_meta( $post_id, '_instructor_name', $storedname );
}
else
    update_post_meta( $post_id, '_instructor_name', $_POST['_instructor_name']);

if ( empty( $_POST['_instructor_email'] ) ) {
    $storedemail = get_post_meta( $post_id, '_instructor_email', true );
    delete_post_meta( $post_id, '_instructor_email', $storedemail );
}
else
    update_post_meta( $post_id, '_instructor_email', $_POST['_instructor_email'] );

if ( empty( $_POST['_instructor_phone'] ) ) {
    $storedphone = get_post_meta( $post_id, '_instructor_phone', true );
    delete_post_meta( $post_id, '_instructor_phone', $storedphone );
}
else
    update_post_meta( $post_id, '_instructor_phone', $_POST['_instructor_phone'] );
}
```

First, you need to check whether this save_post action is being called as a result of an autosave. If it is, you don't need to process the custom fields yet, so you return the post ID and exit the function.

Second, check the post type. The save_post action is called when any post is saved, but you don't need to check for these custom fields if a post or a page is being saved. If the post type is something other than 'course', you can again exit the function.

Third, check the user's capabilities. Does the current user have permission to edit courses? Back when you created the course content type, you had the option of specifying an edit capability other than edit_post. Since you didn't, that's the capability you need to check here.

Last, you need to check the nonces you created in the form field functions. The `check_admin_referer()` function would usually take just one argument, the key you provided when you created the nonce. However, since you're using two, you need to use the second argument (the unique identifier). If either nonce fails verification, you again exit the function without saving the fields.

Once you know that you're allowed to save the data, you need to check whether there's anything in each field. If there isn't, you call `delete_post_meta()` to remove its row from the `wp_postmeta` table. This function requires three arguments: the post ID, the meta key, and the previously stored value. You can again use `get_post_meta()` to fetch the stored value so you can pass it to `delete_post_meta()`.

If the fields aren't empty, you need to update them. The `update_post_meta()` function requires the ID, the meta key, and the new value.

That's it! You can now edit and save the custom fields in their own meta boxes instead of the main Custom Fields box.

Changing Edit Screen Columns

Since you've added the instructor's name to the course, it would be great if you could see it on the Edit Courses screen. Adding columns to the edit screen is a two-step process: first, define the column headers, and second, define the contents of the new column.

Changing Column Headers

The code to add a new column is fairly simple. Listing 14-19 shows how to add a column for the instructor's name to the Edit Courses screen.

Listing 14-19. Changing Column Headers for the Course Content Type

```
add_filter('manage_edit-course_columns', 'course_taxonomy_columns');
function course_taxonomy_columns( $defaults ) {
        return $defaults + array( 'instructor' => __('Instructor') );
}
```

First, you call the appropriate filter, in this case `manage_edit-course_columns()`. (Replace `'course'` with the name of your content type.) You're filtering an array containing the names of the column headings. To add a column, all you have to do is add an item to the array. However, that would place this column at the far right side of the table, after the comment and date columns. To make this page look more like the Edit Posts screen, you need to rearrange the columns. Listing 14-20 shows how to manipulate the array of columns to add the course code in between the checkbox and course title; remove the comments, author, and date; and the instructor name as the last column.

Listing 14-20. Rearranging Column Headers

```
add_filter('manage_edit-course_columns', 'course_taxonomy_columns');

function course_taxonomy_columns( $defaults ) {
        // preserve the first column containing the bulk edit checkboxes
        if ( isset( $defaults['cb'] ) )
                $cb = $defaults['cb'];

        // remove some default columns
        unset( $defaults['cb'] );
        unset( $defaults['comments'] );
```

```
    unset( $defaults['date'] );
    unset( $defaults['author'] );

    // insert checkbox and course code columns
    $newcolumns = array( 'cb' => $cb, 'course_code' => __('Code') );

    // followed by remaining defaults
    $newcolumns += $defaults;

    // then append custom field columns
    $newcolumns += array( 'instructor' => __('Instructor') );

    return $newcolumns;
}
```

In this example, the first thing you need to do is preserve the contents of the checkbox column, so you can restore it when you're done. Next, remove the unwanted columns from the $defaults array. Then, add your custom column for the course code. Last, add back the original columns in the order in which you want them to appear.

The resulting column arrangement is shown in Figure 14-15.

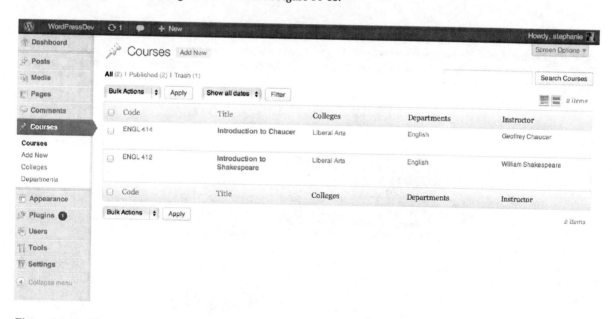

Figure 14-15. *The new Edit screen column*

Displaying Column Contents

Now that your new column is in place, you need to fill it with some information—in this case, the course code and instructor name. Listing 14-21 shows the necessary filter function.

Listing 14-21. Displaying the College Taxonomy Terms in the New Edit Screen Column

```
add_action('manage_posts_custom_column', 'course_custom_column', 10, 2);

function course_custom_column( $column, $id ) {
        switch ( $column ) {
                case 'course_code':
                        $code = get_post_meta( $id, '_course_code', true );
                        if ( !empty( $code ))
                                echo esc_html( $code );
                        break;
                case 'instructor':
                        $name = get_post_meta( $id, '_instructor_name', true );
                        if ( !empty( $name ) )
                                echo esc_html( $name );
                        break;
                default:
                        break;
        }
}
```

Here, you use a `switch()` statement to make sure that you're working with the proper column. (This hook runs on all the columns on the Edit screens; you wouldn't want to print the instructor's name in the Comments column!) Then, you retrieve the custom field data. If it exists, you print it to the screen, escaping the HTML to prevent security issues.

Figure 14-16 shows the completed Edit Courses screen.

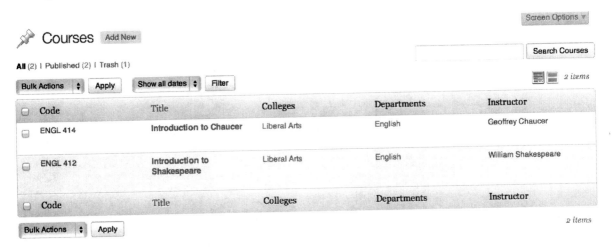

Figure 14-16. *The Edit Courses screen with the completed course code column*

Making Columns Sortable

Wouldn't it be nice to be able to sort the Edit screen by the course code as well as the title? To make the new column sortable, you need to hook in two more functions, as shown in Listing 14-22.

Listing 14-22. Making the Course Code Column Sortable

```
add_filter( 'manage_edit-course_sortable_columns', 'course_column_sortable' );

function course_column_sortable( $columns ) {
    $columns['course_code'] = 'course_code';
    return $columns;
}

add_filter( 'request', 'course_column_orderby' );

function course_column_orderby( $queryvars ) {
    if ( isset( $queryvars['orderby'] ) && $queryvars['orderby'] == 'course_code' ) {
        $queryvars = array_merge( $queryvars, array(
            'meta_key' => '_course_code',
            'orderby' => 'meta_value'
        ) );
    }
    return $queryvars;
}
```

The first function simply tells WordPress that the course code column is a sortable one. The second, `course_column_orderby()`, is where the magic happens. Here, you start with the query variables WordPress expects to work with. You merge this array with a new one containing the sort parameters you want to use. Refer to the WP_Query documentation (`http://sleary.me/wp92`[2]) for the possible ways to sort the query.

All Together

The complete Course Post Types plugin is available for download at `http://sleary.me/cpt`.[3] It registers the course post type, adds the college taxonomy, displays the college taxonomy and the course code on the Edit Courses screen, and adds the course code, instructor name, and instructor e-mail meta boxes to the Courses ➤ Edit screen.

Once you've edited your courses to take advantage of the new fields, you also need to modify the `archive-course.php` template. Listing 14-23 shows a revised template that displays the courses in a table, and Figure 14-17 shows the result.

Listing 14-23. The New Course Archive Template Using Custom Fields

```
<?php get_header(); ?>
        <section id="primary" class="site-content">
                <div id="content" role="main">
                <?php if ( have_posts() ) : ?>
                        <header class="archive-header">
                                <h1 class="archive-title">Course Listing</h1>
                        </header><!-- .archive-header -->
                                <table>
```

---

[2]`http://codex.wordpress.org/Class_Reference/WP_Query`
[3]`http://sleary.me/downloads/plugins/course-post-types.zip`

```
                               <thead>
                                      <th>Code</th>
                                      <th>Title</th>
                                      <th>Instructor</th>
                               <thead>
                               <tbody>
                <?php
                     while (have_posts() ) : the_post(); ?>
                     <tr id="post-<?php the_ID(); ?>" <?php post_class(); ?>>
                        <td><?php echo esc_html( get_post_meta( get_the_ID(), '_course_ ➥
code', true) ); ?></td>
                        <td><a href="<?php the_permalink(); ?>" title="<?php ➥
 the_title_attribute(); ?>"><?php the_title(); ?></a></td>
                        <td><a href="mailto:<?php echo esc_attr( get_post_meta ➥
( get_the_ID(), '_instructor_email', true) ); ?>"><?php echo esc_html( get_post_meta ➥
( get_the_ID(), '_instructor_name', true) ); ?></a></td>
                     </tr>
                <?php endwhile; ?>
                              </tbody>
                     </table>
                <?php endif; ?>

            </div><!-- #content -->
        </section><!-- #primary -->
<?php get_sidebar(); ?>
<?php get_footer(); ?>
```

COURSE LISTING

Code	Title	Instructor
ENGL 414	Introduction to Chaucer	Geoffrey Chaucer
ENGL 412	Introduction to Shakespeare	William Shakespeare

Figure 14-17. *The completed course table*

Further Reading

There is so much more you can do with custom post types. Here are a few particularly informative articles and tutorials.

- Enabling Quick and Bulk Edit for custom fields: http://sleary.me/wp93[4]

- Querying multiple taxonomies: http://sleary.me/wp94[5]

---

[4]http://rachelcarden.com/2012/03/manage-wordpress-posts-using-bulk-edit-and-quick-edit
[5]http://ottopress.com/2010/wordpress-3-1-advanced-taxonomy-queries

- Creating a faceted search form using taxonomies and Relevanssi: `http://sleary.me/wp95`[6]

- Creating relationships between posts with Posts 2 Posts: `http://sleary.me/wp96`[7]

- The Custom Meta Boxes and Fields class, which makes developing custom field boxes much easier: `http://sleary.me/wp97`[8]

Summary

In this chapter, I've shown you how to move beyond the built-in content types in WordPress—way beyond! You can add small custom fields to posts and pages or create entirely new content types of your own, and you can categorize and tag them with many sets of taxonomy terms.

You now have all the tools you need to create a completely customized database of content, all with the same user-friendly editing interfaces that have made WordPress famous. I hope you build something amazing. Good luck!

[6]`http://wp-evangelist.com/2011/02/extending-wp-search`
[7]`https://github.com/scribu/wp-posts-to-posts/wiki`
[8]`https://github.com/jaredatch/Custom-Metaboxes-and-Fields-for-WordPress`

■ ■ ■

Recommended Plugins

There are thousands of plugins and themes you can use to extend WordPress. You'll find most of them in the official plugin repository at wordpress.org. I've provided URLs only for those plugins that can't be found easily by searching for their names. See Chapter 3 for information on installing and configuring plugins.

Editing: Inline, Rich Text, Reusable Content, and Attachments

Front End Editor and **Inline Editor** allow posts and pages to be edited without having to enter the dashboard.

TinyMCE Advanced allows you to add a number of buttons to the rich text editor, including a complete set of table buttons.

MCE Table Buttons is a simpler plugin that adds a row of table buttons to the rich text editor.

Post Snippets and **Reusables** allow you to define bits of reusable content that can be included in a post via shortcode and/or rich text editor buttons.

List Child Attachments (code.google.com/p/list-child-attachments/) provides a template tag and shortcode that lists all the files attached to a post or page.

Gallery Metabox shows a meta box on the post editing screen with a quick preview of the images attached to the post.

PJW MIME Config lets you configure the types of files that users (other than administrators) are allowed to upload to the media library.

Revisions

Revisionary allows users to revise a published post or page without immediately publishing the change. Instead, the updates are submitted to an editor or administrator for approval.

Revision Control allows you to limit the number of revisions WordPress will keep. The site-wide setting can be overridden for individual posts.

Excerpts

Advanced Excerpt modifies the the_excerpt() tag. It allows you to preserve HTML in excerpts, define the excerpt length, and change the ellipsis character.

the_excerpt Reloaded (robsnotebook.com/the-excerpt-reloaded/) provides a new template tag for excerpts. You can preserve specified HTML tags in excerpts, define the excerpt length, and choose what 'more . . .' text to display.

PJW Page Excerpt provides the excerpt box on page write/edit screens and allows you to use the_excerpt() for pages.

Custom Post Types, Taxonomies, and Fields

Custom Post Type UI provides an options page that allows you to create and manage both custom post types and custom taxonomies.

Convert Post Types and **Post Type Switcher** allow you to convert your old posts and pages to new content types.

More Fields and **Advanced Custom Fields** provide a simple user interface for creating meta boxes for custom fields.

Page Order

Simple Page Ordering provides a simple drag-and-drop interface for rearranging the order of pages on any single level of the page hierarchy. A drop-down menu allows you to choose pages that have children and rearrange the pages on that level.

Hierarchy replaces the usual WordPress Edit menus with an outline-like overview of all your content, including all custom post types, and lets you dig deeper into each section from there.

Post/Page Lists and Navigation

Exclude Pages provides a checkbox on the edit page screen that allows you to explicitly include or exclude pages from WP's page list functions.

Page Links To redirects posts or pages to another URL.

Yoast Breadcrumbs provides a template tag for breadcrumb navigation on both posts and pages. Pages display the page parents; posts display the category hierarchy.

WP-SNAP provides alphabetical listings of posts by title within a category.

Post2Post creates one-to-many or many-to-many relationships between posts (including pages and custom post types) and allows you to display the related posts in your theme.

Permalinks and Short URLs

Pretty Link turns your WordPress site into a URL shortening service of your own and can track visitors to the short links.

Jetpack includes wp.me, WordPress.com's URL shortening service.

Workflow and E-mail Notifications

Subscribe to Comments allows visitors to receive e-mail notifications of follow-up comments on individual posts.

Subscribe2 allows registered users to receive e-mail notifications of new posts.

Clean Notifications reformats e-mail notifications in HTML, removing extraneous information and providing useful links.

Notifications to All Administrators sends all the common notifications to all users with the administrator role, not just the one whose e-mail address is shown under Settings ➤ General.

Peter's Collaboration E-mails sends a message when an author submits a post for review, and when a pending post is approved, scheduled, or changed back to a draft.

Editorial Calendar provides a calendar grid interface showing your scheduled posts.

Edit Flow includes an editorial calendar, configurable e-mail notifications, and new post statuses. It lets you create a more complex workflow for submitting and approving posts.

Forms

Contact Form 7 allows you to create e-mail contact forms with Akismet spam protection.

Gravity Forms (www.gravityforms.com) and **Formidable Forms** offer a great user interface, file uploads, e-mail autoresponders, and confirmation pages with data passed from the form input. Gravity allows user-submitted posts (with images, categories, etc.). *Gravity Forms is a commercial plugin. Formidable is free with a limited feature set; the full feature set is available in the commercial Pro version.*

Users, Permissions, and Login Screens

Members provides on/off toggles for all capabilities and allows you to define new roles. It also adds several features relating to private content.

Sidebar Login provides a login form widget.

Login Redirect allows you to reroute users (by username or by role) to a specified URL on login.

Registered Users Only requires users to log in before viewing your site.

Private Suite allows you to change the prefixes on private and password-protected post/page titles, set which roles can read private content, and create private categories.

User Contact Control lets you configure the contact fields on user profile pages.

Visitor Statistics

Google Analyticator includes the Google Analytics code in your footer and provides checkboxes for advanced Analytics options, such as AdSense integration, tracking file downloads, outbound links, and admin visitors. It also adds a graph and some information about your most requested pages to your Dashboard.

Jetpack includes wordpress.com stats, which provides a graph of visitors and search queries as a dashboard widget.

Media and Podcasting

Audio Player provides a Flash-based player for audio files.

Blubrry PowerPress provides extra fields for podcast and iTunes data, adds the necessary tags to your feeds, and displays media players for audio and video. It allows you to create separate podcasts from categories.

Social Media

Jetpack includes a number of social media tools, including sharing buttons and a Twitter widget.

Twitter Tools provides a widget that will display your tweets as well as a number of advanced options such as autotweeting when you post to your blog, shortening URLs via bit.ly or other services, and adding a hashtag in tweets.

Sociable and **Share This** add a configurable row of buttons below your post that will allow users to quickly share your post with specified social networking services.

Social Networks

BuddyPress turns your WordPress site into a complete social network.

Events and Calendars

The Events Calendar allows you to create events (and optionally make a post for each) and display them as a small sidebar calendar, a large calendar in a post, or a sidebar list of upcoming events.

Events Made Easy lets you create events with location data and Google maps, RSVPs, with iCal and RSS feeds.

GigPress (gigpress.com) is designed for listing tour performances, but might work for general events. It includes microformats, RSS and iCal feeds, and CSV export.

Caching

WP Super Cache includes WP Cache and adds a number of other features: file locking, GZIP compression, cache rebuild options, and more.

W3 Total Cache uses APC or Memcached to cache database queries rather than files.

Batcache also uses Memcached and works on distributed servers.

WP Widget Cache speeds up page loads by caching widgets' output.

Performance, Security, Maintenance, and Diagnostics

Better WP Security suggests changes to your site's configuration to improve its security. It also includes a database backup tool.

Maintenance Mode displays a simple maintenance message to everyone except administrators.

WP-DB-Backup provides a button to quickly back up specified database tables and can be scheduled to back up to a specified directory.

Optimize DB performs MySQL's automatic optimization routines on your database from the admin area.

P3 Plugin Profiler helps you identify performance problems.

Search & Replace allows you to replace text in chosen database fields.

Broken Link Checker runs a background process that periodically checks your site for broken links.

Show Template lets you know which theme file is being used to generate a particular page.

Hook Sniffer lets you see which actions and filters are involved (and in what order) as WordPress is generating a page.

Developer checks your installation for various development-related plugins and suggests others that might be helpful.

Debug Bar adds a debugging console to the admin bar.

Core Control lets you inspect several of WordPress's internal processes, including filesystem access, HTTP requests, cron schedules, and upgrade routines.

WP Security Scan monitors file permissions, database security, and user passwords to help mitigate security vulnerabilities.

WordPress Firewall 2 examines incoming requests and rejects those that match well-known attack vectors.

Login Lockdown and **Login Security Solution** allow you to limit failed login attempts.

Mobile

WPtouch provides an iPhone app-style theme to mobile users.

Widgets

Display Widgets allows you to display the widget's contents selectively based on the page context, essentially providing a per-widget UI for the conditional functions.

Monster Widget adds all the built-in widgets to a sidebar in one click, allowing developers to set up widgets more quickly when testing themes.

Dashboard Notepad creates a Dashboard widget where you can store and share notes.

Search Engine Optimization

Google XML Sitemaps generates XML sitemaps (plain and/or gzipped) according to the `sitemaps.org` specification.

Yoast SEO and **All in One SEO Pack** reverses the order of the page/post and site names in titles, sets canonical URLs, generates metatags, and more.

Importing Content

Import HTML Pages imports HTML files as posts or pages.

CSV Importer imports posts from a comma-separated values file and can be used to import content from Excel.

Import Users from CSV allows you to add users in bulk.

Add Linked Images scans posts for image tags and imports the images to the media library.

See `http://codex.wordpress.org/Importing_Content` for many other import plugins.

Network Sites

Domain Mapping allows users to map their own domains to their network subdomains.

Proper Network Activation runs plugins' activation routines on all network sites

Multi-Site allows you to create multiple networks from one WordPress installation. Each new network can have its own site administrator and subsites.

■ ■ ■

Community Resources

Development Philosophy

The core developers set the feature agenda for major releases based on Trac tickets, known problems, and user surveys. Planning for the next version doesn't begin until a week or two after a major release. The development schedule and weekly meeting agendas are kept on `http://make.wordpress.org/core`. The weekly developer meetings take place in the #wordpress-dev IRC channel on the Freenode network. Anyone can join in the meeting, but they must respect the agenda.

If a new feature can be handled by a plugin, the developers are less likely to consider it for inclusion in the core. Core is for features most people need, or frameworks developers can build on.

If you want a bug fixed, writing a patch for it yourself and submitting it to Trac is the fastest way to get it done.

Single-point versions like 2.9, 3.0, 3.1, and 3.5 are all considered major releases, although some might include more new features than others. Minor versions like 3.3.1 are bug fix and security updates. Old releases do not get security updates, which is why it's so important to keep your installation up to date.

Documentation, Discussion, and Help

Codex: `http://codex.wordpress.org`

Forum: `http://wordpress.org/support`

IRC Channels: `https://codex.wordpress.org/IRC`

Mailing Lists: `http://codex.wordpress.org/Mailing_Lists`

Development Blogs: `http://make.wordpress.org`

WP StackExchange: `http://wordpress.stackexchange.com`

News and Events

WP Candy: `http://wpcandy.com`

Planet WordPress: `http://planetwordpress.planetozh.com`

WP Daily: `http://wpdaily.co`

wpMail.me newsletter: `http://wpmail.me`

WordCamp Central: `http://central.wordcamp.org`

Developer Blogs

Andrew Nacin: `http://nacin.com`

Peter Westwood: `http://westi.wordpress.com`

Samuel Wood (Otto on WordPress): `http://ottopress.com`

Mark Jaquith: `http://txfx.net`

Silviu-Cristian Burcă (Scribu): `http://scribu.net`

Pippin Williamson: `http://pippinsplugins.com`

Aaron Campbell: `http://ran.ge/blog`

Index